GW01606511

TECHNIQUES OF FILTERS AND SPECIAL EFFECT PHOTOGRAPHY

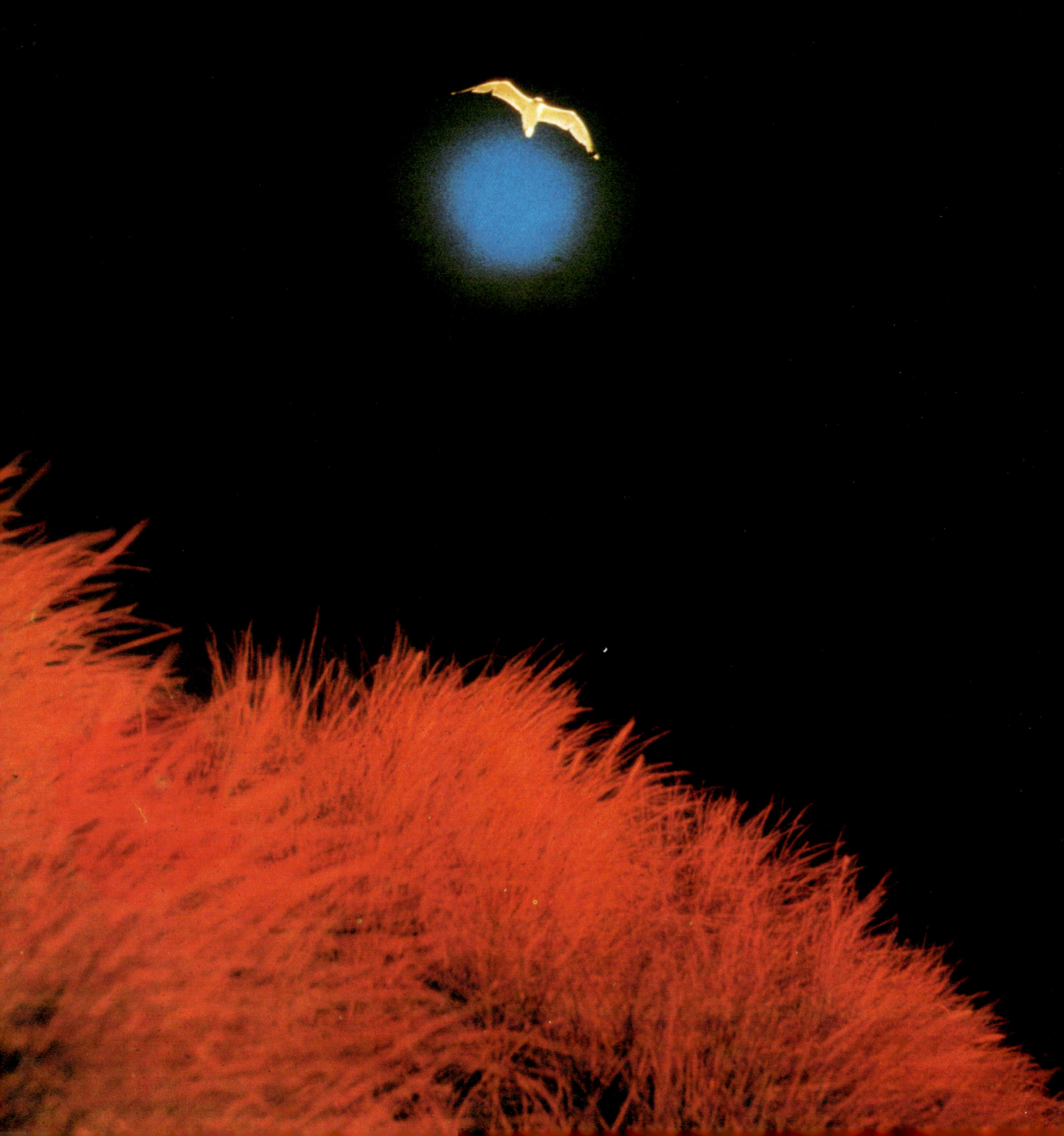

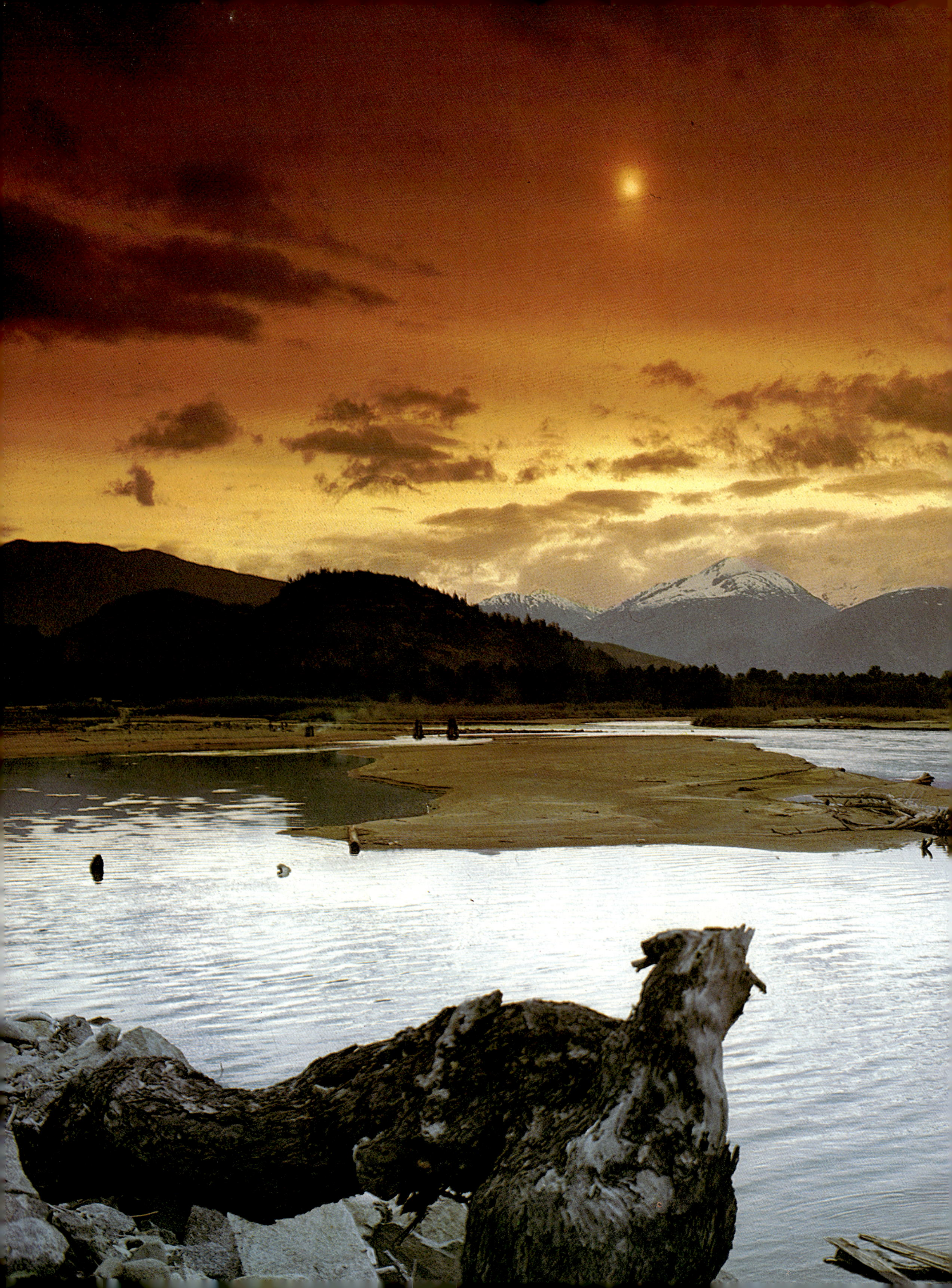

TECHNIQUES OF FILTERS AND SPECIAL EFFECT PHOTOGRAPHY

Colin Glanfield

Designed by
PHILIP CLUCAS MSIAD

Produced by
TED SMART and DAVID GIBBON

COLOUR LIBRARY BOOKS

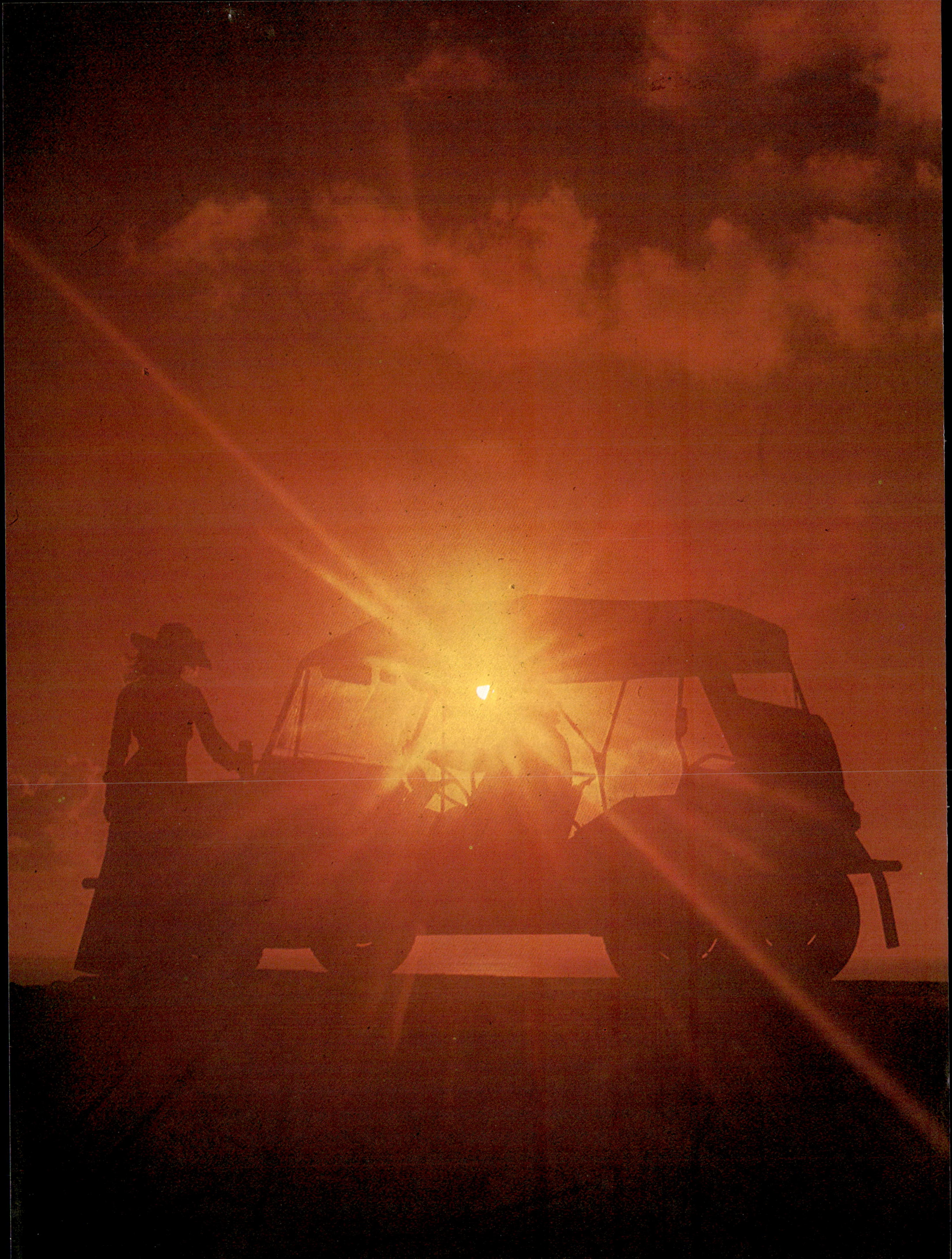

CONTENTS

THE NATURE OF LIGHT

Most of us probably learned the initials R.O.Y.G.B.I.V. whilst at school, (perhaps as 'Richard Of York Gave Battle In Vain'). Maybe we can still remember that they also stand for the constituent colours of white light – or, more likely, the colours of a rainbow. Either way, both have photographic applications. The former relates to filtration, whilst the latter perhaps gave the inspiration for diffraction gratings (rainbow filters) or prismatic (colour fringe) lens attachments.

R.O.Y.G.B.I.V. stands for red, orange, yellow, green, blue, indigo and violet, which is the visible spectrum. To this can be added infrared and ultraviolet, when 'visible' is in a photographic context. Some educationalists and scientists now exclude the indigo category, for reasons best known to themselves, whilst other scientists object most strongly to white light being separated into six or seven segments. They point out, quite rightly, that there is no such colour as red, only shades of red, etc. For example, both vermilion and carmine can be considered as being reds, yet the latter is an impure red, not found in the spectrum. The difference between theory and practice is that, in photographic terms, pure red, blue and green filters do exist, which for our purposes neatly divides the spectrum into three parts. These have been the basis of additive tricolour photography since before the turn of the century. When it comes to subtractive colour photography, which is the vast majority nowadays, then the spectrum is once more divided into three sections. Two of these colours are 'cocktails', namely cyan (blue plus green) and magenta (red plus blue), whilst the third colour, yellow, comes neither shaken nor stirred.

Again, it must be stressed that this arbitrary division only relates to photographic rather than general science. The reason for this is that red, green and blue can be absorbed by cyan, magenta and yellow filters respectively, which is where the term complementary colours comes in. The importance of this will be described in the next chapter.

***Photographic emulsions do not** respond to colour in the same way as does the human eye. As can be seen from the graph **below,** the eye is most sensitive to the yellow/green area of the spectrum, whilst black and white panchromatic emulsion is particularly sensitive to blue light. Filters can be used to alter this response, the classic example being the use of a yellow filter to bring out clouds in what otherwise would be a plain grey sky. **Facing page:** A graphic illustration of the breakdown of white light into its constituent colours.*

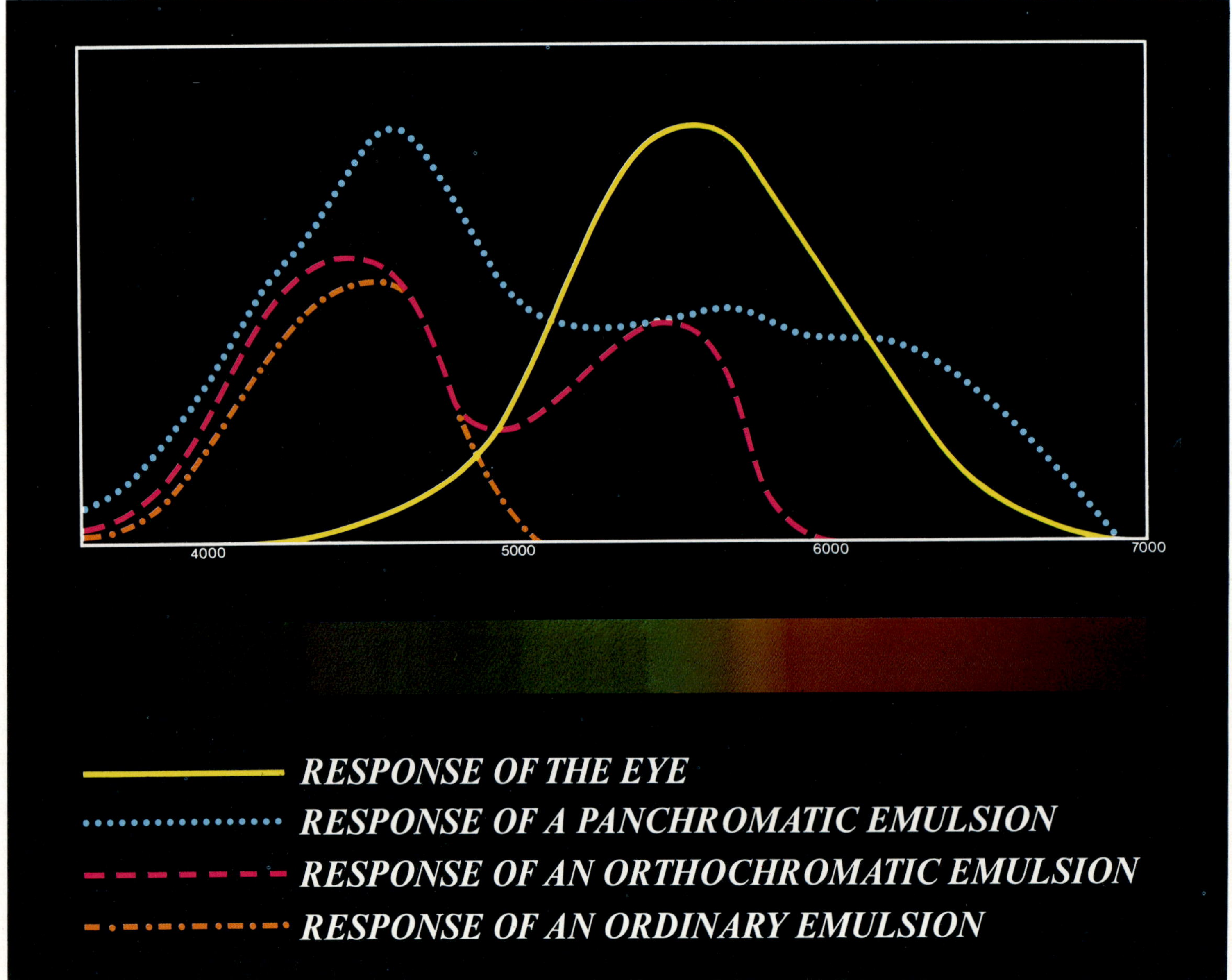

RESPONSE OF THE EYE TO COLOUR

For some still unknown biological reason, the eye is more sensitive in the yellow to green area of the spectrum than in other regions. This phenomenon explains the use of fluorescent and sodium lighting, yellow car headlight bulbs and night driving glasses, yellow-green darkroom safelights and the fact that yellow Automobile Association road signs are more legible than the blue of the Royal Automobile Club! As lighting levels become lower, the colour sensitivity of the eye becomes monochromatic in the sense that images received by the retina become apparently more black and white.

As the brain is part of our optical system, it compensates to the degree that we can see a colour as we wish to see it and not as it actually is. A photographic emulsion does not have this advantage. With experience we learn to compensate for this compensation. Practised photographers, who can see the yellow-green cast of a 'white' fluorescent tube, always use a daylight-balanced transparency viewing box and examine colour swatches under the light source to be used for the photograph. Even with this precaution, the human eye/brain can be fooled. Modern technology has produced inks and dyes which contain amounts of fluorescins. These have the effect of making certain materials and products impossible to photograph to any degree of colour fidelity. Try telling a scientifically illiterate client that just because he can see it does not mean one can necessarily photograph it – yet this may well be so nowadays. In the same vein is the designer who wants a colour object photographed on the same colour background and is then disappointed with the result. Whilst a certain amount of compromise can be achieved in lighting, there is no argument that a pair of eyes see stereoscopically whereas the camera lens is strictly mono. You may have seen a photographer squinting one-eyed at a subject. Now you know that the poor chap isn't afflicted, just being professional – or using experience!

Evaluation of colour can be a subjective matter – or simply personal taste – yet against this, any of us can be colour blind to an extent to which we are not aware. One of my uncles, quite late in life, purchased an expensive brown Harris tweed suit at an absolute bargain price. Arriving home, he was at a loss to understand why his family were horrified at his new peacock blue attire. Likewise, I have worked with a photographer who continually complained to Kodak, Agfa, Nikon, our colour lab and anybody else who would listen, that his results always had a green cast. Perhaps the acid test is to look at the tuning of friends' and family's colour TV sets. But then, just like yours of course, my colour vision is perfect!

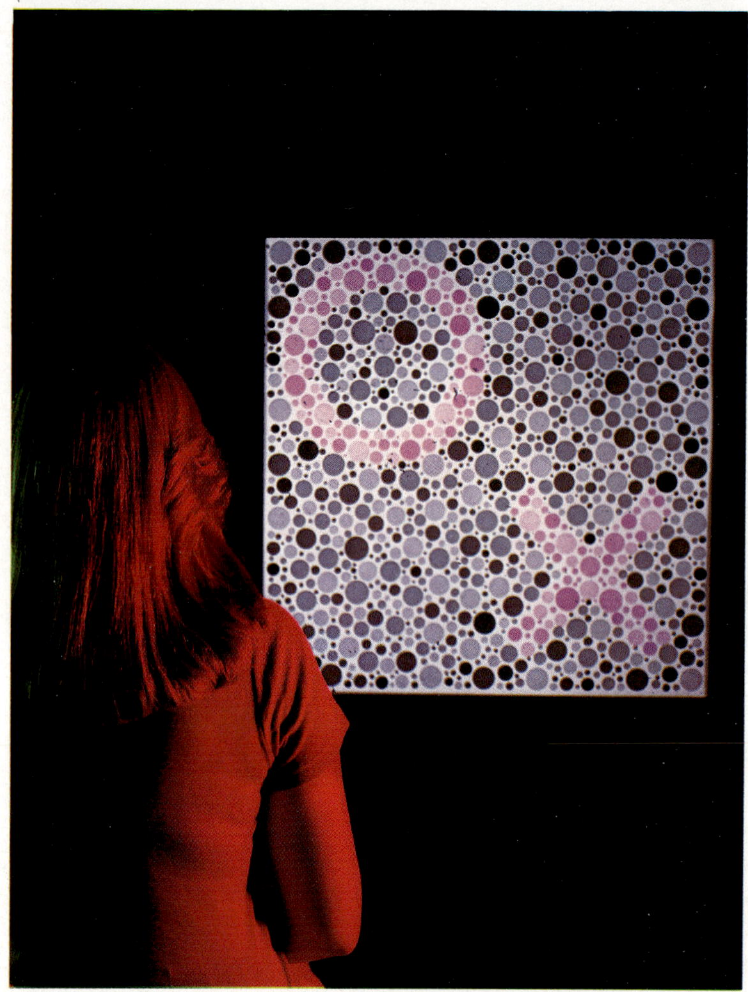

Colour blindness is the *inability to distinguish between colours or, at its more severe, to see them at all. This affliction, of which the sufferer may frequently be unaware, can be tested for by using various charts. Shown* ***above*** *is the British American Optical Company colour blindness test.*

RESPONSE of BLACK AND WHITE PHOTOGRAPHIC EMULSIONS to COLOUR

The colour sensitivity of modern emulsions falls into four main categories. These are shown in the table below.:

EMULSION	SENSITIVITY	SAFELIGHT
Super Panchromatic	+ Red Blue Green Yellow	Not advisable
Panchromatic	Red Blue Green Yellow	Blue-green (with care)
Orthochromatic	Blue Green Yellow	Red
Ordinary	Blue	Orange/yellow

35mm users may well ask why all these categories are mentioned, since ortho and ordinary emulsions are not available in cassettes. The short answer is that they are available in bulk lengths, and, since it is easy to load cassettes and develop the results under a safelight, it may be a subject worthy of experimentation for real enthusiasts or those business executives, scientists, doctors, academics and historians, who use audio-visual means of data presentation and recording. For the latter, the availability of high contrast (or line) emulsions is a plus factor.

'Super Panchromatic' was a pre-war designation for the fastest films around at that time. Designed primarily for low light level photography under tungsten sources, the net result was an over-sensitivity to the red end of the spectrum. This category of emulsion still exists today, though don't expect verification of this statement from the manufacturers of 400 ASA black and white films! The practical result of Super-Pan films was a lightening in tone of lipstick reds – generally worn only by the fairer sex, but also not unknown in the theatrical profession. To counteract anaemic rendition of lips – or the necessity to wear black lipstick – various manufacturers developed the pale blue 'half-watt' filter. This gave the effect of darkening red toned make-up to a satisfactory degree, but did have the disadvantage of reducing emulsion speed by around half a stop. Though (as far as I can ascertain) half-watt filters no longer exist in manufacturers' catalogues, the current equivalent for experimenters would be a Kodak Wratten CC20 or 30 Blue gelatin filter.

RESPONSE OF BLACK AND WHITE FILMS TO COLOUR

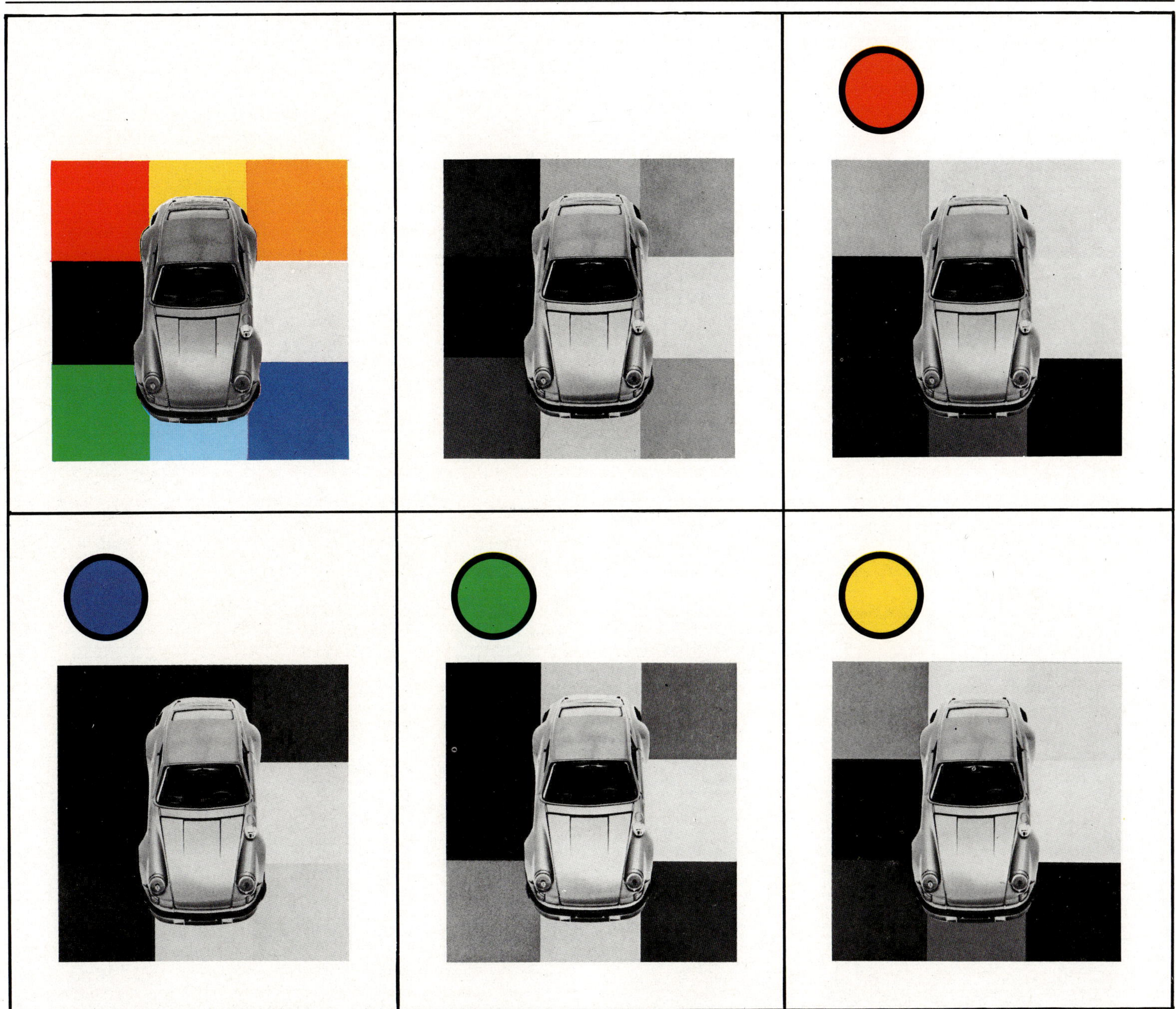

Panchromatic films have the best balanced response to light of all colours, though, in common with all photographic materials, there is an excess of sensitivity to blue light. This is best explained by the photographic phenomenon of a blue sky with white clouds being rendered as a very pale grey non-event, or, in other words, a yellow 'cloud' filter is still necessary, even though it will effectively halve the film speed.

Modern orthochromatic emulsions have a spectral sensitivity extending into orange, although using an orange filter will require a much higher factor than for a panchromatic film. Ortho emulsions in sheet film form can have the same superb tonal gradation as the best panchromatic films, which can be important in copy negative work. When contrast variation is necessary, this can be more easily achieved by visual development under a safelight. Ortho films, like Ilford's obsolete Selochrome, were widely used by medical photographers for fine detail rendition, with increased contrast of various skin conditions. If your nearest and dearest have freckles, avoid experimenting with orthochromatic portraits. The unflattering result will look like somebody's Syndrome.

Coloured filters, when used in *black and white photography, will lighten similar colours in the subject and darken their complementaries. The series of pictures* ***above*** *demonstrate this principle, each being the filtered rendering of the original colour picture* ***top left.*** *The picture* ***centre top*** *shows the tone separation of the unfiltered panchromatic emulsion.*

Ordinary emulsions (blue sensitive only), as found in bromide papers, black and white 'positive' films and some recording films, were historically the first. They are sometimes referred to by the misnomer of 'non-colour sensitive' emulsions – isn't blue a colour? Like some ortho films, they can have a superb tonal range. O.K., they are only suitable for recording black and white original images. However, should you ever wish to copy, say, airbrushed art work, line and wash, pencil drawings and X-rays, there is no better emulsion to use. Development by inspection is even easier than with ortho films – the safelight is brighter! The disadvantage, as stated, is the monochromatic colour sensitivity. Most old books on photography will show the 'black' daffodil to illustrate this point.

COLOUR TEMPERATURE

Colour temperature is a measurement of the incandescence of that heated black box, so beloved by physics teachers. It is expressed in degrees Kelvin, these in themselves being degrees Centigrade +273. Having got this over, it concerns photographers in that it is also a measurement of the degree of redness or blueness of a light source. Lighted candles, at one end of the scale, give a somewhat warm rendition, even on artificial light balanced colour film. Whilst at the other extreme is the sky – which looks pretty blue on a good day. This somewhat crude analogy can also be expressed in tabular form:–

Domestic lamps	ca. 2650 to 2850°Kelvin
Tungsten Halogen	3200°K
Photofloods	3400°K
Blue flashbulbs	ca. 5000°K
Mean noon sunlight	5400°K
Blue sky	12–18000°K

Tungsten type colour films are now balanced to 3200°K, whilst daylight films are for a 5400°K light source. For some international standards reason this was measured at Washington USA in June at noon.

It is also worth mentioning that the colour temperature of tungsten lamps becomes lower with age and with voltage drop. Whether this ever in fact shows up on a colour picture is a matter for conjecture. For the really fussy, there are colour temperature meters on the market. These can be very useful when colour fidelity is important. They do have the disadvantage that they are unable to measure the discontinuous spectrum of fluorescent and other discharge lamps, which is a pity.

Electronic flashes are theoretically balanced to daylight colour films. In practice, even studio units can vary wildly between 5000 and 6500°K. If your results are consistently too red or too blue, use a correction filter taped over the flash head. The reason for this is an excess of ultraviolet, which the eye cannot see but the film can. Obviously with black and white film this is of no importance.

The only other bit of theory relating to colour temperature, which photographers may meet, is mired values. These indicate, numerically, a shift in colour temperature which is constant regardless of starting point. Mired values are either positive or negative. Amber or yellowish filters, which lower colour temperature, have a positive value, whilst bluish filters, which raise colour temperature, have a negative value.

As an example, 5400°K colour temperature has a mired value of 185. At 3200°K the mired value is 312. A Wratten 85B conversion filter is +131 mireds. A Wratten 80A conversion filter is −131 mireds. These are near enough to the 127 mired difference between daylight and tungsten balanced colour films. It follows therefore that a film used in a light source for which it was not designated can, with the appropriate filter, give adequate results. Some German and Japanese filter makers also use mired values for their red to blue correction filter ranges.

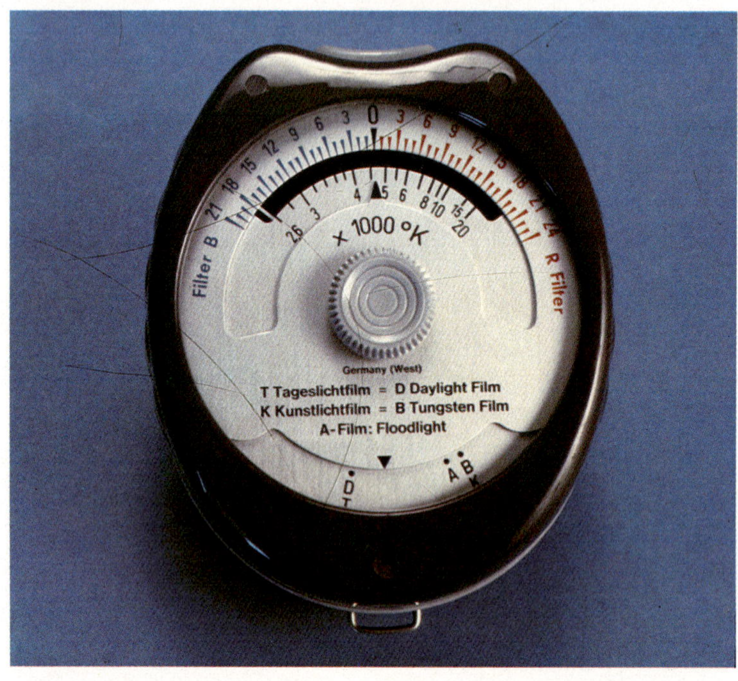

A colour temperature meter, *such as the Sixticolor* ***above*** *tells us, once we know the temperature for which our film is balanced, how 'blue' or 'red' is the prevailing light. Filters, indicated by the meter dial, can then be used to apply correction so as to bring the film into balance with the light.*

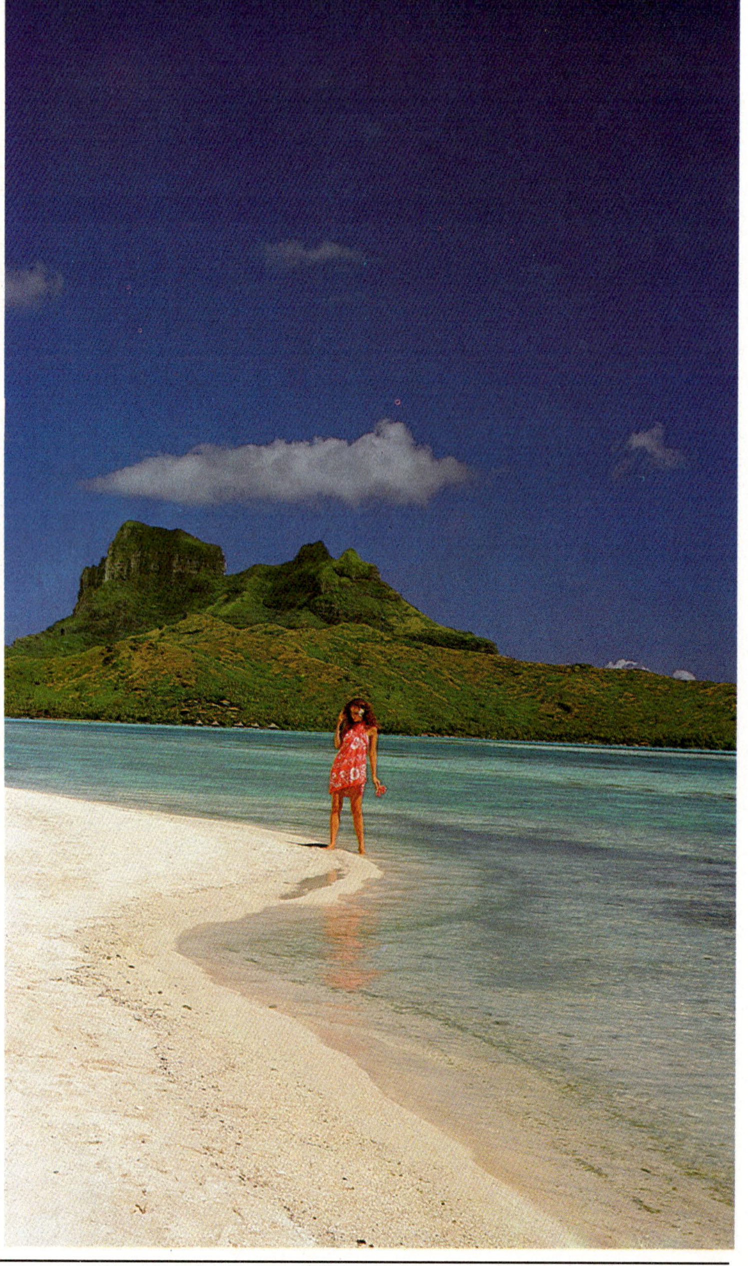

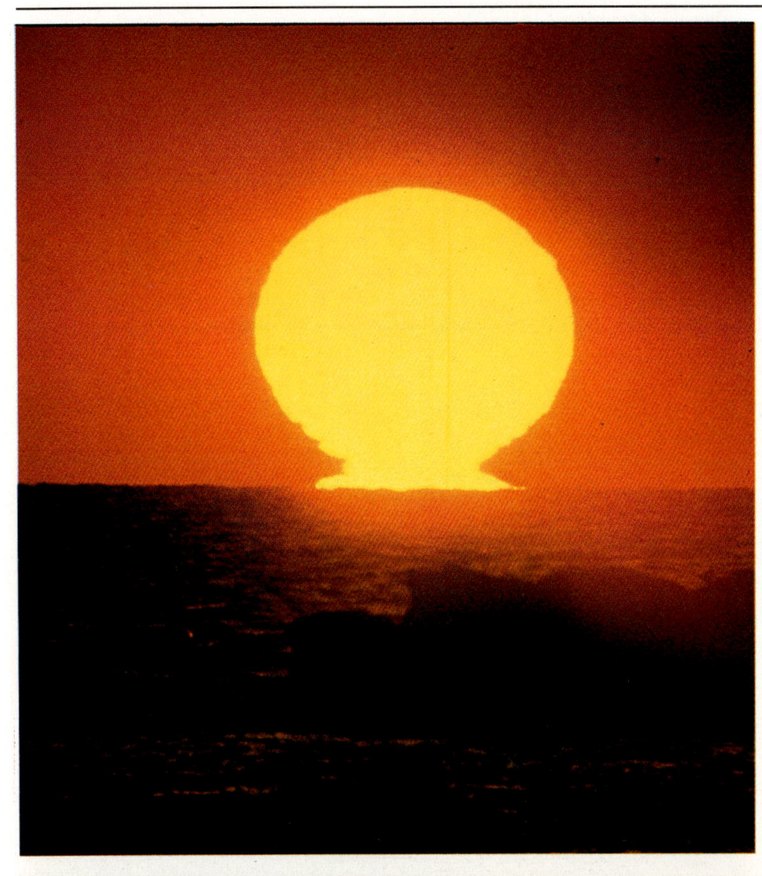

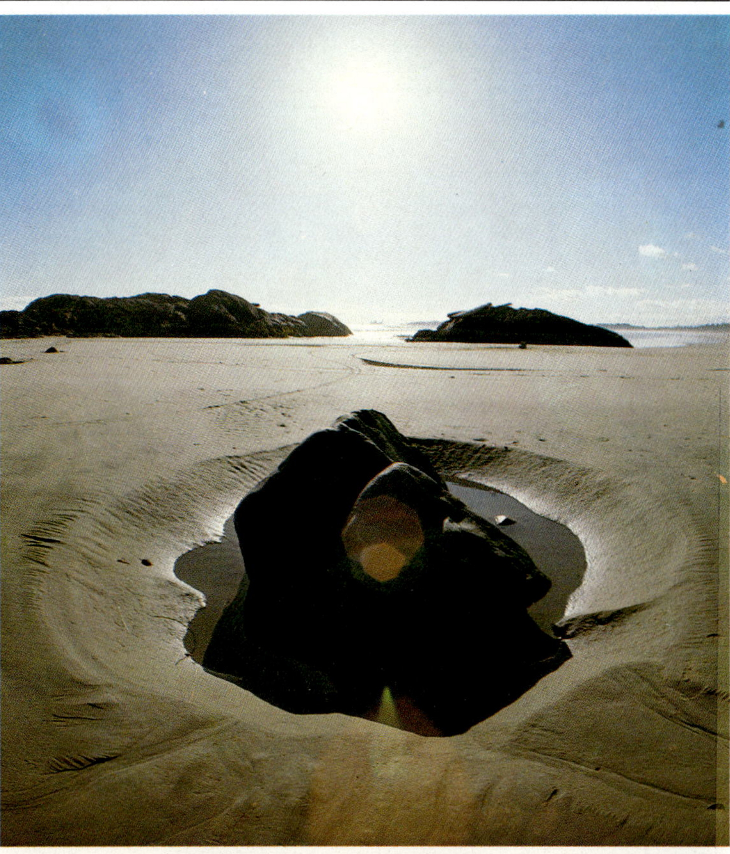

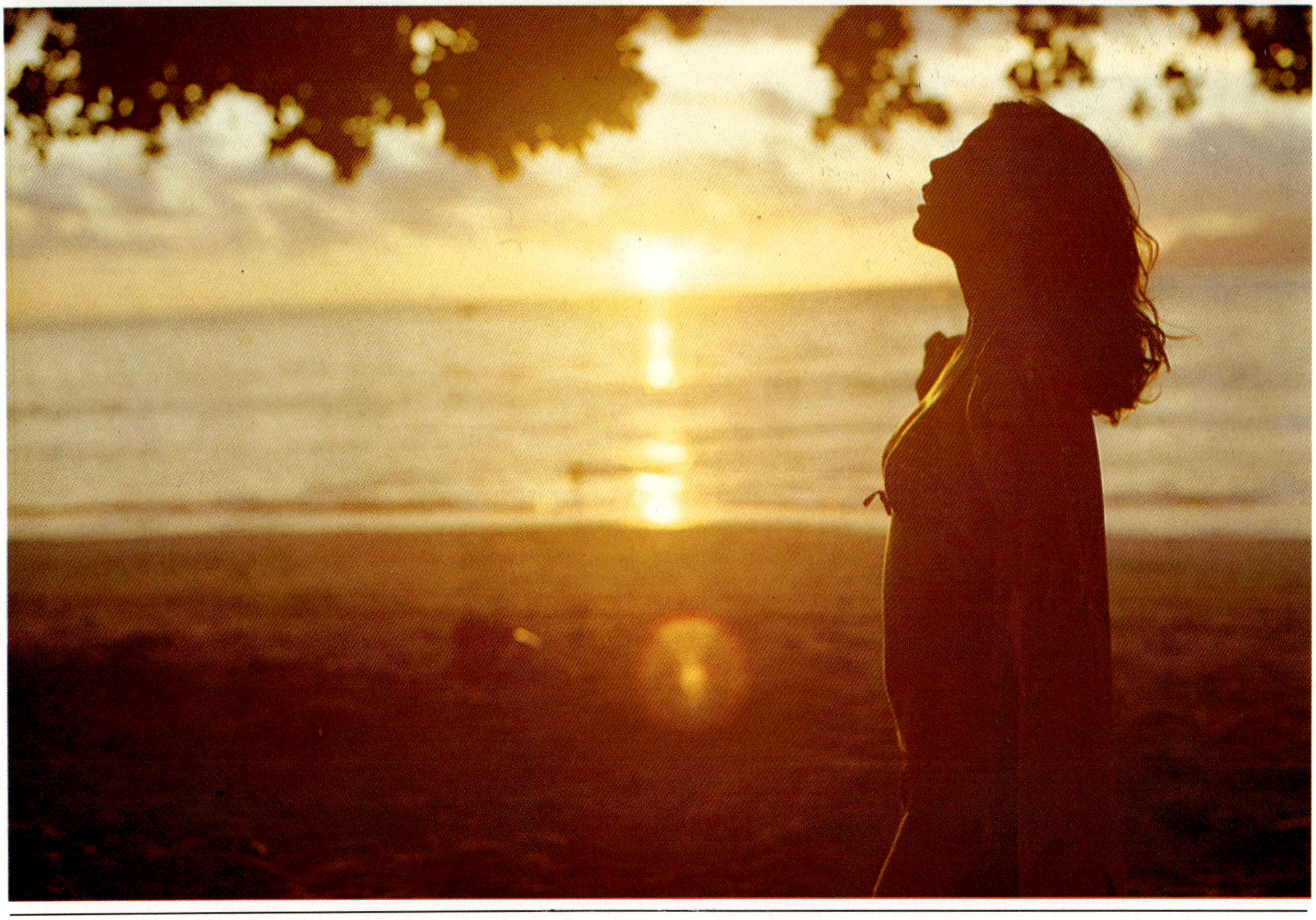

FILTER EXPOSURE FACTORS

Now that we have discussed the main parameters affecting the usage of filters, it is possible to relate these to an explanation of how filter factors work.

These can best be described as the increase in exposure necessary in relation to filter colour and density, emulsion sensitivity, and the light source to be used.

Unfortunately, even with this information, there is still some theory to come. Those of you who have had enough can skip the next part and come back later.

A filter factor can be shown as being 2X, 3X, 4X, 5X and so on, sometimes in ½X or ⅓X increments. As long as it is a 2X, 4X,

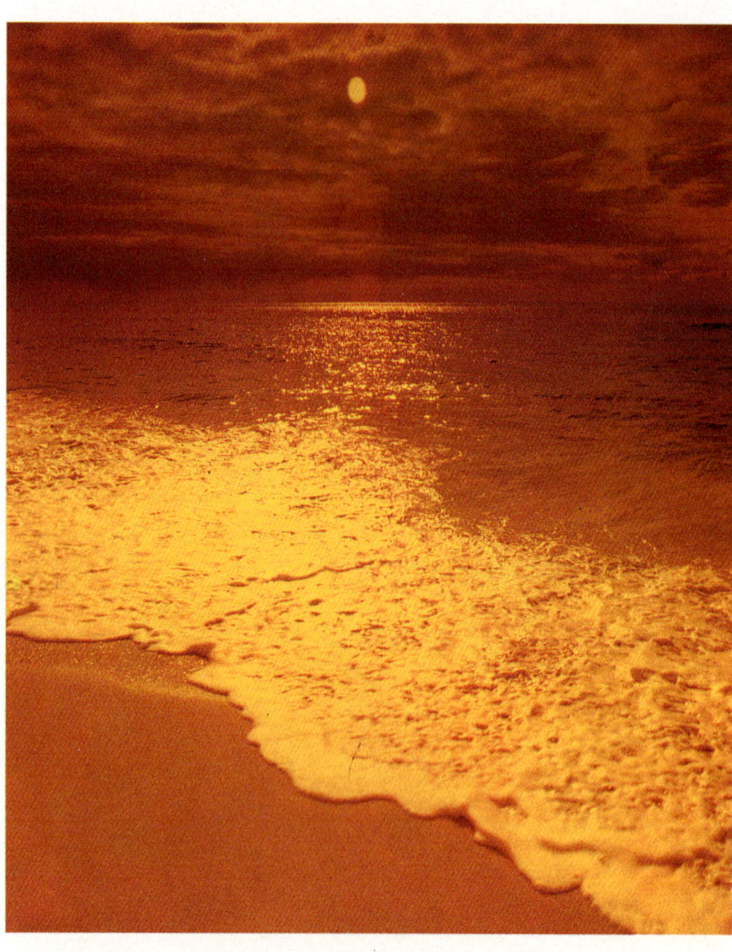

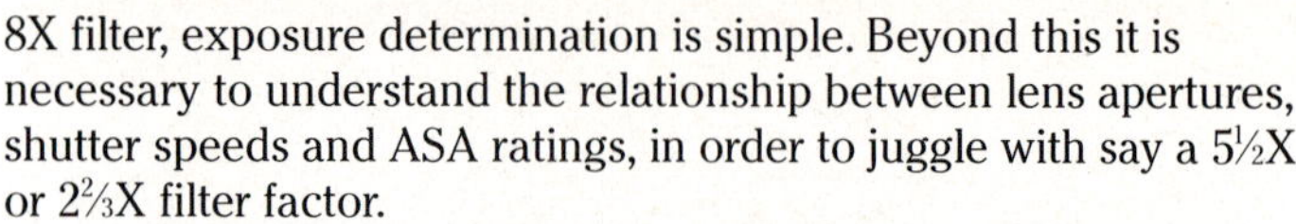

8X filter, exposure determination is simple. Beyond this it is necessary to understand the relationship between lens apertures, shutter speeds and ASA ratings, in order to juggle with say a 5½X or 2⅔X filter factor.

A question I am often asked is 'Why do I have to know about filter factors, when my camera's TTL meter will compensate automatically?' The answer, I am afraid, is that it will not do so in all cases. It may well cope adequately with blue, green and yellow filters, sometimes with magenta, seldom with orange, and not at all with red. This is due to the colour sensitivity – or lack of it – of the measuring cell employed. Reputable camera makers, like Nikon, will admit that exposure compensation is necessary for certain filter colours, and tell you how much extra to allow.

Most modern lenses use the International scale of apertures in the following progression, f1, 1.4, 2, 2.8, 4, 5.6, 8, 11, 16, 22, 32, 45 and so on. This was arrived at in 1910 after nearly thirty years of International Congress of Photography squabbles. However, it was not until after 1945, after the Internationals had won the war, that the rival Continental system was dropped. This progressed through f1.25, 1.8, 2.5, 3.5, 4.5, 6.3, 9, 12.5, 18, 25, 36, and so on. In practice, these two systems slot neatly between each other, in half stop increments, thus it is possible to express a 3X filter factor at a metered f16 as needing an aperture of f9 – or midway between f8 and f11.

There is, however, a modern tendency to express this as 'f8 and a half', which is equally valid. Most modern small format lenses are calibrated in one stop increments, with a half stop indication (or click stop) – if you are lucky. Large format lenses, nowadays, indicate one third stop divisions – with or without clicks! This is in line with professional E6 emulsions, which can

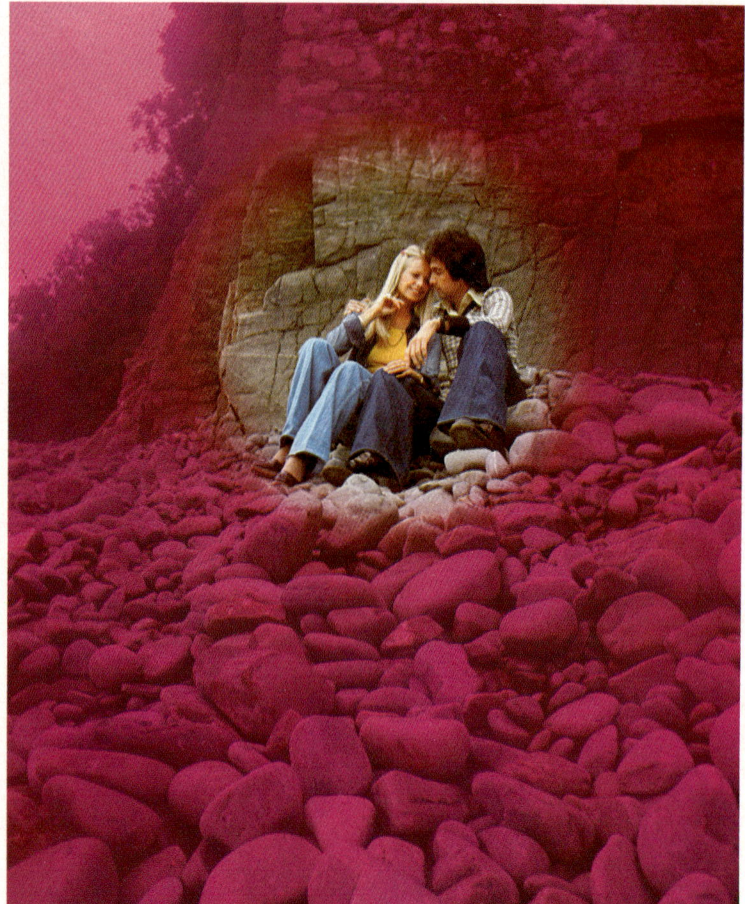

Exposure measurement should *always be made before adding a graduated or spot filter* ***above*** *to the front of the lens. Taking a reading with such filters in position will result in overexposure of the unfiltered part of the shot.*

theoretically have up to a one sixth of a stop tolerance, but in practice a third. Shutter priority exposure metering systems invariably work to around a half stop tolerance. Better makers like Canon and Leitz can improve on this.

Shutter speeds double up or halve temporally between marked values. A very few high precision camera makers allow for intermediate settings within stated limits. Some electronically controlled shutters, when part of an aperture preferred metering system, give stepless speeds. These cope beautifully with those filters which include halves or thirds in their factor – providing that the metering colour sensitivity is compatible with the filter employed.

When it comes to time exposures a filter factor becomes easier to allow for. Assuming that the basic exposure reading can be adjusted to show a shutter speed of one second – at one of the possible shutter/diaphragm combinations, the following table shows how simple exposure compensation for filter factors can be:–

Basic exposure +	Filter factor =	Adjusted exposure or	Equivalent exposure increase in stops
1 second	1X	1 sec	0
1 second	1½X	1½ secs	+½
1 second	2X	2 secs	+1
1 second	3X	3 secs	+1½
1 second	4X	4 secs	+2
1 second	5X	5 secs	+2¼
1 second	6X	6 secs	+2½
1 second	7X	7 secs	+2¾
1 second	8X	8 secs	+3

ASA increments are in thirds, which gives yet a further way of compensating for filter factor increases in exposure. There is, however, a very great danger in that failure to reset the ASA dial of camera, or meter, can result in ruining the rest of the film by over-exposure when the filter is removed. The same applies to those cameras which have an exposure compensation dial. These are usually calibrated in half stops within a range of −2 to +2. 'Against the light' buttons, fitted to some automatic exposure cameras, are of plus one stop (2X), or sometimes plus two stops (4X), value. Again, a TTL system will not compensate correctly for some filter colours. If in doubt then bracket your exposures towards over-exposure.

The following table shows what happens when an ASA scale is used for filter factor compensation. An ASA 400 film has been used as the norm.

ASA setting	400	320	250	200	160	125	100	80	64	50
Filter factor	1X	1⅓X	1⅔X	2X	2⅔X	3⅓X	4X	5⅓X	6⅔X	8X
Equivalent exposure increase in stops	0	+⅓	+⅔	+1	+1⅓	+1⅔	+2	+2⅓	+2⅔	+3

Colour photography is where we finally meet all those filters with one third and two third fractional increases of factor – in profusion! As previously mentioned, there is less latitude, i.e. exposure tolerance, in colour than there is in a black and white emulsion. Furthermore, a pale filter over the lens has a far greater effect on colour balance than the same filter would have on monochromatic tones. Hence the one third fine tuning.

The last part of this section is by way of an explanation. Related only to black and white photography is the question of the light source and emulsion colour sensitivity affecting the filter factor.

Daylight at 5400°K contains more blue and ultra violet, yet at sunrise or sunset can be as red as 2000°K. Artificial light at 3400°K and below, contains more red and yellow than daylight. The green content of both sources is about the same.

All black and white emulsions are, if anything, over sensitive to blue light – this is where they get their daylight ASA rating. Consequently when used in artificial light which contains less blue, there is a drop in emulsion speed. This doesn't really matter with 35mm and 120 rollfilm, where a thinner negative has advantages. It does matter with sheet film and Polaroid materials, where perhaps as much as a one stop loss of emulsion speed becomes critical. Because of this situation, it follows that filter factors can be of different values between the two light sources. The table below is an average of several manufacturers' data.

DAYLIGHT FILTER FACTORS	**FILTER** Red	Orange	Yellow	Green	Blue
Medium speed panchromatic	8X	4X	3X	3½X	3X
Medium speed orthochromatic	–	NR	5X	4X	3X
ARTIFICIAL LIGHT FILTER FACTORS					
Medium speed panchromatic	5X	2½X	1½X	3X	5X
Medium speed orthochromatic	–	NR	2½X	3½X	5X

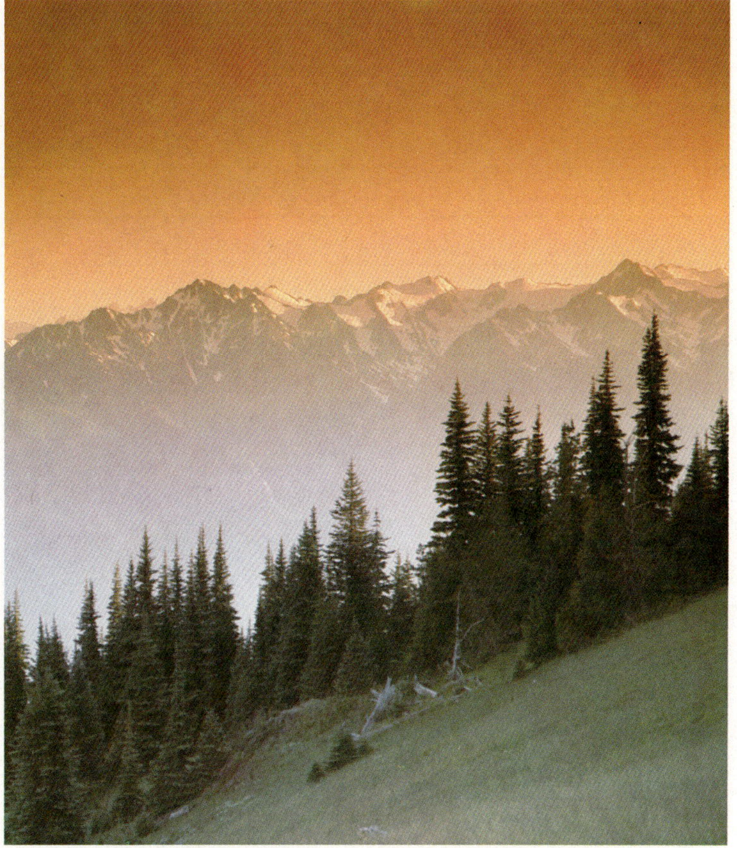

Whilst we probably all realise *that using colour filters means increasing exposure, this is not so for grads or spots. Colour effects filters on colour transparency film depend for their success on the colour they impart to the image, so err on the side of underexposure for maximum effect.*

Throughout the latter part of this chapter there may appear to be some mathematical inconsistencies, and I admit to a certain amount of rounding up and down. This is in line with practice, rather than the theory of academics arguing methods of calculation and decimal points. Whilst it is possible to measure the difference between exposures made at f1.4 and f1.5, between 1/100 sec and 1/125 sec, and between ASA 400 and ASA 450, most of us use our eyes for assessment rather than densitometers.

QUALITIES OF FILTERS

All lens manufacturers go to great lengths to produce the best optical performance which their marketing structure will stand. Yet having purchased a standard of optical excellence which their forbears would have committed murder for, both professional and amateur photographers alike will then deliberately go about destroying that image quality with a layer of organic glass (i.e. plastic) in a suitable attachment. All in the interests of creativity. Never let it be thought that I am against sticking things in front of a lens; throughout my professional career these very devices have often made the difference between success and failure – and in consequence between eating and starving. Nevertheless, I can assure those who have not tried it that it is possible to see a marked difference in definition between transparencies taken with and without a plastic filter – even with the naked eye. Of course, the larger the format the more likely one is to get away with it!

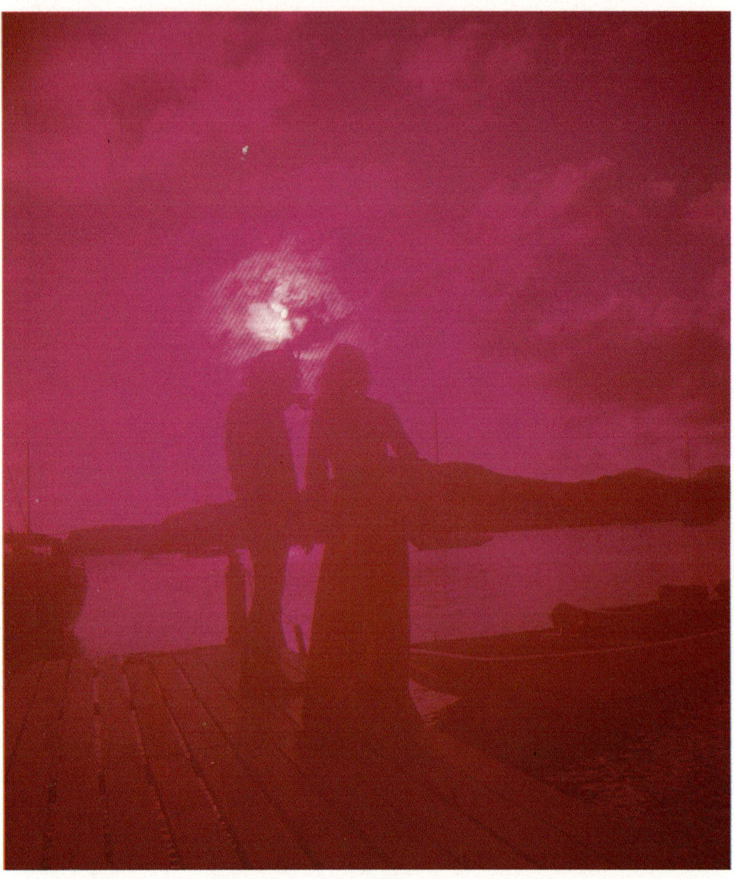

Twenty odd years ago Leica enthusiasts argued and discussed, in print, the question of filters debilitating image quality – and this with Leitz! To be fair, Leitz probably produce the finest filters around – even with Zeiss still in the market, yet the progenitors of the Leica eventually admitted that although their superb filters were plane parallel to within a few microns (i.e. very flat indeed), in optimum photographic terms there was still some slight image degradation.

This debate began long before the advent of multi-coating; a technique which has helped to alleviate those problems which occur by adding what is in effect an extra lens element and air space! To sum up, it can be said that a good quality multi-coated glass filter will have little apparent effect upon image quality, provided that a good sized lens hood is also used. Plastic filters, partly by their nature, and more so because of the ingenuity of Jean Coquin, whilst existing in a sophisticated range at budget prices, can be discounted by optical purists only at their creative peril. The movie business, because of the limitation of using a single shutter speed, i.e. 24 frames per second – or 1/60 sec., has traditionally been far more expert in the use of filters than even the most advanced stills photographer.

For the last forty odd years, ciné cameramen have used special filters to give exactly the on-screen effect that they – or more likely, the director, requires. To this day, certain camera operators have 'secret' filter combinations made up. One such could be, say, a combination of Wratten 85 + neutral density + graduated neutral density + crosstar. Of course, with the Hoyarex, Cokin and other systems one can build up the same combination, but shooting through perhaps as much as 10 to 12mm of plastic gives an effect perhaps most kindly described as interesting. By comparison, glass/gelatin/glass sandwich movie filters are about half this thickness, and although they may cause slight focus shift, they will have less effect on definition and

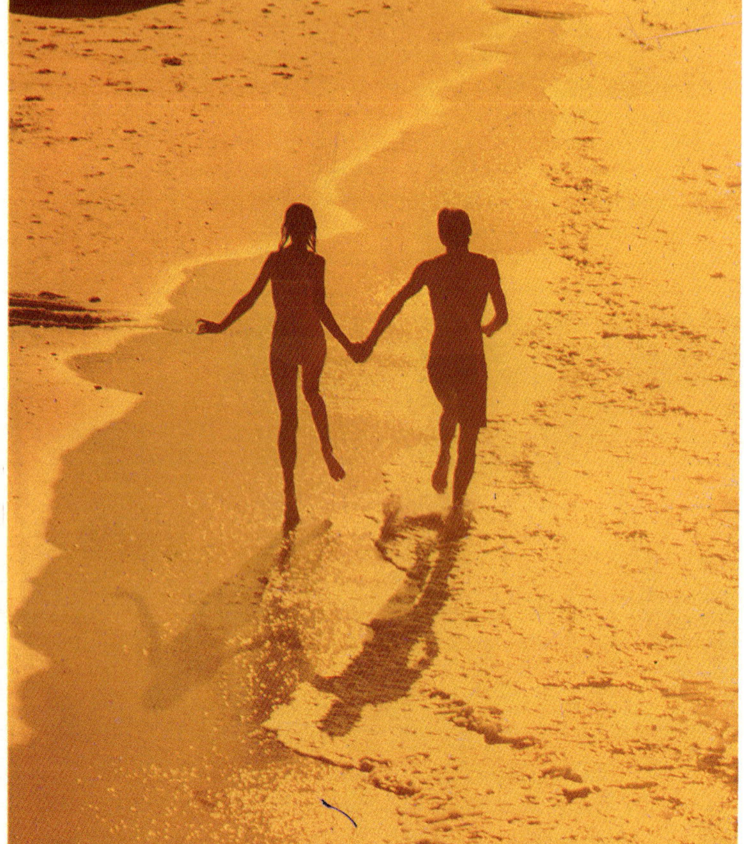

image contrast. We are of course talking about big image magnifications rather than the snapshotter's postcard-sized colour print.

Gelatin filters, extant since the early days of photography, are fragile – even though lacquer coated, and whilst becoming as expensive as organic filters, are still much cheaper than glass. So where is the advantage? 'Gels' have little effect upon the definition of a lens, being nominally only 0.1mm thick, even when two or three are used together. They exist in a huge range which is totally unmatched by any other filter system. They cannot be multicoated and need a deep lenshood for this reason. Plate camera users invariably attach gels to the back element of a lens – ergo inside the camera, or sometimes even between the lens elements. This is not as horrific as it sounds, having been standard plate maker practice since the year dot.

With careful handling, gelatin filters can last for many years and furthermore take up little space in the gadget bag. I have

Kodak Wratten gels which are around twenty years old and still in usable condition. Keep gelatin filters in all their original packing and ensure that they remain flat and dry. The colour of synthetic organic dyes used may change in time, though my oldest gels show no marked colour difference when compared to a freshly purchased filter of the same designation.

Acetate filters of similar appearance to gelatin, are now marketed in a big enough colour correction range to rival Kodak's Wratten series. Whilst they are supposedly as optically clear as gelatin filters, my feeling is that, in comparison, they are slightly cloudy. This suspicion does not show up in practice, and after all, acetate has been used as a rollfilm base material for many years. Certainly, most colour printing filters are made of acetate for its greater resistance to heat.

C.P. filters, however, are not optically suitable for use over a lens. Cokin make an acetate 'Creative filter' set, and state that – 'optical definition is not the same as normal optical filters.' Cemented filters are the oldest type around. They appeared in various shades of yellow as soon as orthochromatic emulsions became available. Used primarily to give an enhanced sky rendering on black and white negatives, they were also known as ortho screens.

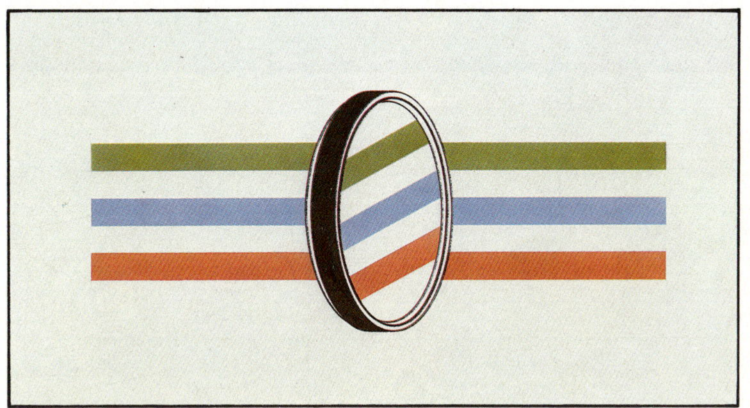

Filters, like lenses, come in *varying qualities, and whilst it is argued that all filters degrade the image, poor examples can produce noticeably inferior results. Cheap glass filters are not always optically flat, leading to fall off in quality, whilst polarisers and neutral density filters may give poor colour rendering. For creative purposes, a second-rate filter may be ideal, in that it can reduce a lens' inherent 'bite.' The diagram above illustrates the effect a poor filter has on the light it transmits.*

A cemented filter consists of a gelatin filter sandwiched between two pieces of thin, optically flat glass, and glued together with Canada balsam. If this sounds somewhat crude, remember that camera lens elements are stuck together in the same way.

These filters are widely used by the cinema industry and to a lesser extent by large format professional photographers. It is not generally known that many proprietary polarising and rainbow (diffraction grating) filters are still made in this way. If you are unlucky enough to drop one and cause it to start separating, you will see the rather nasty, characteristically blotchy appearance of the now useless filter.

Special combination filters and very large sizes can still be supplied to special order. In fact if you are prepared to pay for it, then anything can be made.

Last, and commonest of all, are the dyed-in-the-mass glass filters. It is perhaps surprising that, in spite of all the ancient stained glass windows around the world, this is a comparatively modern process. For some reason (other than the Leica and Contax), coloured glass filters first appeared in Germany in the late nineteen twenties, being generally available in colours other than yellow by 1935, when exotic coloured glasses like graduated green or yellow, infrared and ultraviolet were catalogued.

Postwar reparations allowed other countries to take advantage of German technology at no cost. In Britain, Chance glass from Pilkington Bros. gave rise to a spate of badly made filter holders and their contents, in a range – other than various yellows, which had been the pre-war pattern. Even the burgeoning French photographic industry could see the logic of this market. America had been producing some dyed-in-the-mass glass filters during the war, though really wedded to the 'home-grown' Wratten cemented filters. It was, of course, the Japanese who finally produced glass filters of a standard equal to pre-war Germany's best, albeit many years later.

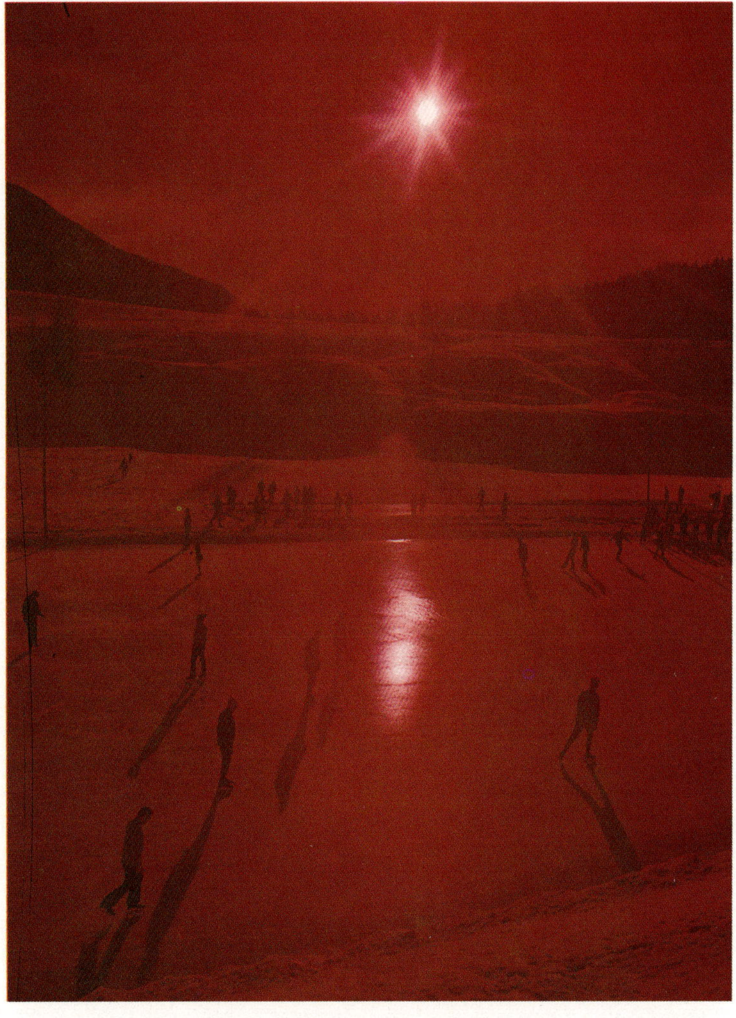

The quality of glass filters still varies enormously. Not only in terms of the glass used, the degree of parallelism between faces, but also ultimately in the thickness of the final product. It is much easier to make a thick filter, for fewer get broken in manufacture. The best glass filters are thin, which means less diffraction, though there is then the problem of fragility. This can be overcome by the use of tension springs to hold the filter glass against the front rim of its mount. Rolleiflex filters, for instance, will rattle when shaken hard, but seldom seem to break when accidentally dropped. At one time, Leitz and Zeiss were so proud of their thin filters that both engraved the company logo minutely on the glass!

WHY USE FILTERS?

When we photographers first encounter filters, there is a tendency to be confused by what we learned in art class, where mixing colours produced the immediate shade we required – well sometimes! A colour cast in colour photography works in the same way, though the film will see the effect more strongly than the eye. Where the confusion between painting and photography occurs is when dealing with complementary colours, an understanding of which is necessary for black and white photography, neg-pos colour printing, the correction of colour casts in transparencies and pos-pos colour printing processes.

The chart below illustrates the make-up (or breakdown) of white light for both additive and subtractive colour photography processes.

ADDITIVE		
	Absorbs	Reflects/transmits
RED (= Yellow + Magenta)	CYAN (= Blue + Green)	RED
BLUE (= Cyan + Magenta)	YELLOW (= Red + Green)	BLUE
GREEN (= Cyan + Yellow)	MAGENTA (= Red + Blue)	GREEN

SUBTRACTIVE		
	Absorbs	Reflects/transmits
CYAN (= Blue + Green)	RED	CYAN (= Blue + Green)
MAGENTA (= Red + Blue)	GREEN	MAGENTA (= Red + Blue)
YELLOW (= Red + Green)	BLUE	YELLOW (= Red + Green)

The triangle below shows the** relationship between colours, with complementaries shown opposite one another. A filter absorbs and hence darkens its complementary colour whilst lightening its own colour. **Facing page bottom:** Square plastic filter systems of the Cokin type are an affordable and flexible method of increasing creativity. Filters and effects can be combined to make even the mundane appear dramatic, as in the filtered fish-eye shot **facing page top.

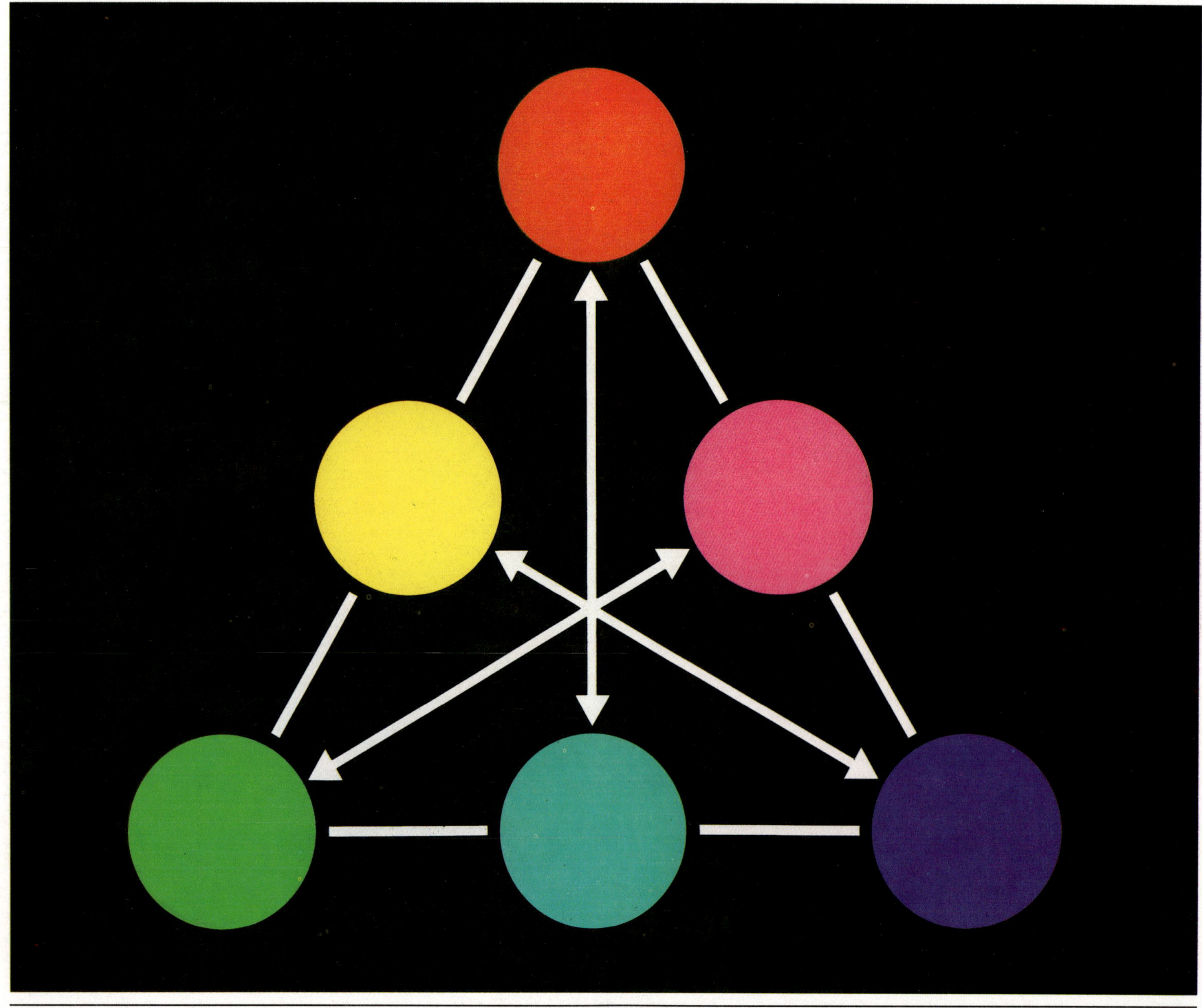

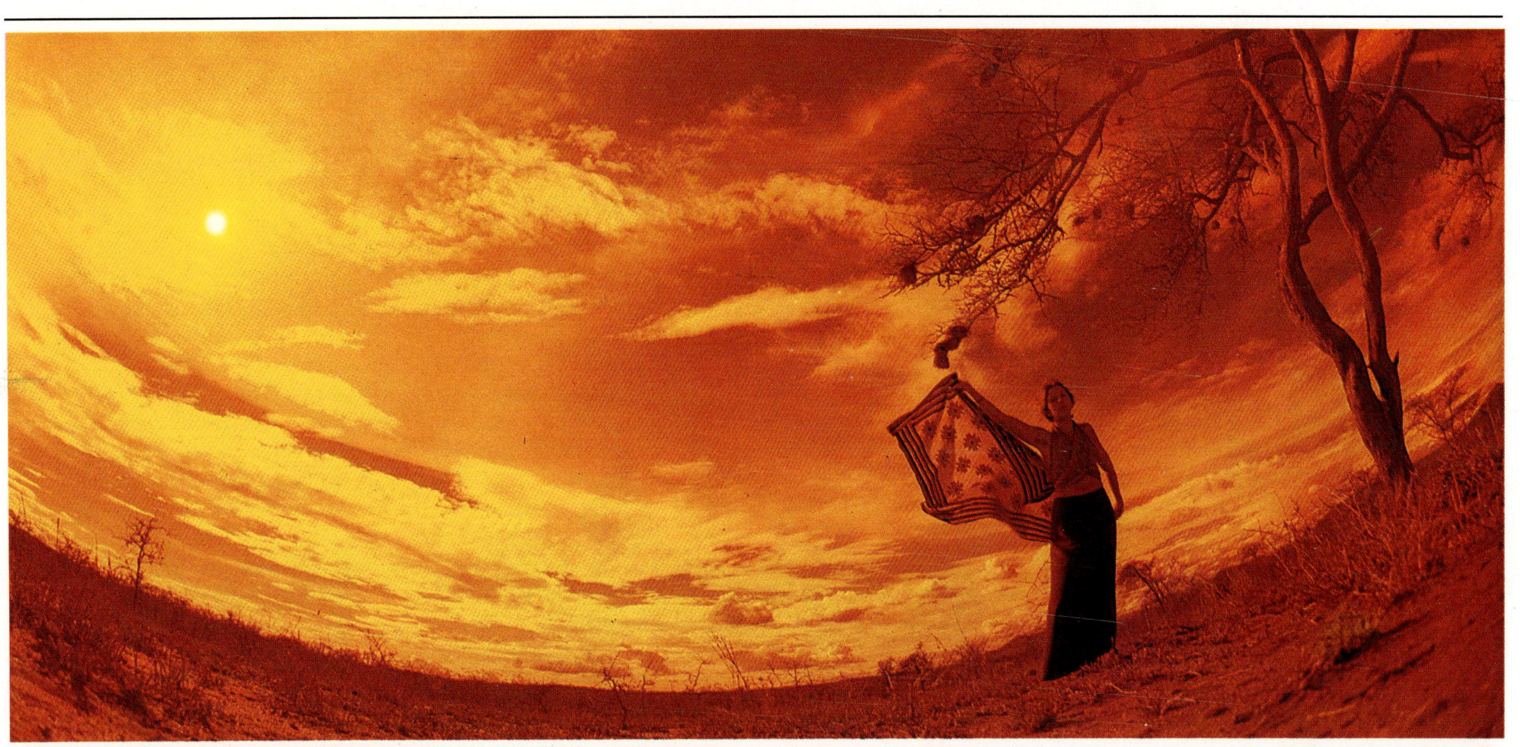

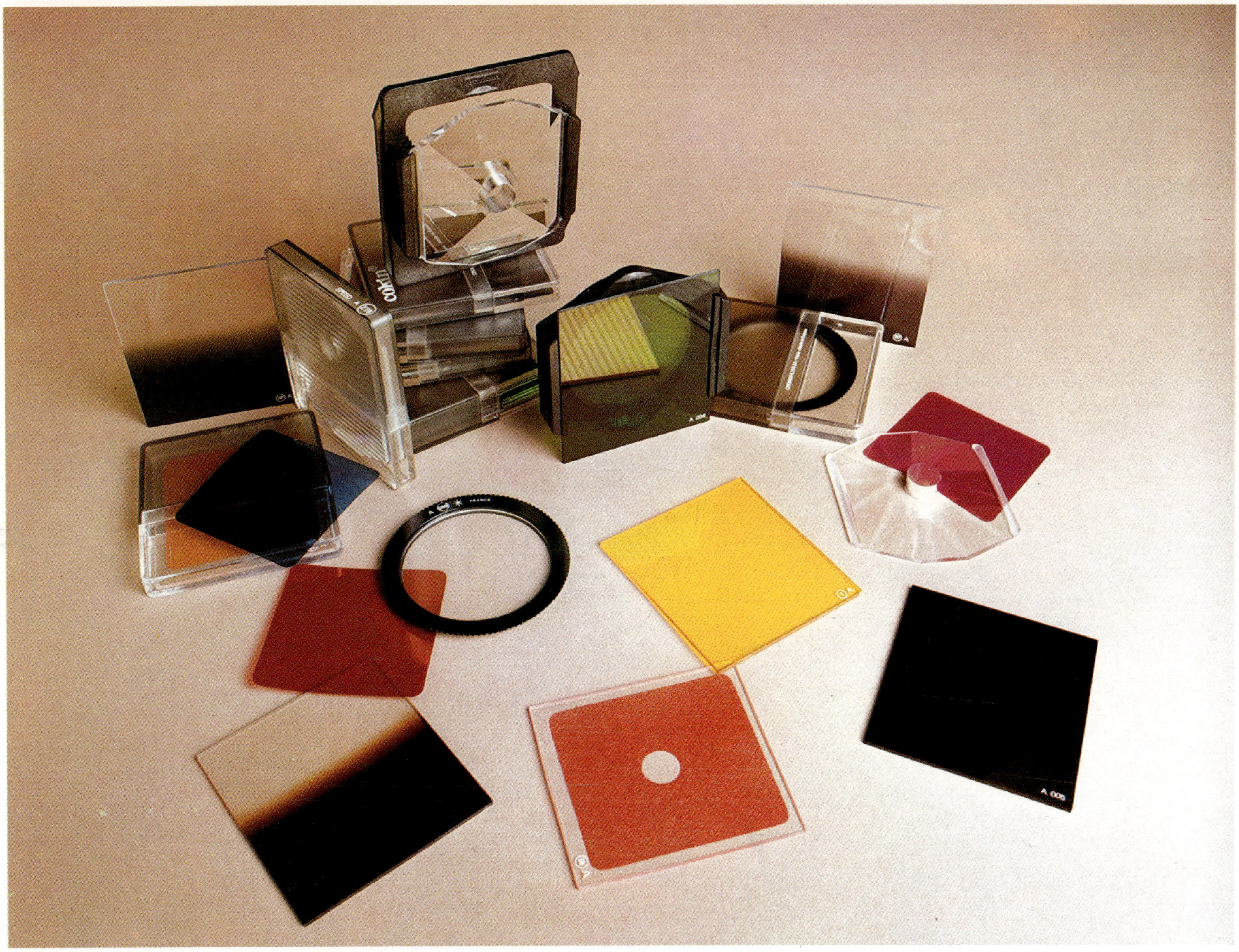

FILTERS FOR BLACK AND WHITE PHOTOGRAPHY

Any good black and white film can record a range of tones in excess of a ratio of 100:1. The figure is still impressive, even when reduced by about half in the final print. These lovely theoretical figures are arrived at by measuring black, grey and white densities from a negative of a black, grey and white original.

Unfortunately, most subjects are composed of colours. It is quite possible to find two colours which, whilst readily separable to the eye, will, when photographed, be rendered in the same shade of grey. To correct this situation we must use a filter. If the subject colours happen to be complementary, then something has to go, in which case we would filter for the colour which needs to be predominantly rendered. It is as well to observe the cardinal rule in filtration, which is: 'A like colour will lighten tone, whilst a complementary will darken.' This in turn can be used to correct, emphasise or exaggerate tones at will. Just to complicate matters further, there is the question of degree. Just how absolute theory differs from practice is shown in the following table:

Subject colour	**Filter to lighten tone** Maximum – minimum (transmits)	**Filter to darken tone** Maximum – minimum (absorbs)
Red	Red-orange-yellow	Green-blue
Orange	Red-orange-yellow	Green-blue
Yellow	Orange-yellow	Blue-green
Green	Green-yellow	Red-orange
Blue	Violet/blue	Red-orange-yellow-green
Violet	Violet-blue	Red-orange-yellow-green

Apart from the use of 'mixed' filters such as magenta and cyan (covered elsewhere), there is also the yellow-green compromise still offered by many filter makers. This has the effect of darkening the sky whilst lightening foliage. Salmon coloured filters were in vogue in the late 1930s, when dramatic skies were all the rage. These gave the effect of moderately darkening a sky and deciduous foliage tones, whilst conifers became virtual silhouettes. The nearest modern equivalents are Wratten CC30 magenta, or a proprietary FLD colour correction filter.

Filters for b/w photography can be placed into four main categories. These are: correction, contrast, detail and haze penetration, all of which can overlap in function to any degree the photographer chooses. Black and white film has a colour sensitivity which differs from the eye in that most emulsions over-react to ultraviolet and blue. We are all aware of the phenomenon whereby a beautiful blue sky with white clouds is recorded as a bald non-event. Whilst this is mostly as a result of the nature of photographic emulsion, it can also be because an area of sky is relatively brighter than other parts of the subject and in consequence over-exposed. Contrasty films, developers and over development can cause or add to this effect. Apart from the aforementioned, the usual remedy is to use a filter to absorb the excess 'blue' light. In ultimate terms, this is normally a yellow-green or medium yellow filter of between two and three times exposure factor.

Contrast filters can fit partly into the correction filter category. Where the subject is a light-coloured building against a blue sky for instance, the use of anything between a yellow and red filter will effectively increase the contrast between subject and background, whereas a flat, hazy landscape, photographed through an orange or red filter will gain in contrast due to the elimination of the softening atmospheric conditions. Monochromatic subjects, such as magenta stained tissue section on a microscope slide, will need a complementary filter – in this case deep green – in order to produce sufficient contrast, and this really is the name of the game. The final result may be a false rendering of the subject, but clarity is the desired effect.

In a different category are the detail filters, where a filter of like colour to the subject is used. Probably the best known is an orange 'furniture' filter, which will bring out the maximum grain detail in stained woodwork. For rosewood or dark mahogany, even a red filter can be used. Careful printing is necessary, as otherwise an object of dark toned wood could appear to have been made of pine or teak!

Haze penetration filters range from the colourless ultraviolet, through yellow and orange to red for maximum effect. It requires considerable experience, or a knowledge of meteorology, to know with some degree of exactitude which to use. As a rough guide, a UV is generally only used at the high altitudes encountered in mountain or aerial photography, where anything stronger will result in a sky which is darkened too much. Nearer sea level, one uses yellow, orange or red filters, depending upon the amount of haze penetration desired and the degree to which a 'normal' to black sky is acceptable. On dull days a red filter can be used, which, whilst darkening foliage will also increase the overall contrast of the scene. Haze filters will not penetrate mist or fog, so if in doubt try the lot!

With the exception of the huge Kodak Wratten gelatin filter list, a quick glance at any top manufacturer's catalogue is likely to provide a range of filters for black and white photography which consists of something like six colours, of which at least two are likely to be supplied in differing strengths. These could well consist of yellow (in three strengths), orange, red (in two strengths), yellow-green, green and pale blue. This is apart from ultraviolet, infrared and those filters primarily intended for colour photography. A summary could well consist of:

Colour	**Approximate factor**	**Use**
Light yellow	1½ x	Mild correction of sky tones. Stronger at high altitudes.
Medium „ Dark „	2 x 3 x	Stronger correction of sky tones with mild haze penetration properties.
Orange	4 x	Over correction of sky tones. Stronger haze penetration.
Light red Red	6 x 8 x	Dramatic sky rendition. Strongest haze penetration. Use for 'moonlight' effects.
Yellow-green	3 x	Standard correction filter. Darkens sky and lightens foliage.
Green	4 x	Similar in effect to medium yellow but lightens foliage to a greater degree.
Pale blue	2 x	For correction of skin tones under artificial light.

For the inexperienced, and long before the days of Polaroid, there were monochromatic (or panchromatic) vision filters. Intended for use in front of the eye, or camera viewfinder, these would render any subject in monochromatic tones, or at least a semblance of such. They would effectively give the photographer a guide as to the rendition of coloured objects on b/w film, or to a subject's tonal differences. Traditionally of deep blue glass, they are nowadays either an olive green colour, or, as Kodak describe their current Wratten 90 P.V. gelatin filter, 'a dark greyish amber.'

Whether panchromatic vision filters are in fact of any use is a subjective matter, though there is no doubt that they do reduce the eye's adaptability in assessing tonal differences.

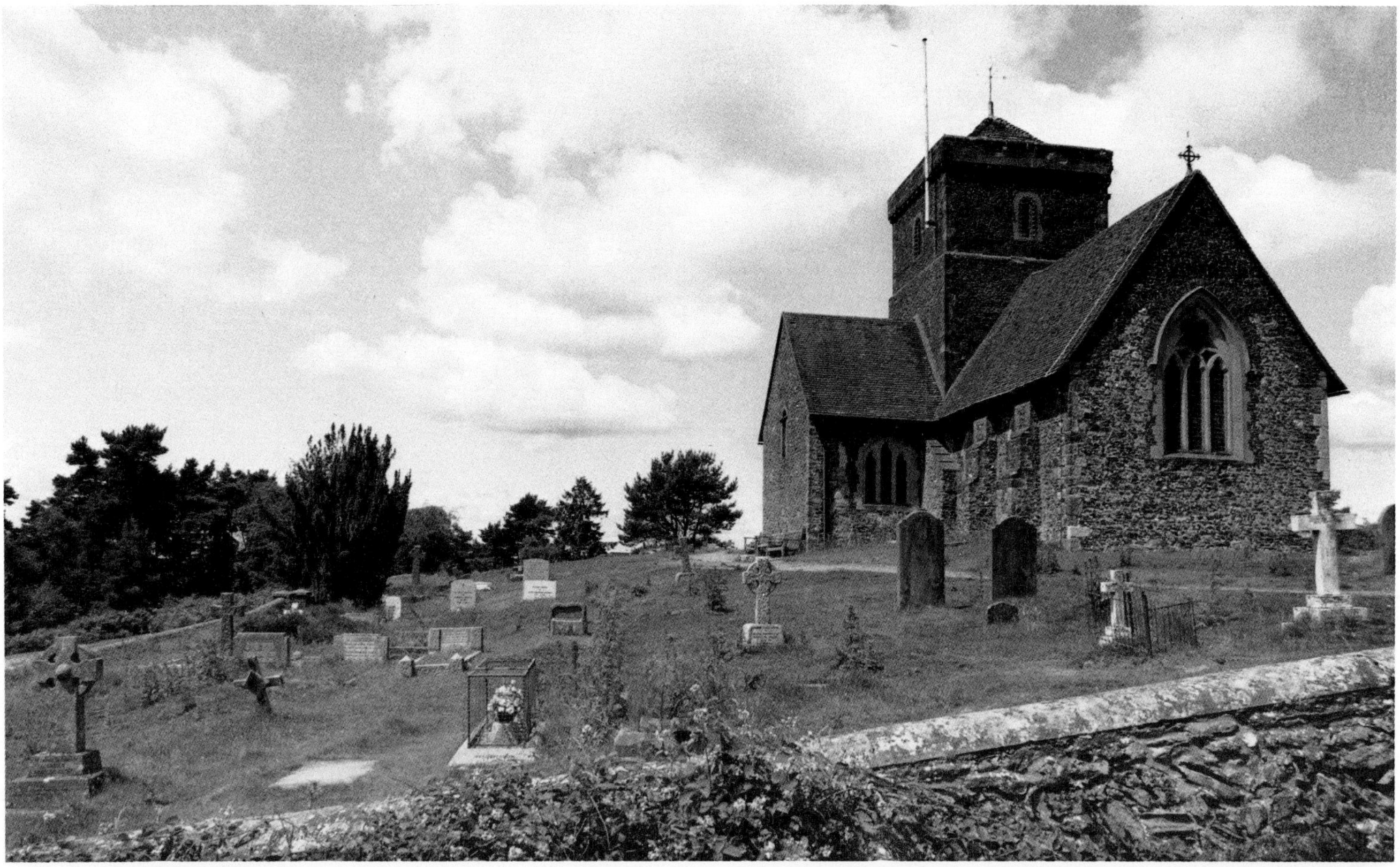

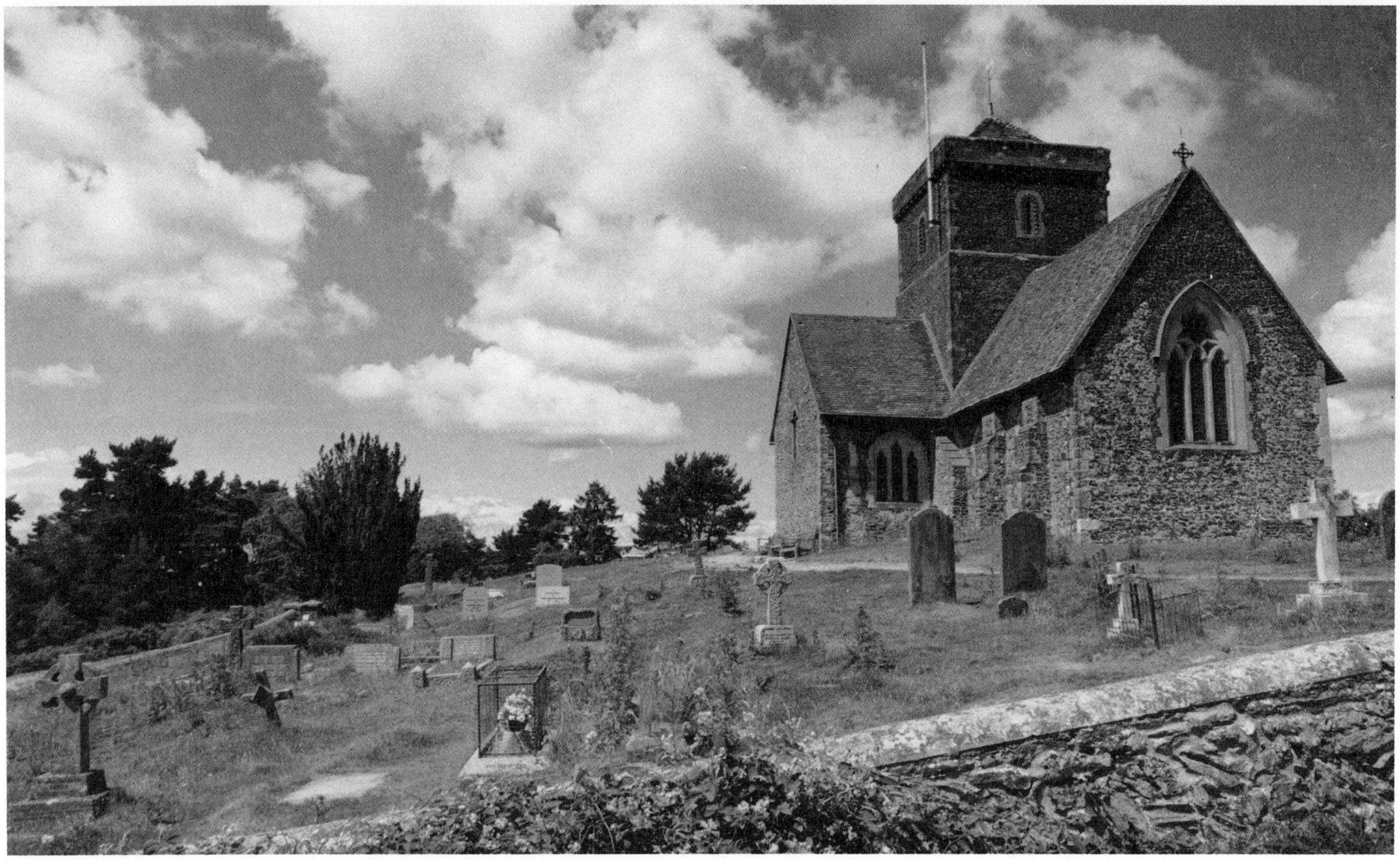

Above: Cloud detail can be enhanced to varying degrees by using yellow, orange or red filters.

COLOUR CORRECTION AND LIGHT BALANCING FILTERS

The whole field of colour correction filters for colour film is generally considered to be a Kodak benefit, even though Wratten designations have become the generic nomenclature. To be fair, although Agfa still make a set of camera filters – primarily intended for their non-E6 emulsions, these are only generally known and appreciated on the European mainland.

Kodak colour correction filters fall into three main categories. There are the 80 series blue filters, intended to convert daylight balanced colour film emulsions to artificial light conditions, and their antitheses the 85 series orange/brown, or amber filters. Apart from their intended use, the 80 filters can be used as 'moonlight' filters in daylight, whilst the 85 series can be used to produce – or enhance – a sunset. In either case do not allow for the approximately one stop filter factor, as this amount of under exposure adds to the effect. A TTL metering system will have to be 'cheated' by use of the ASA setting if a reading is taken with the filter attached.

The second category of Kodak filter is the warming 81 (brown) and 82 (blue) series of filters. Primarily intended for colour temperature correction, these are designed to work in smaller increments than the 80 or 85 conversion filters. The 81 family are widely used by fashion and portrait photographers as suntan filters. The exposure factor of ⅓ to ⅔rds of a stop is ignored, thereby producing a slightly dark and warm transparency.

Colour negatives produced with 81 filtration will make the final printing easier – if this is the effect you are after – but in this case allow for the filter factor. The 81EF filter, as the strongest of the range, is generally used only in very overcast daylight conditions where the light is decidedly blue. The lighter 81C and 81B are my preferred filter strengths for general use, rather than the still paler 81 and 81A.

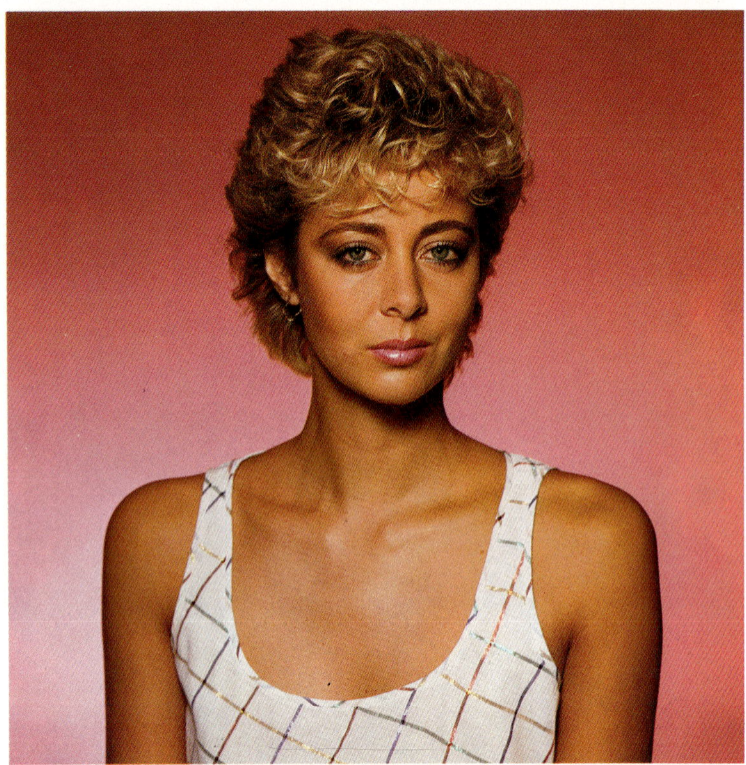

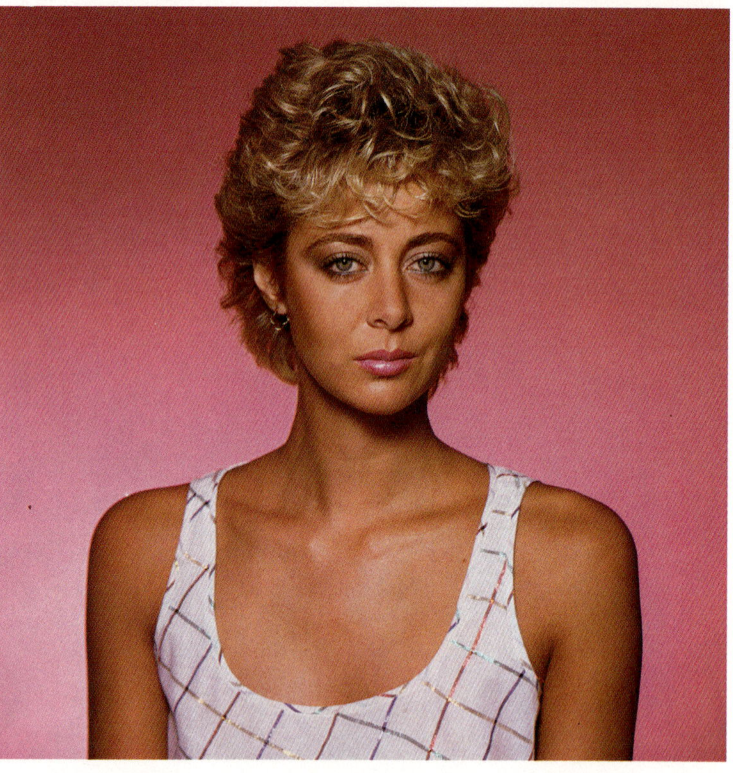

KODAK LIGHT BALANCING FILTERS

These filters are intended for use over the camera lens to raise or lower the colour temperature of the light reaching the film by much smaller increments than conversion filters.

Filter Colour	WRATTEN Filter Number	Exposure Increase in stops*	To obtain 3200K from:	To obtain 3400K from:	Mired Shift Value
	82C + 82C	1⅓	2490K	2610K	- 89
	82C + 82B	1⅓	2570K	2700K	- 77
	82C + 82A	1	2650K	2780K	- 62
Bluish	82C + 82	1	2720K	2870K	- 55
	82C	⅔	2800K	2950K	- 45
	82B	⅔	2900K	3060K	- 32
	82A	⅓	3000K	3180K	- 18
	82	⅓	3100K	3290K	- 10
	No filter necessary		3200K	3400K	—
	81	⅓	3300K	3510K	+ 10
	81A	⅓	3400K	3630K	+ 18
Brownish	81B	⅓	3500K	3740K	+ 27
	8C	⅓	3600K	3850K	+ 35
	81EF	⅔	3850K	4140K	+ 53

*These values are approximate. For critical work they should be checked by practical tests, especially if more than one filter is used.

Chart reproduced by courtesy of Kodak Ltd.

Blue 82 filters are frequently used in early morning, late afternoon or winter sun conditions to take out the excess warmth of the light, particularly when any degree of subject colour fidelity is necessary. Under these conditions, a certain amount of experience, or experimentation, is necessary in the absence of a colour temperature meter, though be assured that any 82 filter will effect some improvement. Unlike the 81 series, 82's can be used in combination for even greater correction.

As mentioned above, manufacturers other than Kodak use 81 and 82 designations. These will not necessarily match the original, but will usually still work in a pleasing manner.

Kodak's third category of colour correction (CC) filters is for even finer tuning of colour transparency materials. The range consists of six colours namely: cyan, magenta, yellow, red, green and blue, in a range of six densities from CC05 to CC50. Each designated density of each colour is roughly comparable in the degree of colour shift, though not in the exposure factor required.

The primary use of CC filters is in correcting mild colour casts. This tends to be the prerogative of professional studio photographers, where there is time to shoot a test transparency. It is not unknown for a colour laboratory to have a consistent processing colour bias. Here the professional will have a constant CC filter pack to correct this. Likewise he may well have a favourite CC filter which suits his particular electronic flash unit or lighting technique. There are also many subjects which do not reproduce on film in the same colour/s as they appear to the eye. The client may well insist that his product does so, which can call for a very odd CC filter combination. Bounced light can produce colour casts which need to be filtered out. A CC15M or 30M (Magenta) is a good starter for correction of a yellow-green fluorescent lighting colour bias on daylight emulsion. Other needs for CC filters are; reciprocity shift – where a long or ultra-short exposure changes the colour balance of an emulsion; underwater photography, which requires a CCR (Red) filter; and the colour corrections required when making duplicate trans-parencies – especially when duping film is employed.

manual exposure compensation. Checking the camera's exposure readout with and without the filter, will show how closely (or otherwise) the meter cell's colour sensitivity copes with the filter makers recommended factor.

Judging which CC filter to use for correction on a test, or clip, transparency is partially subjective but mostly a matter of experienced colour vision. The first essential is that the transparency is examined on a daylight corrected viewing box, or even by projection. Holding a 'tranny' up to a window or fluorescent ceiling light is not good enough, even if it is the common practice of people who should know better.

Colour corrected fluorescent tubes are made by Phillips (and others) specifically for the graphic arts and photographic trades. They are not much more expensive than conventional tubes. I should add that they are only for viewing, and are not suitable for use as a photographic light source.

Let us assume that a test transparency is too blue, but of

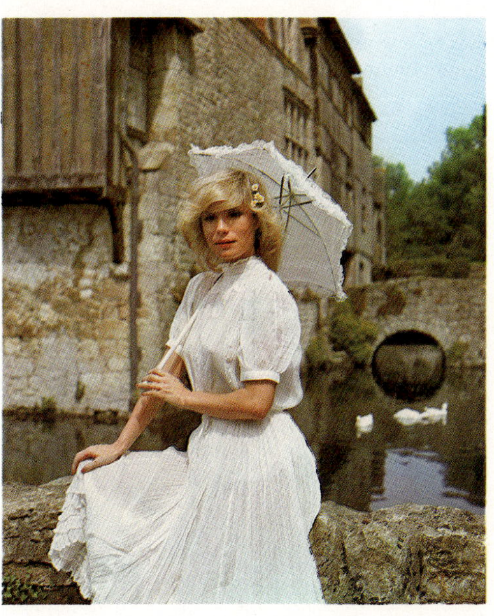

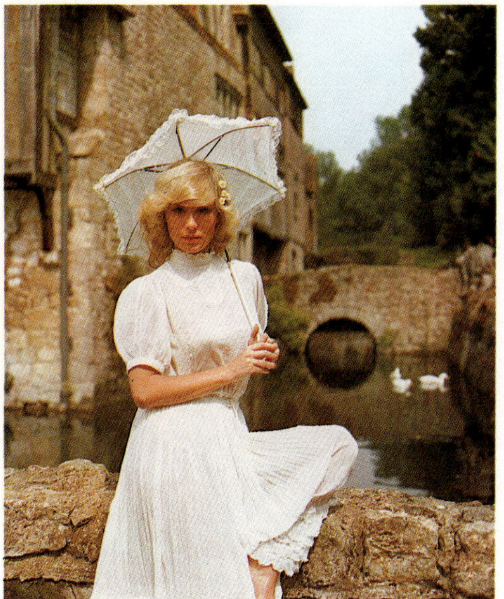

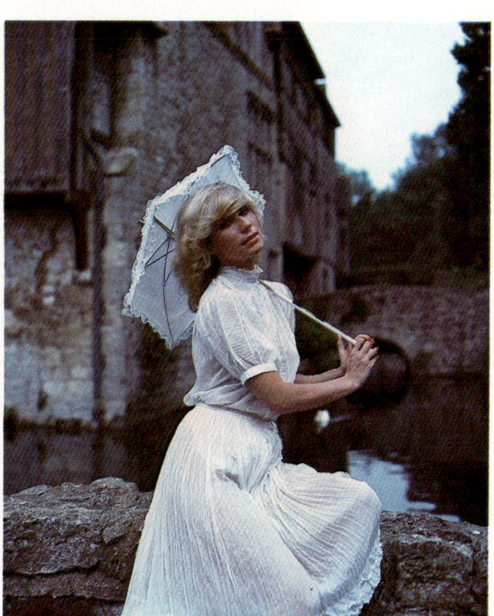

With transparency materials, it *is important to consider the final colour effect that you wish to achieve.* ***Facing page:*** *An 81 brown warming filter was used in the top shot to enhance skin colour without upsetting the overall colour balance. The three pictures* ***above,*** *from left to right, show the effect of using daylight film unfiltered, with 85C orange colour correction filter and with 80B blue filter, normally used with such film under tungsten light.*

The list of uses for CC filters is almost endless – at least in the studio, where after making a test shot, one always ensures that the final photograph is taken on the same film batch number as the test. Oh yes, I nearly forgot to mention that professional colour emulsions can vary in colour rendition from batch to batch!

KODAK COLOUR COMPENSATING FILTERS

Cyan	CC05C	CC10C	CC20C	CC30C	CC40C	CC50C
Exposure Increase*	⅓ stop	⅓ stop	⅓ stop	⅔ stop	⅔ stop	1 stop
Magenta	CC05M	CC10M	CC20M	CC30M	CC40M	CC50M
Exposure Increase*	⅓ stop	⅓ stop	⅓ stop	⅔ stop	⅔ stop	⅔ stop
Yellow	CC05Y	CC10Y	CC20Y	CC30Y	CC40Y	CC50Y
Exposure Increase*	–	⅓ stop	⅓ stop	⅓ stop	⅓ stop	⅔ stop
Red	CC05R	CC10R	CC20R	CC30R	CC40R	CC50R
Exposure Increase*	⅓ stop	⅓ stop	⅓ stop	⅔ stop	⅔ stop	1 stop
Green	CC05G	CC10G	CC20G	CC30G	CC40G	CC50G
Exposure Increase*	⅓ stop	⅓ stop	⅓ stop	⅔ stop	⅔ stop	1 stop
Blue	CC05B	CC10B	CC20B	CC30B	CC40B	CC50B
Exposure Increase*	⅓ stop	⅓ stop	⅔ stop	⅔ stop	1 stop	1⅔ stop

*These values are approximate. For critical work they should be checked by practical test, especially if more than one filter is used.

Chart reproduced by courtesy of Kodak Ltd.

As CC filters – up to a 30 density – are not intense in colour, most TTL exposure metering systems will compensate for the filter factor automatically. The 40 and 50 densities in red (particularly) and magenta (sometimes) will usually need

correct density. Place it on the viewing box and try putting a CC20 yellow filter over half of it, the idea being to bring the blue cast back to a neutral grey. Upon examination, the CC20Y overcorrects, producing a yellow rather than grey tone. Next try a CC10Y, which looks just about correct. Some photographers prefer to wave the filter to and fro across one eye, whilst viewing the transparency. Whichever method is preferred, we still end up with a CC10Y correction. The trick then is to use HALF the visual density, i.e. CC05Y, over the lens. The reason for this is the different response of an emulsion in comparison to the eye.

Transparency evaluation by projection works in a similar fashion, except that in this case the test filter is held over the projection lens. It is quite possible to bind a gelatin correction filter together with the transparency, thereby saving a reshoot. Here one would of course use a visual correction density. Transparency retouchers are capable of dyeing a CC density into a transparency, but this is a skill beyond the ability of most photographers and best not attempted except in desperation.

ULTRAVIOLET FILTERS

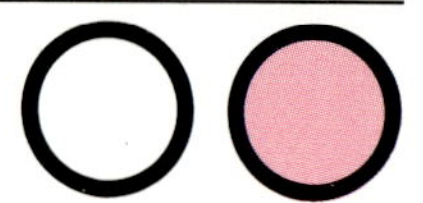

The wavelength range of the normal photographic spectrum falls between 3250 and 7000 on the Ånström Scale(AU), or can be measured in Nanometres (nm), which are numerically the same, less a zero! The response of the eye falls approximately between 4200 and 6800AU, whilst the ultraviolet region is between 3250 and 4000. It therefore follows that photographic emulsions, with their high sensitivity towards blue and ultraviolet, can produce a result which the eye cannot appreciate until it sees the photograph!

Any sunlit long distance subject, such as mountains or water, is likely to show both a loss of contrast and definition, and in the case of colour films, a blue cast. This is because under these conditions a high proportion of ultraviolet radiation becomes scattered in the atmosphere to produce haze. This should not be confused with mist and fog where there is water vapour and/or dust present as well. Atmospheric haze scatters very little red, little yellow, some green, more blue and a helluva lot of ultraviolet. Conversely, and perhaps confusingly, there is less of a problem with UV at altitudes above 6,000ft (2,000m), for, though the UV content is higher – as sunburn enthusiasts will attest, the atmosphere is thinner, so the scatter is correspondingly lower. This is, however, not true for aerial photography where pictures are taken through the atmosphere towards the ground.

The reduction of ultraviolet can be achieved in several ways. The development of rare earth glasses, some with UV absorbing properties, multicoating techniques and even UV absorbing lens element cements, have all contributed to the modern lens' 'warm' colour rendering, with its reduction in ultraviolet effect. Many current lenses in fact no longer need an ultraviolet absorbing filter for normal use. The practice of using a UV filter at all times is unnecessary. I appreciate that there is the excuse of lens protection, but what are lenscaps for? All too often an expensive lens is degraded by the use of a cheap filter. If you

The ultraviolet filter can be *virtually ignored where filter factors are concerned. The extra exposure required is minimal and camera meters will allow for this automatically. There are several different filters marketed under the general term 'ultraviolet.' They reduce to some extent the blue cast caused by ultraviolet rays but the effect of all but the stronger varieties is negligible except at high altitudes or by the sea. They do serve, however, as efficient lens protectors, but this must be balanced against the fact that, being mounted on the front of the lens, a lenshood is particularly important to counteract flare.*

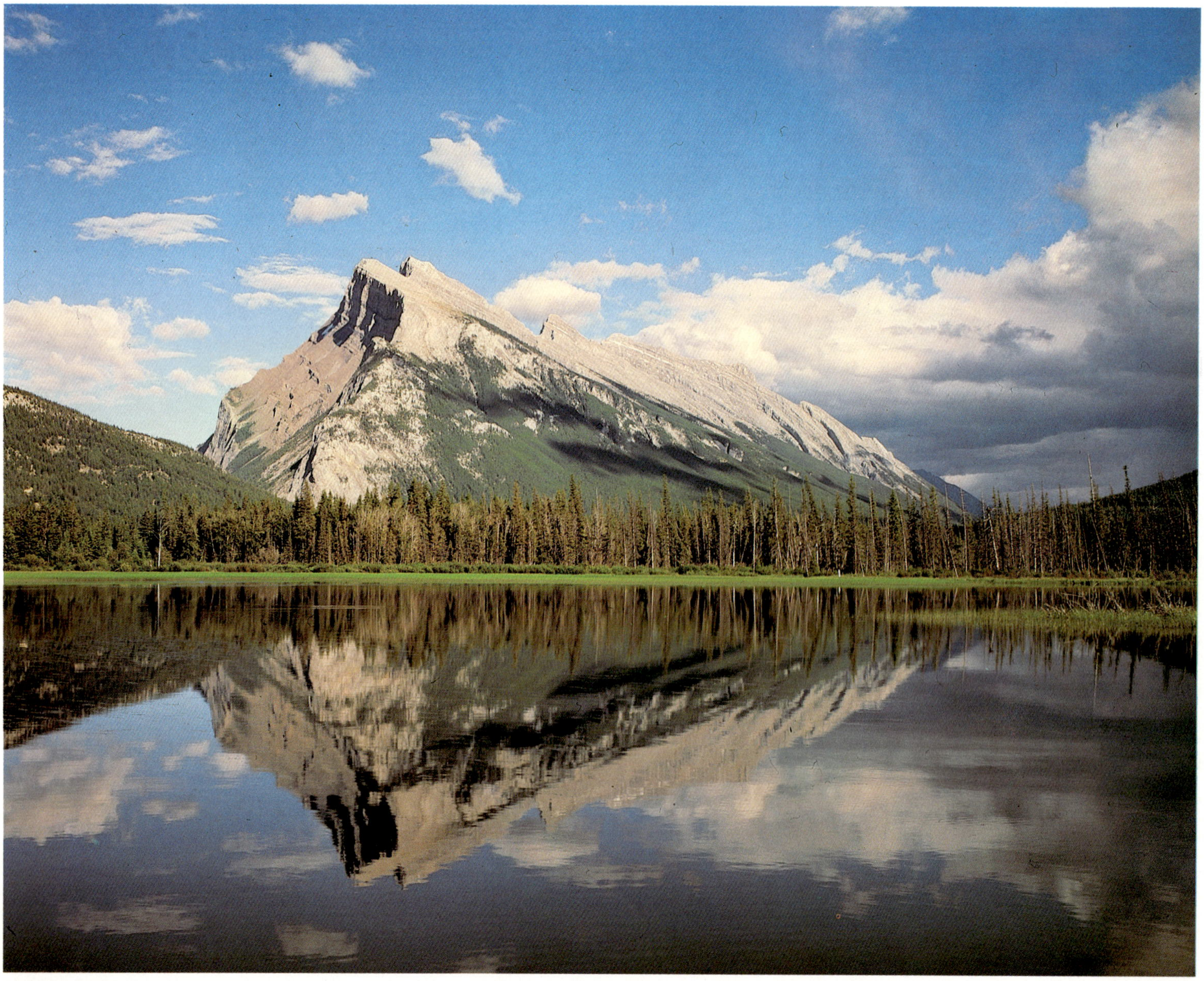

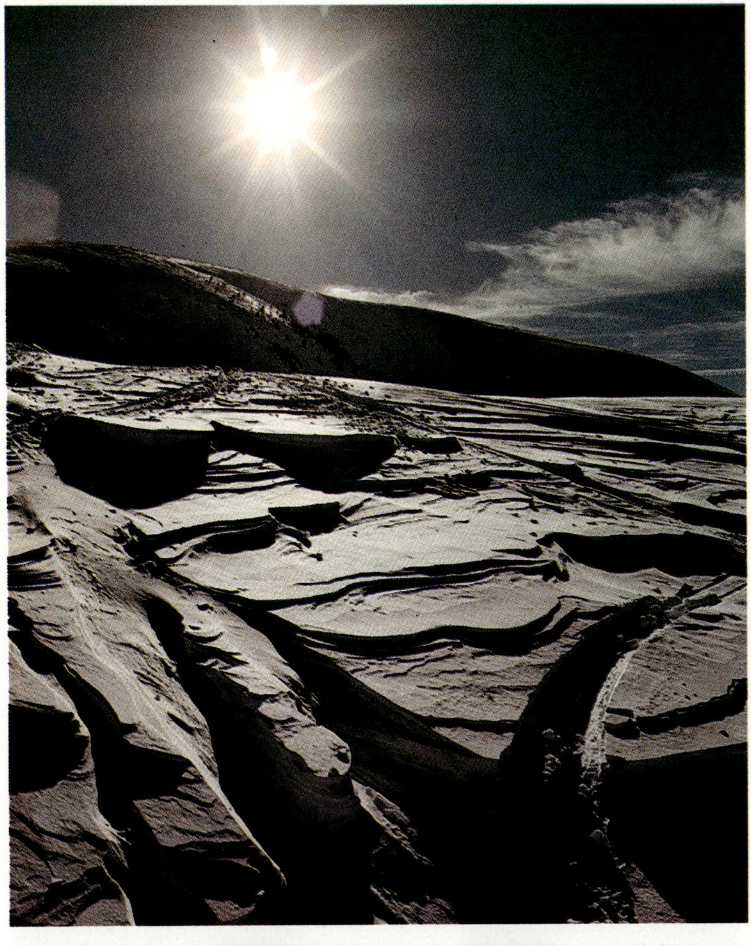

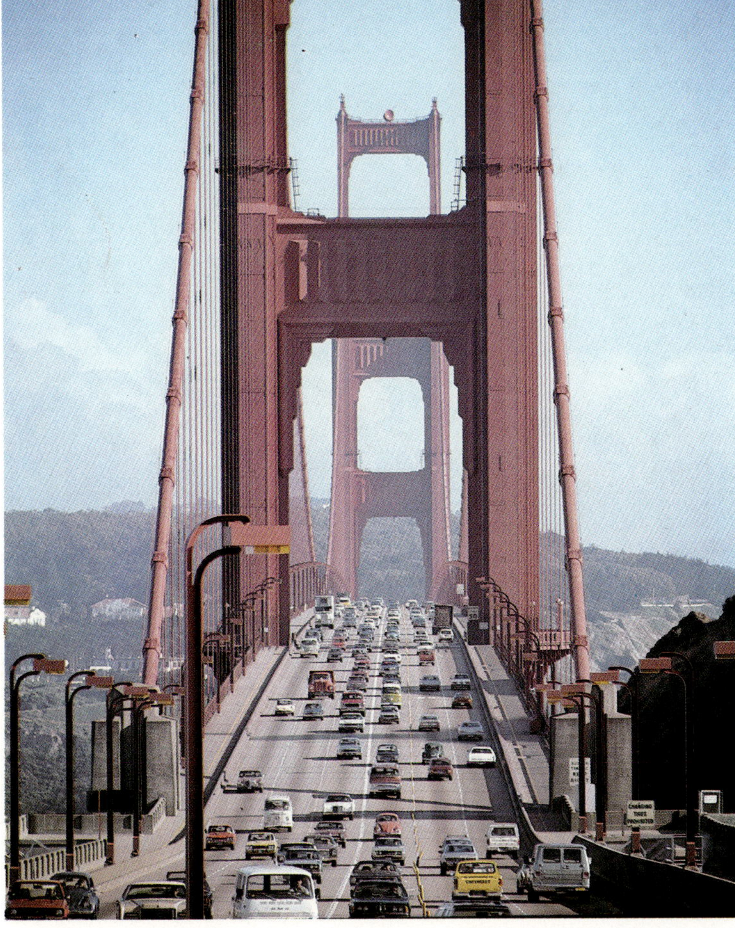

must pursue this route, then buy the best multicoated filter around.

UV filters fall into several different categories:

Filter colour	Suitable film	Approximate factor	Typical example
Clear	B/w only	1.1 x	Nikon L37, L37C
Clear (stronger)	B/w only	1.2 x	Nikon L39
Very light yellow	B/w only	1.3 x	Kodak 2A
Very light yellow (stronger)	B/w only	1.5 x	Kodak 2B
Pinkish	Colour + b/w	1.2 x	Kodak IA (skylight)
Pinkish (stronger)	Colour + b/w	1.25 x	Nikon LIBC
Very pale amber	Colour + b/w	1.3 x	Kodak 81, Nikon A2
Very pale red	Colour + b/w	1.5 x	Hasselblad CR1.5, Kodak CC 05 Red
Very pale magenta	Colour only	1.3 x	Kodak CC 05 Magenta

As these filter factors are so low, they can in most cases be safely ignored.

The loss of definition and contrast due to ultraviolet scatter in black and white work can be corrected to any degree the photographer wishes. On the other hand, it can be left alone - or even enhanced - if this gives the desired effect.

Assuming that a reduction is required, then there is a choice of colourless and yellow filters, through to the over-correction of orange and red if maximum haze penetration is the name of the game. Colourless UV filters are primarily used at high altitudes where anything stronger will produce an over-dramatic sky rendition. This is particularly true in winter sunlight, where the sky is an intense blue anyway. 1A skylight and 1B filters are virtually interchangeable with their colourless counterparts. Very pale yellow filters fall somewhere between these and a 2x yellow or yellow-green tone correction filter. Pale amber or red filters perform about the same function as a skylight, whilst a CC05M has virtually no effect.

Colourless UV filters for b/w work can be used with colour films, though the effect is negligible except at high altitudes; much better to use an 1A or 1B. Pale amber, red or magenta filters all absorb about the same degree of ultraviolet and are primarily used to add a degree of colour correction as well. German lenses used to give a bluer rendering than their warmer Japanese counterparts - some still do. This is where the additional warmth of amber, red or magenta may be preferable. Their other use is with telephoto and long focus lenses, where haze is apt to be amplified, or with zoom lenses of low contrast characteristics.

Colour films also have some degree of colour bias between 'warm' and 'cool,' which can affect their sensitivity towards ultraviolet and its subsequent rendering. This is just as much a subjective matter as over-blue mountain or seascape pictures. All too often the photographer's memory is short and he will accept the final result as truth. Likewise, there are those who prefer snowscapes with blue shadows as a result of too much UV. "They are more picturesque, even if incorrect," I was once told by an art editor!

Ultraviolet casts can also occur with electronic flash, particularly with powerful studio units, where a standard filter pack could be, say, a Wratten 1A + Wratten CC05 Yellow. As any colour cast can be a combination of lens, film, flash unit and colour lab, this is a matter for experimentation, though as a rule there is no harm in always using a skylight filter when an electronic flash is employed. It is usually possible to tape a gelatin filter over the flash head and forget it.

POLARISING FILTERS

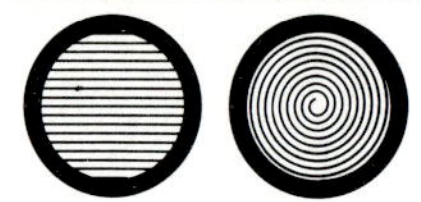

Synthetic polarising material was developed in 1934 by the brilliant Dr Edwin Land of sunglasses and instant picture fame. The first such camera filters were produced by Leitz and Zeiss a few years later. Light is composed of a wave motion vibrating around a central axis. If it is restricted to one plane, we have polarised light, which can be obtained in several ways. One is by reflection from a non-metallic surface such as water, glass or paint – where the effect is greatest when reflection takes place at angles of between 30° and 40°; is less at other angles and disappears altogether at 0° and 90° Light is also polarised quite strongly in those sectors of the sky at a 90° angle to the sun. At other angles the effect is weaker and vanishes at 0° and 180° to the sun. Another method is the use of a special screen. What this polarising filter does is to suppress light vibrating in one particular plane, whilst freely passing light vibrating in a plane at 90° to it.

In practice, by revolving a pola filter on the lens, it becomes possible to reduce or eliminate a reflection by coinciding the plane of suppression of the filter with the plane of reflection of the subject. In the case of a sky the result is similar in that removal of flare or reflection effectively darkens that subject.

For those who are interested, polarising material consists of a gelatin film holding in suspension a multitude of double-refracting, dichroic, ultra-microscopic and similarly-orientated crystalline needles of luteocobaltic periodosulphate.

Yes, Well!!

The cobaltic bit explains the bluish tinge of the better pola filters. A greenish tinge in a cheap filter will produce a corresponding colour cast.

All polarising filters have to be laminated between optical glass flats, though Kodak do sell the original in gelatin form. Polarising filters destroy a certain amount of resolution, so adding

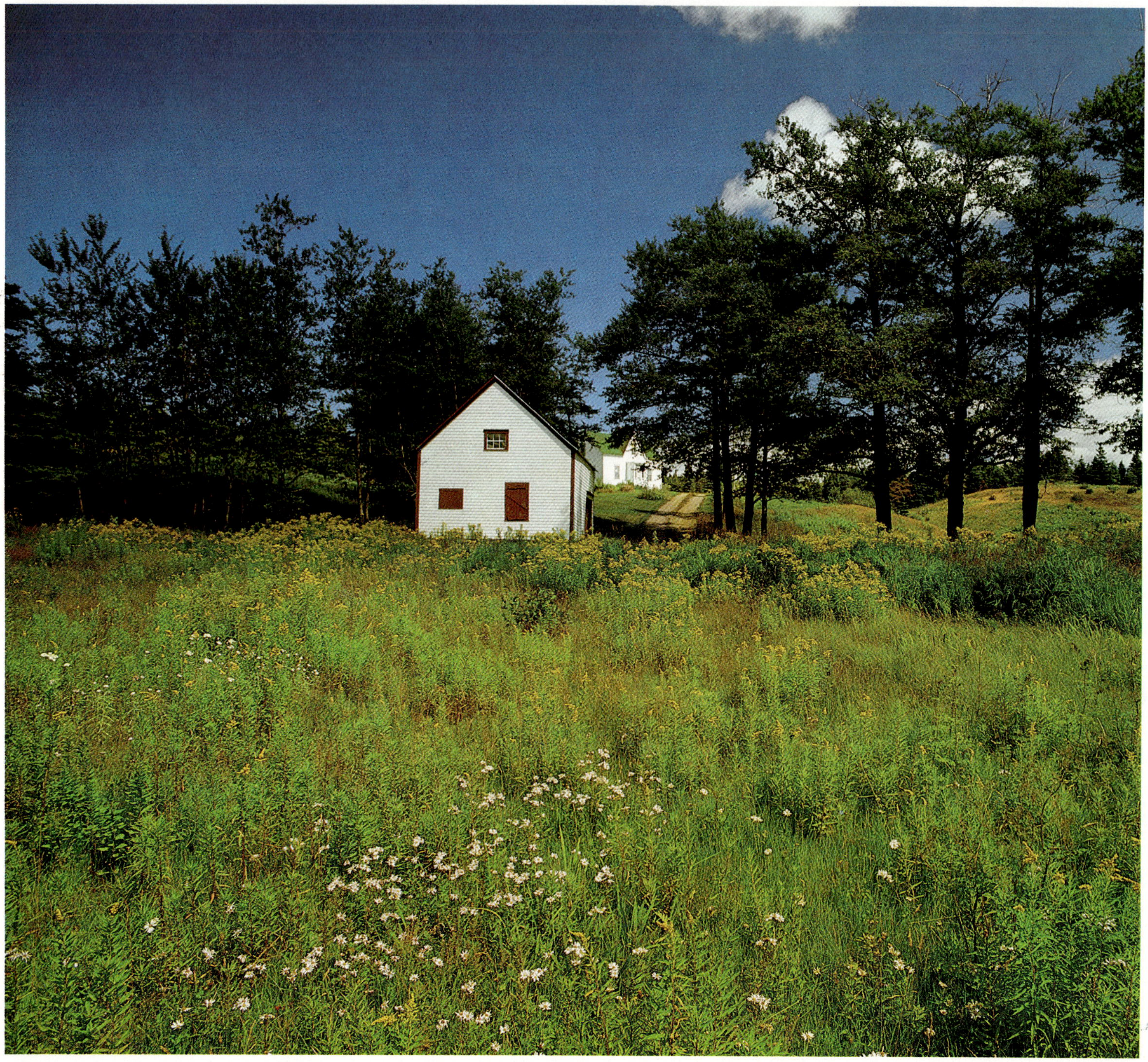

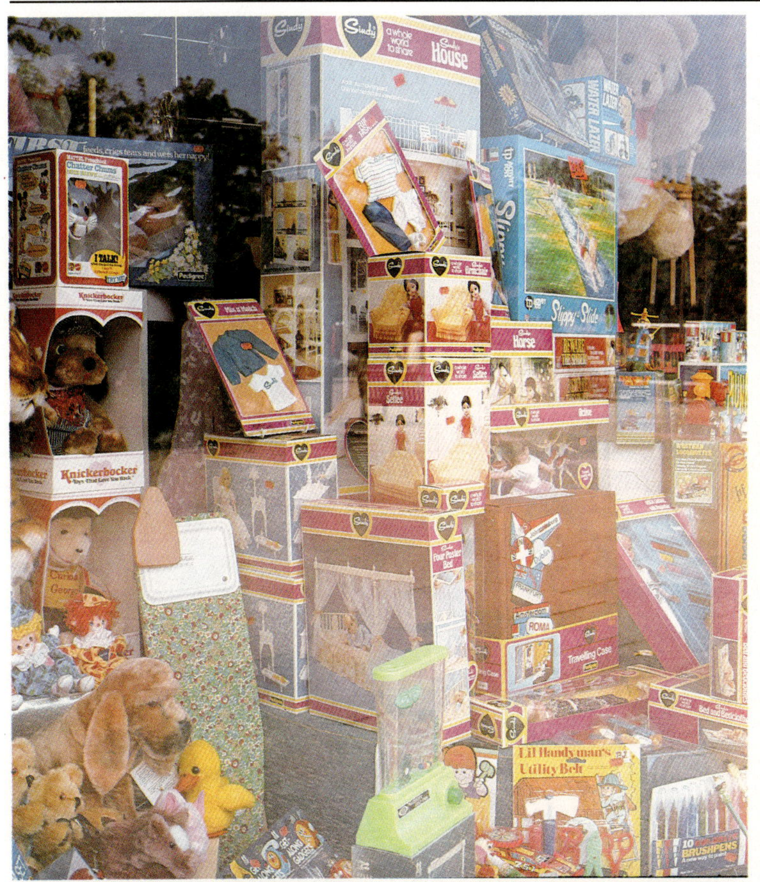

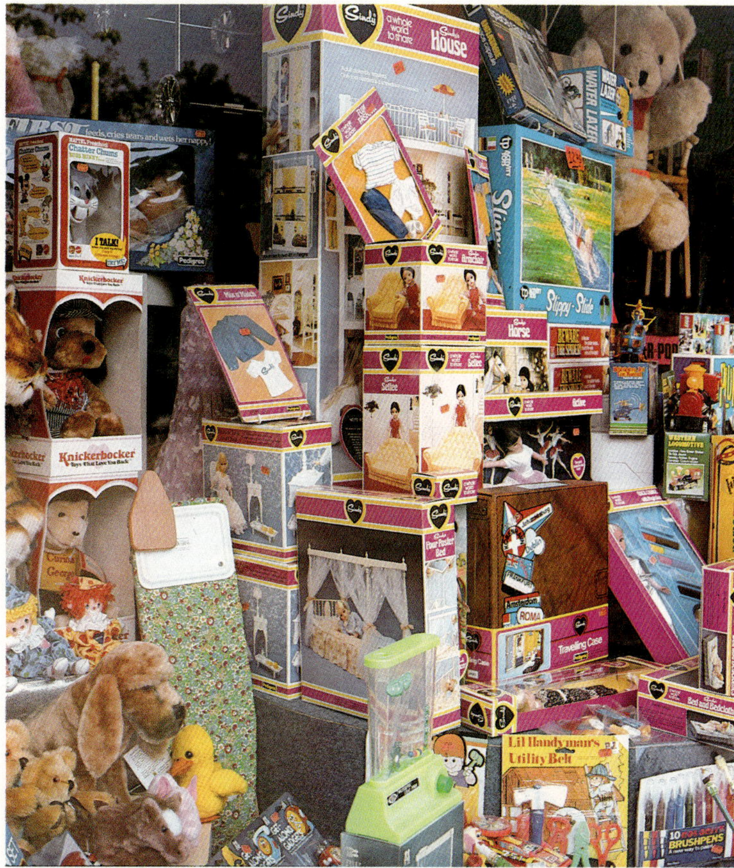

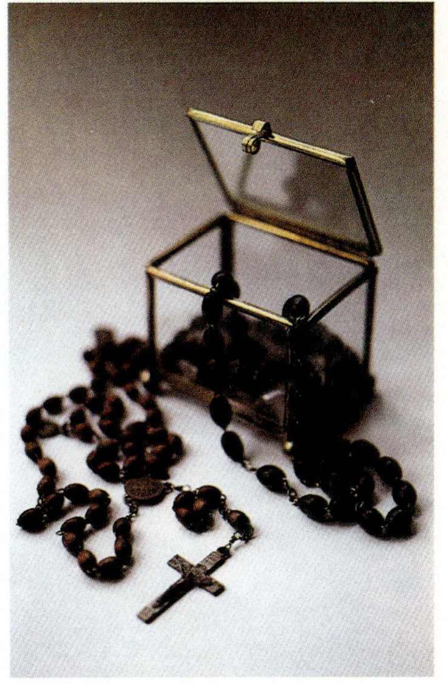

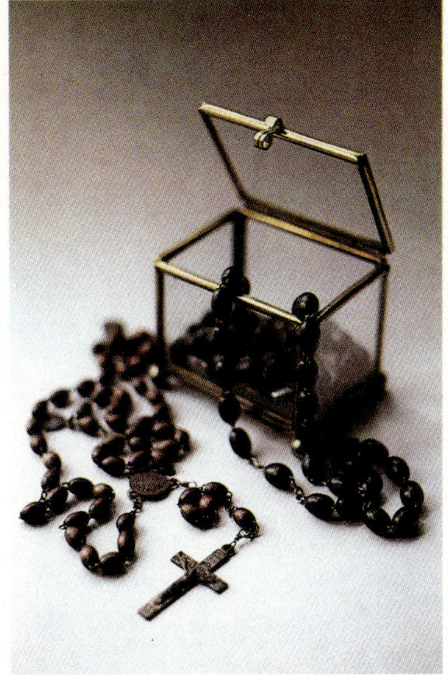

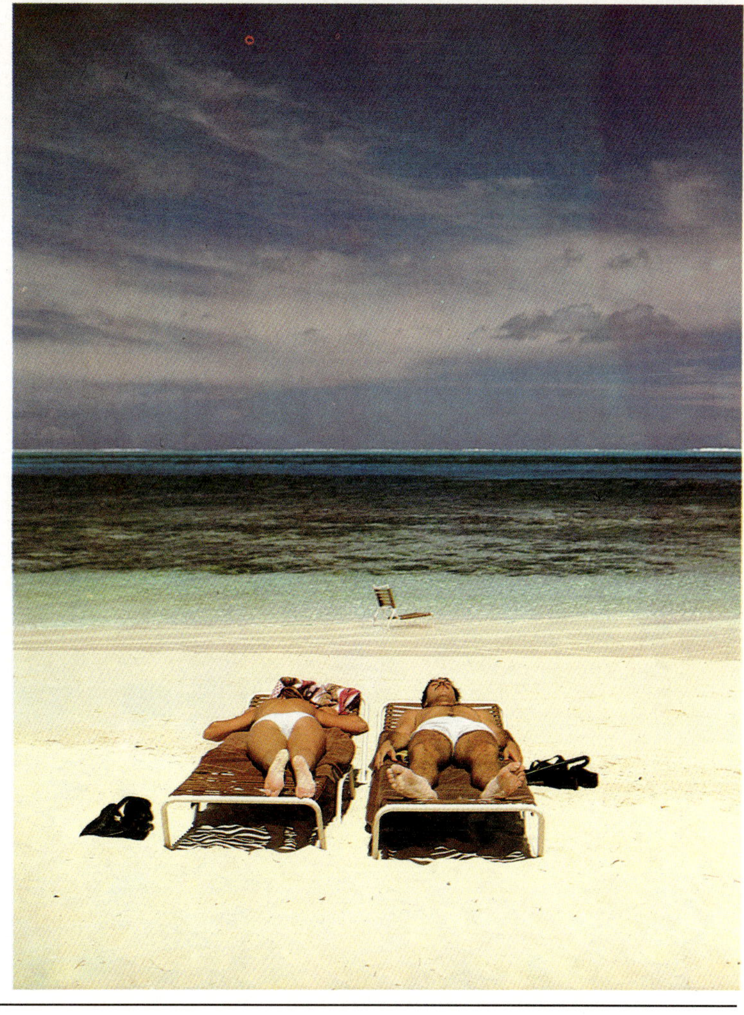

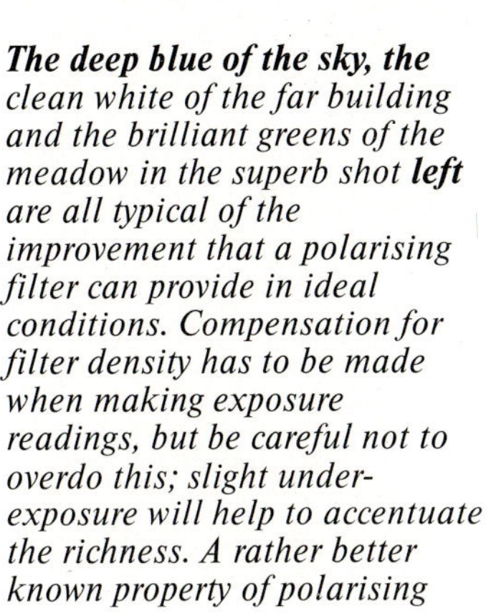

The deep blue of the sky, the *clean white of the far building and the brilliant greens of the meadow in the superb shot* ***left*** *are all typical of the improvement that a polarising filter can provide in ideal conditions. Compensation for filter density has to be made when making exposure readings, but be careful not to overdo this; slight under-exposure will help to accentuate the richness. A rather better known property of polarising filters is their ability to reduce, or eliminate, reflections in surfaces other than metal. The most obvious example is that of glass, in which reflections can be very distracting. In the pair of pictures* ***top*** *the reflections* ***left*** *have been considerably reduced* ***right,*** *allowing the contents of the shop window to be seen more clearly. In the pictures* ***above*** *the reflections in the lid of the box* ***left*** *have been completely eliminated* ***right.***

POLARISING FILTERS

this factor to poor quality glass flats, colour and mount, means that a cheaper filter is capable of pretty nasty results. Likewise, because they are of cemented construction (or should be), there is a possibility of separation should the filter be dropped or subjected to heat and/or damp. The better manufacturers use edge sealing and multicoat the optical flats, which all helps. Nowadays polarising filters are produced in two variants – the traditional linear being augmented by the more recent circular type. The latter works in exactly the same way, but is designed for use with those TTL metering systems which utilise polarising matter as part of the light receptor. The use of a conventional linear polariser in such cases will produce errors in exposure readings. The camera makers handbook should warn of this. Among the independents who produce both types are Hoya and B + W.

Because of the necessary density of polarising material there must also be an exposure increase. This will be between 2.5X and 4X. Strangely, perhaps, the lower factors come from the better manufacturers. Two polarising filters may be used together, but watch out for vignetting, particularly with wide angle lenses. When polarising filters are used in tandem, they can become a variable density ND filter, or be used as a ciné fading device. The loss of resolution can, however, be high.

Pola filters have three distinct uses, with both black and white and colour films: the elimination or reduction of reflections and flare, to darken a sky, and to increase contrast and colour saturation.

Reflections can work both ways for the photographer. On the one hand he may wish to take a reflection out of a shop window – fine – on the other hand he wishes to photograph a blue sea and sky. Perhaps the shot would look better with a darker sky, so out comes the polarising filter. The sky has now been rendered darker but the sea has gone dirty grey. Quite simply he has polarised the blue reflection of the sky out of the sea. Had he been using black and white film, then the effect would have been similar to using a medium yellow filter, i.e. a darker sky and some elimination of haze to increase overall negative contrast. The result would be at its strongest with the sun behind him.

The toughened glass screen of a motor car can show up with a pattern when photographed with a pola filter. Though this tends to occur mostly in a studio situation, I have had it happen when shooting through both coach and aircraft windows.

Fortunately there is no need to expend film when trying a polarising filter, as the eye gives an accurate indication of what the film will see. Non-reflex camera users have had to use this technique since pola filters were invented, first obtaining a setting, and then transferring filter to camera at the same setting.

A rather specialist use for polarising filters is in the photography of oil paintings. No matter how one lights them, there will always be highlights somewhere. Using a conventional, ninety degree, two light copy set-up, with pola filters over each light and on the camera, gets over this problem.

Expensive but nice!

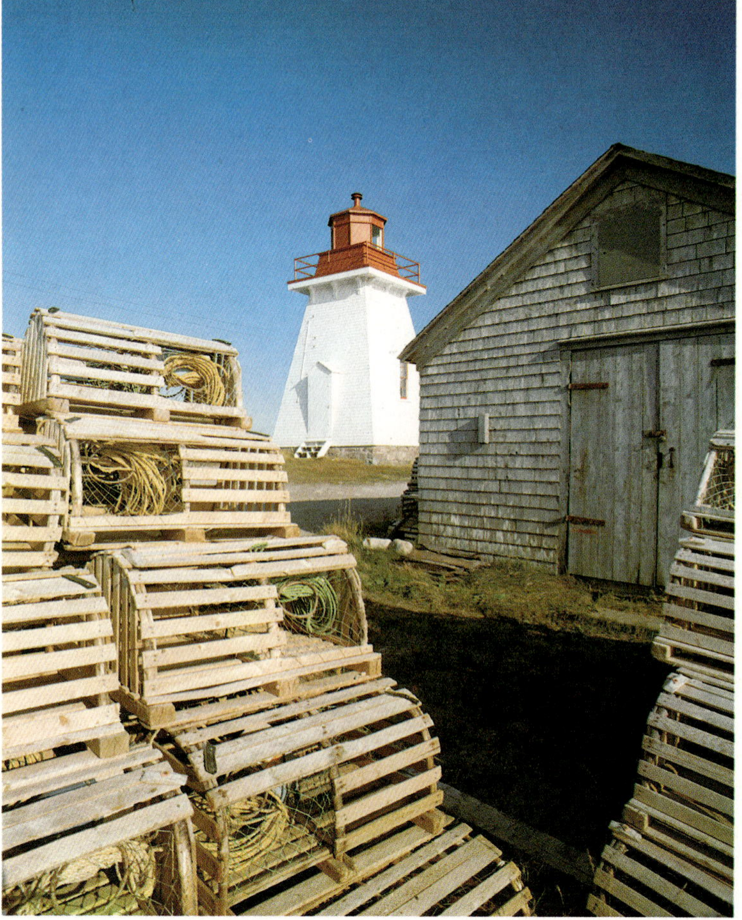

A polarising filter, for rather *complex scientific reasons, polarises, as its name implies, light passing through it. One of the ways this particular property of polarising filters affects us as photographers is that it intensifies and cleans colours. This is most noticeable in skies, which take on a much deeper blue, allowing clouds to stand out quite dramatically. On dull days, however, it has no such effect; instead it simply cuts down the light reaching the film and can, in fact, serve as a weak neutral density filter.*

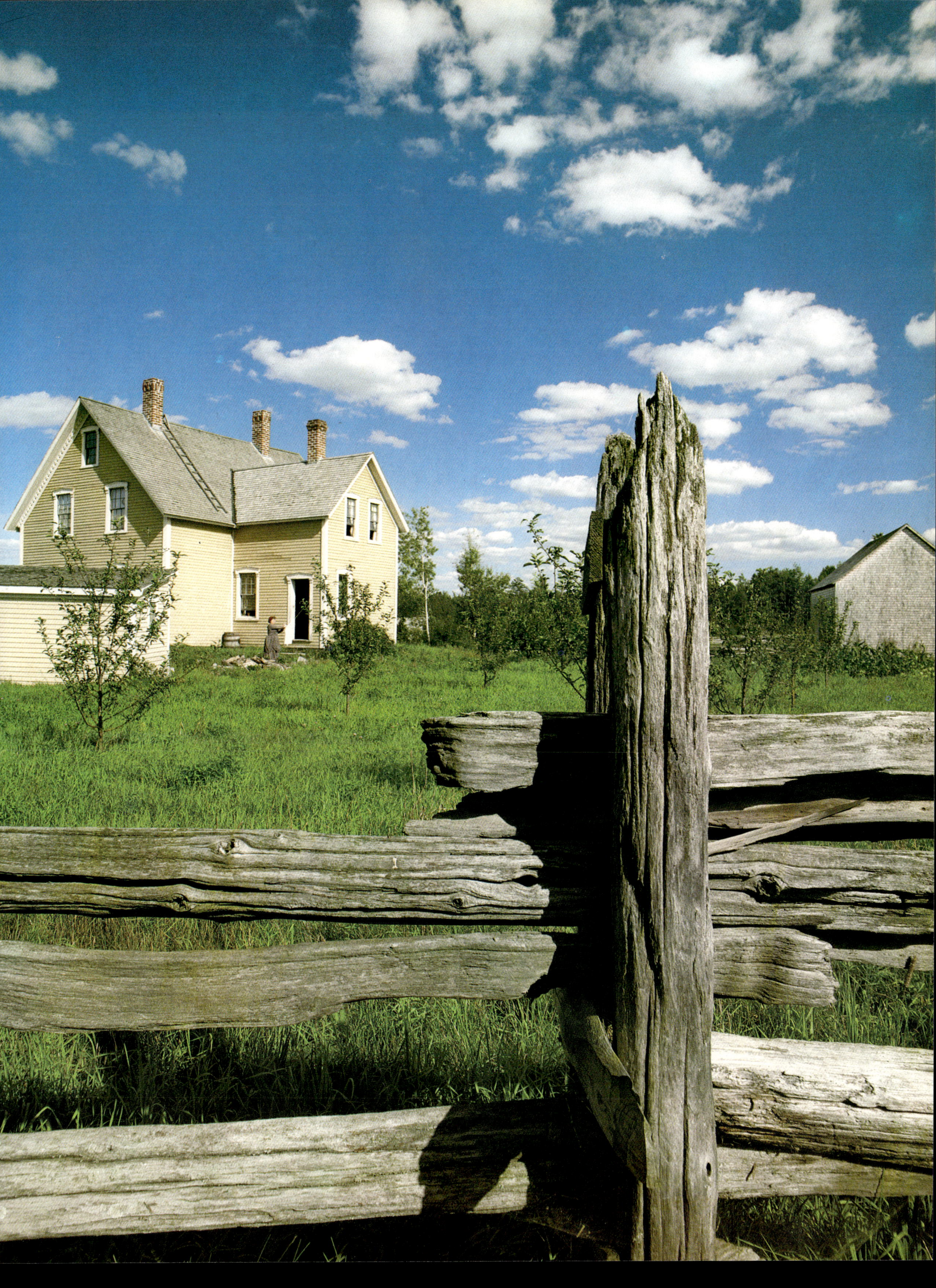

NEUTRAL DENSITY FILTERS

The use of neutral density filters started in the film industry many years ago. A fixed shutter speed of 1/30 sec (now 1/60 sec), meant that depth of field – controlled by the lens' iris diaphragm, could not be varied except by reducing light intensity, which in daylight was not possible. Nowadays, with a still camera – loaded with 400 ASA film – and a trip to the beach, the same situation exists. Too much depth of field can be a detraction to an outdoor portrait, or any other subject which needs to be 'lifted' from its surroundings. An analogy is the picture which looked great (at fl.8) in the SLR viewfinder, but when processed (in f8 form) is disappointing!

Neutral density filters can be obtained in strengths from an arbitrary 1¼x to a massive 10,000x factor. Or from ¼ stop to 13½ stops. Even denser N.D's can be used for Solar and other scientific photography. Neutral density filters can be marked in exposure factors like, say, 2x, 4x, or 8x, or may frequently be found with density marked in a geometric progression, such as 0.3, 0.6 or 0.9. This goes back to the days of black and white cinematography, where a one stop increase in exposure corresponded to a 0.3 increase in negative density.

Whilst most N.D. filters can be used with either b/w or colour materials, they do vary in colour from maker to maker.

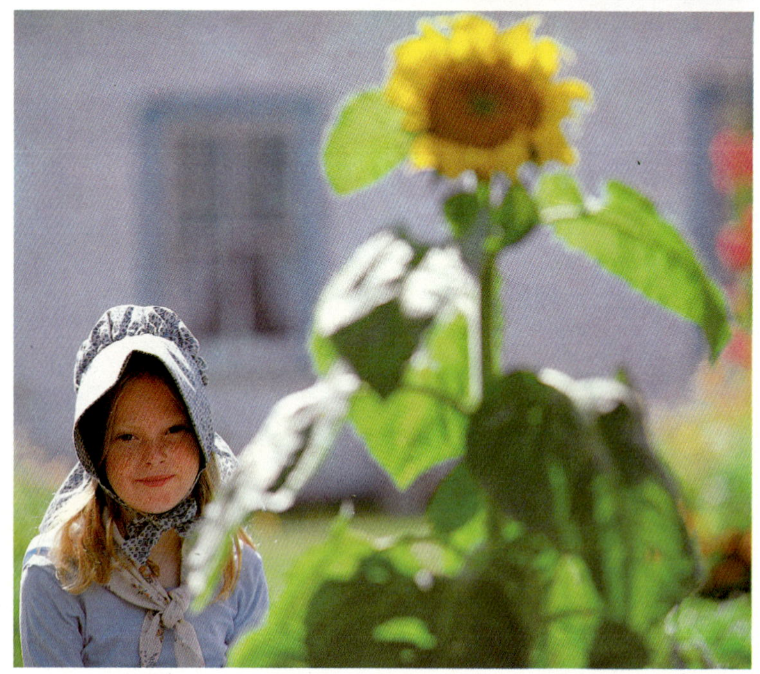

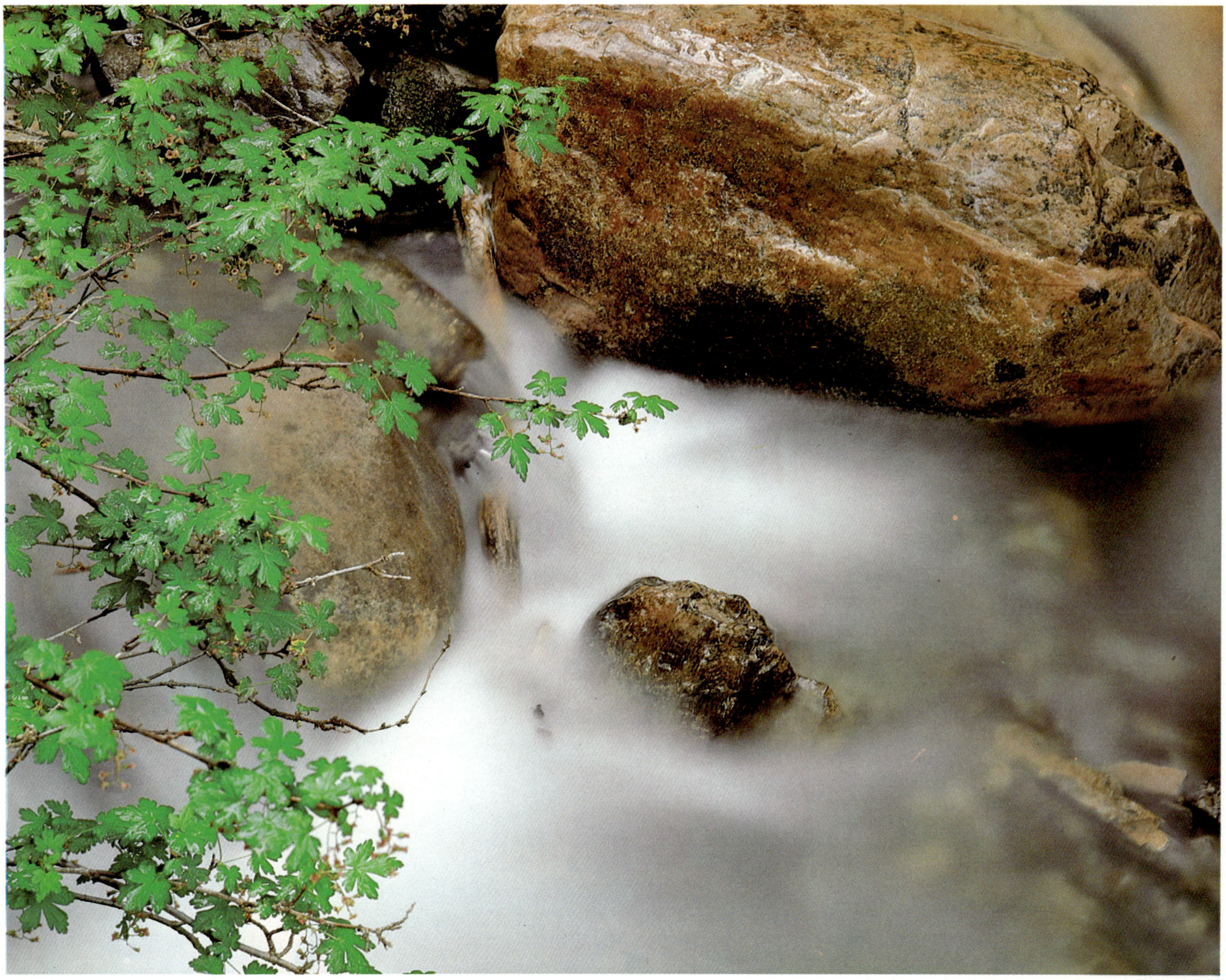

There is a tendency for the cheapest to give a slightly green cast, or occasionally blue. This doesn't matter for b/w work or for colour prints, where the printer can make the correction. In colour transparencies, a green cast can do nasty things to skin tones. 'Warmer' emulsions, like amateur Ektachrome, Fujichrome, and Agfachrome 100 can cancel out a slight green cast. Obviously the greater the filter density the greater the colour cast. Additionally there is the question of optical clarity. If you habitually use a deep N.D., I would recommend the use of an expensive glass, or appositely a cheap gelatin filter!

Variable density N.D. filters are a combination of polarising and N.D. technology. In their simplest state they use cross polarisation between two pola filters in order to produce a darker image. Rotating one filter in relation to the other can produce varying exposure factors of say 2x to 4x. When a N.D. filter is also included, the factors can rise to a 3x to 8x range. Cinematographers use Vario-N.D. filters to fade a scene in or out. Professional stills photographers use them to adjust the ASA speed of Polaroid materials to match the emulsion intended for the final photograph. In both cases neither loss of definition or colour cast is important.

SLR users will find one big disadvantage in using the deeper neutral density filters, in that the viewfinder image also becomes 2x, 4x, or what have you, darker. This can be overcome by using a frame – or optical – viewfinder in the camera's accessory shoe, and framing the subject this way. A more expensive alternative is another camera body loaded with slower film!

NEUTRAL DENSITY FILTERS

'Wratten' 96 Filters

Neutral-density filters absorb light of all wavelengths throughout the visible spectrum and thus permit the reduction of light intensity by a definite ratio. They have many uses in all branches of photography and scientific optical work. These filters are not intended for use in the ultraviolet or infrared regions of the spectrum. Density values, percentage transmissions and approximate filter factors of Neutral-density filters are given below. Other densities can be built up by combining two or more filters, e.g. ND 5.0 can be obtained by combining ND 1.0 and ND 4.0.

Name	Density	Percentage Transmission	Filter Factor	Exposure Increase (in stops)
ND 0.1	0.1	80	1¼	⅓
ND 0.2	0.2	63	1½	⅔
ND 0.3	0.3	50	2	1
ND 0.4	0.4	40	2½	1⅓
ND 0.5	0.5	32	3	1⅔
ND 0.6	0.6	25	4	2
ND 0.7	0.7	20	5	2⅓
ND 0.8	0.8	16	6	2⅔
ND 0.9	0.9	13	8	3
ND 1.0	1.0	10	10	3⅓
ND 2.0	2.0	1	100	6⅔
ND 3.0	3.0	0.1	1,000	10
ND 4.0	4.0	0.01	10,000	13⅓

Chart reproduced by courtesy of Kodak Ltd.

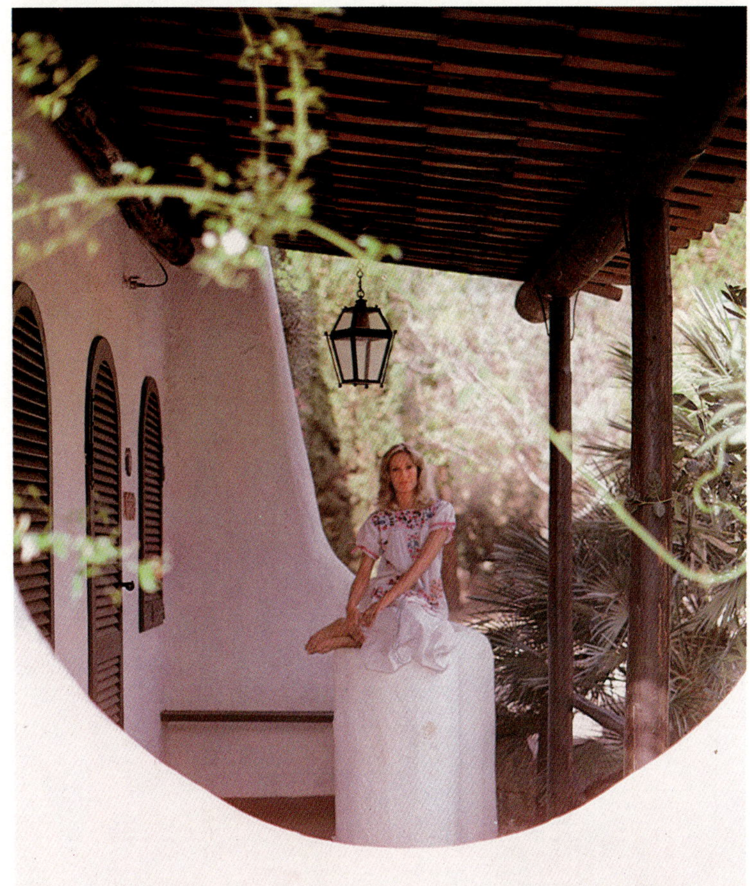

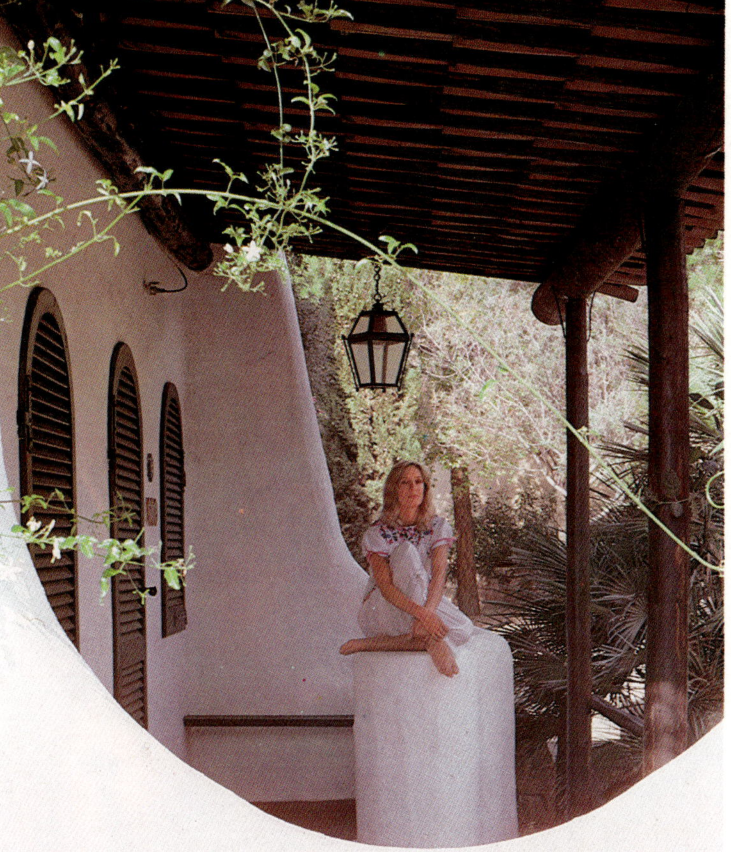

If the light is very bright, or we** have loaded with fast film, and require either a wide aperture, slow shutter speed, or both, then an answer is the neutral density filter. For the pictures on the **facing page** a wide aperture was required **top** to show only the child in sharp focus, and a shutter speed of seconds was needed **bottom** to blur the running water. Neither would have been possible without neutral density filters. Foreground, subject and background sharp **above,** and separated via wide aperture/ neutral density **above left.

INFRARED BLACK AND WHITE

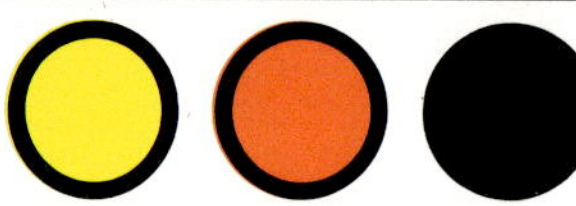

Infrared filters, for black and white photography, vary in density from deep red to the visually opaque, and must be used with a special infrared sensitive film. Infrared emulsions were introduced in the middle nineteen thirties for aerial photography, since one property of using these long wavelengths is the penetration of haze. Other properties include the ability to differentiate between deciduous and coniferous foliage and between them and camouflage! There are medical uses, where for instance it is possible to photograph the subcutaneous layers of human skin in order to show vein, and sometimes artery, configuration. Inevitably, as soon as infrared emulsions became available in 35mm form, the process was also exploited by pictorialists and newspaper photographers. An infrared landscape has a black sky, with grass and deciduous trees being rendered as white. Photo-journalists were quick to discover that pictures could be taken by this so-called 'black light,' leaving the subject unaware that a photograph had been taken. There was a spate of pictures taken of cinema audiences, and the like, illuminated by means of a flash bulb covered with an infrared, and therefore visually opaque, lacquer. There were also oblique aerial photographs, taken from over London, which showed the south coast over sixty miles away.

One classic infrared photograph, taken in the Himalayas, 'reached' a distance of one hundred and fifty miles. During the last war, German photographers took pictures across the English Channel, which clearly showed the opposition's radar installations. Since infrared is also heat, there were gimmick photographs taken by the 'light' of an electric iron. In fact everybody had fun!

Since infrared is a long wavelength, camera lenses do not give correct focus at their engraved settings so an adjustment must be made. Most lenses will have a correction mark for infinity, which is an increase in camera/lens extension of 1/300th of the lens' focal length. This same rule applies for the

Dark skies, white grass and *foliage as well as tremendous haze penetration are what can be expected from black and white infrared film. Conventional black and white developers can be used in processing, and pronounced grain should be expected. The film should be kept refrigerated, loaded in darkness and if used in a viewfinder camera with cloth shutter, the lenscap should be kept on between exposures. Because of the density of some of the appropriate filters, extended exposures may be necessary. Bracketing is recommended in this somewhat imprecise area of photography.*

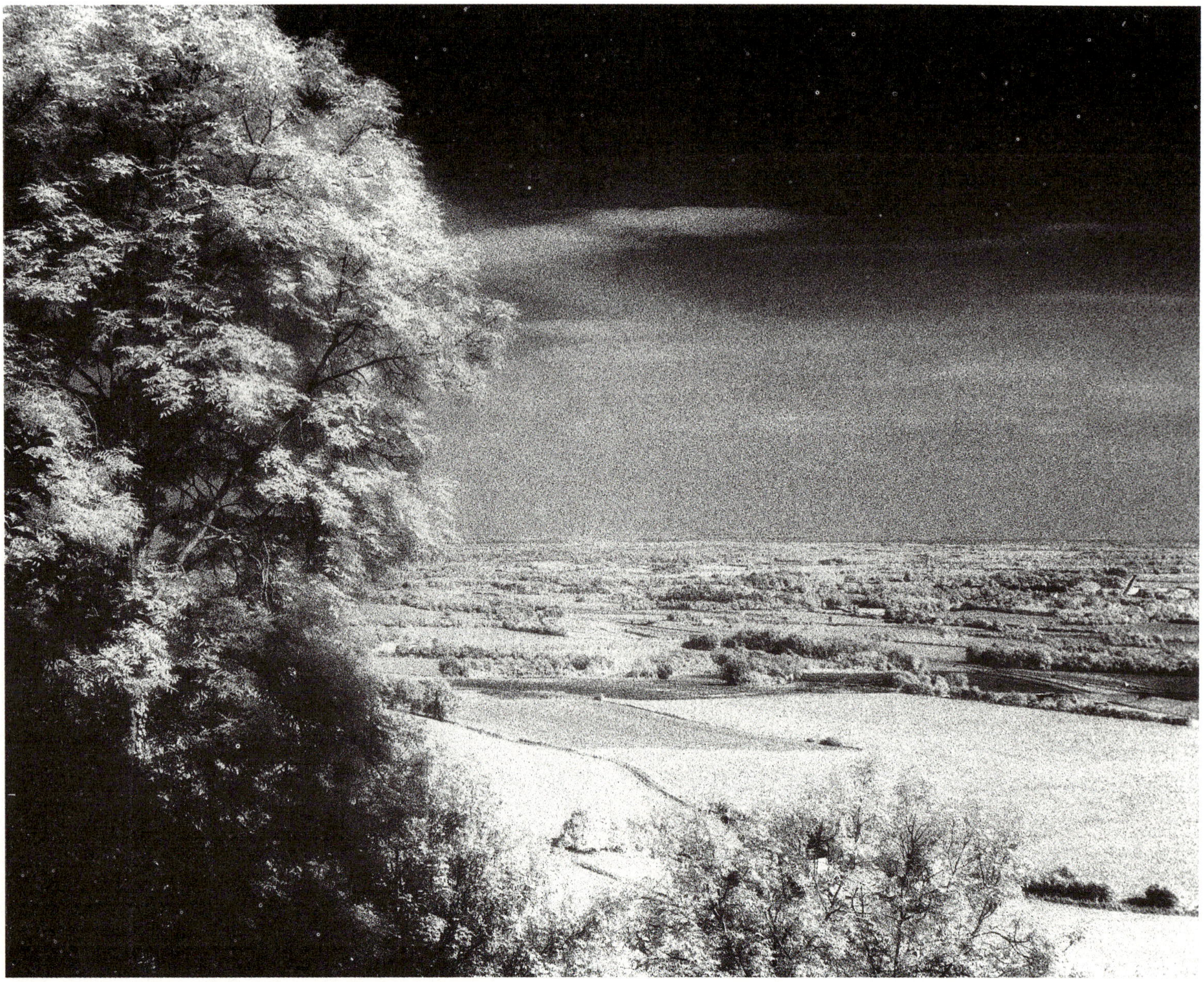

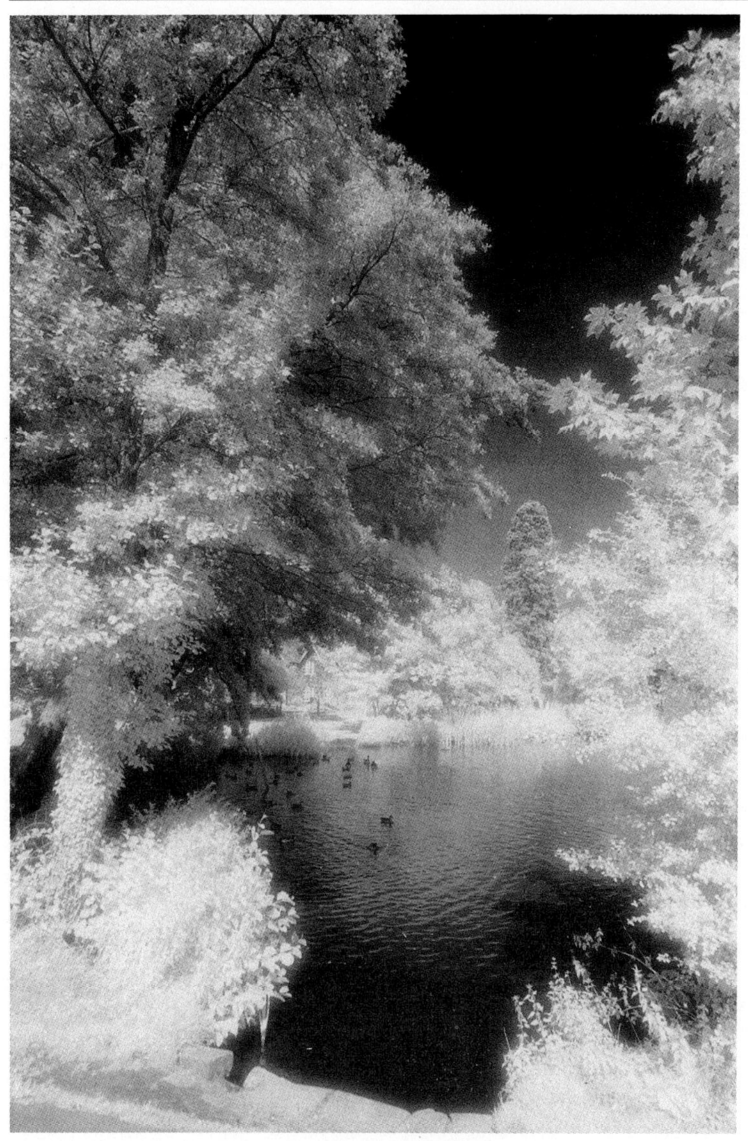

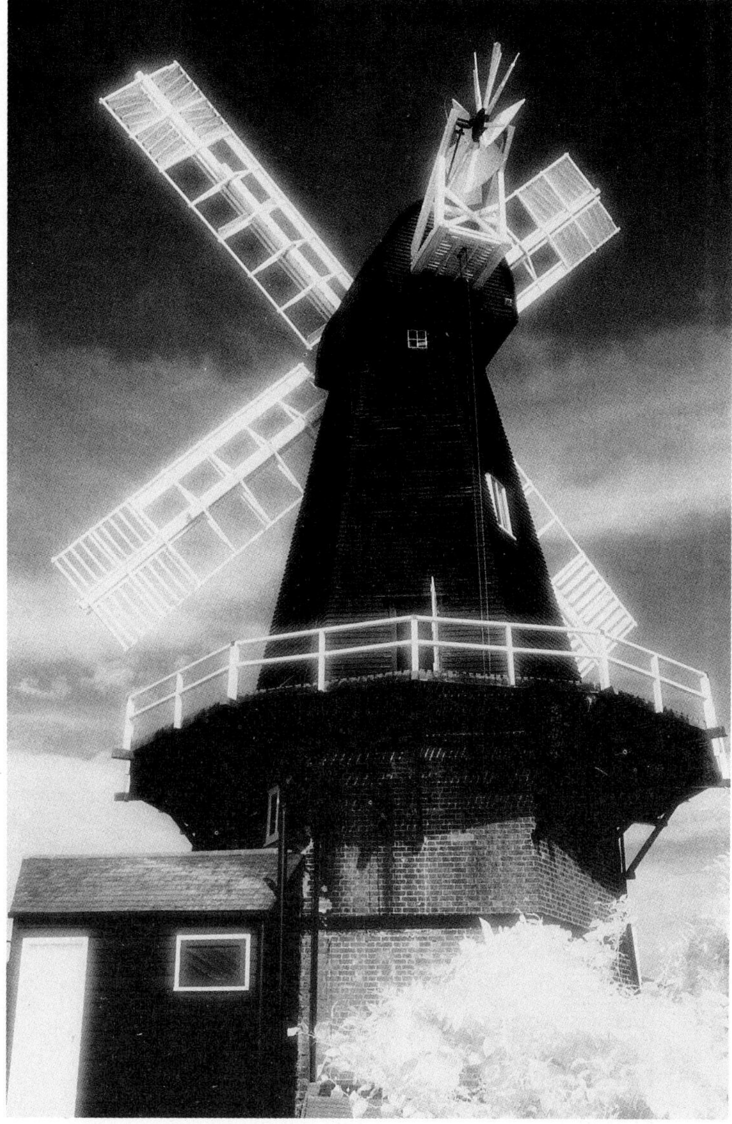

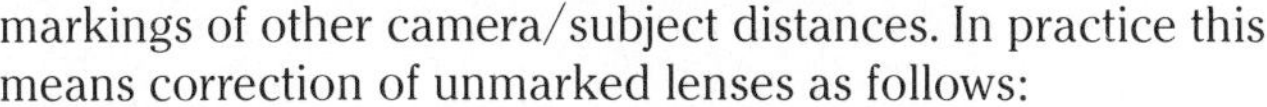

markings of other camera/subject distances. In practice this means correction of unmarked lenses as follows:

Focal length when infinity setting is required

35mm use	33ft (or 10 metres) setting
50mm use	50ft (or 15 metres) setting
90mm use	90ft (or 27 metres) setting
135mm use	132ft (or 40 metres) setting
200mm use	200ft (or 60 metres) setting

Since the 'feet' settings roughly correspond numerically to the focal length of the lens, this is an easy one to remember. Thank you Leitz!

Shorter than 35mm focal lengths need no correction from the normal infinity setting, provided the aperture used is not wider than f11 – f16.

The ubiquitous SLR must be used on a tripod, since viewing through the necessarily dark red, or opaque, infrared filter is impossible. The alternative is to use an optical viewfinder in the camera's accessory shoe. Coupled rangefinder cameras are easier to use – with one exception. Bellows are not opaque to infrared for anything other than a short time. It is sometimes possible to wrap them in aluminium foil for protection. Keep the lenscap on for protection if your camera has a rubberised cloth focal plane shutter.

Before loading an infrared film into the camera, read the instructions. These will tell you that the camera must be loaded in total darkness. The felt light trap of a 35mm cassette is not opaque to infrared. Likewise, since infrared is also heat, the film should be kept cool in order to avoid fogging. Its shelf life is short, so if you do not intend to use it soon after purchase keep it in the refrigerator. Six months is about the maximum storage time, though I have used Kodak film which had been refrigerated for a year, with satisfactory results.

Infrared film is grainy and of low contrast. You should increase development by 20% when using a Kodak D76 or Ilford ID11, MQ Borax type of developer. If using Kodak D19B, or other contrast developer, then times can be normal. Finer grain developers are not recommended.

The intensity of infrared within daylight or artificial light cannot be accurately measured, so it is always advisable to bracket exposures by at least one stop, and preferably two, over the normal meter reading. Most infrared films are around 40 ASA when used with an 8X deep red filter, less with the ultimate opaque type. Leitz, for instance, quote the exposure factor of their deepest filter as being between 8X and 60X in daylight.

The whole technique of infrared photography may sound complex, yet it is something that every photographer should try at least once – preferably in the summer when there is more foliage about.

INFRARED COLOUR

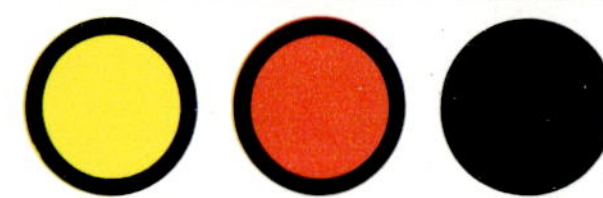

The techniques of using infrared colour film – or false colour as it has been described – are not so very different from the black and white version except in filtration. Perhaps surprisingly, the standard filter is a deep yellow, which means that an SLR is usable! The reason for this is in the sensitization of the basically Kodak Ektachrome three layer emulsions. Infrared Ektachrome was developed during the U.S.A.'s space programme. It is now widely used for surveying and forestation work as well as for military purposes.

Using the normal deep yellow filter again separates the camouflage from the trees. Conifers are rendered as a deep red. A further benefit is that tree and crop disease can be recognised by a colour difference from the norm due to a change in infrared reflection from the foliage. Inevitably someone had to try changing the filter colour, or leaving it off altogether. The results can be of a startling science fiction nature. Skies can become green or magenta or yellow, whilst the infrared reflection qualities of everyday subjects have to be tried to be believed. There is no alternative but to use a lot of film, experimenting with filter changes as well as subjects. The whole exercise must be regarded as a gamble, but when it comes off – wow!

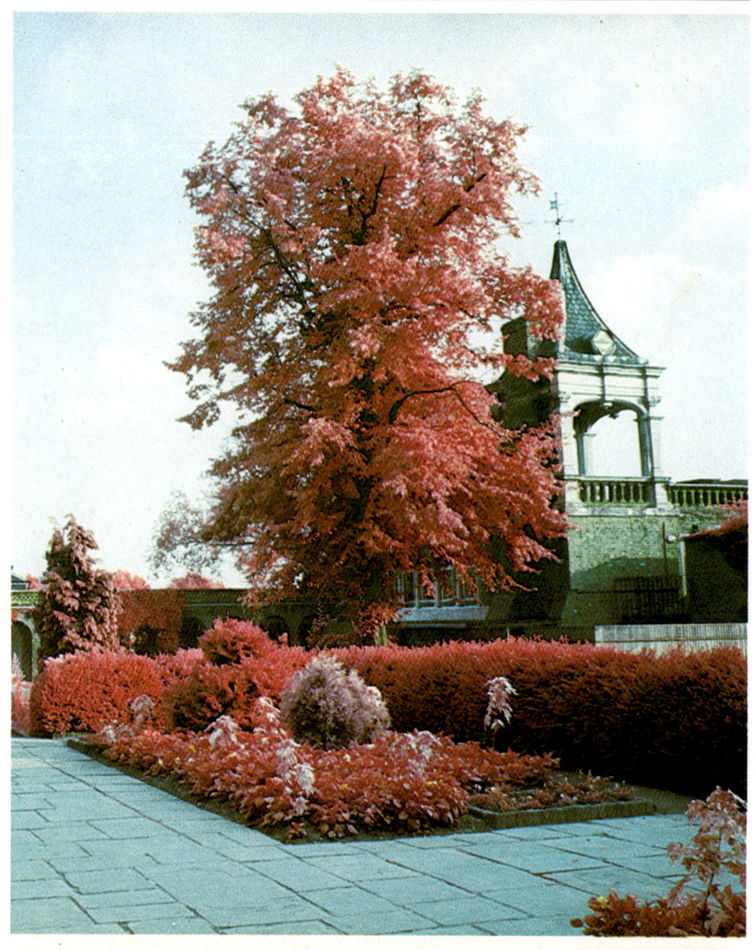

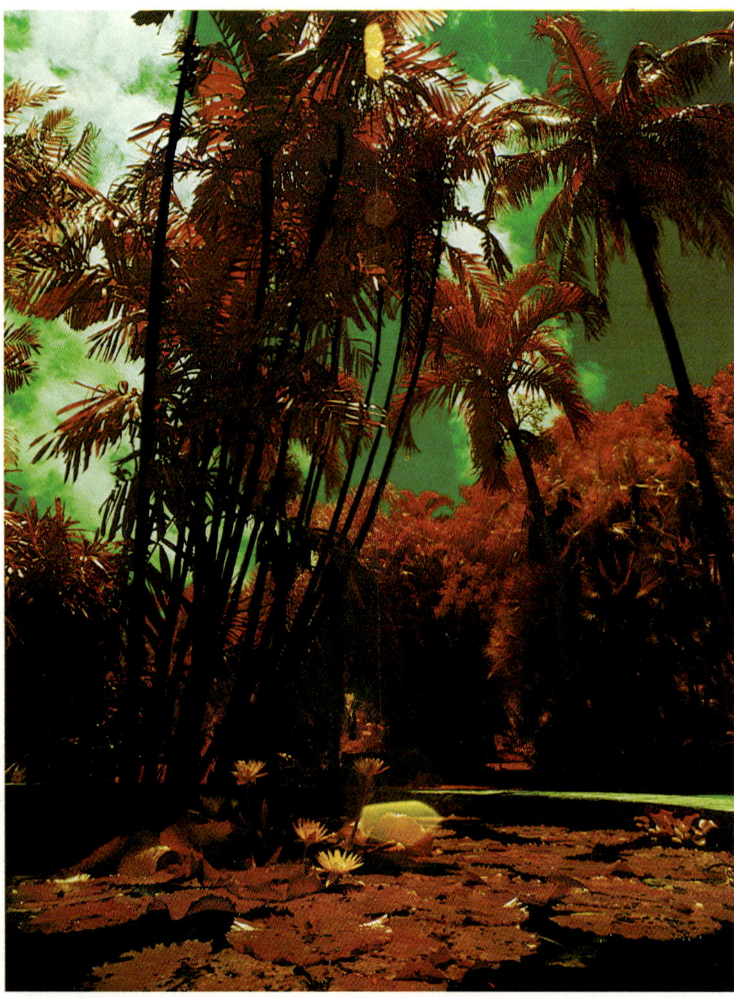

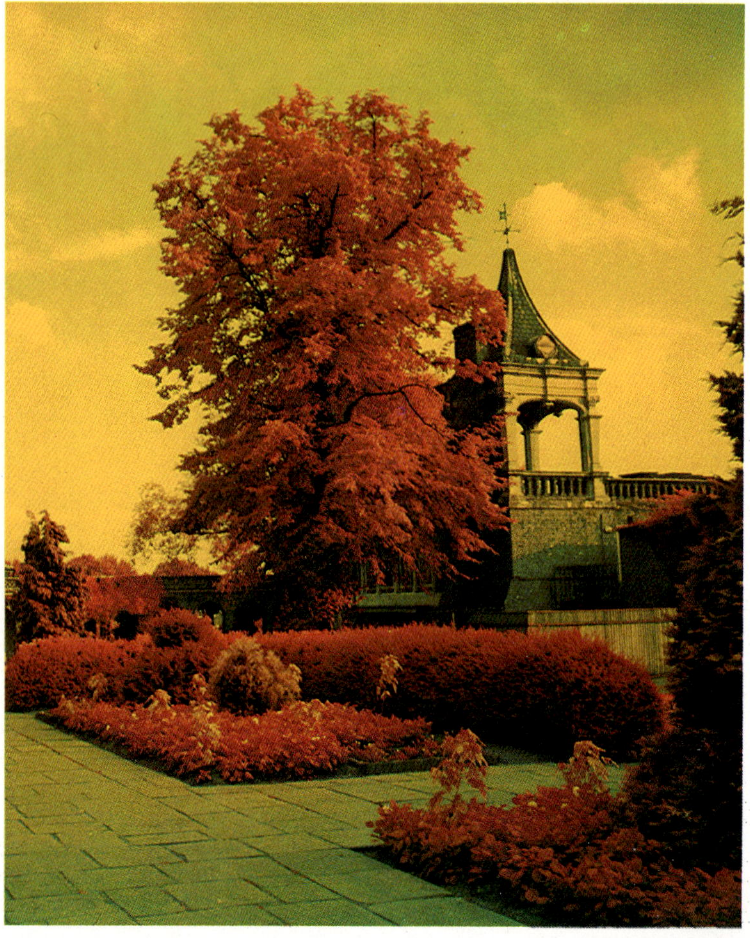

Developed primarily for *scientific purposes, infrared colour film can nevertheless be used to great effect in pictorial photography. The key to success with this unpredictable medium is experimentation. For focusing, distances should be set against the R mark on the lens. Dramatic colour shifts can be obtained by altering filtration, suggestions for this being given in the leaflet packed with the film. The pictures shown* ***top and bottom right,*** *were taken using Y2 and No. 11 Wratten filters.*

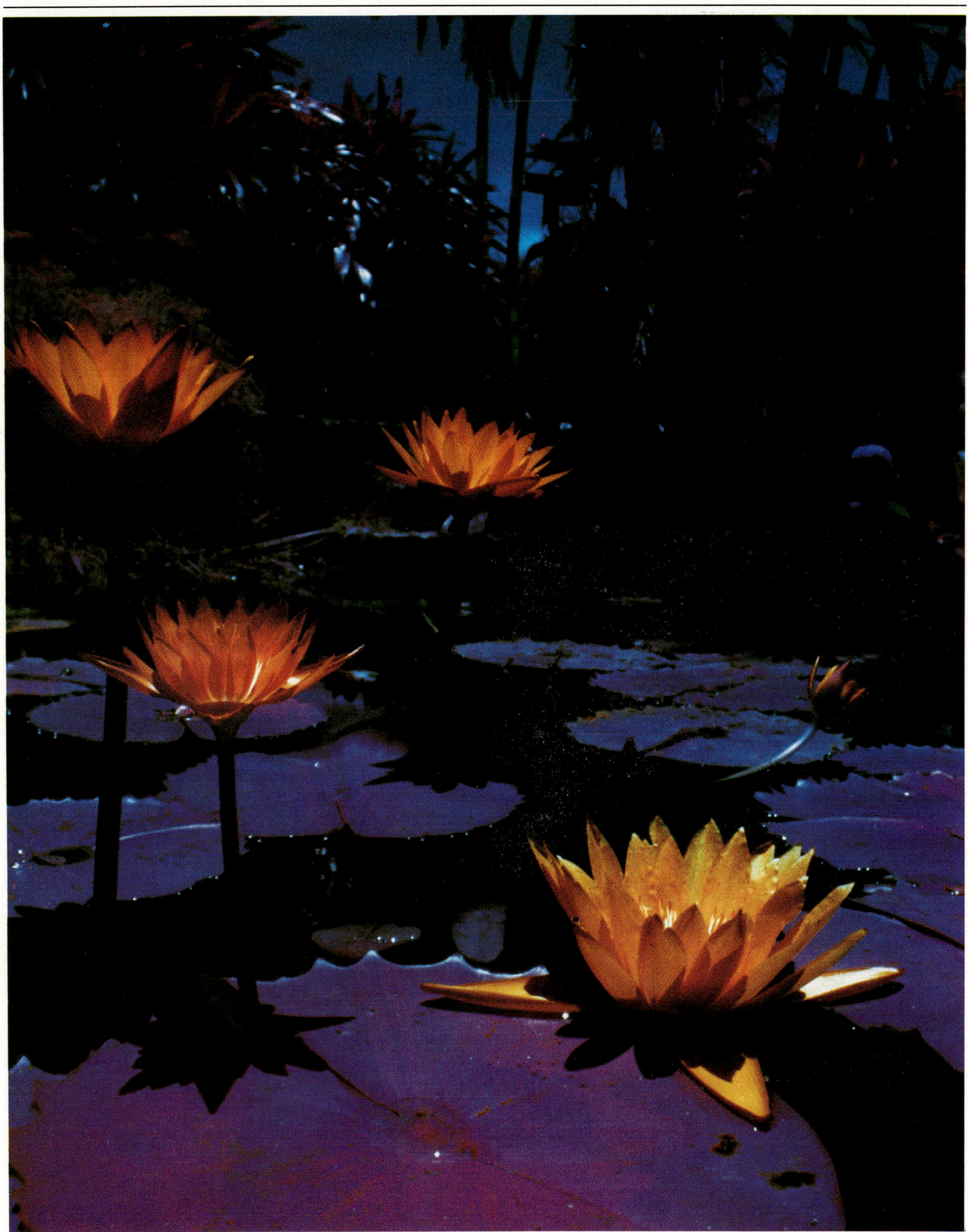

FOG FILTERS

Fog filters are the antithesis of UV and haze filters in that they artificially induce a degree of 'mistiness'. Made in two forms, the earliest and still current, fog filters are blue or violet in colour. What these do is enhance the over-sensitivity towards blue and violet light possessed by all black and white emulsions, with a consequent loss of contrast in the negative. With an exposure factor of between 4x and 10x it hardly seems worthwhile.

In comparison, the more modern dichroic fog filter has a lower exposure factor and is usable with both black and white and colour films. Invariably produced in at least three grades – often more, the dichroic fog filter can have a factor of between 2x and 6x. If there is any snag, it is a certain loss of definition, but then the very nature of the filter makes this unimportant. For once, a lack of coating does not matter either, so the cheapest fog filters work as well as the best. My only proviso to this statement is that if you intend to use, say, a sky filter in conjunction with a dichroic, then better quality filters will produce less overall degradation of the image.

With perhaps a choice of five grades of fog filter, as in the GOYO/TORA range, it may be difficult to decide which one to choose for 'starters'. If in doubt, purchase a mid range density. Fog filters can be used in tandem, subject to the usual warning about the possibility of vignetting with wide angle lenses.

You will find that the milder grades of fog filter can sometimes be used to produce a different kind of portrait. Because of their nature, it becomes possible to use much more contrasty lighting than usual: indeed, a single light technique is often adequate. Used out of doors, it is as well not to use a fog filter on a subject which has clearly defined shadows. Even after these are degraded, the result will look more like an accident rather than a deliberate attempt at producing something different. Perhaps surprisingly, I have yet to meet a fog filter which produces a cast on colour film, and (for once) TTL exposure meters will compensate automatically for the filter density. However, there is a strong case to be made for overexposing by half a stop, which adds to the fog effect. For the sake of an extra frame, try it both ways at your first attempt and take it from there. Finally, for the impecuneous, it is possible to use an evenly fogged b/w negative for experimentation before purchasing the real thing.

Some of the most attractive *landscapes can be taken in foggy, or misty, conditions. As usual, however, just as when we don't want fog we get it, so, when we want it it's not there! This is the time to employ the fog filter, which is available in varying strengths, and certainly imparts an impression of mistiness to a subject, as may be seen in the comparative shots* ***below,*** *and the beautiful subject* ***right.*** *Filters, of course, cannot show recession in the same way as real mist, and you should choose a day when there are no strong shadows, as their presence immediately gives the game away.*

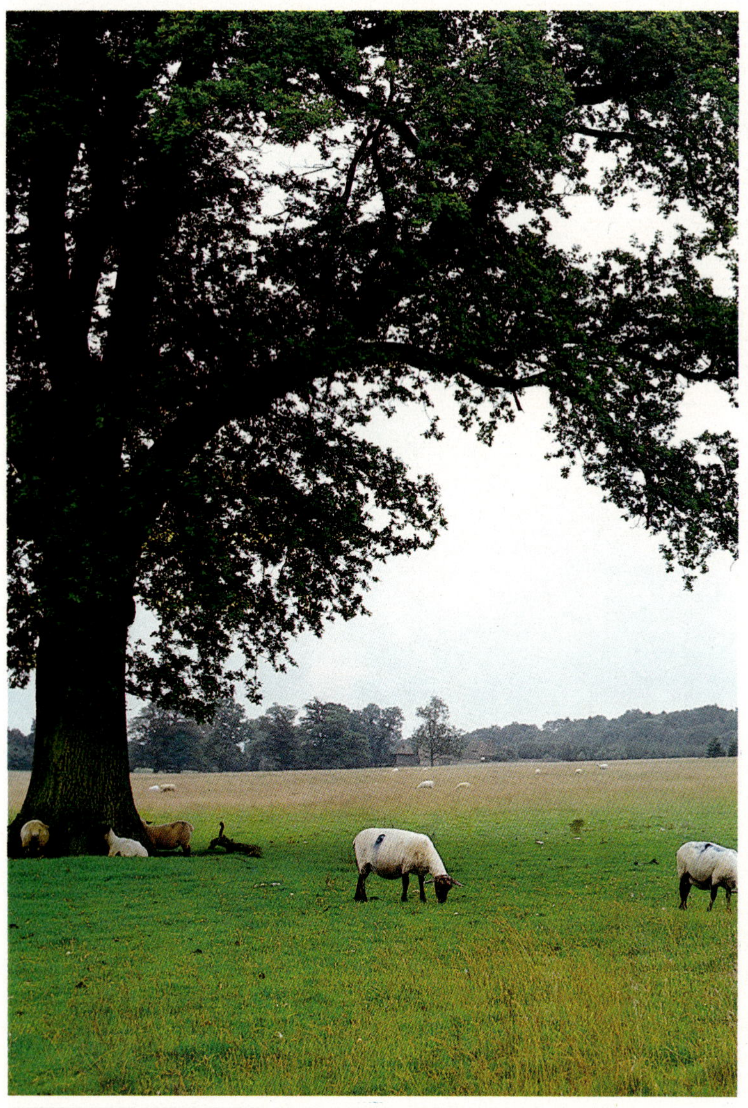

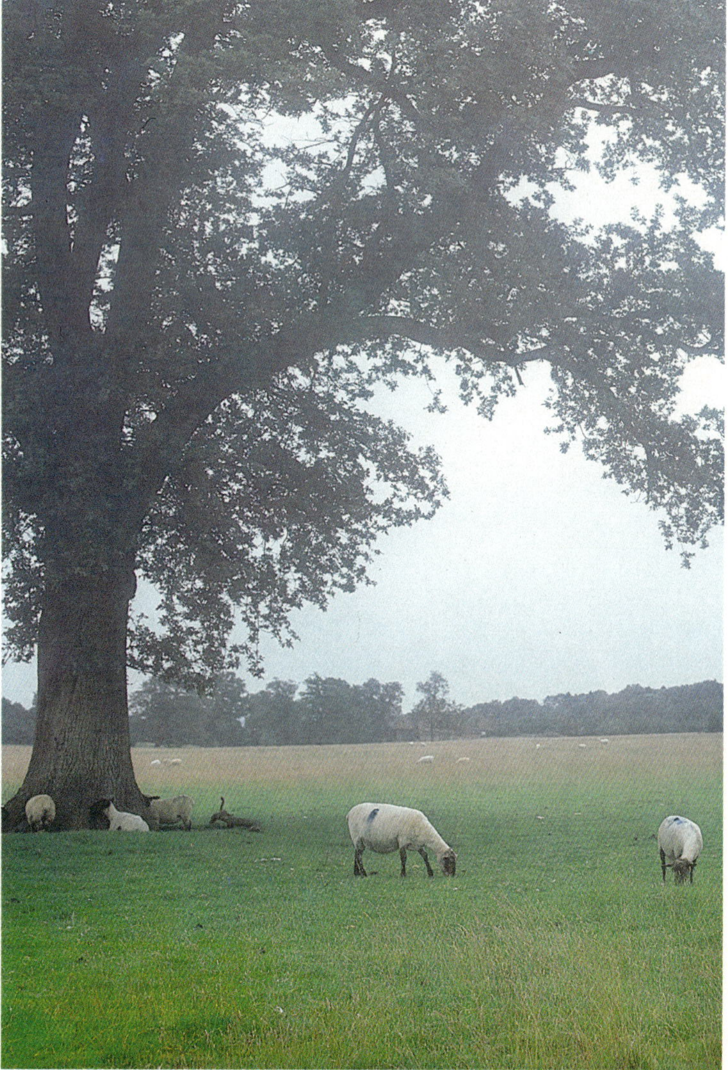

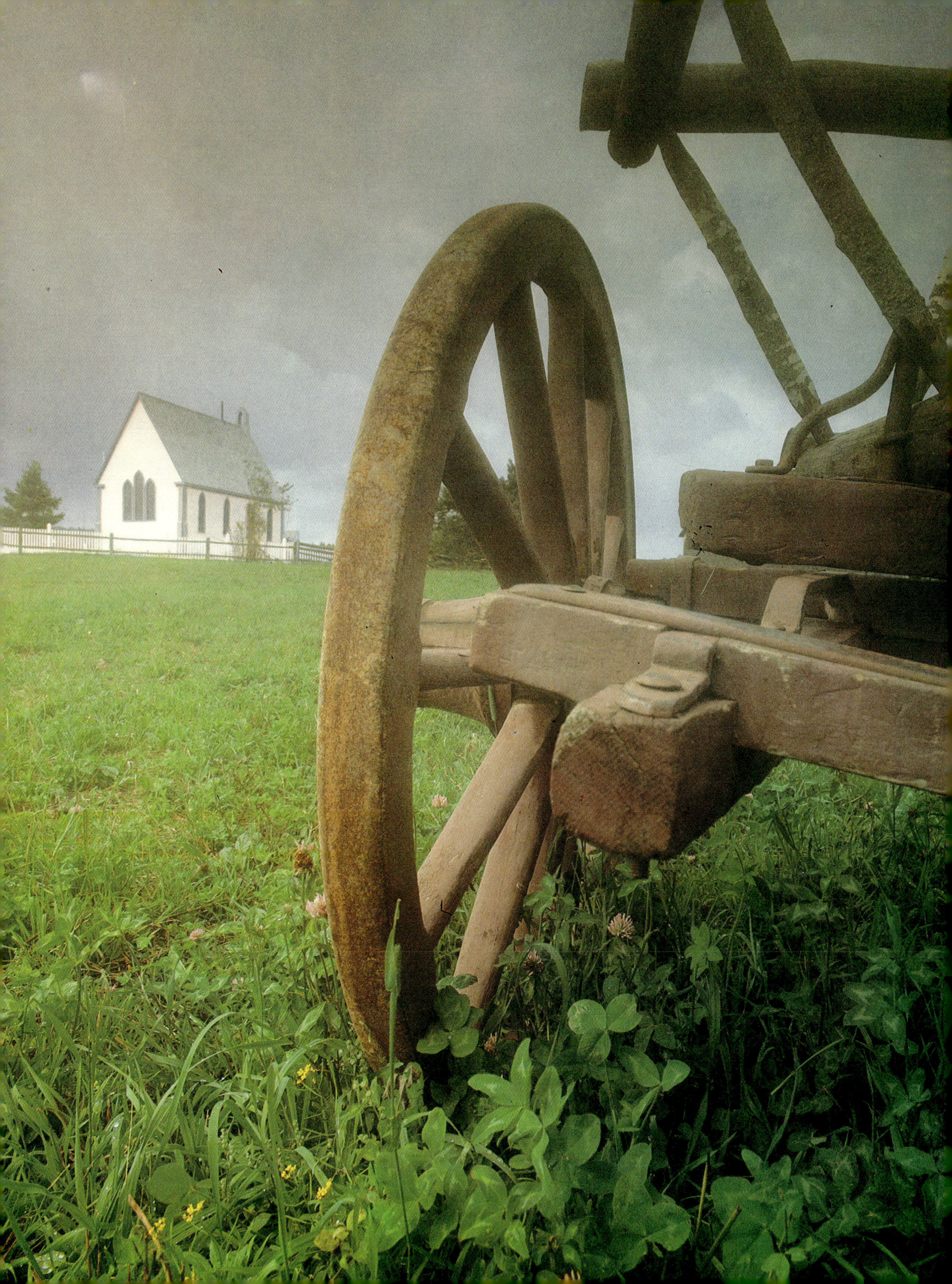

GRADUATED FILTERS

Graduated filters have become a college student, amateur and 'art' photographer's cliché – which is a pity. Not that they and M. Coquin are entirely to blame, as art directors have been requesting fall-off backgrounds for years now, so that a headline can be reversed out of an advertisement, brochure or showcard. 'Grads' were invented by film cameramen many moons ago. At first they were homemade from neutral density filters until technologists found not only ways of graduating without steps, but also how to do it in glass as well as plastic and gelatin. Most graduated filters around today are plastic.

Apart from the usual neutral, blue, green, orange, red and yellow types, there are exotics like pink, emerald, mauve and tobacco. Cokin hold the record with a range of 14 filters, by providing two densities of each shade, whilst B + W make eight colours and two neutral density filters in glass. Cokin is unique in marketing two graduated fog filters which are very useful for those not wishing to go the whole fog!

The Actina/Filtek catalogue not only lists ten graduated filters but offers the same range of colours plus the added ingredient of slight fog. Known as pastel grads, they give more gradation than other filters of this type.

Grads are available in either circular or rectangular form, the latter having the advantage that the 'horizon' of the filter is invariably adjustable in the mount. Both types can be revolved

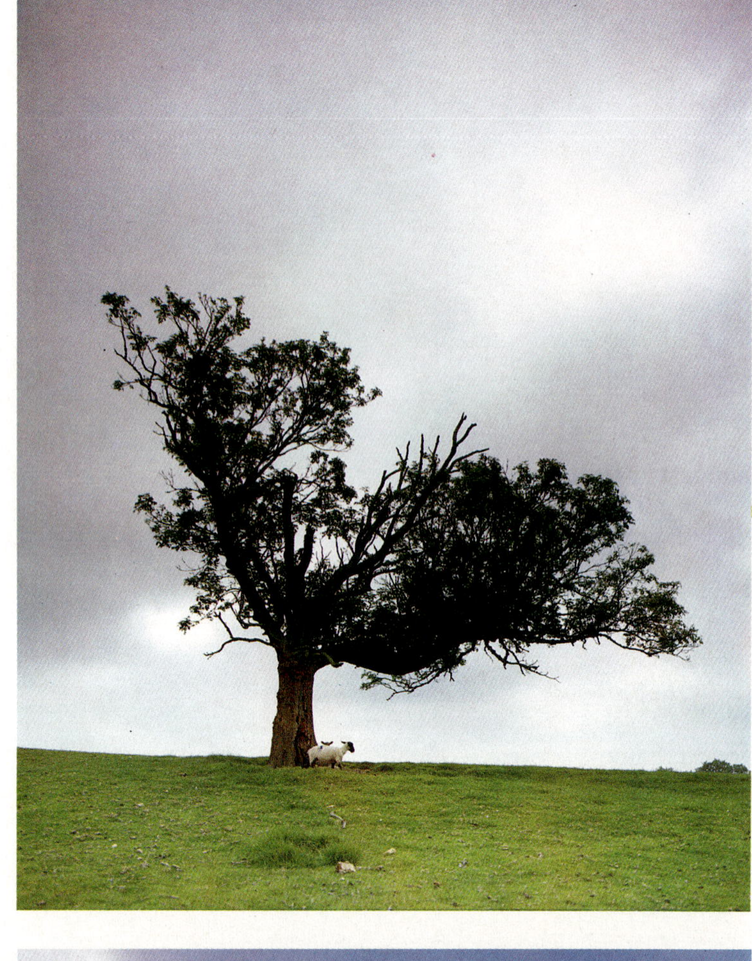

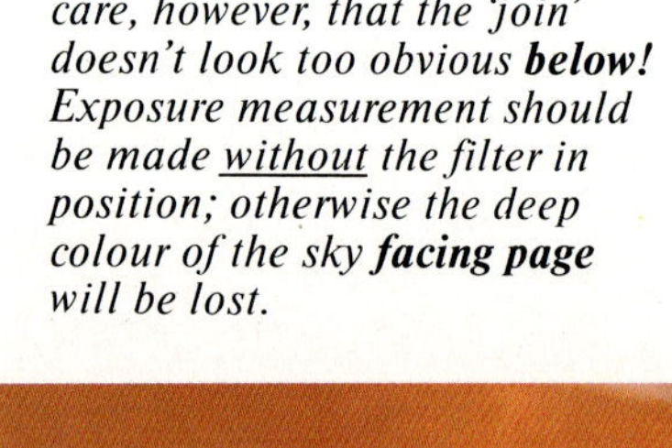

Graduated filters are an *extremely useful addition to any photographer's creative armoury. Available in a variety of colours, they can transform a rather dull shot* ***right*** *into a dramatic one* ***below and below right.*** *Take care, however, that the 'join' doesn't look too obvious* ***below!*** *Exposure measurement should be made without the filter in position; otherwise the deep colour of the sky* ***facing page*** *will be lost.*

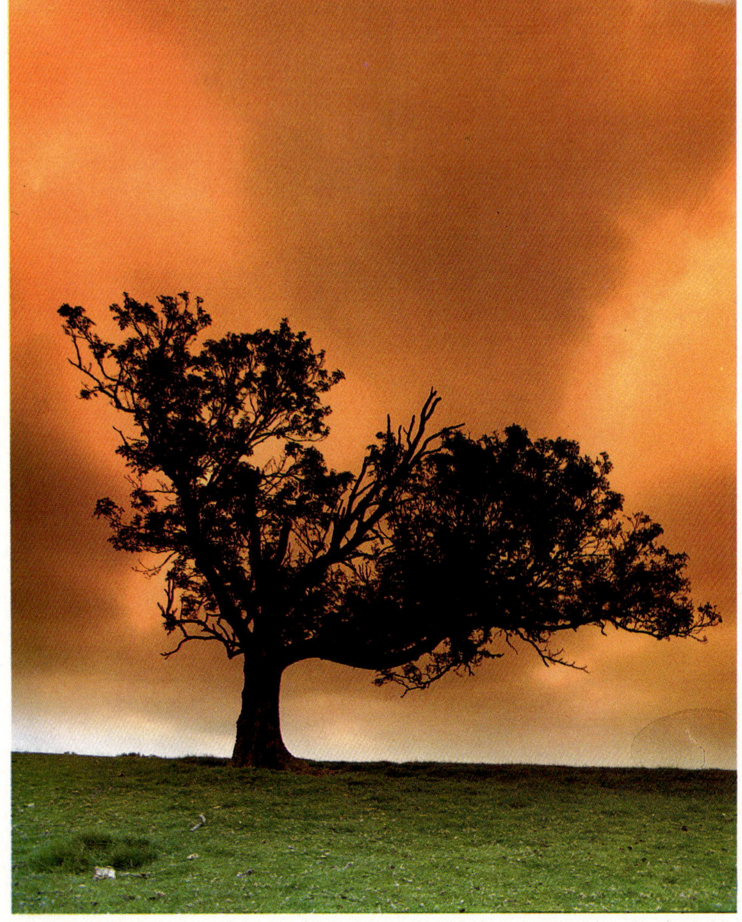

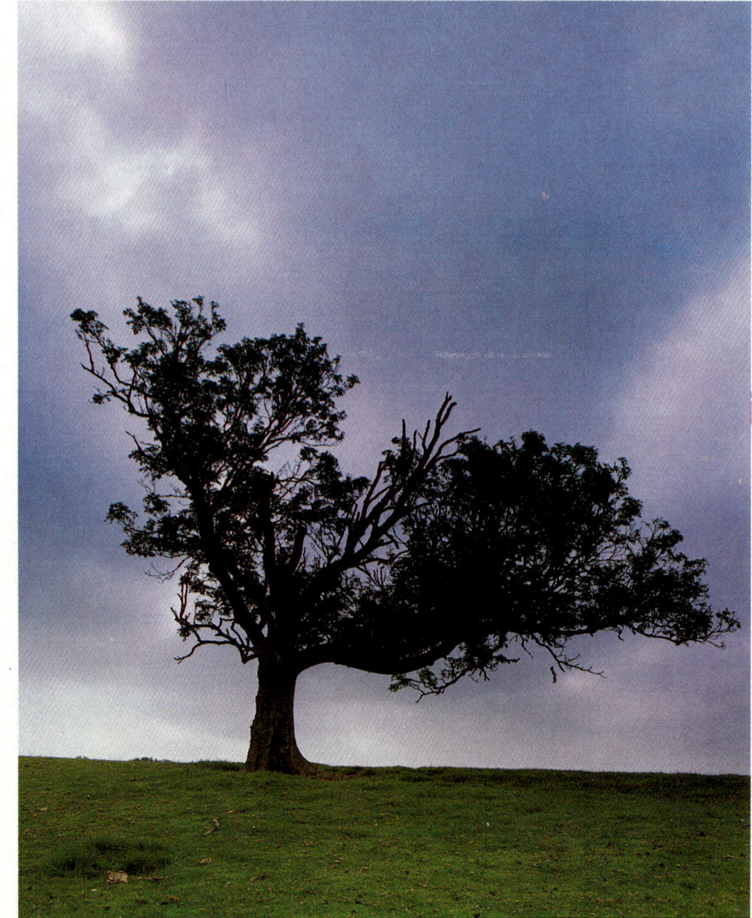

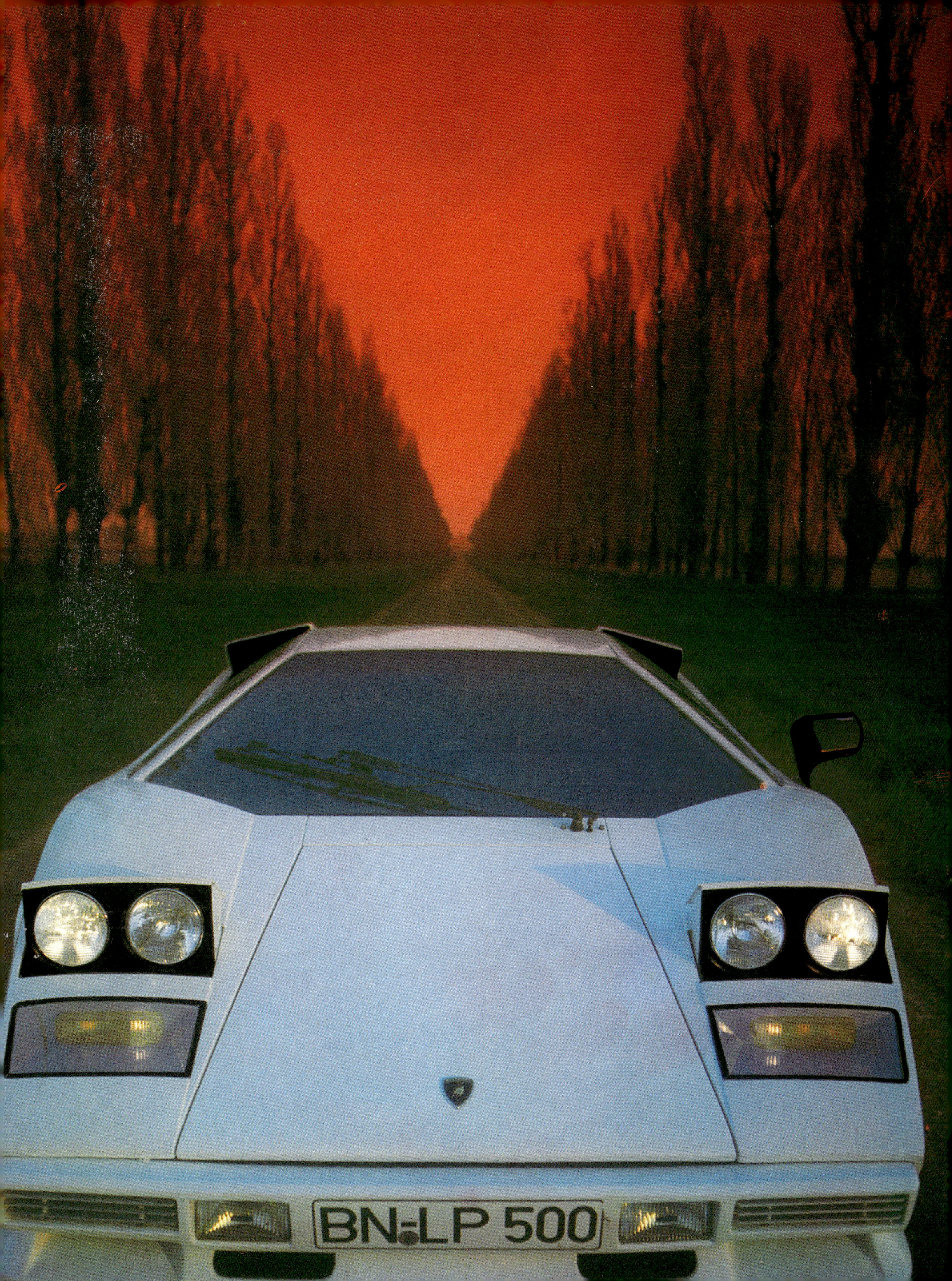
BN-LP 500

GRADUATED FILTERS

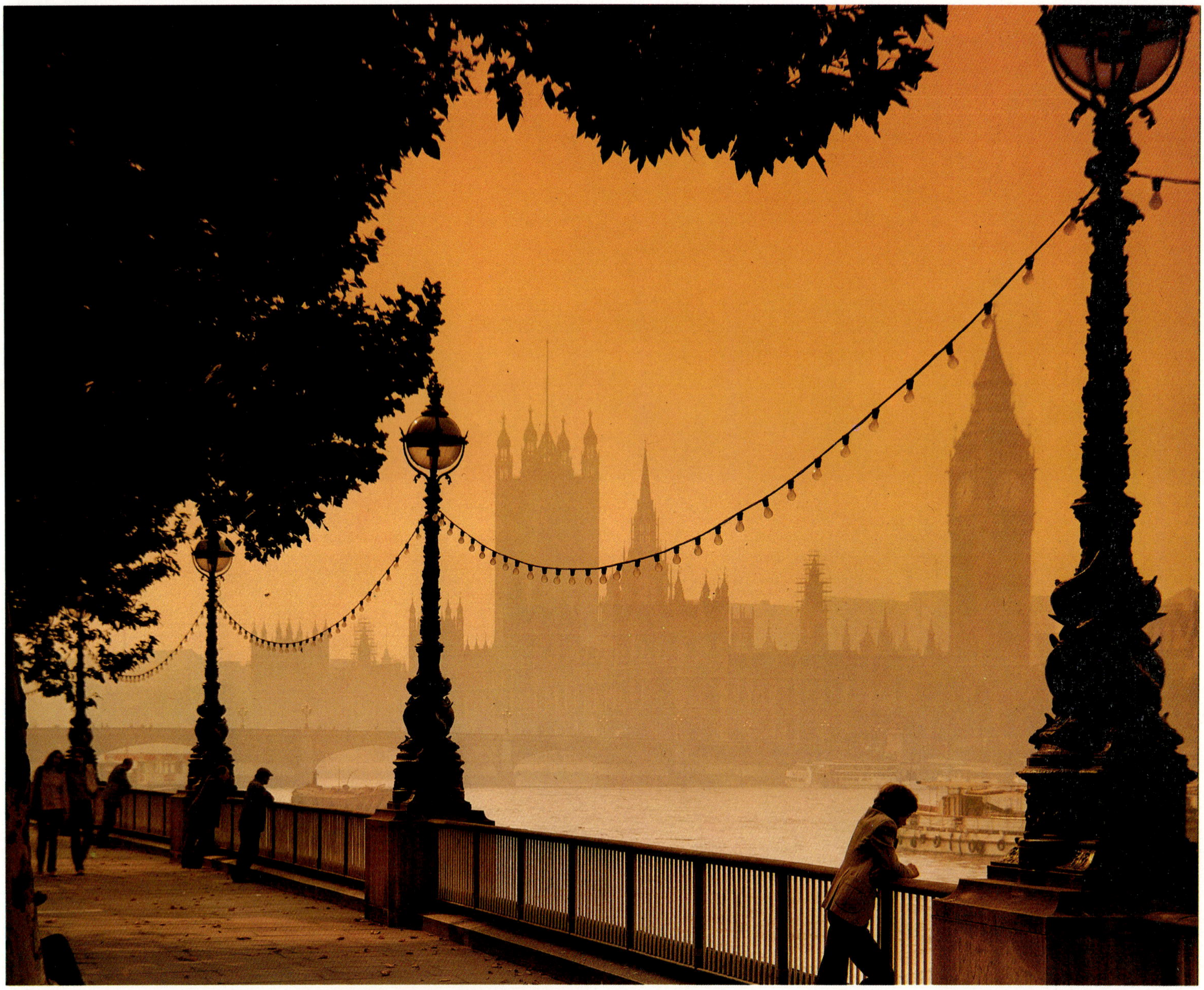

When using graduated filters, *unless you want to produce an obviously unreal, and startling, result, try to match the mood and feeling of the location to the colour of the filter. The various strengths of 'tobacco' graduated filters, used for the pictures on these pages, are usually very effective; they don't jar the eye and are not too far removed from nature's colouring – given a little imagination! The picture* ***right,*** *had a filter not been used, would have been almost monochromatic and, it might be argued, far less interesting. All these 'grads' can, of course, be used to colour one side of a shot if that is what is wanted.*

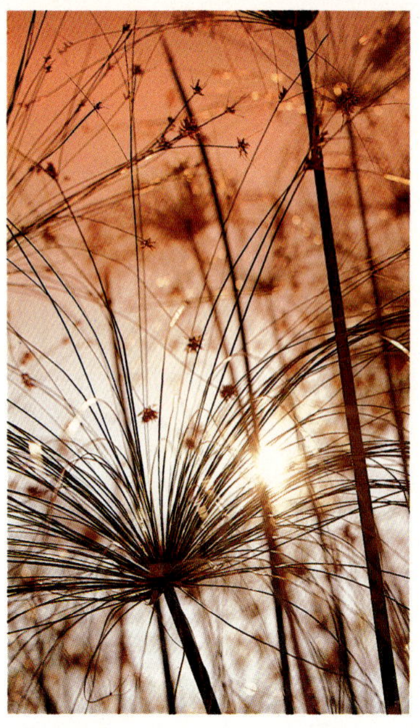

through 90° used upside down or at an angle. Square and oblong filters are usually large enough to be used with most lenses, including wide angles, and have the advantage that they can be used (with adaptors) on several different lens mount sizes.

The first rectangular graduated filter for still photography was made for the Rolleiflex camera over 40 years ago, and as it had an adjustable 'horizon' mount, no exposure increase was necessary. The same is true today providing a TTL reading, made without the filter attached, can be held on manual or memory. Otherwise a half stop decrease to the indicated reading is the usual compensation, in order to avoid over-exposure.

Graduated filters are affected more by focal length than aperture. Compared to the standard lens, a wide angle will produce a sharper 'horizon' whilst a telephoto, or long focus lens, will provide more graduation, providing it is not used at its smallest aperture. To a certain extent this is also true for any normal focal length lenses.

Any graduated filter can be used on black and white film. The tonal effects upon the parts of the subject being 'filtered' are just the same as if a full filter of the same colour was used, except that that portion of the subject will be rendered darker. The

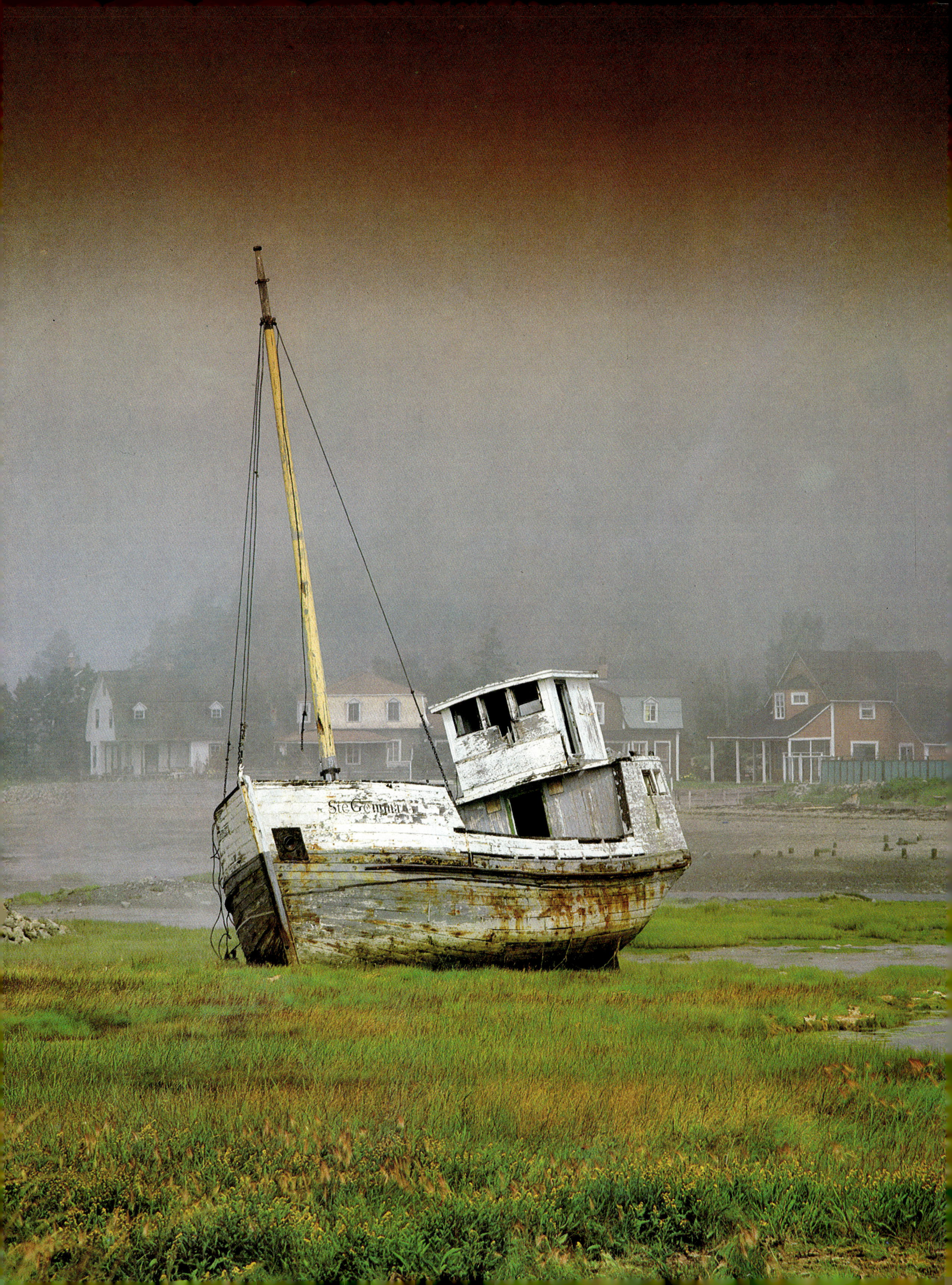
Ste Gemma

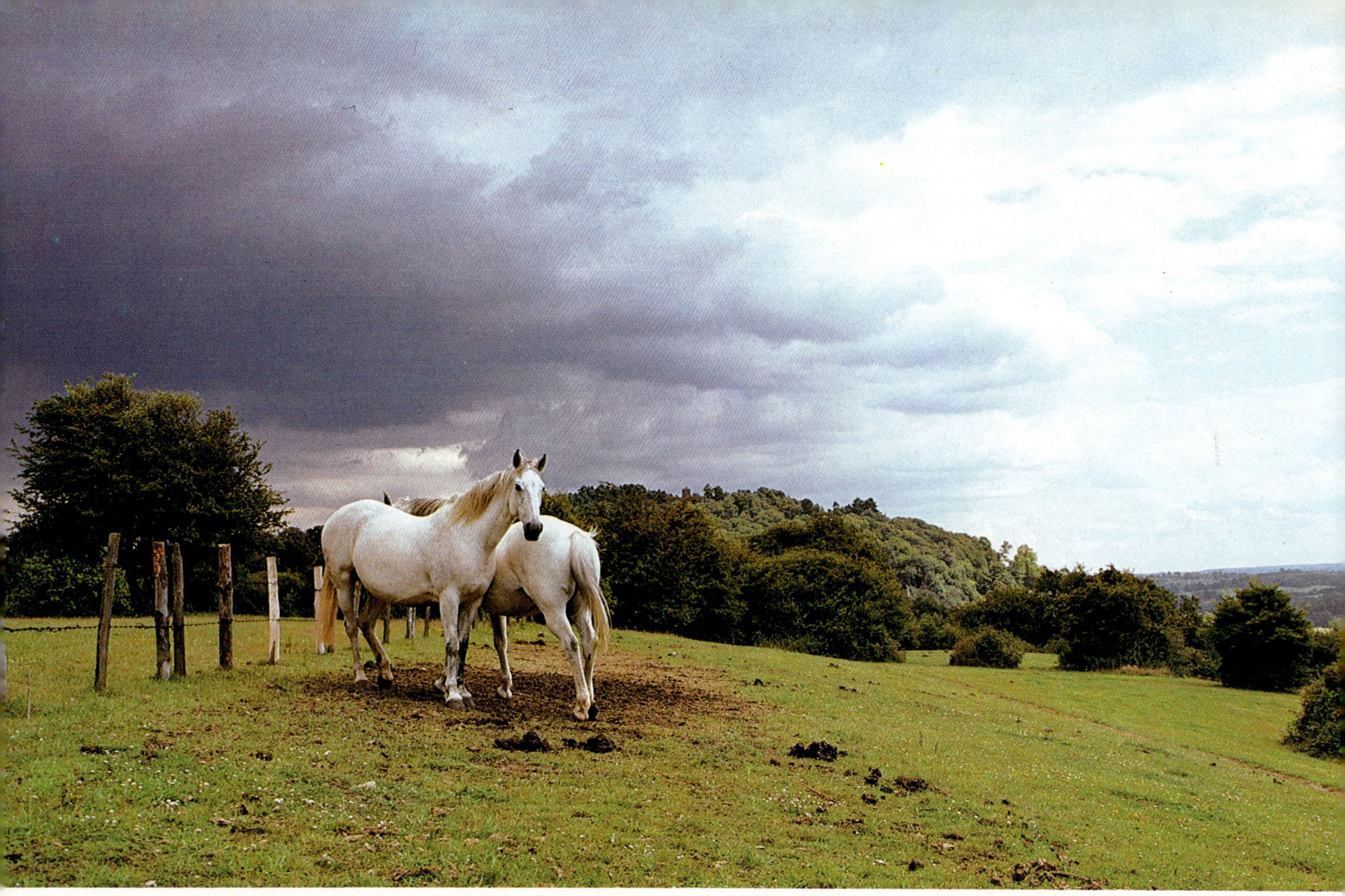

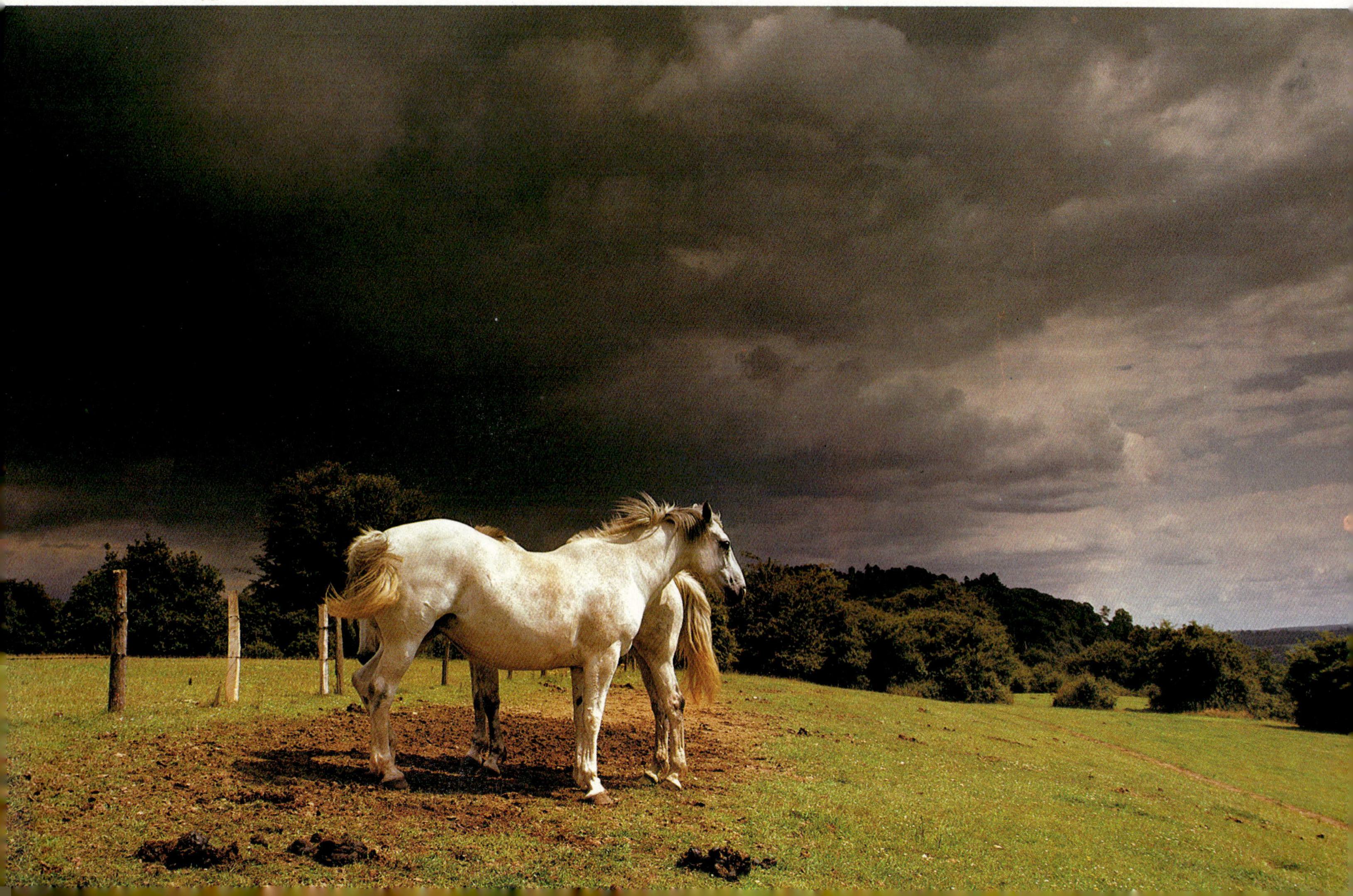

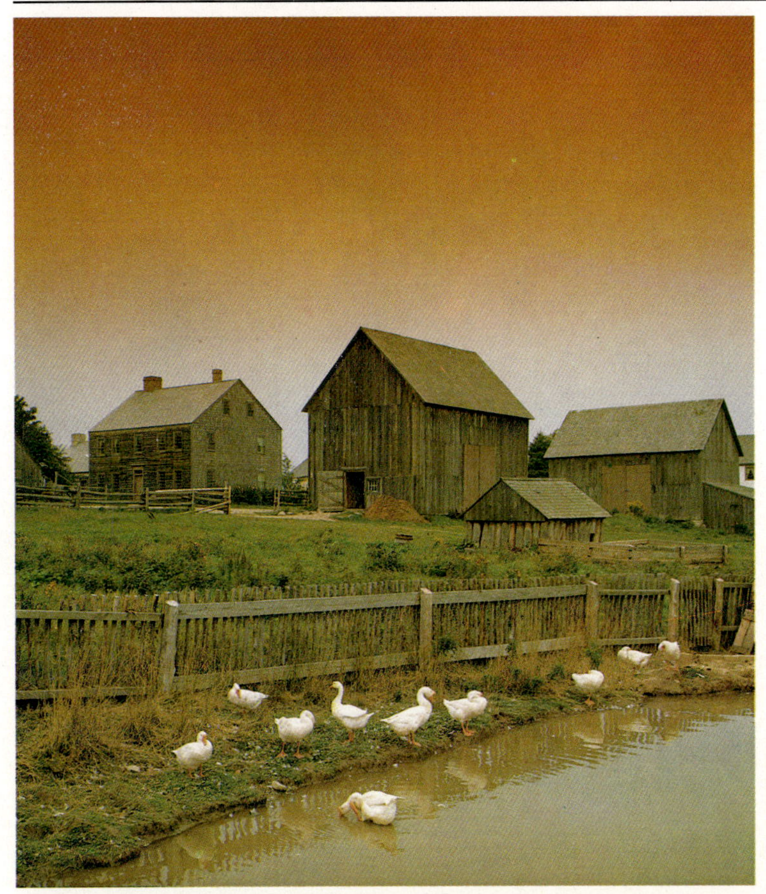

degree of darkening will depend upon the colour and density of the graduated filter.

When used with colour film, the filter colour will add a cast of the same colour to the subject area covered. Here the mix of colours is similar to a paintbox. For instance, a yellow filter over a blue sky will produce a green sky, and a red filter over green foliage will produce brown foliage. This is, of course, a matter of degree, and some very intense grads are quite capable of obliterating the subject colour.

It is possible to use graduated filters in tandem, so that a subject can be tinted in two colours. Likewise, two same colour filters, or a colour with a neutral density can be used to make a more intense filter. Doing this with plastic filters will ensure a loss of definition which may or may not be acceptable.

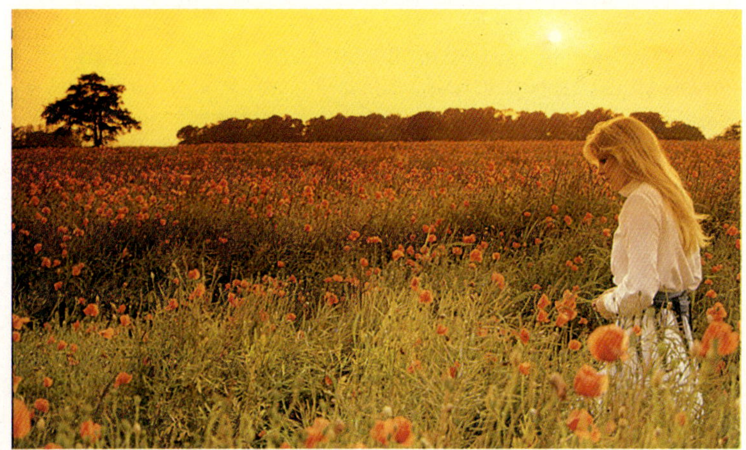

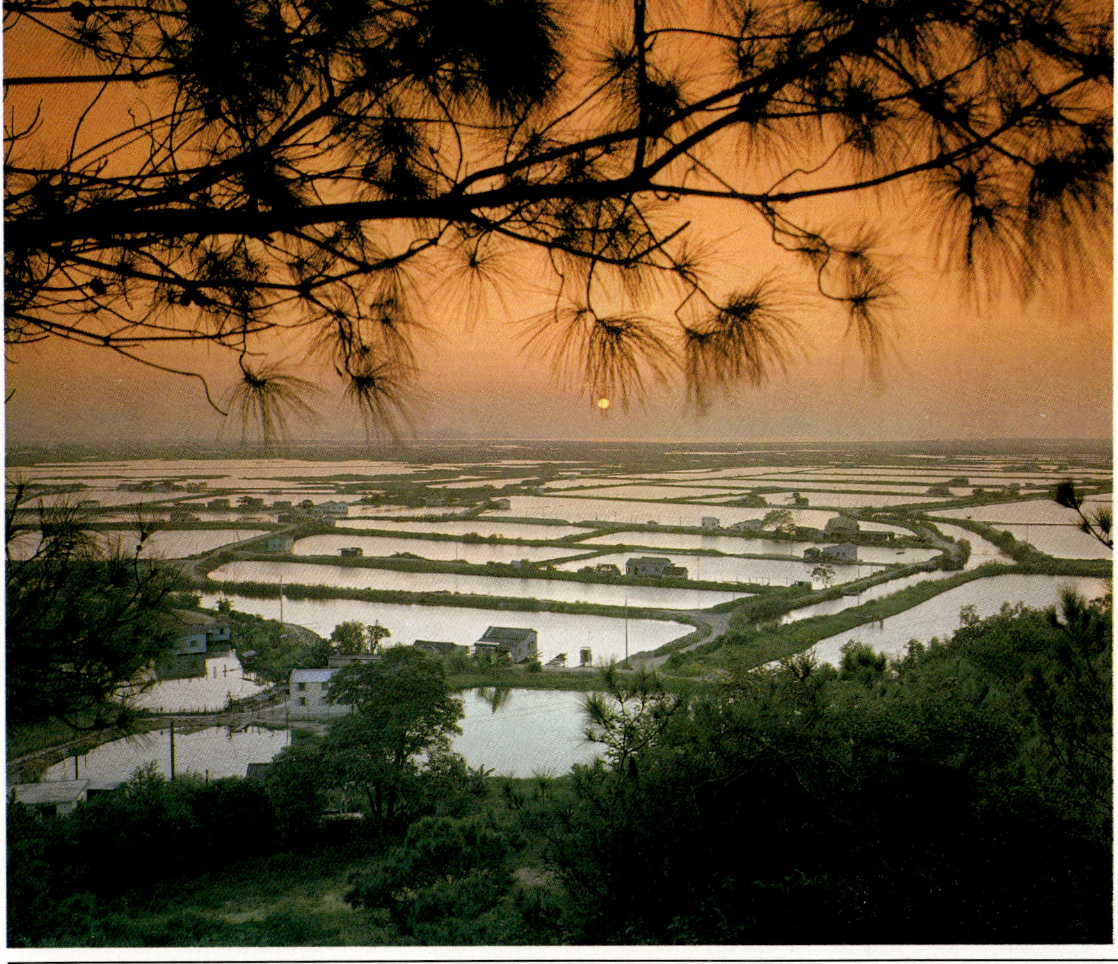

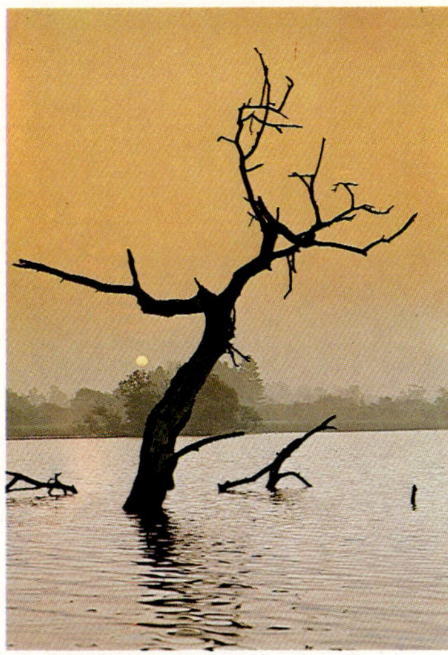

The landscape with horses facing page, top *is certainly attractive as it stands. The lower picture, however, shows just how dramatically the whole mood can be changed by the use of a graduated grey filter. Now the sky is dark and threatening, and the horses stand out in sharp contrast. Shown on* ***this page*** *are some further examples of the change that can be affected by the use of yellow, orange and tobacco graduated filters.*

HALF, DUAL AND TRI COLOUR FILTERS

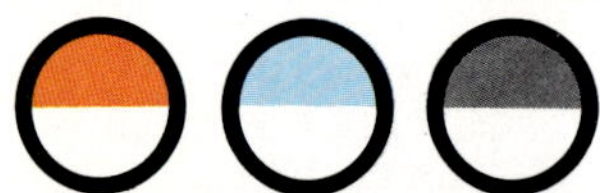

Half colour, dual colour and tri-colour filters come into the same category of construction in that they all consist of a glass/gelatin/glass sandwich. Half colour filters have a single colour 'gel' across the mount aperture. Most makers give a choice of about four colour options, whilst Hoya have a range of eleven, including two neutral density filters. Some makers allow for rotation of the mount, whilst cheaper alternatives require the filter holder to be partially unscrewed from the lens mount. The effect of a half colour filter is to add a colour tint to either a foreground or background – or for that matter to either side, or even diagonally. An increase in exposure is seldom necessary unless the effect required is to lighten the foreground. This is achieved by allowing for the filter factor of the coloured half.

Dual colour filters perform a similar function, except that each half is (usually) in somewhere near complementary colours. Typical combinations are: Red/Blue, Orange/Green, and Yellow/Mauve. Obviously, since the filter is totally coloured, an increase in exposure is necessary. This can vary from 2X to 6X, depending upon the individual makers colour densities. A third variant of this filter form is the Tricolour. In this instance, the filter

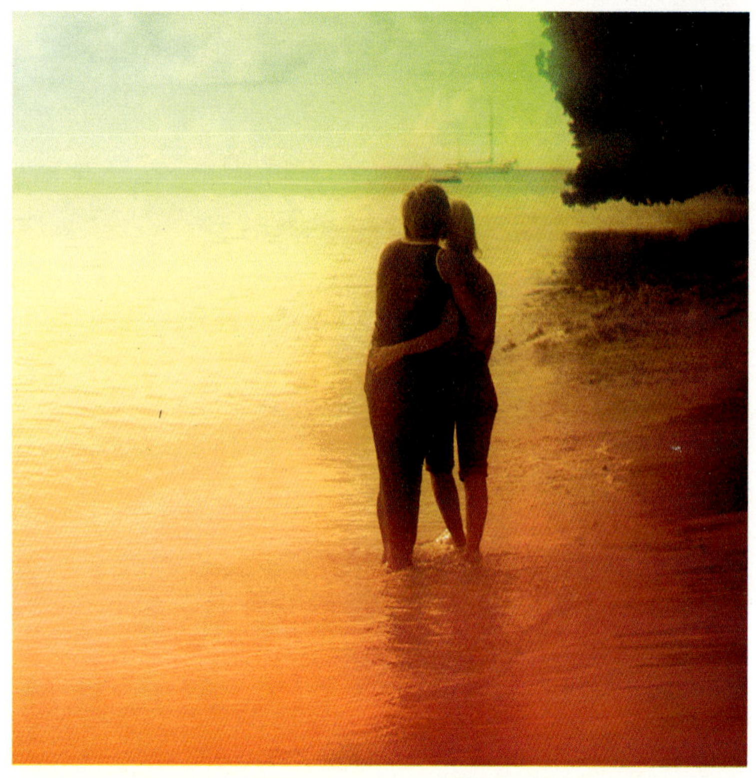

***The pictures featured on these** pages, whether they are universally liked or not, are certainly arresting, and this is often the purpose of the photographic image. Plenty of film should be shot when attempting subjects like these, with exposures bracketed and slight changes of filter position; most of them are not identically repeatable.*

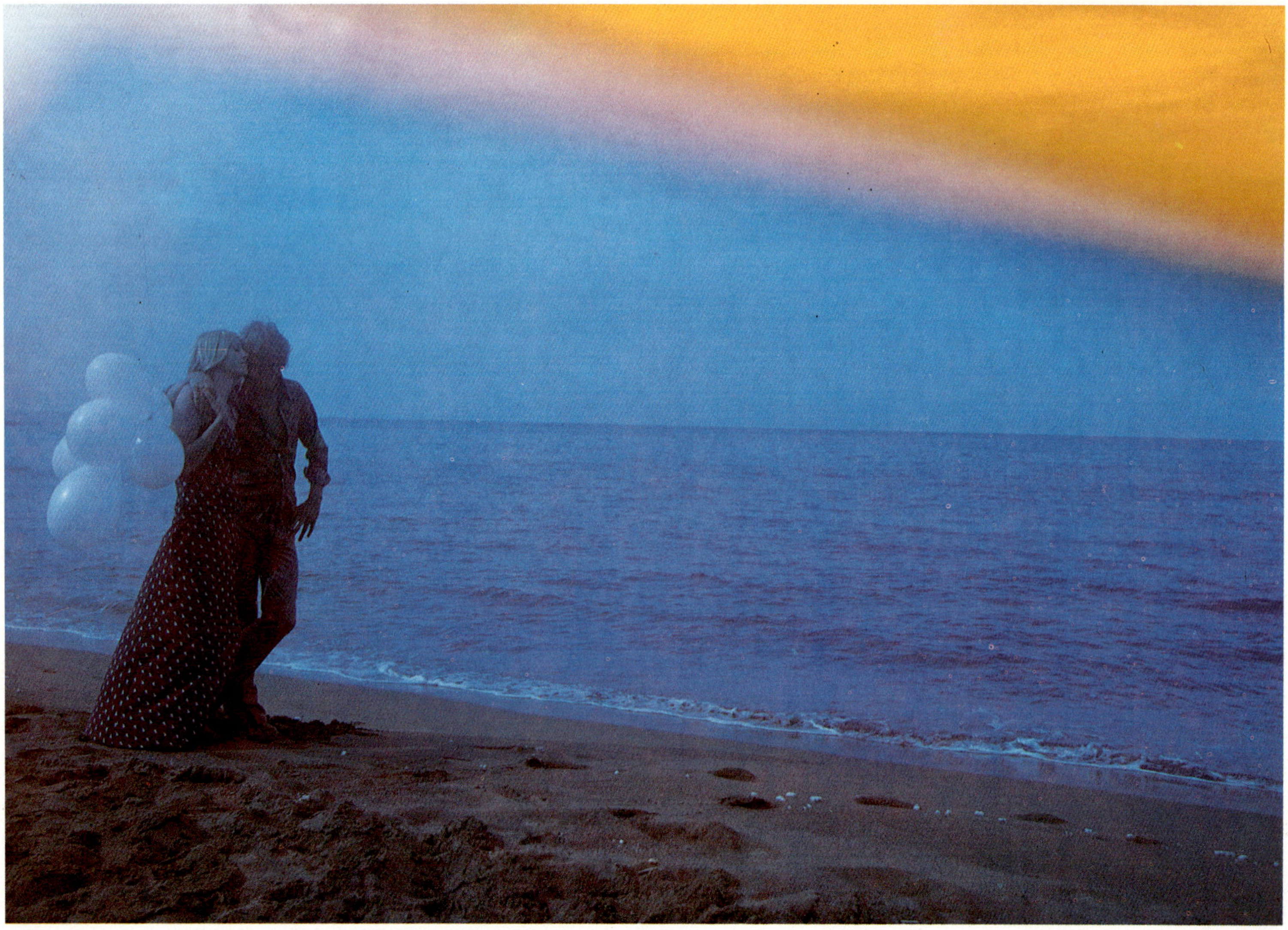

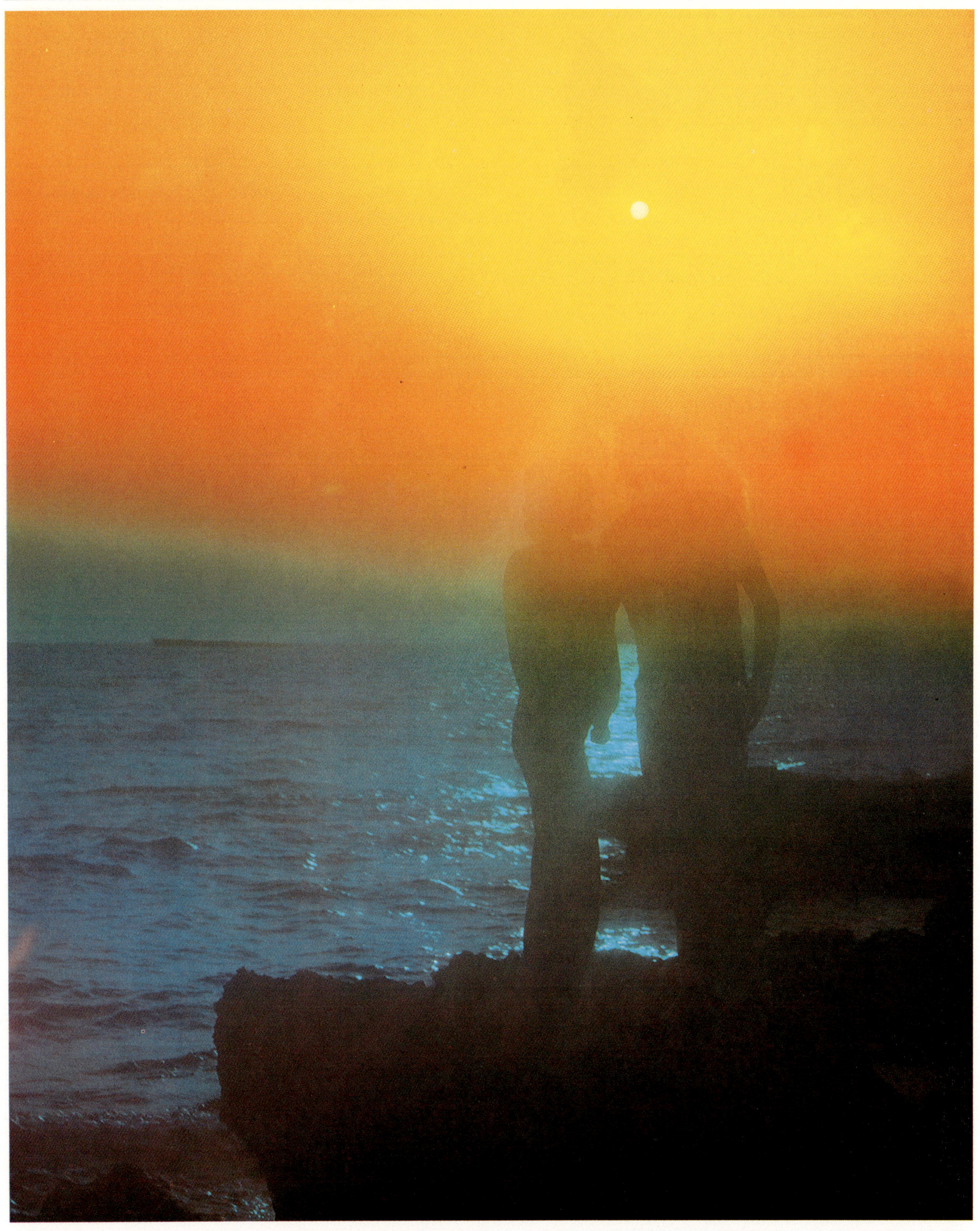

HALF, DUAL AND TRI COLOUR FILTERS

glass is divided into three colours in either three plane parallel or 120° segmented form. A rotating mount is normally fitted as standard.

Using any of these filters requires a certain amount of experimentation before they can be mastered. The effect of lens 'taking' aperture is drastic. When viewing with an SLR camera at full aperture, the effect may be either too gradual or just right. But, by the time the lens is shut down to its smallest stop, then the division(s) in the filter glass will be rendered sharp in the final result. As reducing lens aperture gradually produces an equally gradual effect, a depth of field preview control on the camera is useful, to say the least, in evaluating the final result. It may be that when using a fast film in bright light, it is necessary to use the camera's highest shutter speed, or even to employ an additional neutral density filter, in order to allow for a wide enough aperture setting.

This effect also varies with focal length, in that longer lenses are easier to use with these filters than wide angles. With the latter, the horizon of a landscape shot may have to be positioned exactly half way up the frame, in order to achieve a pleasing division of tone.

Whilst half colour filters do not theoretically require any increase in basic exposure, it may be that a TTL metering pattern will not now read correctly. It is as well to note the exposure readout with and without the filter in place, and to note any discrepancy for future reference. Dual colour and tri-colour filters alike may also fool the camera's metering system, since colour sensitivity of TTL meters varies from maker to maker. The camera's handbook should mention any compensation needed for orange and red filters, as these are the usual culprits. Again, a practical preview can well save future disappointment.

As far as professional *photography is concerned, the use of strong filters, especially mixes of colour such as can be produced by half colour, dual, or even tri-colour filters, is usually at the request of a client or art director, or an attempt by the photographer to create something 'different.' Many photographers spend a good deal of their time photographing girls or couples by the sea and, after all, one seascape is much like another. Different models, clothes and ideas all help – as do special effects filters. The combination of colours can be startling, restful – or however you choose to interpret the feeling.*

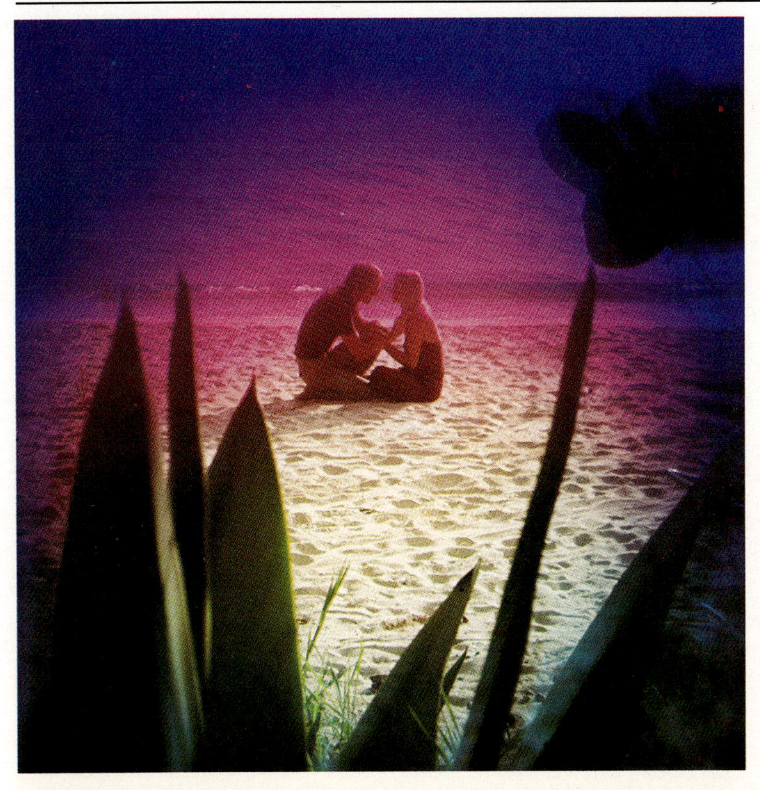
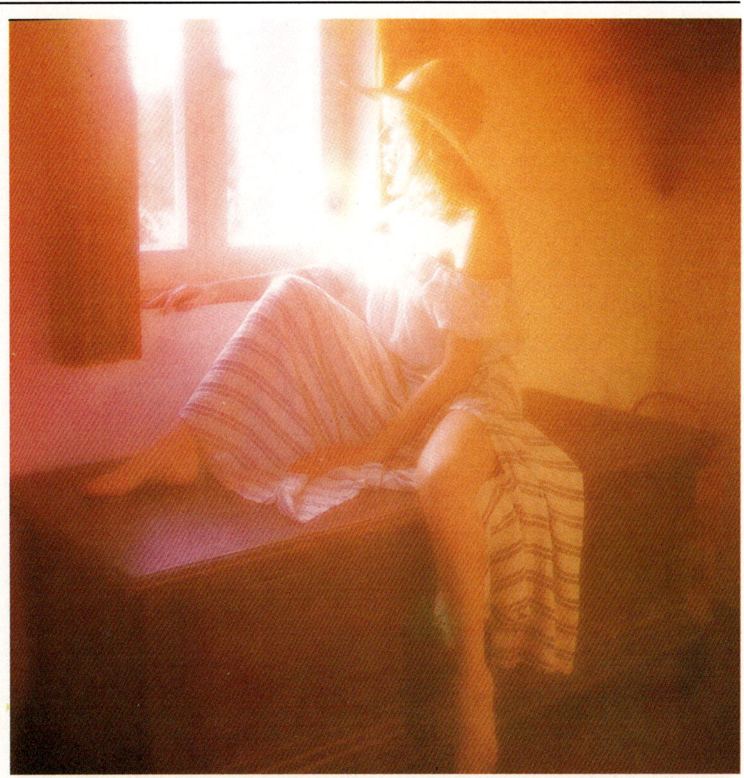
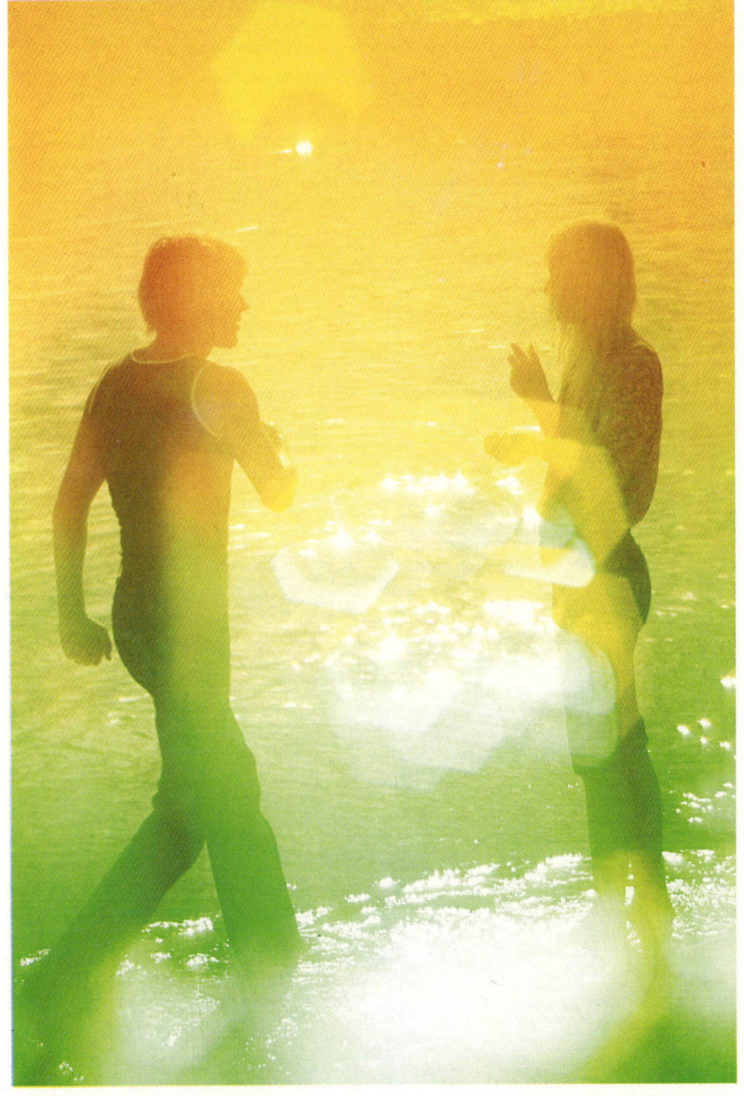
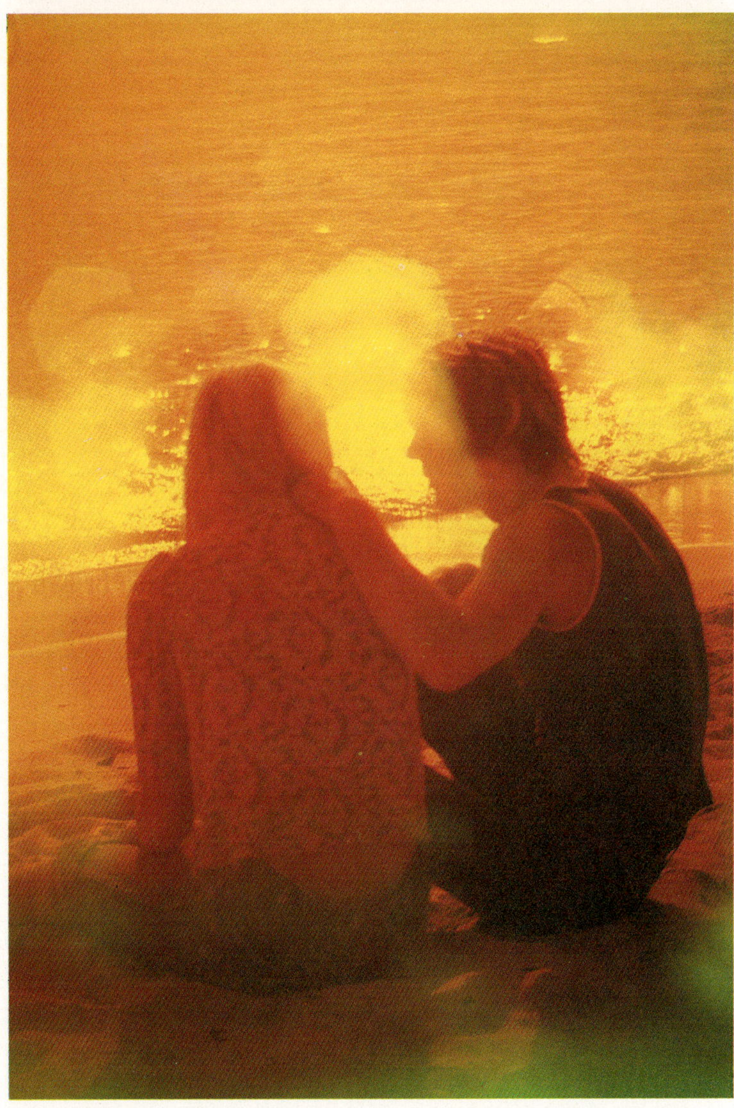

HALF, DUAL AND TRI COLOUR FILTERS

Although many of the effects *created by half or multi-coloured filters can appear weird and unreal as, indeed, they should – that is often the intention – they can also be used simply to enhance what already exists in the picture. This is true of the beautiful, geometrically-composed shot* ***facing page*** *of Muttart Conservatory in Edmonton, Canada. Another example is shown by the picture* ***below,*** *with its dramatically deepened sky and sea. The picture* ***right*** *was taken through a tri-colour filter and, additionally, a multi-image prism.*

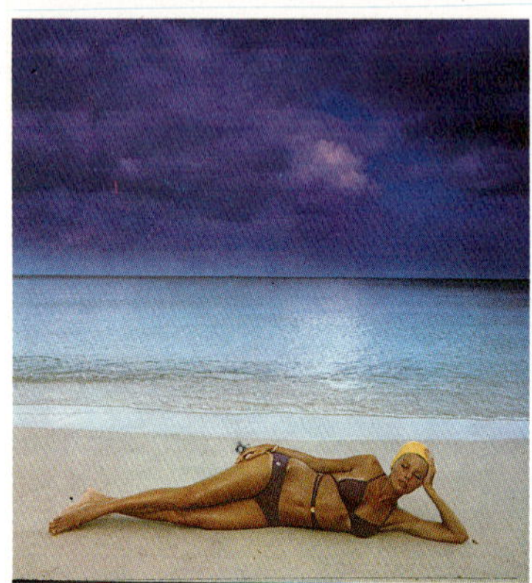

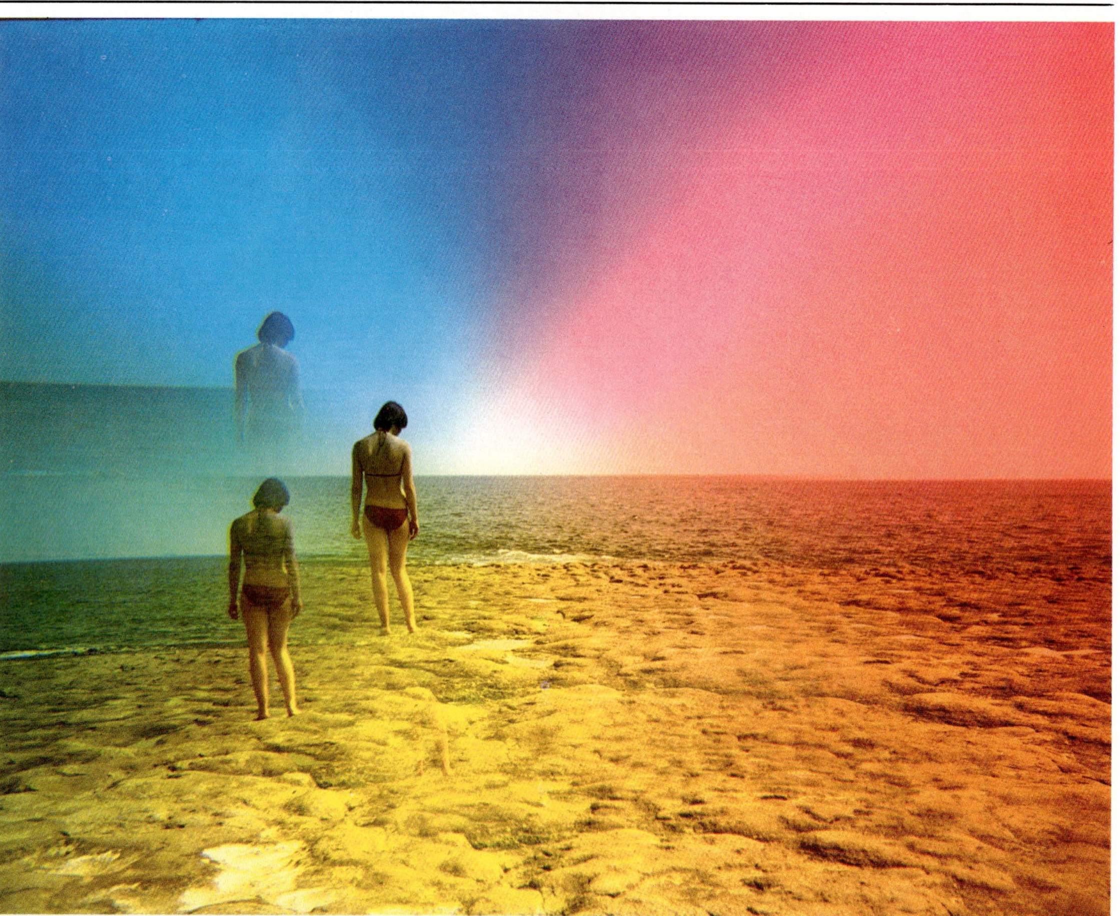

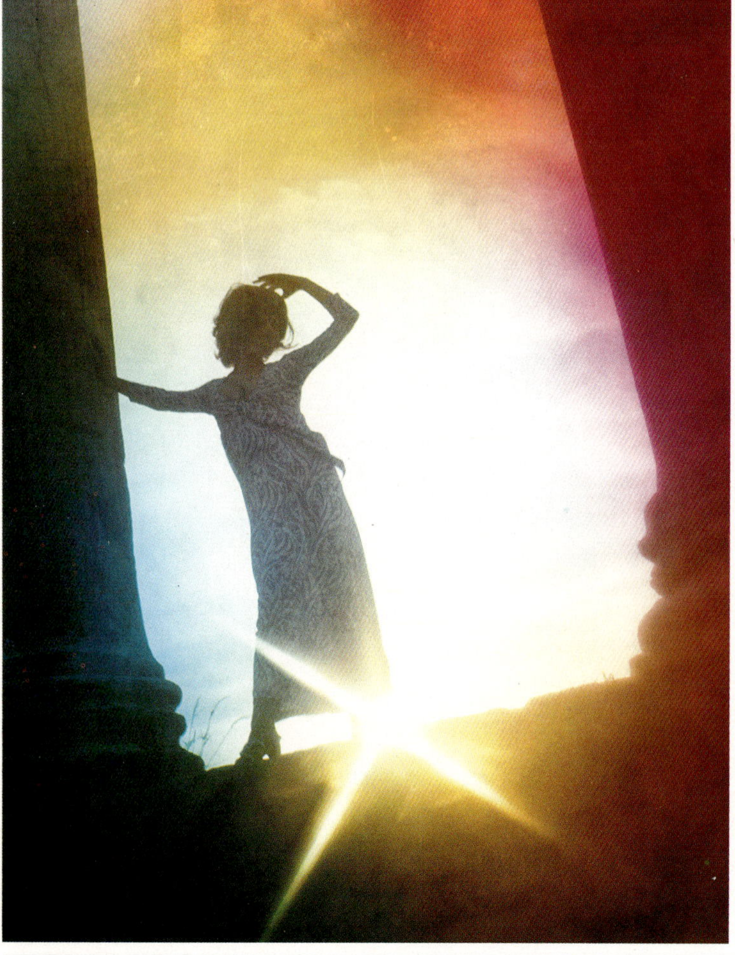

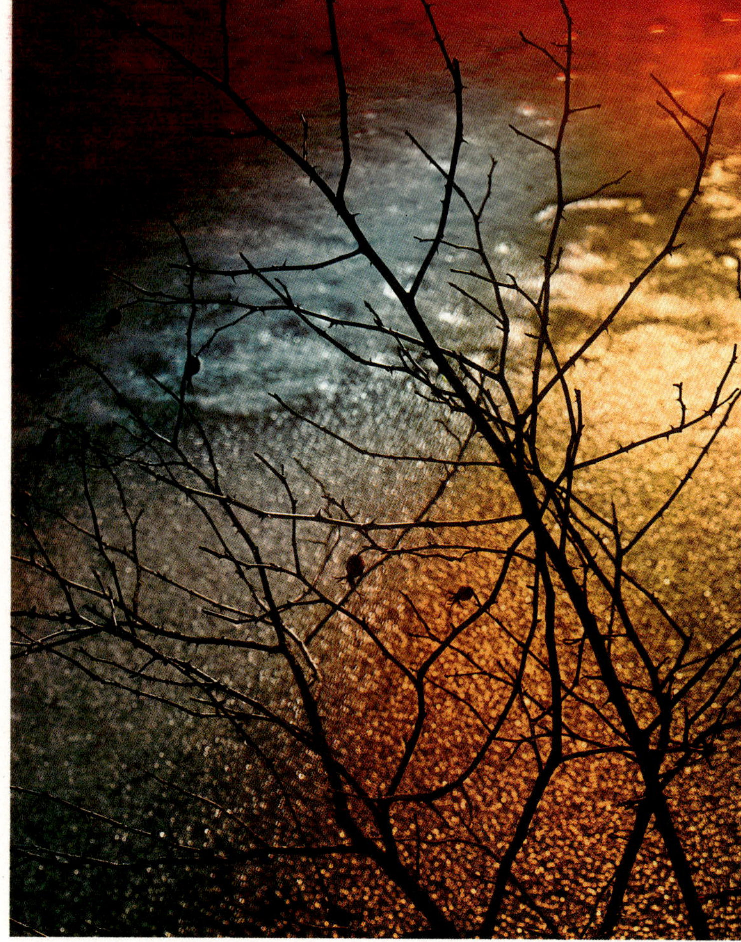

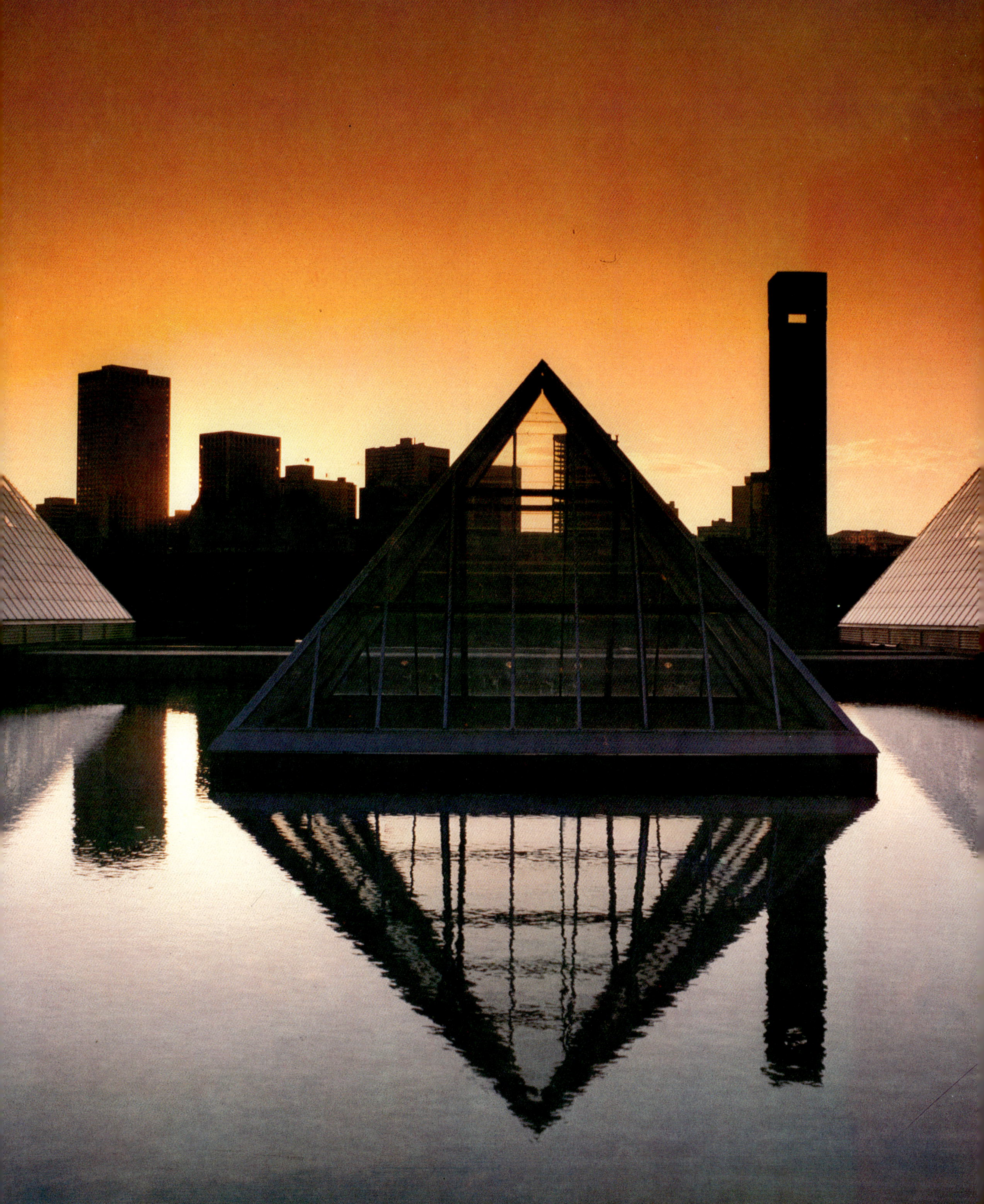

POPS, PASTELS AND SEPIAS

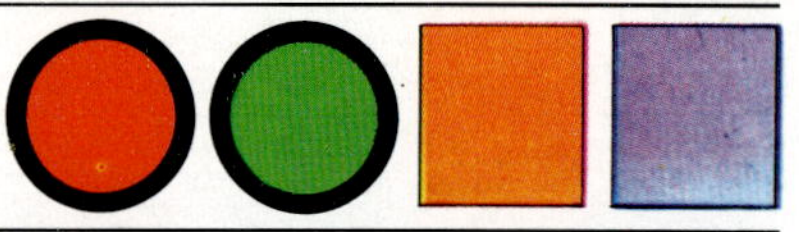

This section is about using those filters primarily intended for black and white work on colour film, or vice versa. Modern marketing techniques have produced a situation whereby these applications have seemingly become a separate photographic entity, whereas in reality the categories of pop and pastel filters, for instance, are in fact only extensions to the uses of filters which have been around for a long time. This statement in no way denigrates those manufacturers who produce these items, indeed they are to be commended for providing an awareness of a creative technique, which has, until recently, nominally only been the province of the experimentally minded or those in the audio visual field.

Any pop, pastel or sepia filter will have its near equivalent in the Kodak catalogue of gelatin filters, albeit that Kodak's intended use was for some abstruse scientific application. Most pop filters for instance can be equated with the following:-

WRATTEN DESIGNATION	COLOUR
11	Emerald Green
21/22	Oranges
15/16	Chrome Yellows
25	Intense Red
30/31	Shocking Pinks
34A	Violet
44	Turquoise
46/47	Intense Blues
58	Intense Green

Some of these filters have a pretty high factor but then so do many pop filters. The oft repeated warning about TTL metering systems still applies.

The result of using pop filters can be startling, though whether one likes the end result is purely a matter of taste. The deeper colours, and red in particular, will give a totally monochromatic result often with an apparent lack of resolution and contrast. Any of the 'combination' colours such as magenta, cyan or yellow-green may allow an intense subject colour to show through. There are no hard and fast rules on this, it is simply a matter of having a go. Two of the most effective subjects can be the sun upon water or a silhouette. Since these are largely monochromatic anyway, a bit of colour enhancement can only add interest.

Conventional red, orange, yellow, blue and green filters for black and white photography can perform the same function as a Wratten or pop filter, providing that there is sufficient intensity of colour, or alternatively that under-exposure (of a colour transparency material) can be employed to heighten the colour enhancement.

Pastel filters too can be equated to the densest Wratten colour correction filters, though the Actina ten-filter pastel range adds three colours which Kodak haven't yet produced in a suitable strength. Pastel filters, like pop filters, work well with subjects of high contrast and yet in addition can produce ethereal results when used in flat lighting conditions, to give an end effect

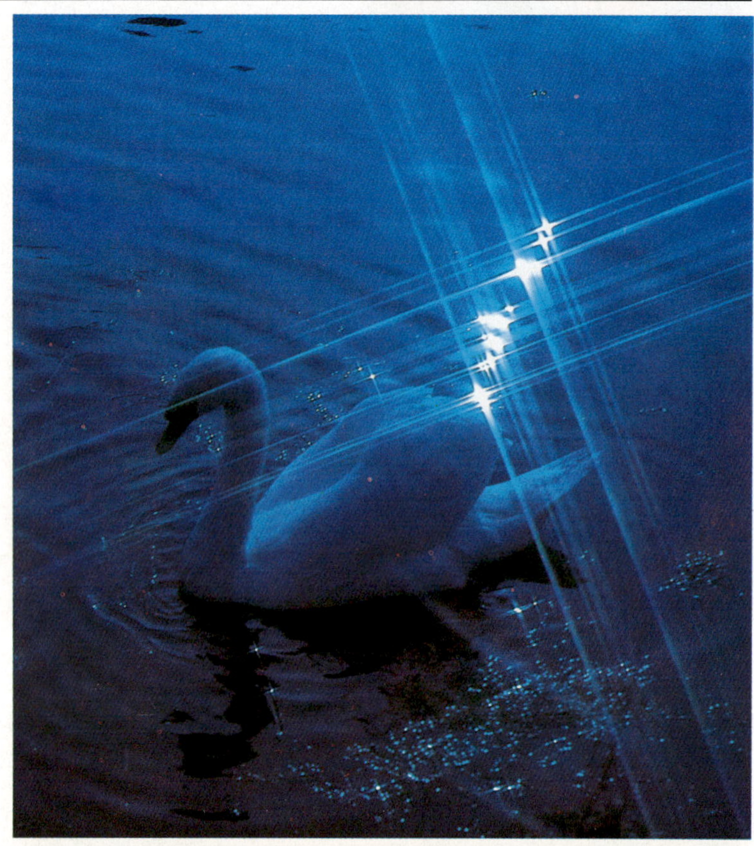

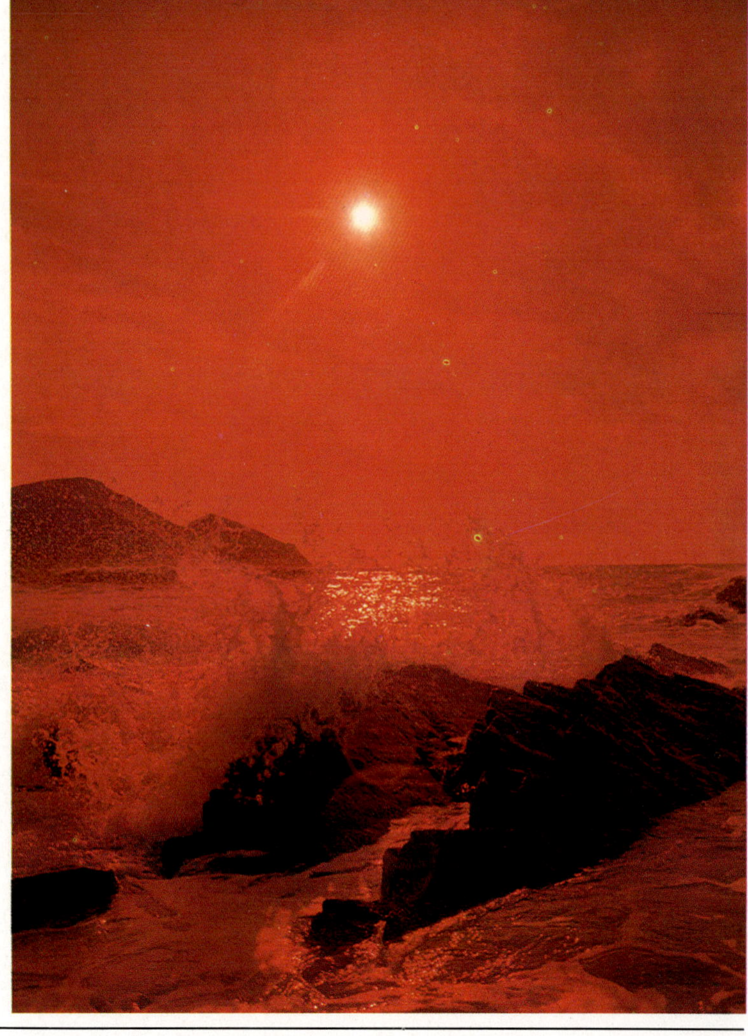

***Once we get into the realms of** bright, or 'pop' colours in filtration there is seldom any doubt that we are going for effect, rather than enhancing reality. Blue swans, green snow, sea and sky are not what we expect to find in nature. Nevertheless, providing you do not attempt to take every shot in this way, startling and attractive pictures can result. Once again, all these filters can be combined with starbursts or any other filters you care to try.*

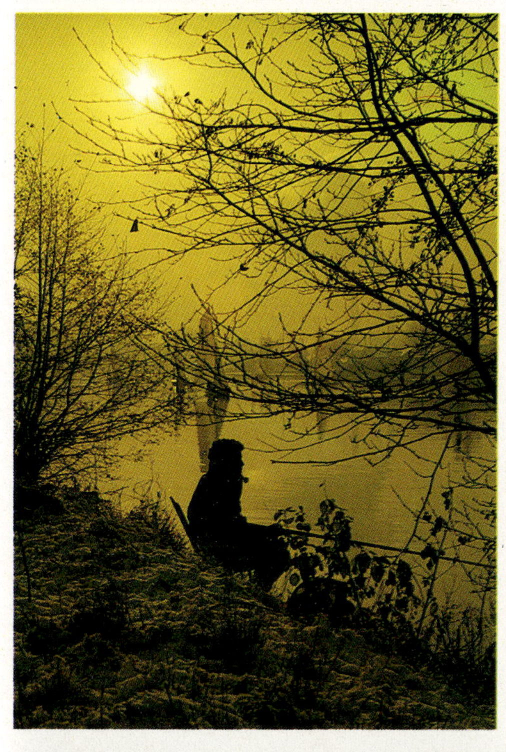
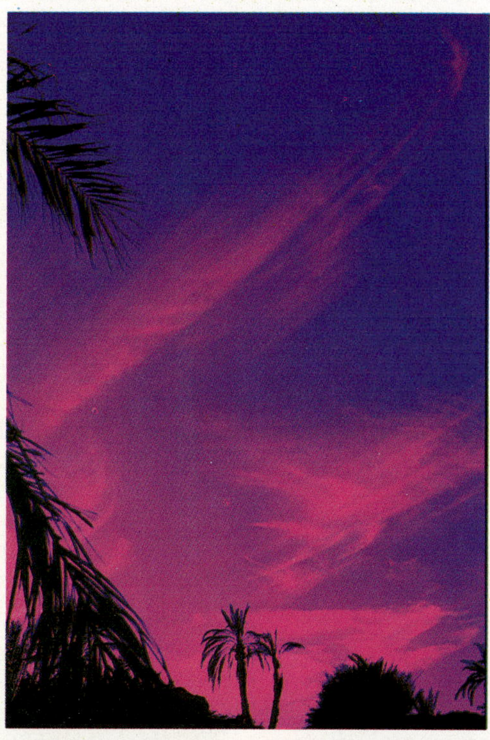
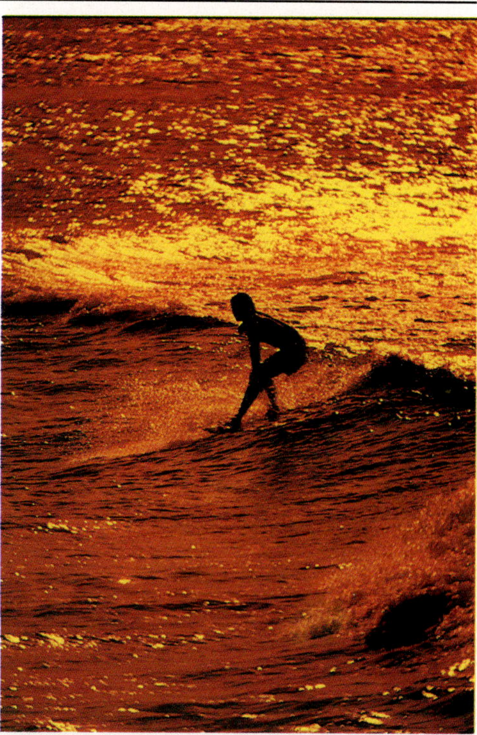
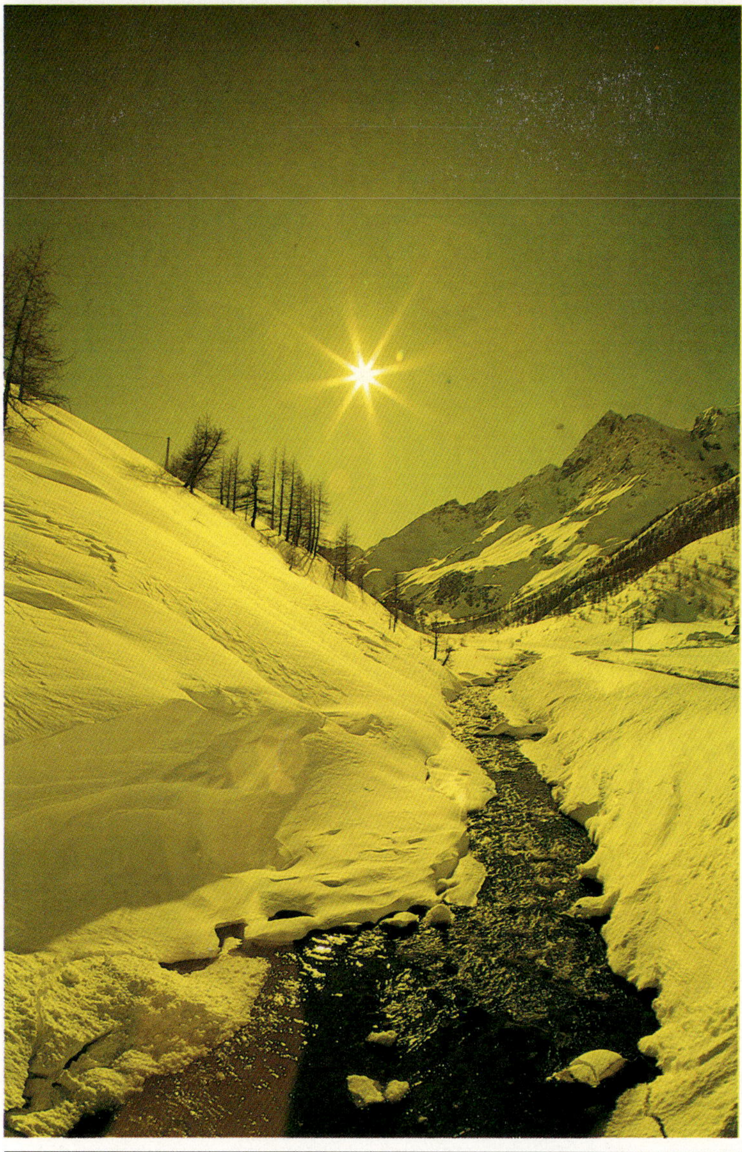
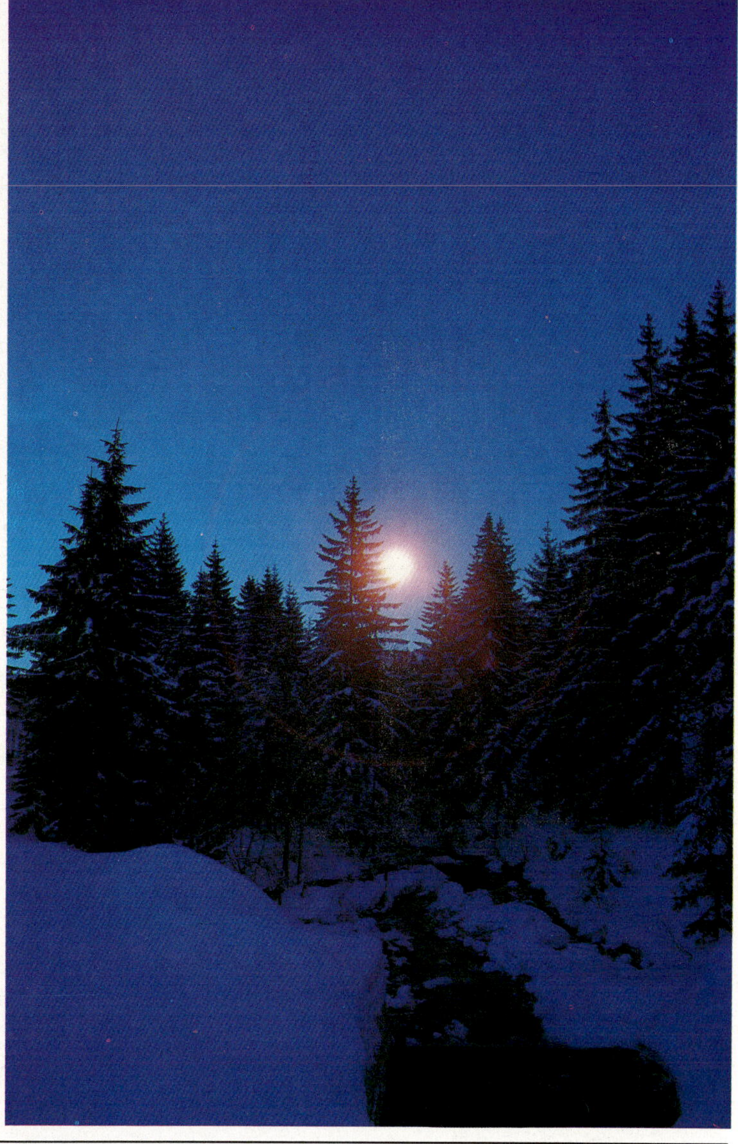

which appears to have been taken in coloured mist. Monochromatic subjects can be considered to work the best, as strong subject colours will show through a pastel. The choice of a sympathetic filter colour can still give a feeling of reality – but enhanced reality. Pastels are also suited to photography of people, particularly when a romantic feeling is required. The addition of a soft focus or diffusing filter will heighten the result, as will a small amount of over-exposure on colour transparency film. Colour negative workers can always make a lighter print.

Pastel filter factors range from virtually one to about +1½ stops. As they are not of high density, most TTL metering systems will cope adequately, though this will vary with differing filter and camera maker combinations.

Sepia filters can be described like 'An 85B by any other name would work as sweetly'! This is the basis, though an 81EF could be added to taste. Using a Wratten 85 series alone will produce a redder sepia tone, adding an 81 will make the result yellower. There is plenty of room for experimentation and plenty of proprietary sepia filters for those who want one off the shelf. Incidentally, as with all other filters, one maker's sepia will not necessarily match another's, and the results are better in daylight and with electronic flash than with tungsten, where the results can be too 'hot.'

I suspect that sepia filtration first occurred in the cinema world, where black and white footage mixes more easily with colour when toned sepia. The same is true for audio visual presentations, or even television – if they can be bothered.

Sepia filters work well in portraiture for special effects. Brunettes become auburn and redheads become very red, whilst blonde hair becomes a colour not found in nature, only in a bottle! Still life sets can work well in sepia, provided that the subject's colours are warm toned, blues and greens are apt to be neutralised.

Exposure factor varies between +⅔rds and + 1½ stops. A half stop under-exposure, on colour transparency stock, can often help by adding richness to the end result. The exception is

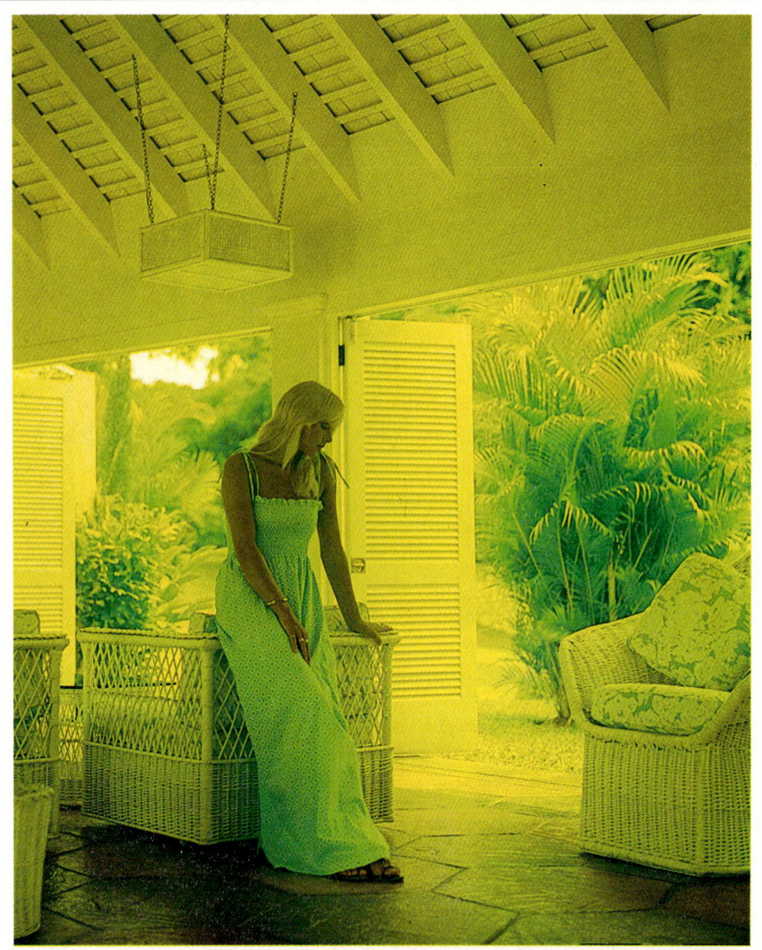

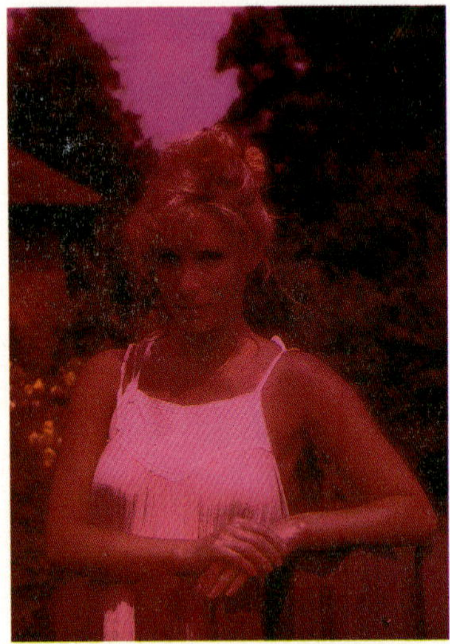

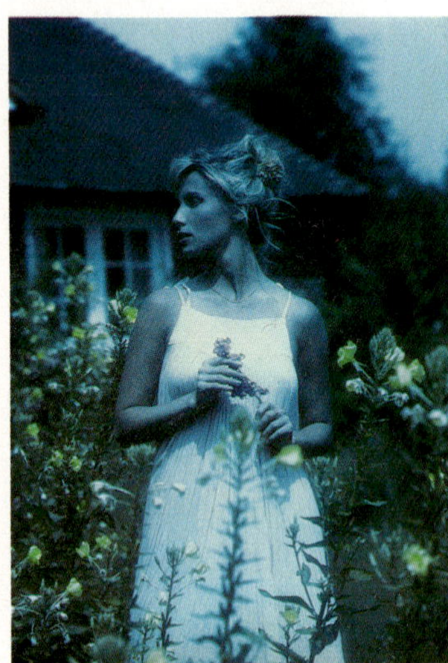

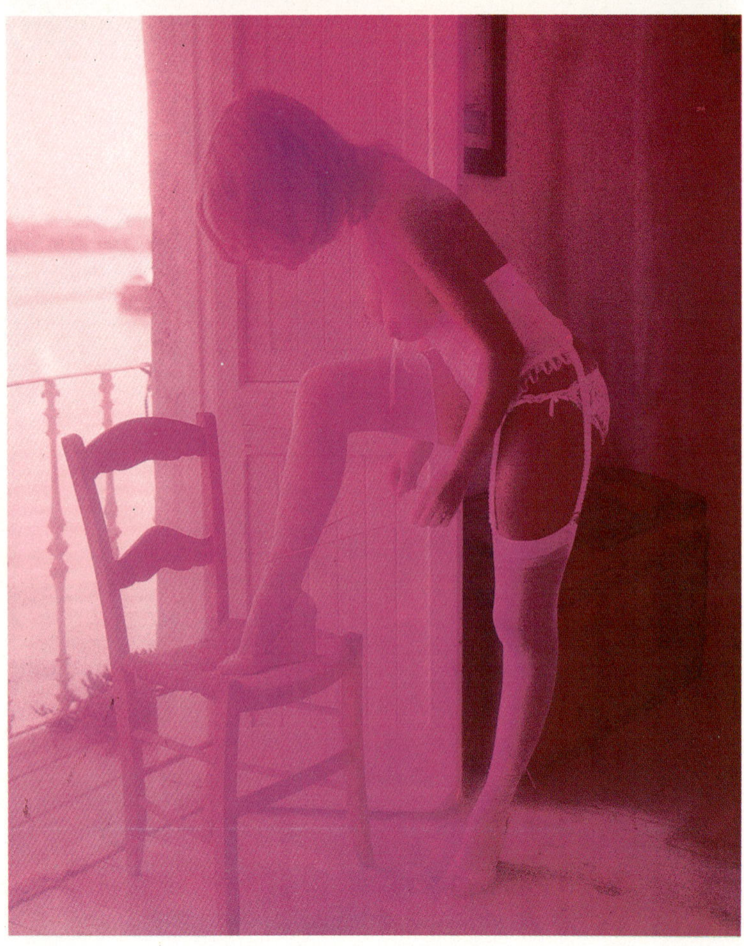

It would be easy to make the *statement that certain colours are better than others for certain pictures, but whether a colour works well or not depends entirely on whether it pleases you and achieves the result you want. However, most people would find the pale yellow/ green* ***top,*** *the pink* ***right,*** *the blue* ***above*** *and certainly the sepia* ***facing page*** *acceptable and attractive, but they would probably be less happy with the heavy magenta* ***above left.***

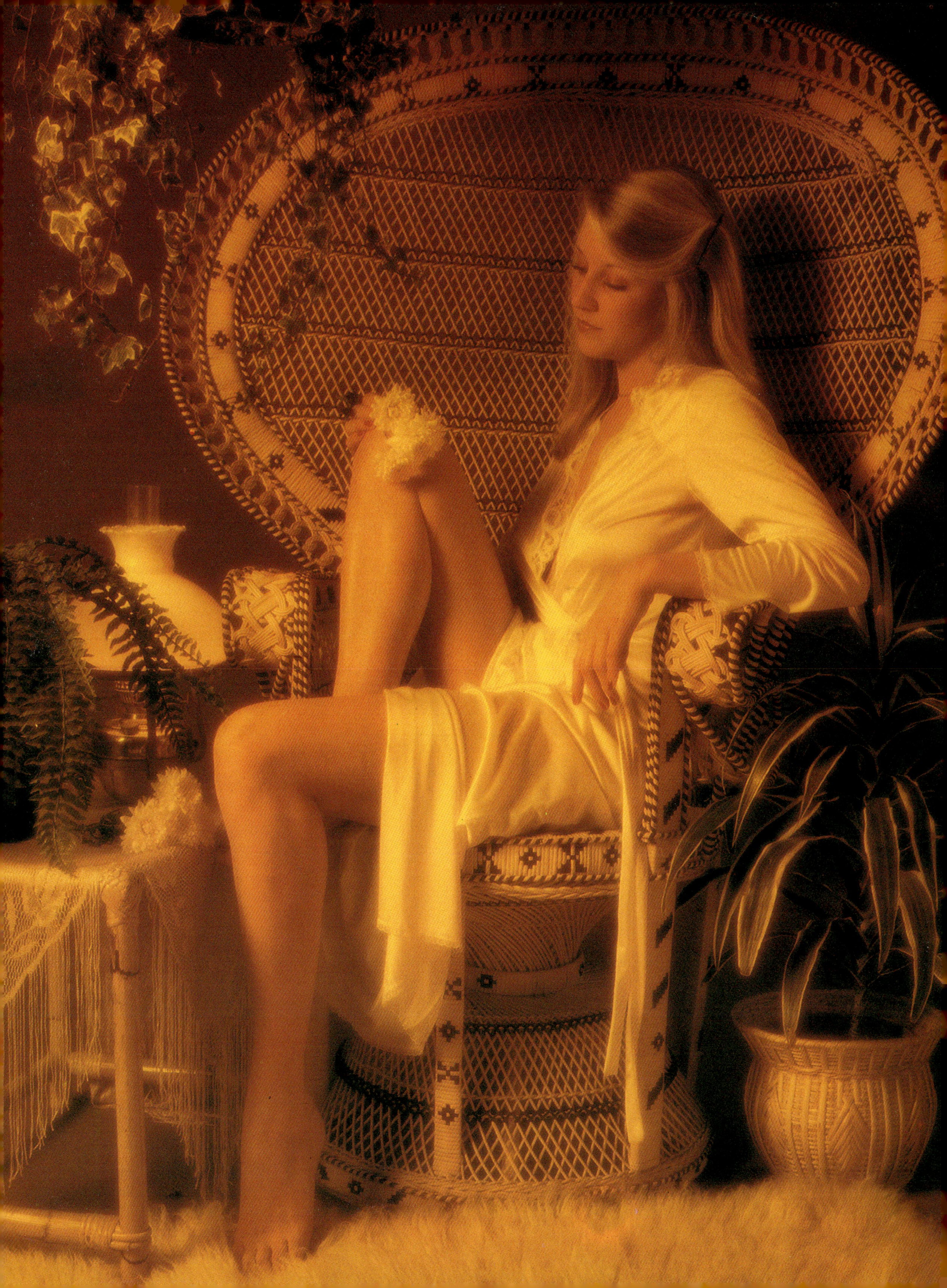

POPS, PASTELS AND SEPIAS

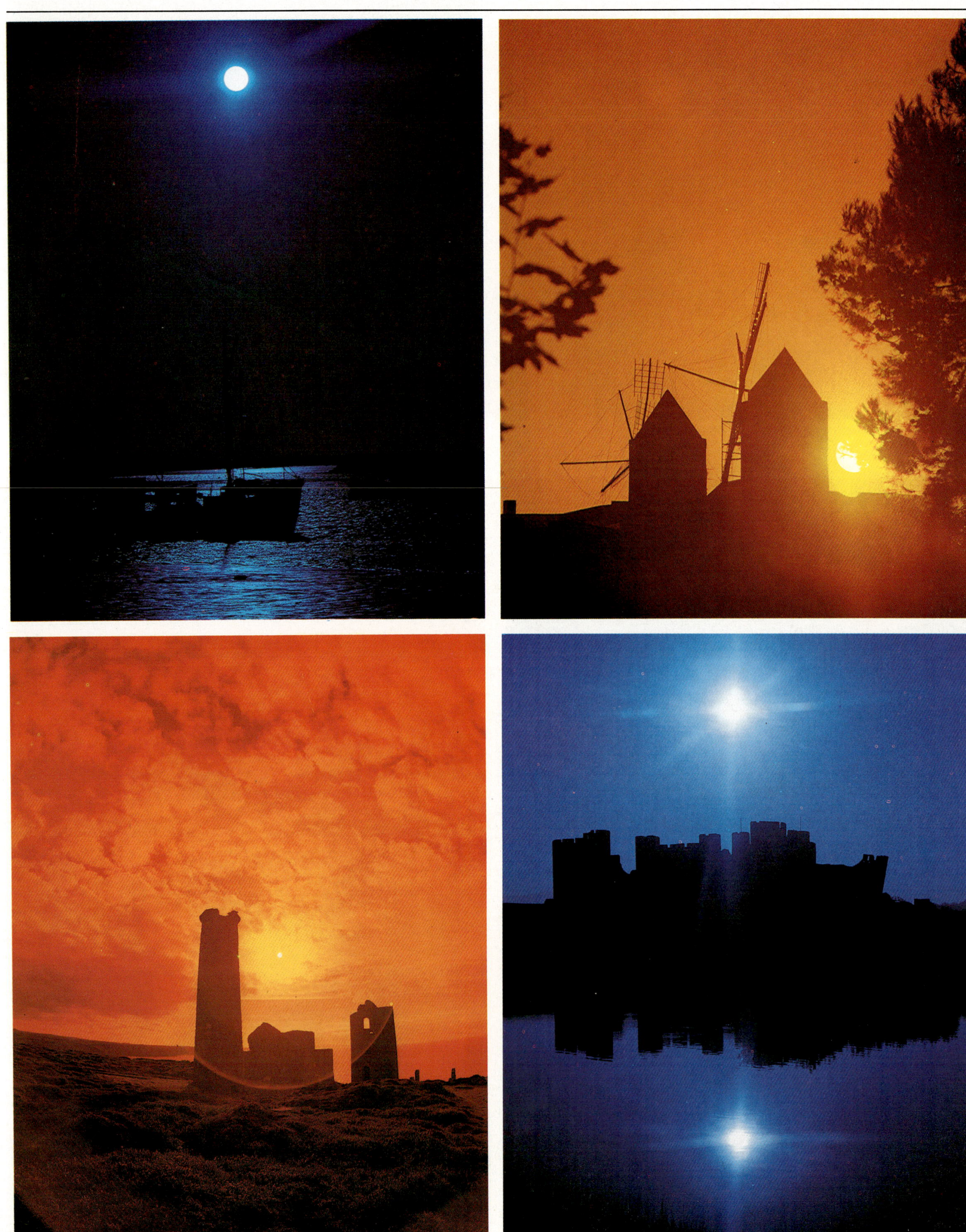

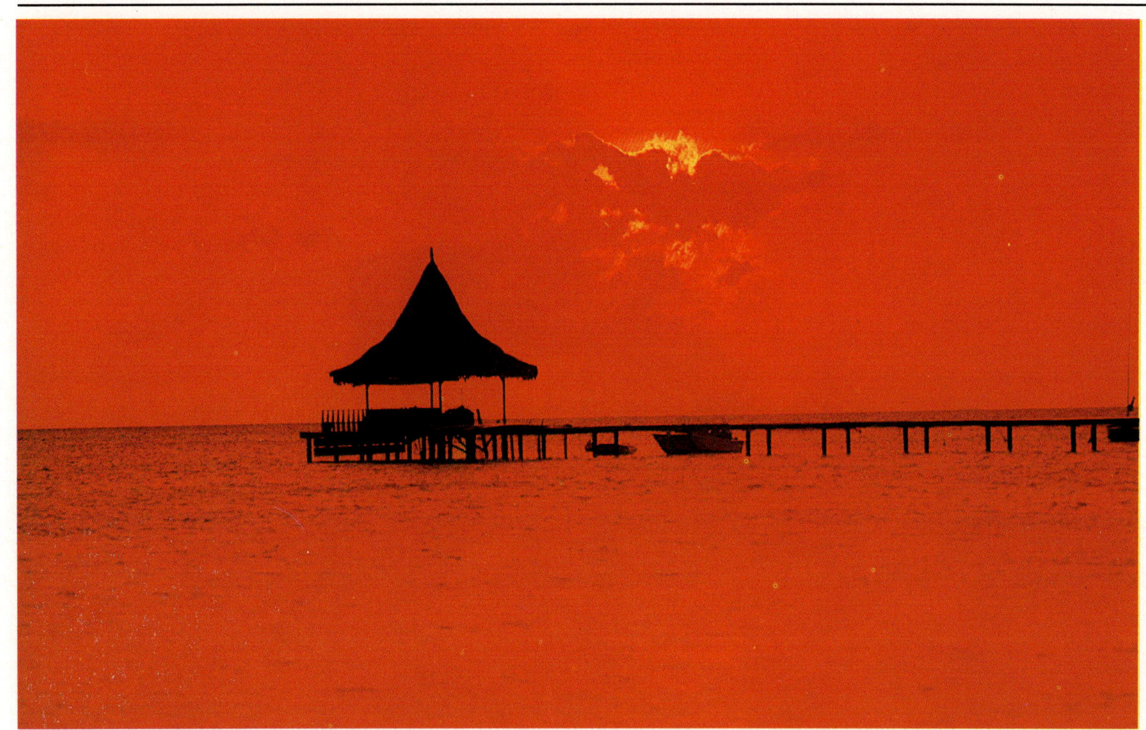

It is best to include strong *shapes in pictures when using strongly coloured filters. The deep colours have the effect of rendering objects as silhouettes; therefore they should be recognisable from their shapes as buildings, ships or whatever. The alternative is to give more exposure so that detail is visible, but this weakens the strong colour. The sun in shot helps to give variation to the colour by providing a lighter tone around it. In the original transparency* ***facing page, bottom left*** *the sun was exactly in the centre of the frame. The lens was stopped right down and this has created the 'halo' visible across the buildings. There is no mistaking any of the subjects on these pages, and 'wine dark seas' – and skies – are yours to command* ***left and below!***

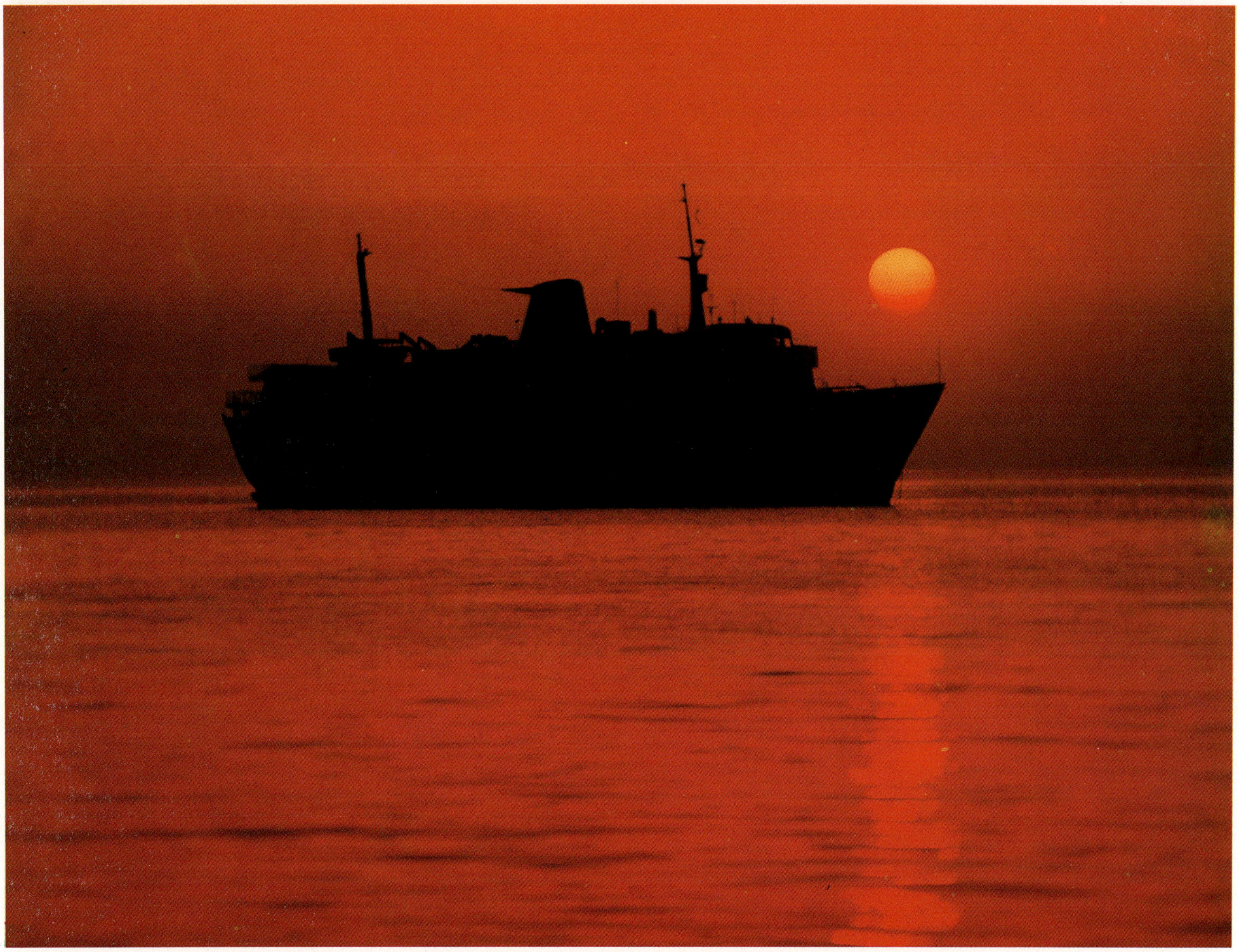

POPS, PASTELS AND SEPIAS

portraiture, where the skin tones should be nearer to nature as the added warmth of the filter colour is sufficient in itself.

Filters specifically intended for colour photography can be used with black and white films. Probably the most useful is an 85B which gives much the same sky rendering as a deep yellow or pale orange. An FL-Day or FL-B filter does the same thing to a lesser degree. The amber 81C and EF work like a UV filter at high altitudes to reduce haze and give a darker sky rendition, whilst the blue 82 filters will act like a half-watt filter for artificial light portraiture on fast panchromatic film. The 80 series blue filters are too strong for anything but colour correction, i.e. strengthening a yellow subject, or alternatively can be used to emphasise haze and fog in a landscape. Only the densest CC filters are of any use with black and white films, and then only for mild tonal correction. Both CC50 Yellow and CC50 Green may be used as sky filters.

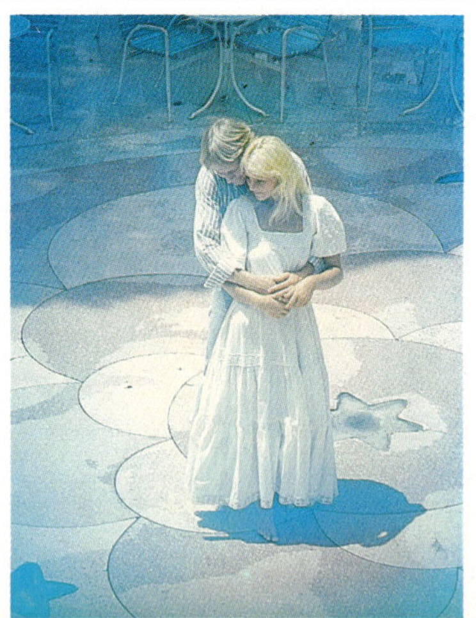

The rather delicate colours in *the pictures* ***left and facing page top right*** *are not intrusive and lend an added feeling of 'romance.' Most fish-eye lenses* ***below*** *are provided with built-in filters. The curvature of the front element and the field of view makes the use of conventional filters impossible. All the pictures in this section should be considered merely as ideas; experiment, combine filters, find out how far you want to go along the special effects road, but remember that good photography is what counts.*

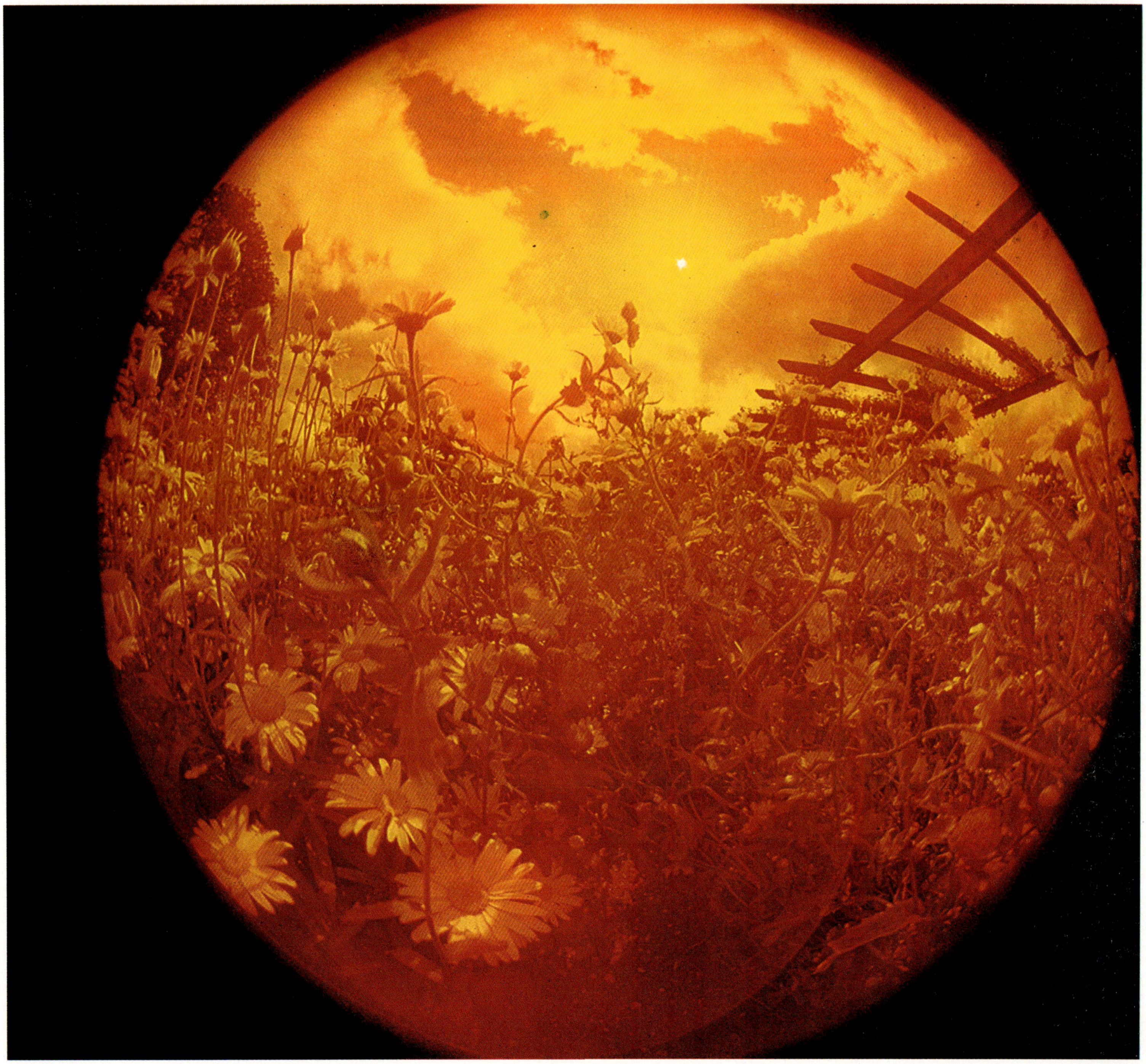

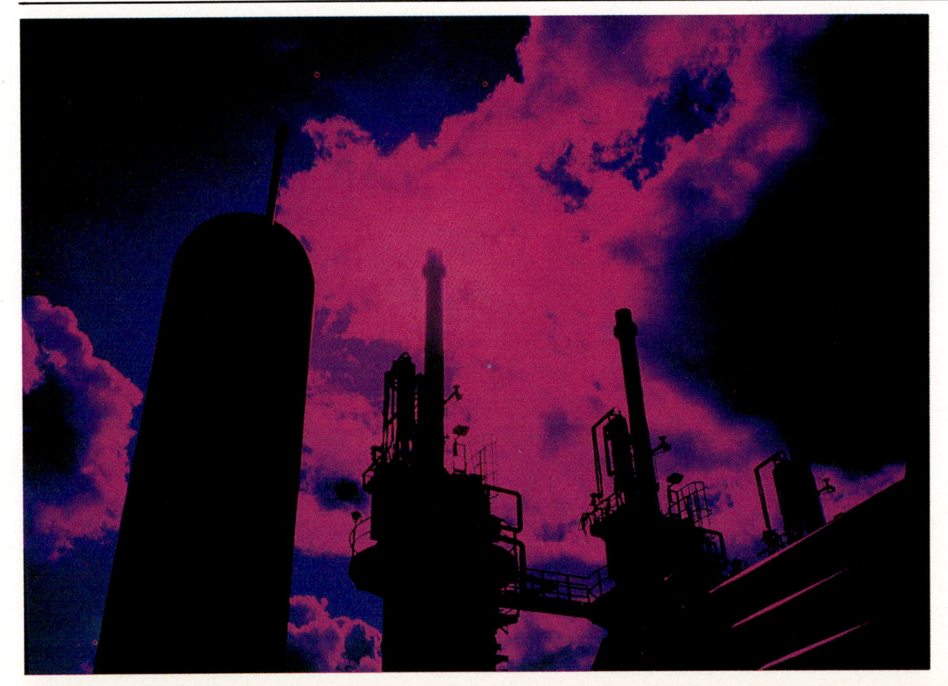
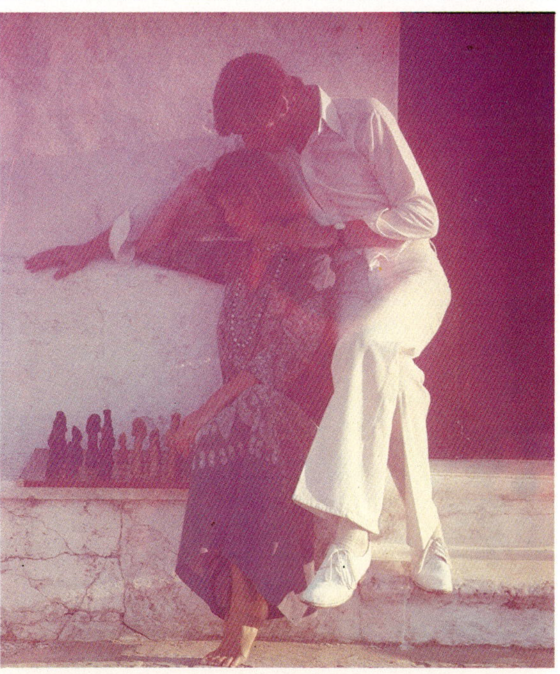

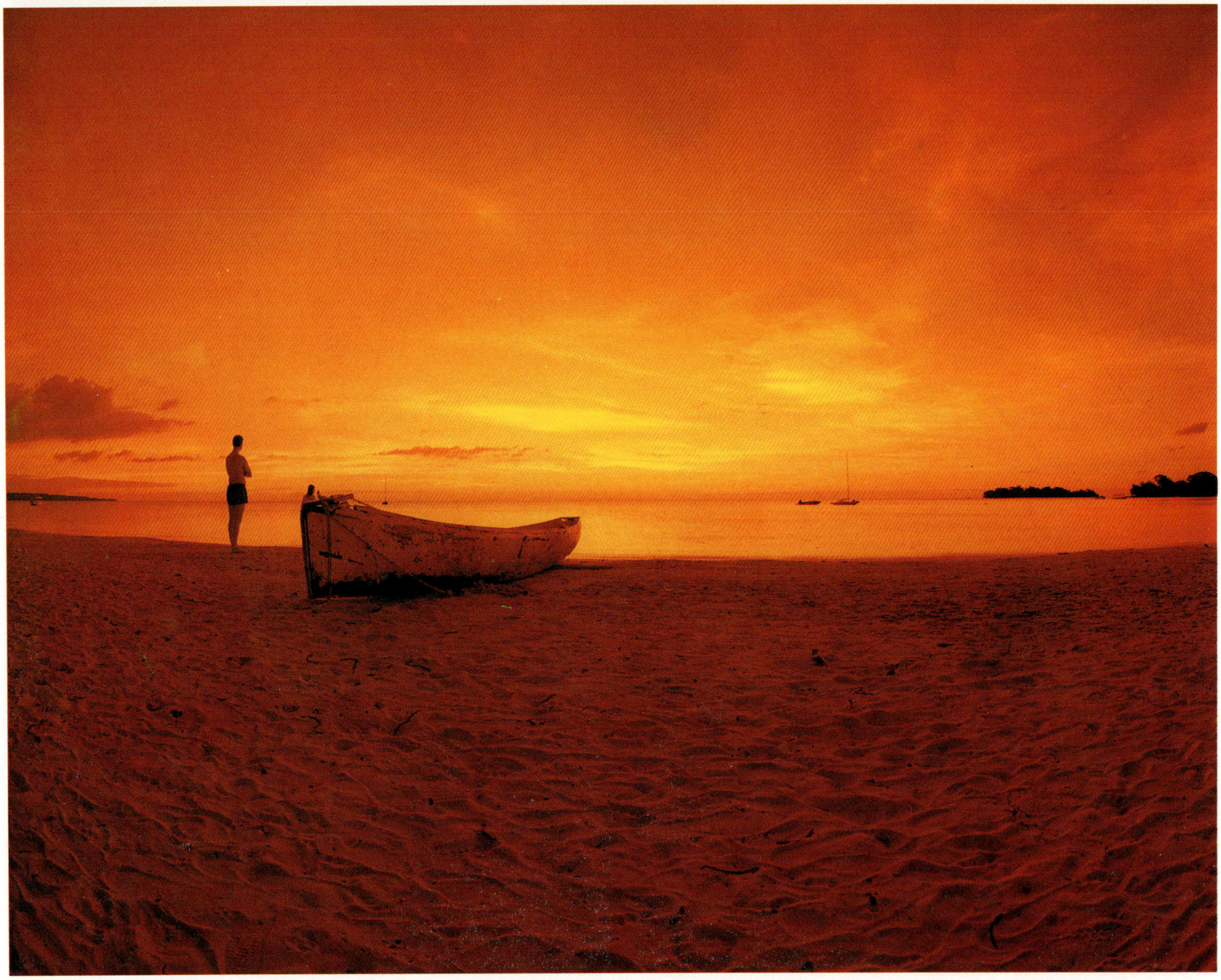

COLOUR BACK

The unique Cokin colour back filter set is a means of colouring the background whilst retaining normal colour in a foreground subject. This set is primarily intended for fashion or portrait photography, but can be adapted for other uses. The principle is to use complementary colours and synchro-sunlight flash technique. For example, if the cyan filter is placed over the lens, this will colour the whole subject in that colour. However, if the flash is now covered by a complementary orange filter, the subject will appear in normal colour, whilst the area of the background not lit by the flash will remain cyan. The Cokin filter set comprises:

mauve + yellow
orange + cyan
cyan + orange
yellow + mauve

The flash and filter sizes are different. Like Jean Coquin, I will give my explanation of this technique in a hypothetical situation. An ASA 64 film exposed in sunlight could need an exposure of 1/125 sec at f11. The subject, a full length figure, is ten feet from the camera. To light this figure correctly from the camera position would require a flash guide number of 110 with ASA 64 film, or in other words, 110 divided by ten feet = f11. Assuming that this is possible, we have a complete synchro-sunlight flash balance. This is the starting point for colour back filters. Each of these pairs of filters has a filter factor which must be allowed for. Here comes another complication and that is, that whilst the orange/cyan pair virtually match in factor, the yellow/mauve filters have about a stop discrepancy between them which must be taken into consideration.

The Cokin brochure quotes 'Be patient, and follow a set method, because even if the principle sounds easy, the application can be quite tricky. So only use these filters if you feel capable of patience and method.' I wholeheartedly agree!

Those of you who read on may care to have a few extra tips. Most modern SLR cameras (excluding the latest Nikon) will only synchronise an electronic flash at a maximum shutter speed of 1/125 sec. This directly relates to the factor of the electronic flashgun which in turn relates to flash/subject distance. There is a lot to be said, in this respect, for using either a medium format or older 35mm camera with a between lens shutter. The ubiquitous Compur will synchronise up to a 1/500 sec (indicated) speed. This has the direct benefit of allowing a lower powered flash unit to be used in bright sunlight conditions. It may be that the old Retina, Vito B or Yashicamat will be brought out of retirement for use with colour back filters, as an alternative to buying a more powerful flash unit.

As usual, TTL metering systems must be used in a manual mode, as must (generally) automatic flash units. There are exceptions but it would be pedantic to quantify this for every situation. Ultimately, the photographer must exercise his own judgement.

Colour back filters are not very intense, so they must be regarded as degrading rather than obliterating the background colours, the exception being when the tones are light or white. Once more, the phenomenon of a green sky (blue + yellow filter) and other combinations of subject and filter colour must be taken into account.

In the controlled environment of the studio, conditions are somewhat easier. A background of white or pale grey can be chosen, which makes life easier, as does the option of flash/subject distance for exposure balance. Shutter/flash synchronisation speed is no longer relevant.

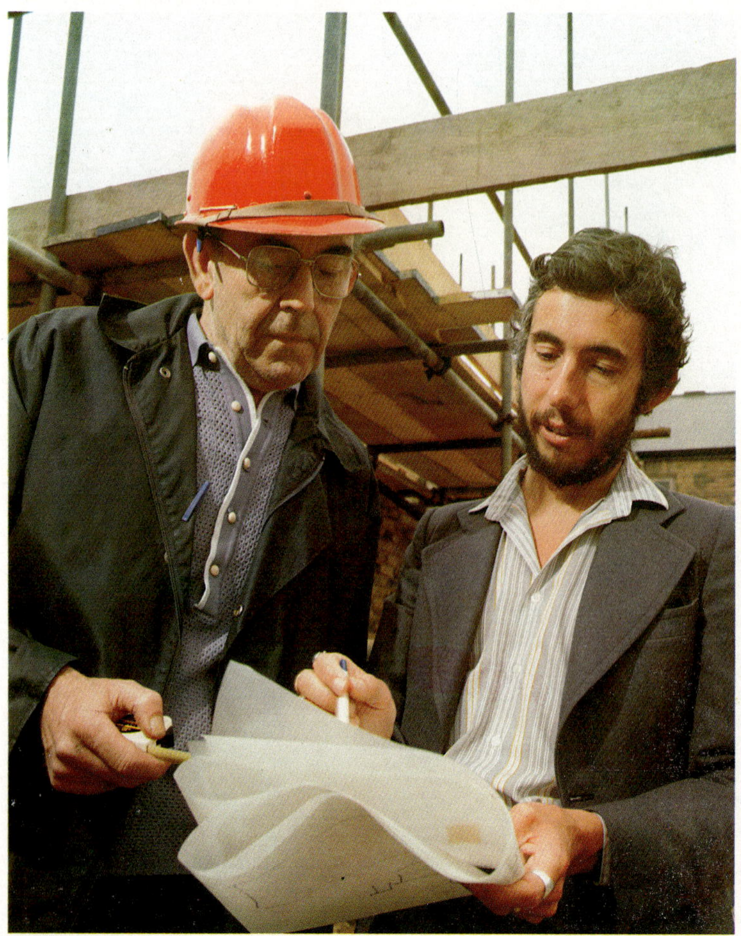

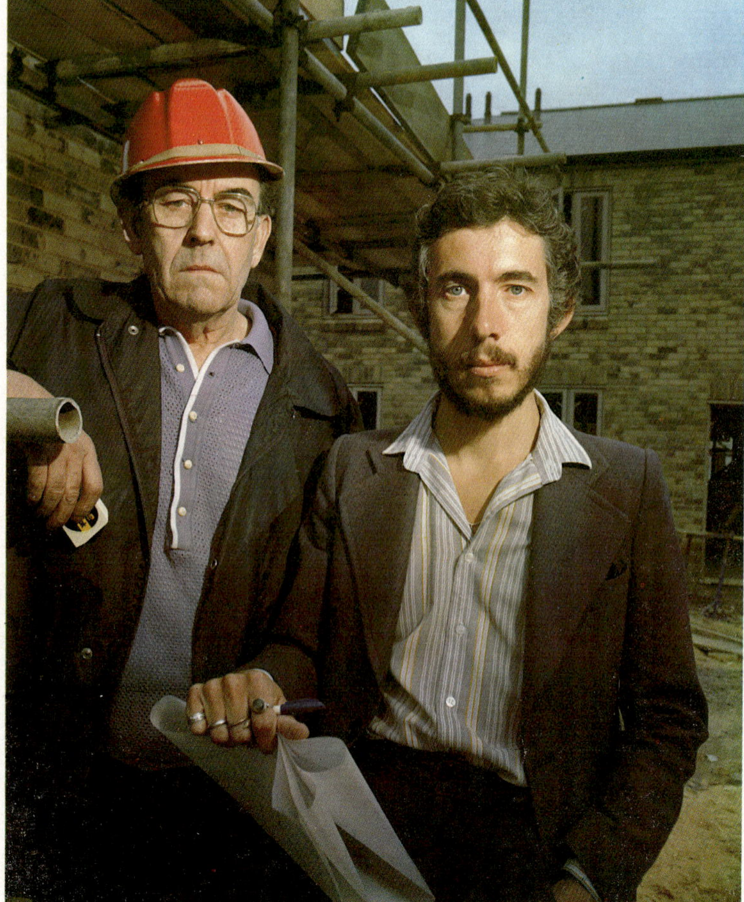

90° MIRROR AND DATE ATTACHMENTS

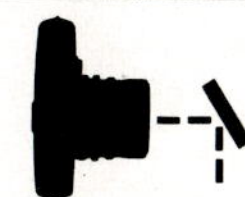

The principle of photographing a subject so that the 'victim' is unaware of the camera goes back over fifty years. Intrepid explorers of the 1920s, having discovered the new lightweight Leitz 35mm camera, also found that the Leica could be fitted with a right angle viewfinder, in order to take pictures unobserved of the shy, reticent or religiously opposed.

The modern 90° mirror attachment performs the same function, but with greater disguise. Consisting of a cylinder with a circular cut-out and a 90° surface silvered mirror set within, the attachment can be used on any 35mm or 6 x 6cm SLR camera, provided that a lens of at least double the normal focal length is used. Use of a shorter focal length will give rise to image vignetting. Some zoom lenses, due to their construction, may also give rise to cut off. As there is no general rule in this case, it must be a question of try before you buy. A single filter may be used, providing it is not in a deep mount, behind the mirror attachment. Exposure loss through the 90° attachment can be up to one stop. A TTL metering system will compensate for this; otherwise make test exposures at plus half and plus one stop over the meter reading.

All mirror devices have a revolving mount, which allows for vertical or horizontal pictures. As well as sideways use, the attachment can be used for taking pictures upwards, or, for foot fetishists, downwards! It is better to make rotational adjustments before taking photographs, in order to avoid oblique pictures.

The 'colour back' system is *described in the text and has many applications. One is shown* ***facing page*** *in which the pale sky has been rendered a deeper blue. The key to the system is patience. Take your time, think about what you are trying to do, and be prepared to experiment.*

Left and below left is shown *the 90° mirror attachment. Longer than normal lenses should be used to avoid vignetting, and the film will show a reversed image of the subject. This item is ideal for use in situations where 'furtive' photography is the only way to get the picture – as in some countries where the inhabitants object to being photographed. The date attachment,* ***below,*** *as its name implies, allows the date to appear in the bottom corner of the picture. If a lot of photography is undertaken it is useful to be able to 'date' the first frame of each day's shoot to ease future identification.*

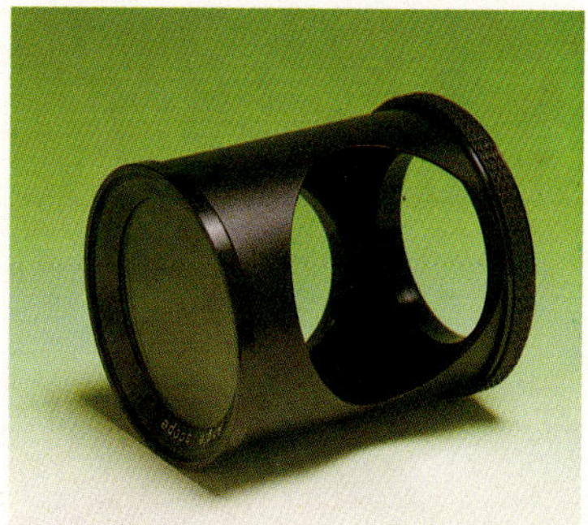

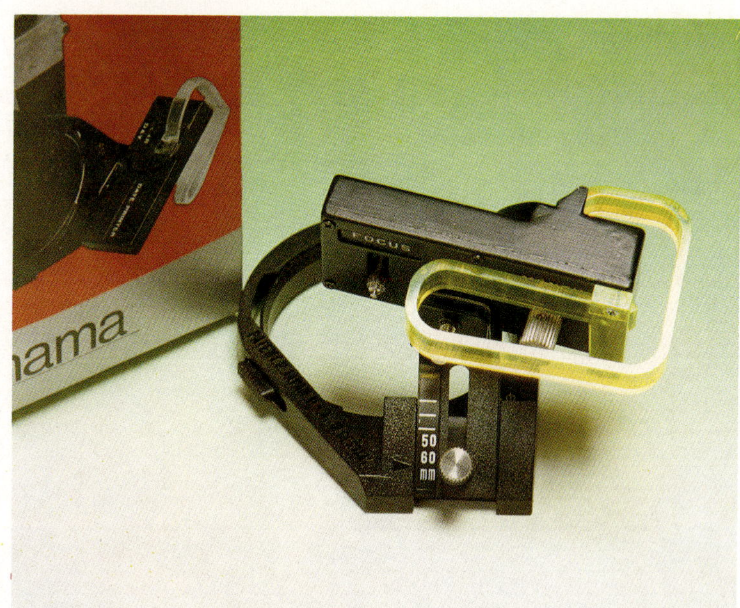

Another unique device from HAMA/Enterprise, enables those with a sense of history, or a scientific bent, to record the date on film, with a relative degree of simplicity. This budget-priced device, at least compared to data backs, can be fitted to 35mm, medium and large format cameras, provided that the lens mount size is between 49 and 58mm.

After fitting the date printer to the lens mount, there is an adjustment for date position, focus of the superimposed image and, of course, day, month and year (up to 1990). An additional control is scaled for focal lengths of between 30 and 60mm for 35mm format, though it is suitable for equivalent focal lengths on other formats.

The date image appears in frame as a blocked out section, in a choice of either top left or bottom right corner, on a rectangular format, or near either edge of any side of a square format. Allow for approximately a 24 x 30mm crop on a 35mm frame if the date is to be excluded for some reason.

The green plastic light collector produces a VDU-like data image on film. When working indoors, it may be necessary to use a separate light source to 'power' the date recorder.

COLOUR, SOFT AND MIST SPOTS

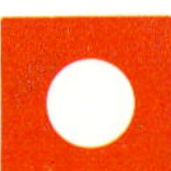 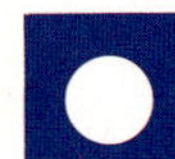 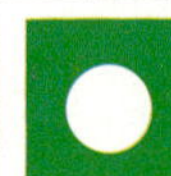 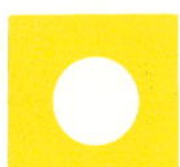

Centre spots can be considered as a filter with a hole or clear area in the centre. This aperture is about a third of the filter width or circumference. Centre spots come in two distinct types: those where the area surrounding the spot is clear neutral density or colour; and those where the surround is a diffuse neutral density or colour. A further variation is for the surrounding area to consist of a fog filter, or sometimes to have a texture similar to a ground glass focusing screen.

Most makers of plastic rectangular centre spot filters have a range which consists of both neutral density and colours. The Filtek catalogue lists 'clear' centre spots of three neutral density and ten colours, whilst Cokin make two mists, two clear neutral density and five clear colours. Hoya produce their mist spots in plastic squares and also a round soft spot, in glass, in a conventional mount.

The function of all these filters is to concentrate attention on the middle of the field, although in the case of rectangular filters the centre of interest can be adjusted within frame. The

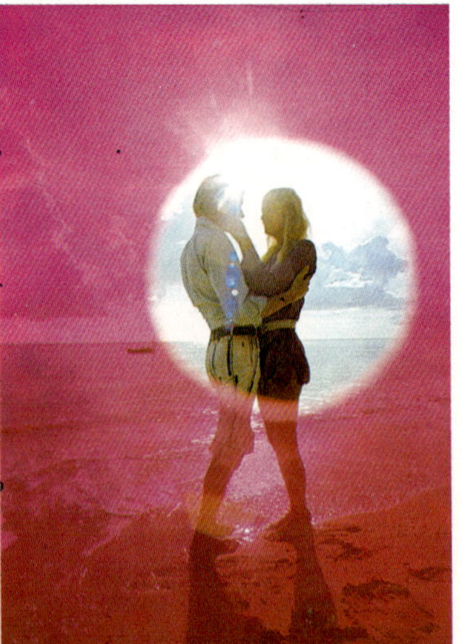

Any coloured filter has the *effect of darkening the photographic image, and we normally compensate for this by allowing extra exposure. It is very important, however, to remember that, in the case of colour filters with clear central areas, taking light readings with the filter in position will mean overexposure of the clear centre – except in those instances where a narrow-angle, spot-metering facility is provided in the camera. In the case of 'mist spots,' where a clear central area is surrounded by a soft area, then exposure readings are not affected.*

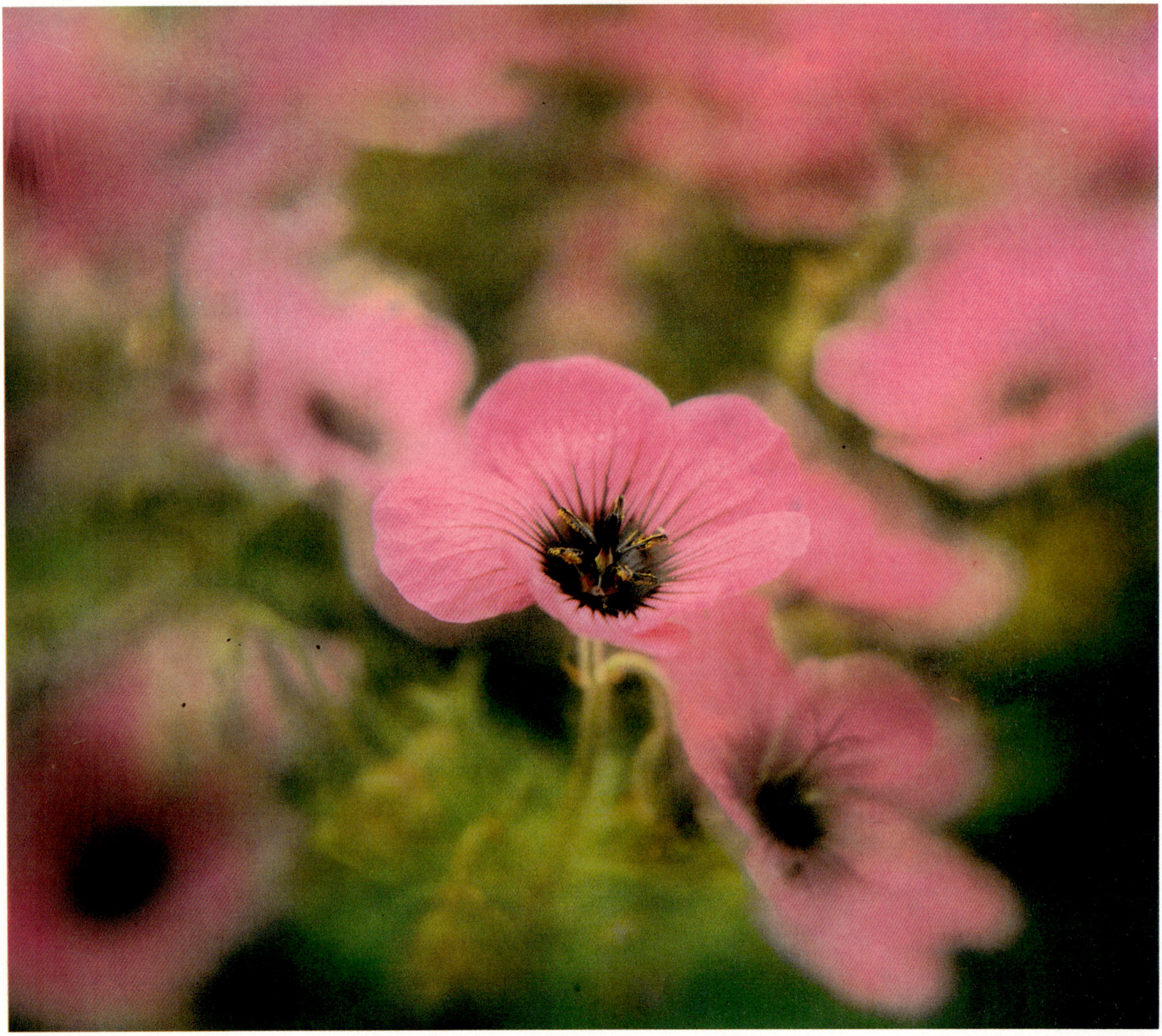

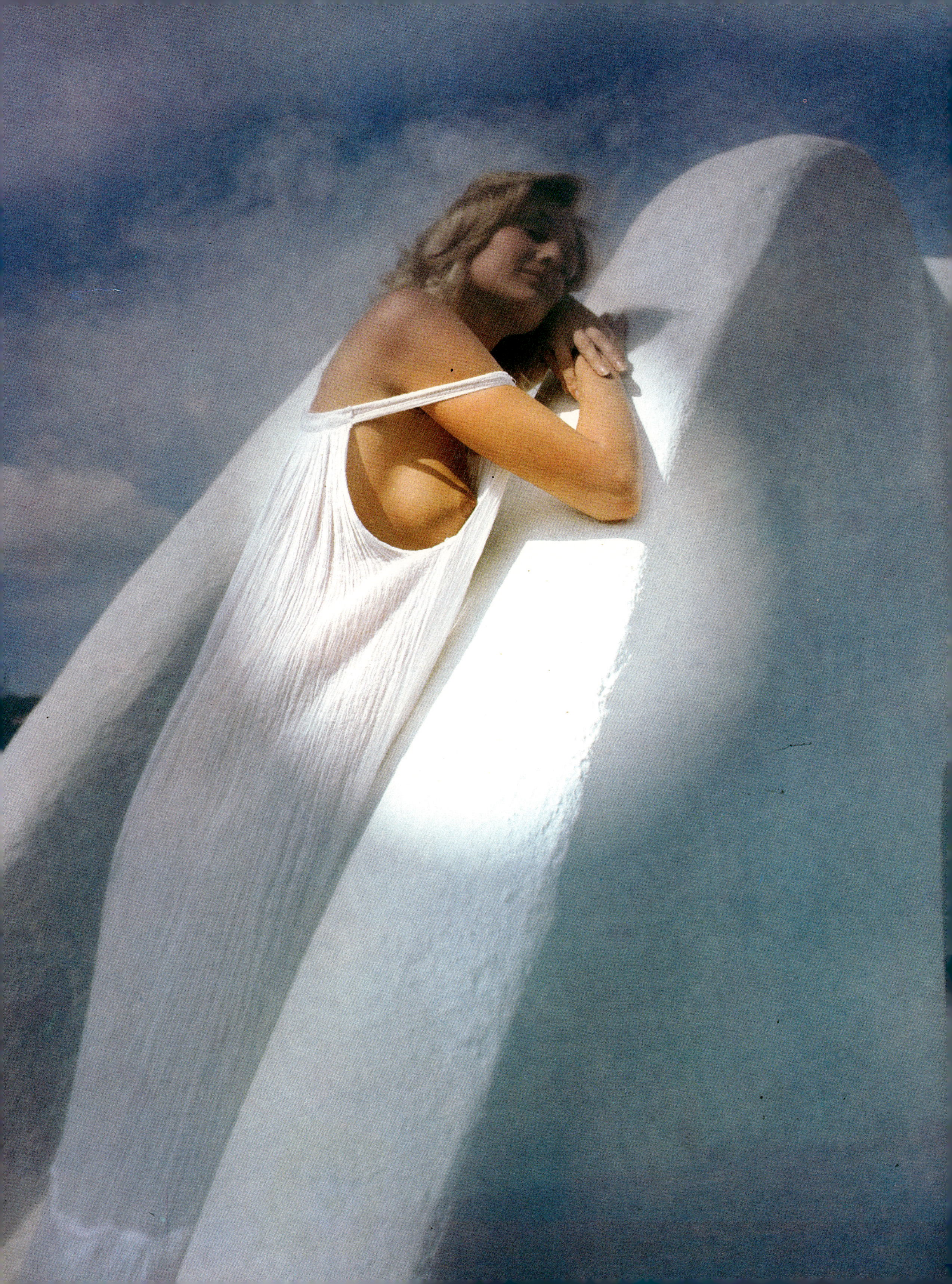

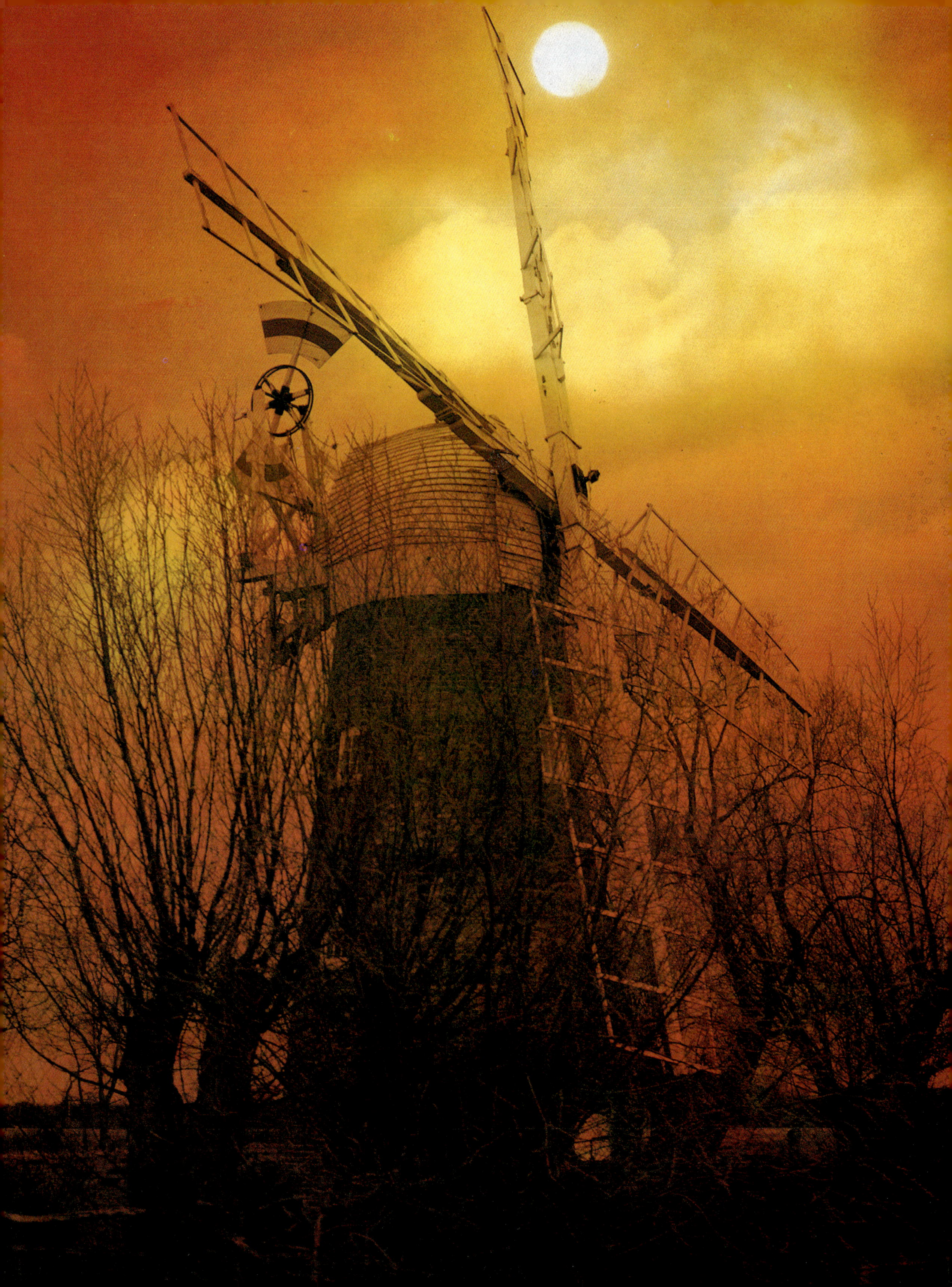

COLOUR, SOFT AND MIST SPOTS

Attachments which provide *clear central areas surrounded by some form of image degradation or diffusion – which may take the same form as a soft focus filter, a diffuser, a fog filter or even a close-up lens – can also be combined with other attachments. Thus, two clear centre spots can be mounted together to increase the out-of-focus effect of the*

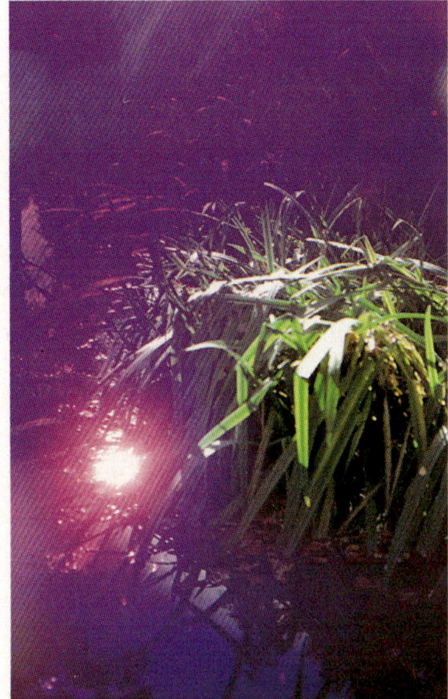

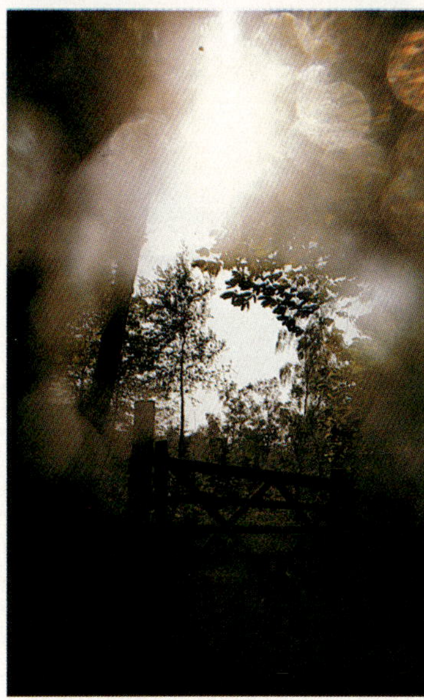

outer area, or a mist spot can be combined with a magenta colour spot filter, and so on. With square filter systems it is not necessary to have the clear area in the centre; it can be positioned wherever you wish to achieve the result you want. All attachments are merely starting points for your own creativity.

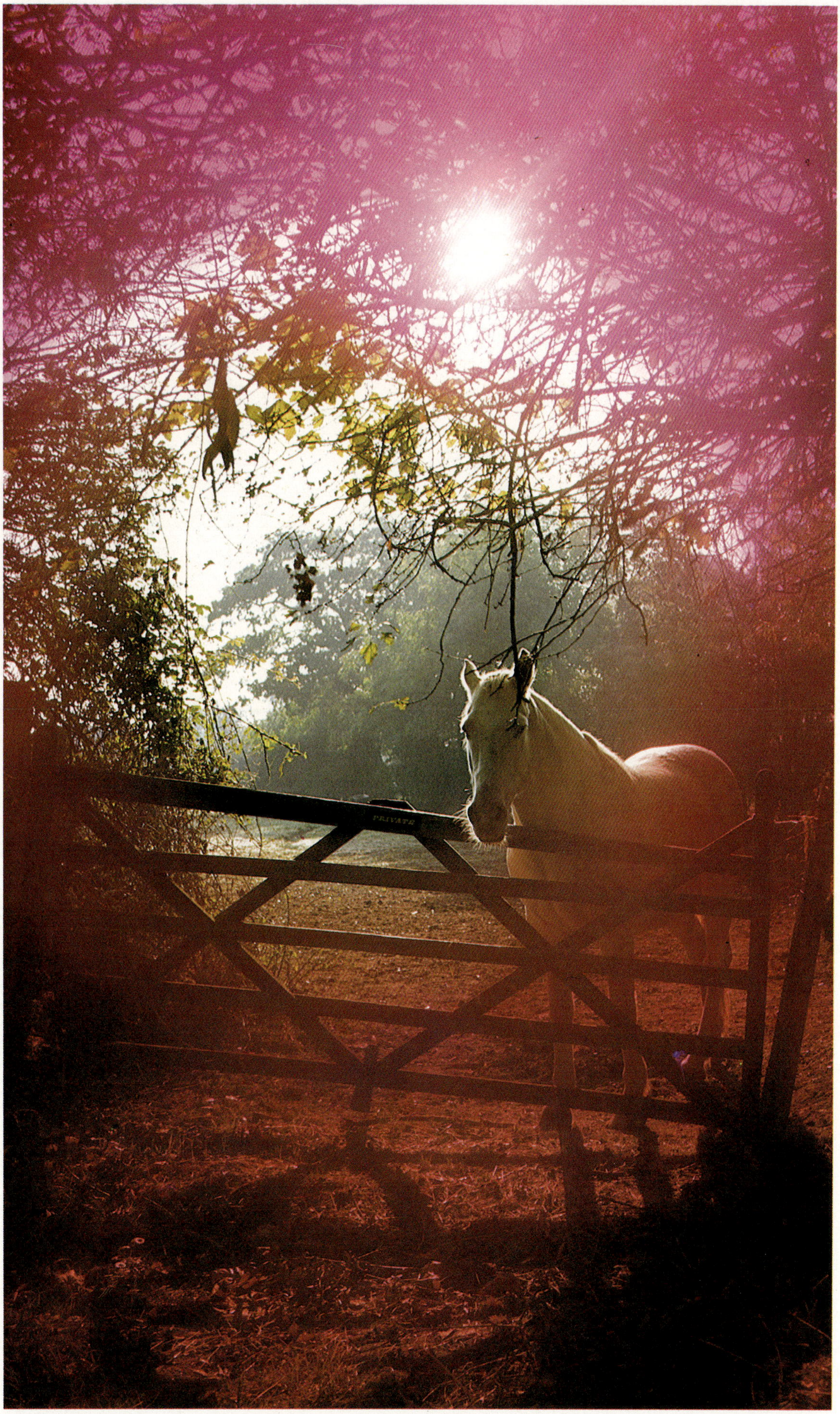

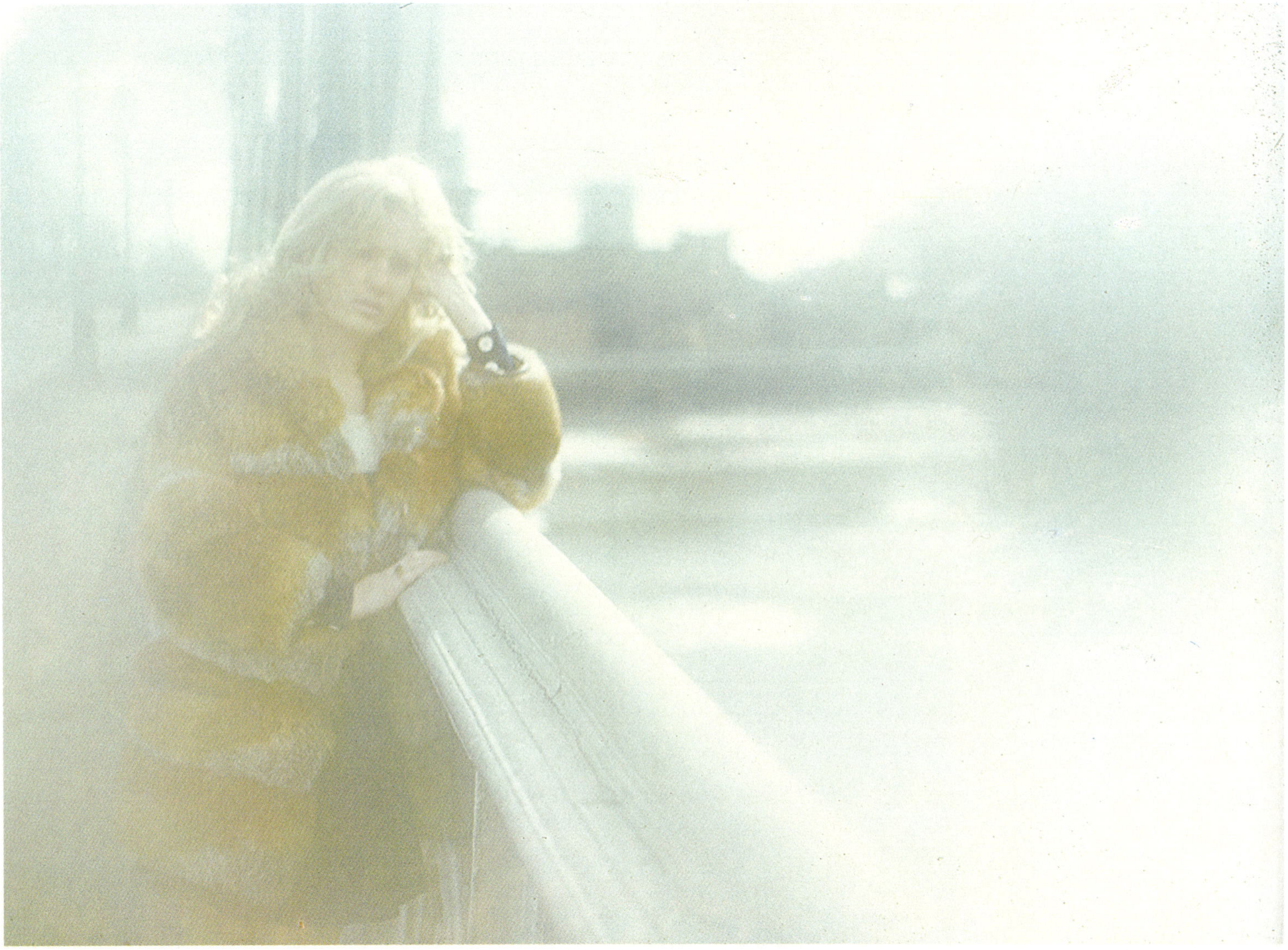

COLOUR, SOFT AND MIST SPOTS

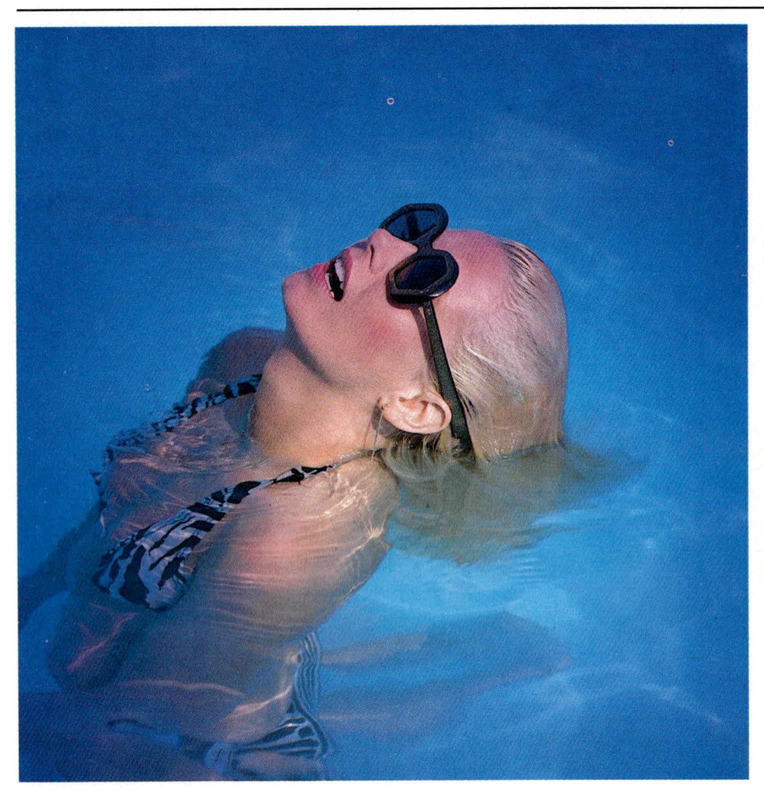

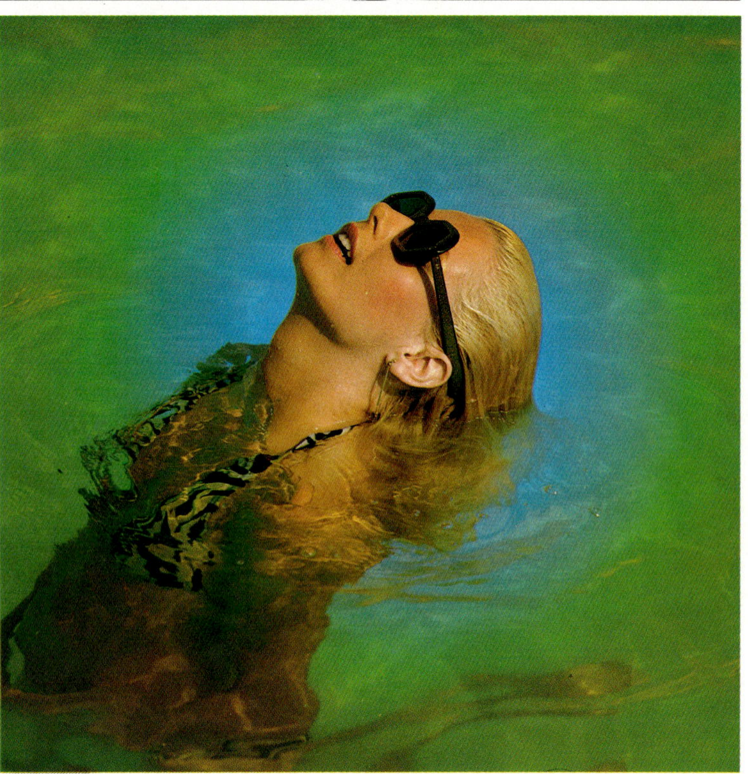

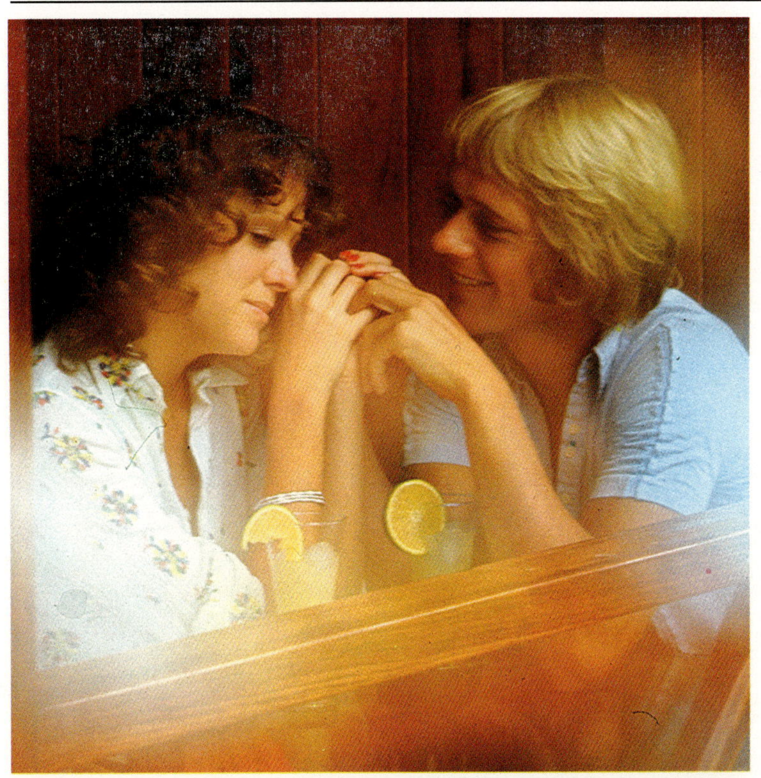

neutral density centre spots darken round the subject, the fog and 'ground glass' types add white flare, whilst the colours simply tint the surrounding area.

Centre spots may be used in combination. Those with an actual hole in the middle provide superior definition for obvious reasons.

These filters are suitable for any focal length of lens. A wide angle will produce a smaller sharper 'hole,' whilst a telephoto, or long focus, lens will do the opposite. Normal and longer focal length lenses can produce more blending between subject and surround, particularly if wider lens apertures are employed.

Once more, I am afraid, TTL metering systems will produce over-exposure of the centre area of the picture unless the filter factor of the surround is allowed for to some degree. The exception to this is those rare cameras which have a TTL spot metering facility. Any camera fitted with a depth of field preview control enables the user accurately to gauge the centre spot effect.

Facing page: A blue centre spot *has the effect of darkening the blue of the water, whilst a yellow combines with the blue to produce a greenish surround. A mist spot was combined with a soft focus filter for the shot below. A clear centre spot surrounded by a close up lens was used to make the pictures on* ***this page,*** *which accounts for the double images and strong softening.*

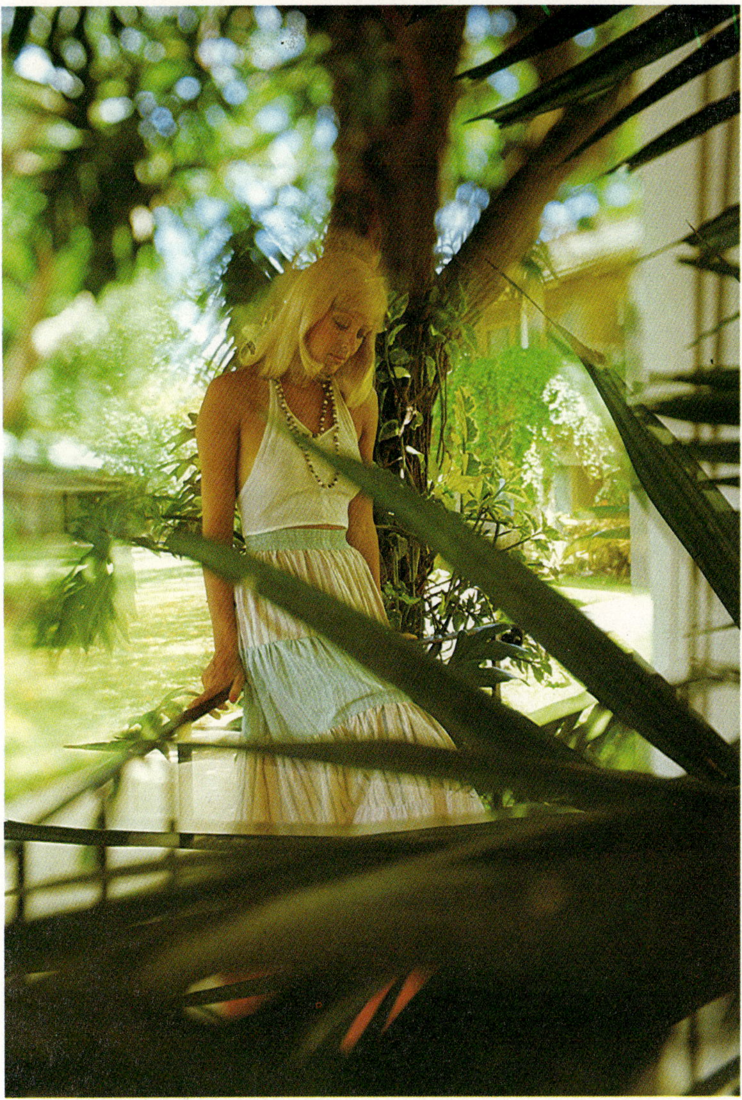

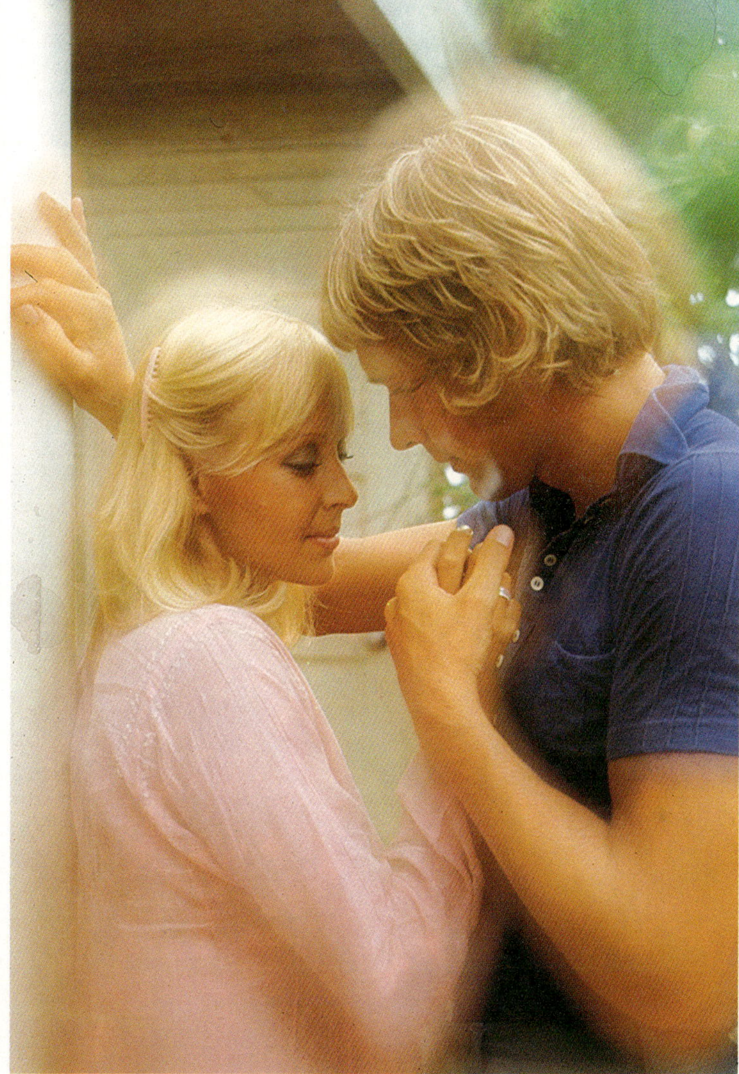

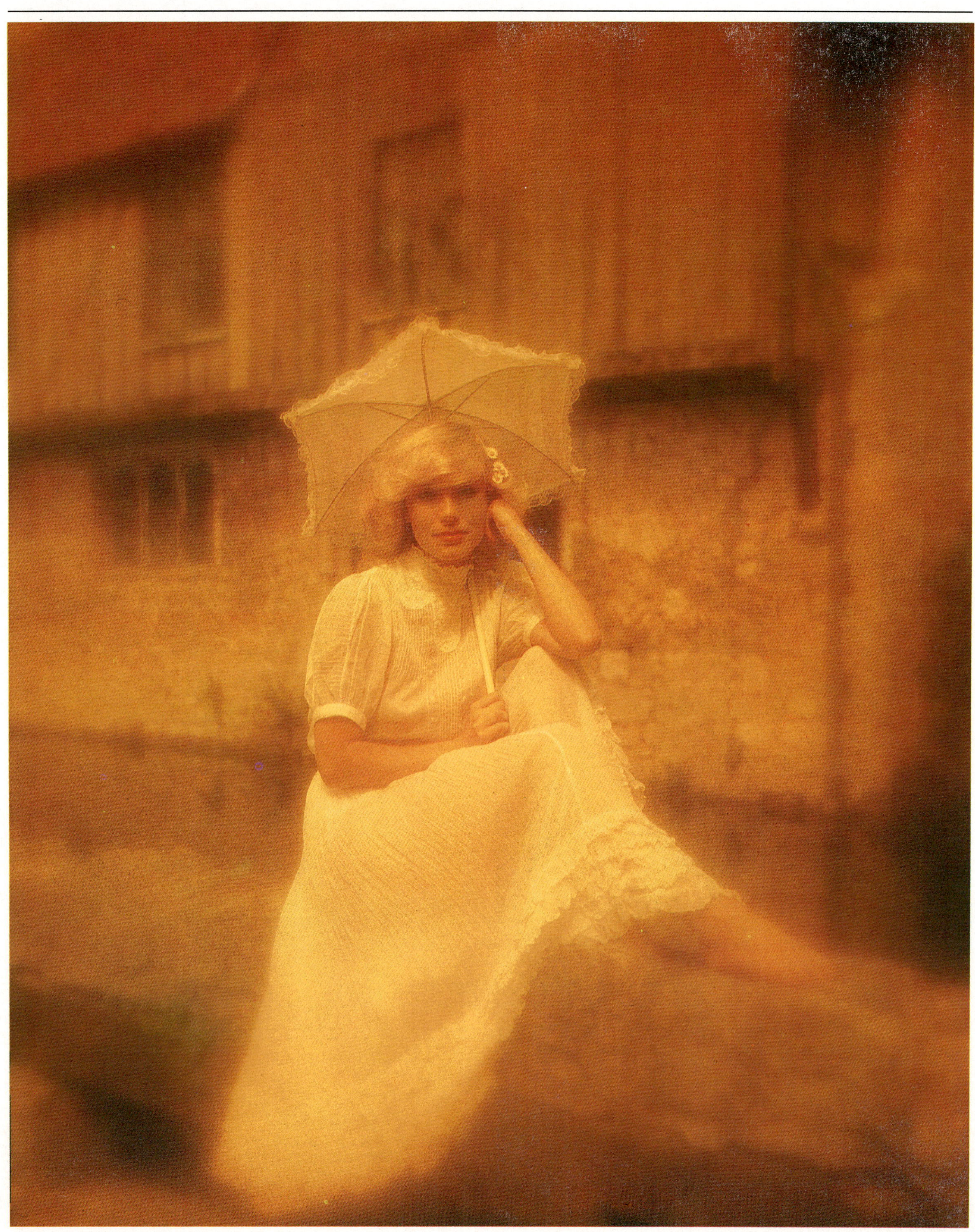

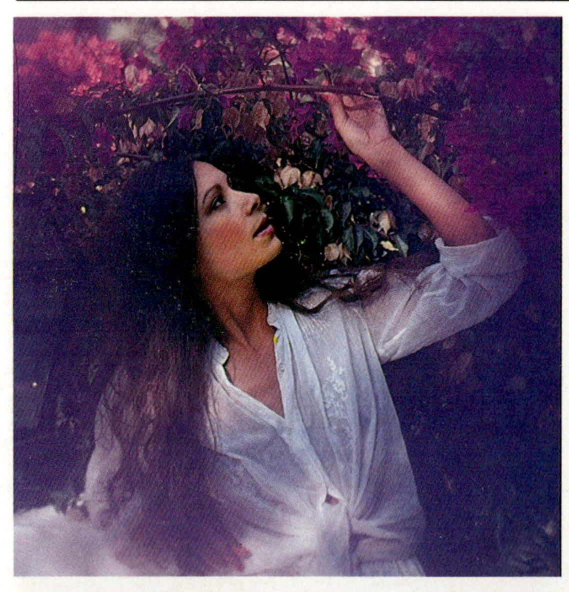

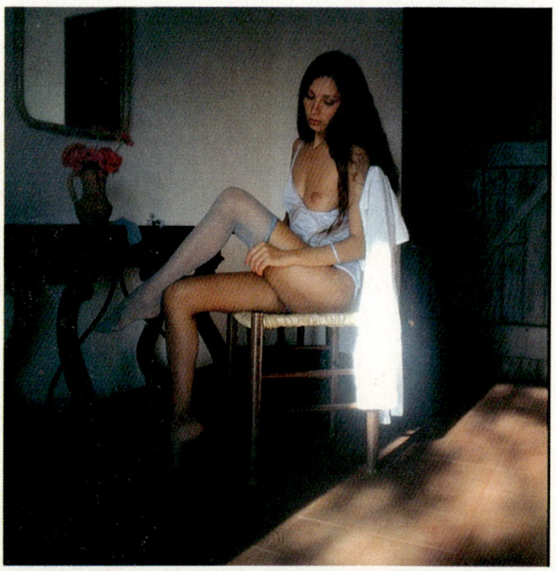

Denise, facing page, is featured *several times in pictures taken specially for this book. For this one the photographer used a sepia filter combined with a soft focus attachment with clear centre spot. The colouring, pose, clothes and props all match the mood and location admirably. For the picture* ***top left*** *a mauve centre spot was used, and for the shot* ***left*** *the model was positioned so that the strong sunlight coming through the doorway spilled onto the white blouse at the edge of the clear area of the soft focus centre spot. An orange centre spot, soft focus and underexposure made the subject* ***below.***

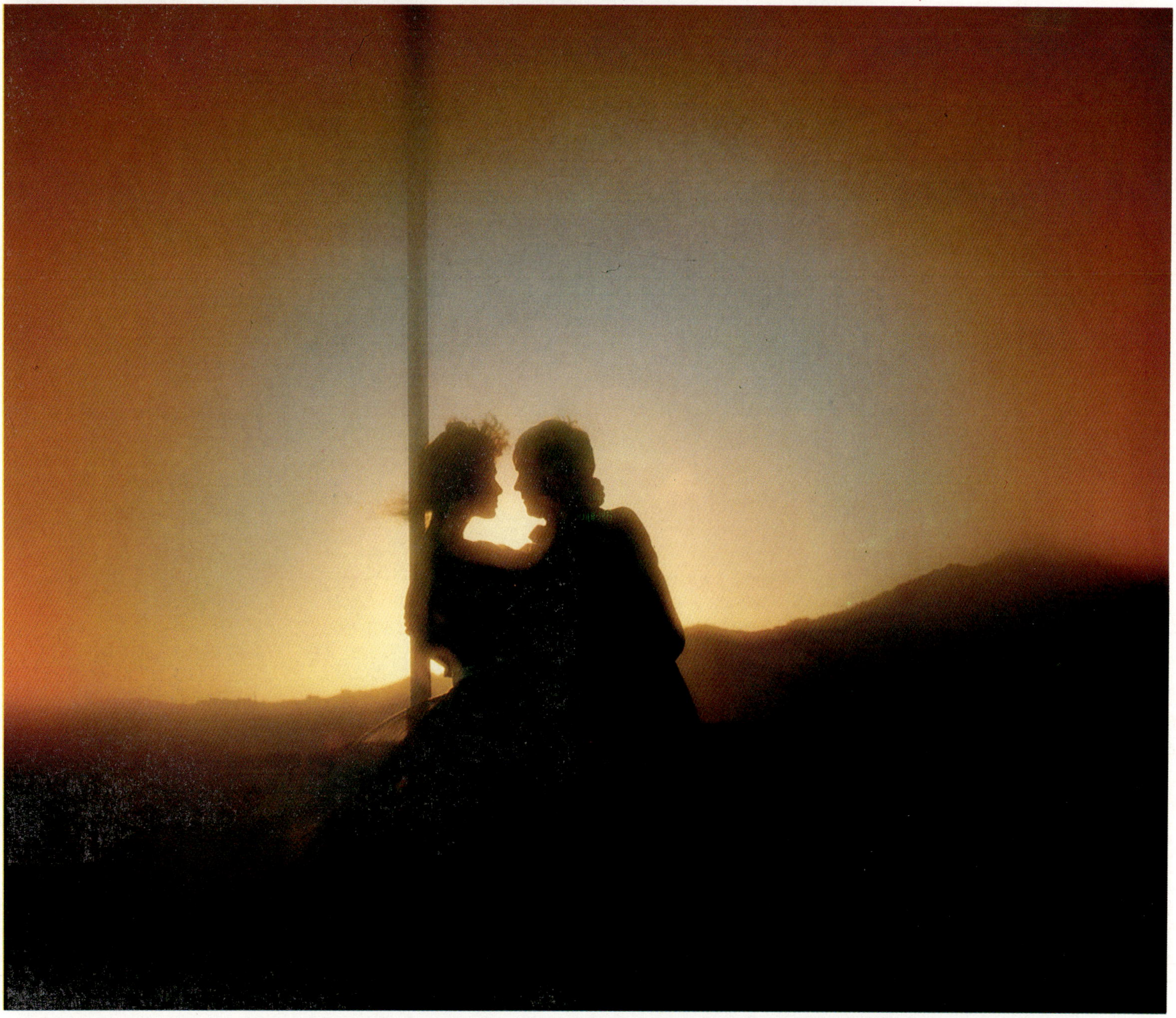

VARIPOL, VARICOLOR, MAGICPOL

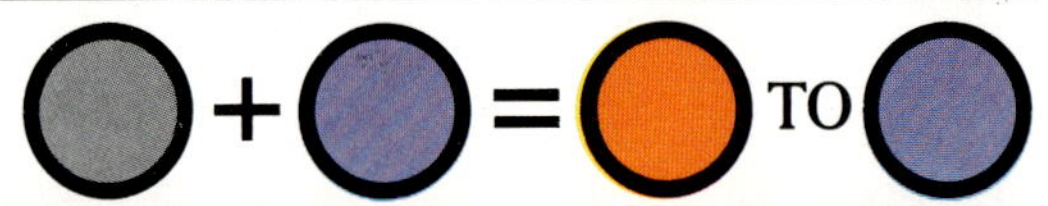

Like so many other categories of filters, there emerges from time to time a generic term to describe a particular type. It may be that one particular manufacturer was first in the field or spent more money on advertising, or whatever: one name will stick with Joe Public, and from then on . . .

The varipol filter consists of one normal polarising filter and one coloured polarising filter. These may be sold in sets comprising a 'master' plus a choice of three colours, or as individual filters. Varipols consist of two types. The single colour variety in red, orange, yellow, green, blue and purple could well be described as dial-a-shade. As with variable density filters (same technical background), it is possible to select a shade of colour amounting to a filter factor range of between approximately 3x and 8x.

Double colour varipols achieve the apparent 'magic' of changing colour as the mount is rotated. This may be achieved by the use of two coloured polarisers. A typical example is the Goyo/Tora range of red to blue, red to green, red to yellow and yellow to blue. B + W make a purple, which miraculously changes the image colour from blue to purple to magenta to orange in that order. If I have any criticism of the varipol filter, it is that, unlike a variable neutral density, there are no graduations which, at least, give an indexed guide to exposure. I have yet to meet a TTL exposure system which can cope with these, and if it is of the type which needs a 'circular' pola filter then manic bracketing or experience is the only way.

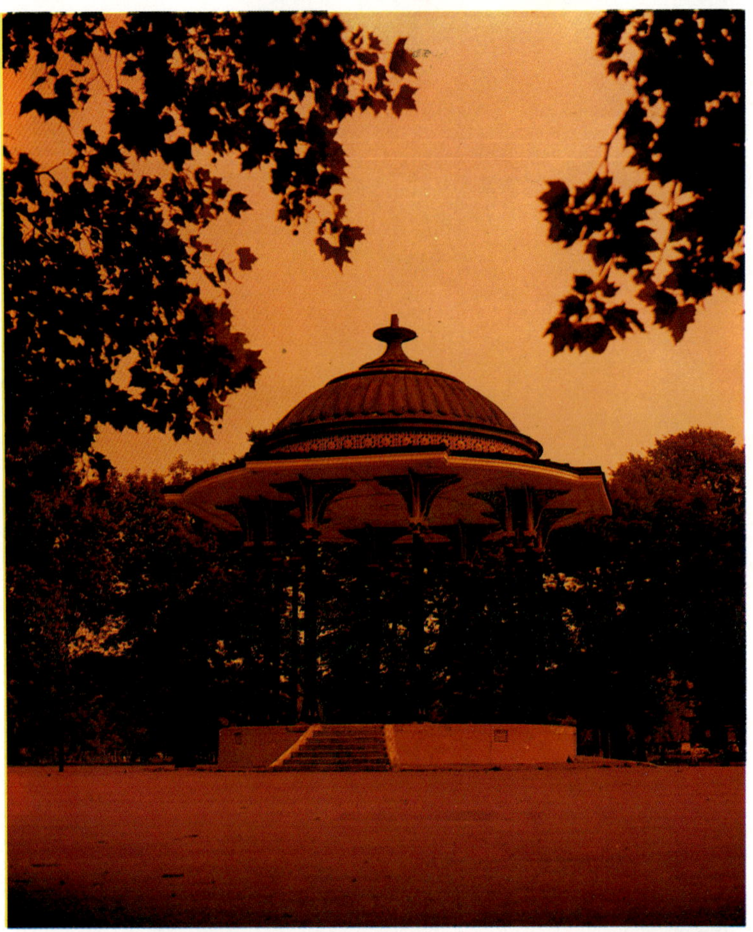

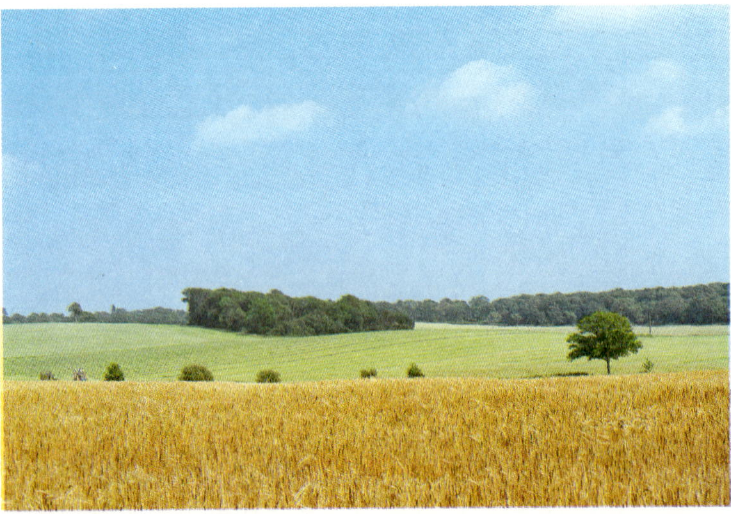

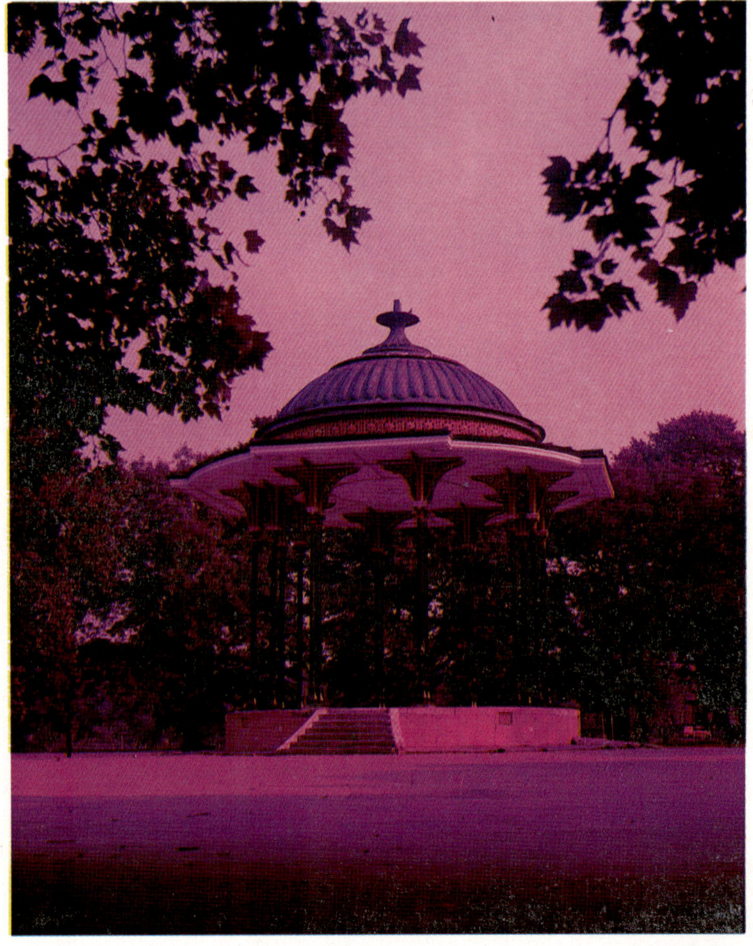

New additions to the ranges of *filters and attachments are constantly being made available. One of these is a combination of grey and coloured polarising filters and yet another makes use of two coloured polarising filters plus grey. By these means colours can be changed by rotating the mount. All the pictures on these pages were made with just the one filter. An unfiltered shot* ***above*** *is included for reference.*

Varipols do not always act as a normal polarising filter when used in their combined form, but separated, a neutral 'master' will. A coloured back half can be used as a monochromatic polarising filter, providing that the mount allows separation without damage. It is sometimes possible to achieve two colours simultaneously by using a bi-colour varipol. This is of necessity a matter of the subject's planes of polarisation being exactly right. There is no guarantee that all makers' products will work this way, for there are too many variables. All I can stress is that when conditions are right the result is unusual, to say the least. All varipol filters can be tried in front of the eye in order to gauge the effect.

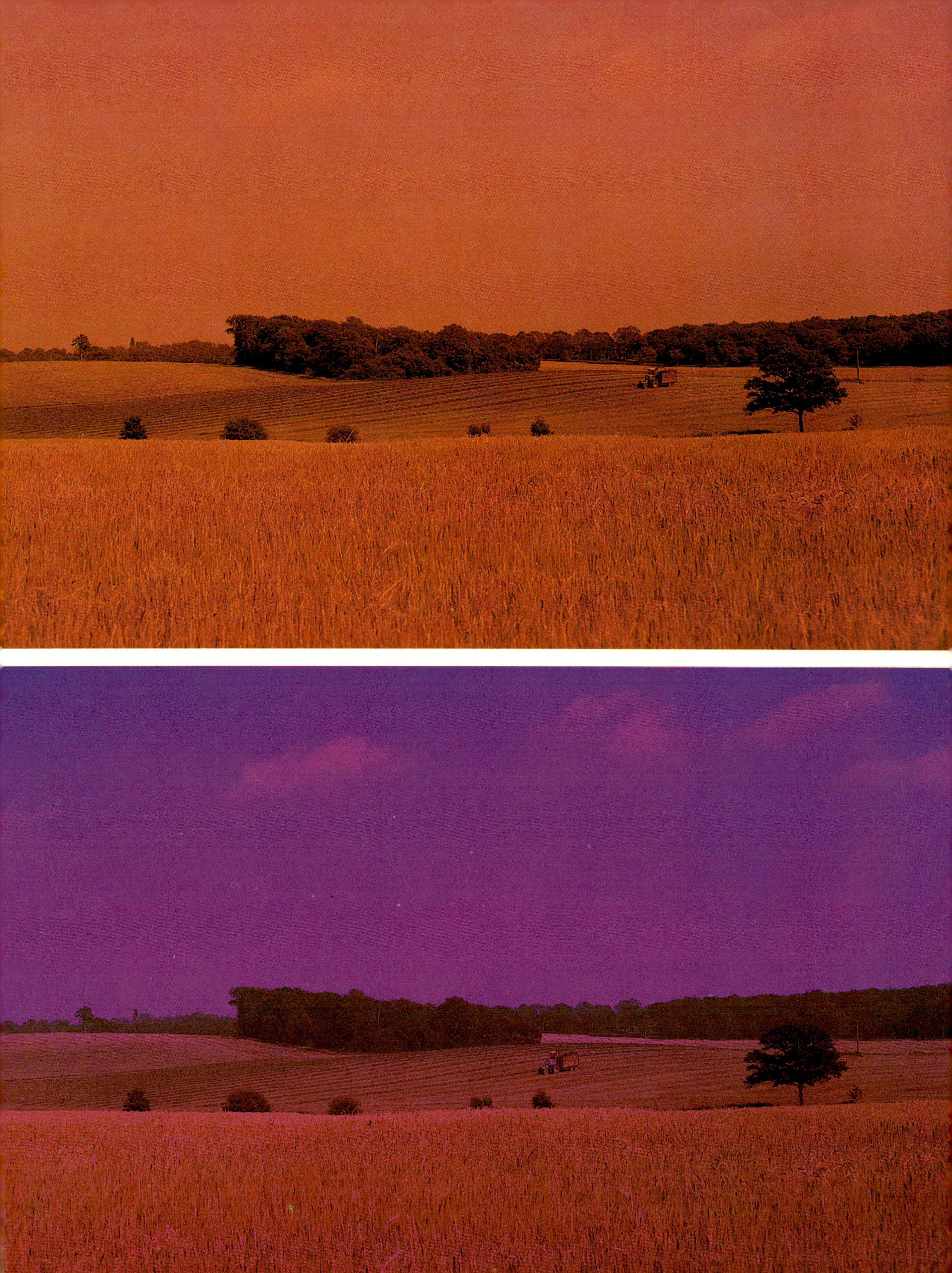

CROSSTARS

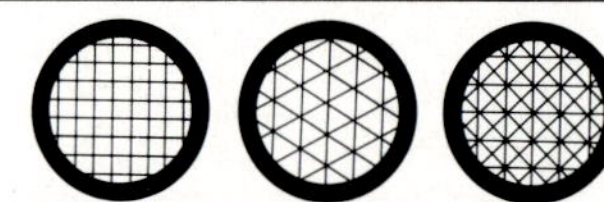

Crosstar has become the generic term for those devices which render a light source as a point with anything between two and sixteen 'beams' emanating from it. These can be produced by scribing, etching or moulding indentations into plain glass. Whilst it is possible for the impecunious to attack the old UV filter with a glass cutter, most manufacturers make a better job of it. However, the do-it-yourself approach is quite valid for special applications.

Commercial crosstars invariably produce regularly spaced beams, though Actina do produce an irregular 6 point star and Goyo a vario-cross, in which the angles of a four point star can be varied at will. It is possible to use most crosstars in combination.

Crosstar masks, in effect, alter the shape of the lens' iris diaphragm. We are all familiar with the TV cliché/sloppiness of thirteen hexagonal blobs racing across the frame when a light source is in shot. Using a zoom lens plus a crosstar mask can produce this effect, but with a star instead of a hexagon.

The last category of crosstar is the radial type which breaks up the beams into a series of crosses – or, if out of focus, a series of blobs. The effect can also produce a photograph which appears to have been printed through a coarse newspaper screen. Lots of light sources in shot are necessary in this instance.

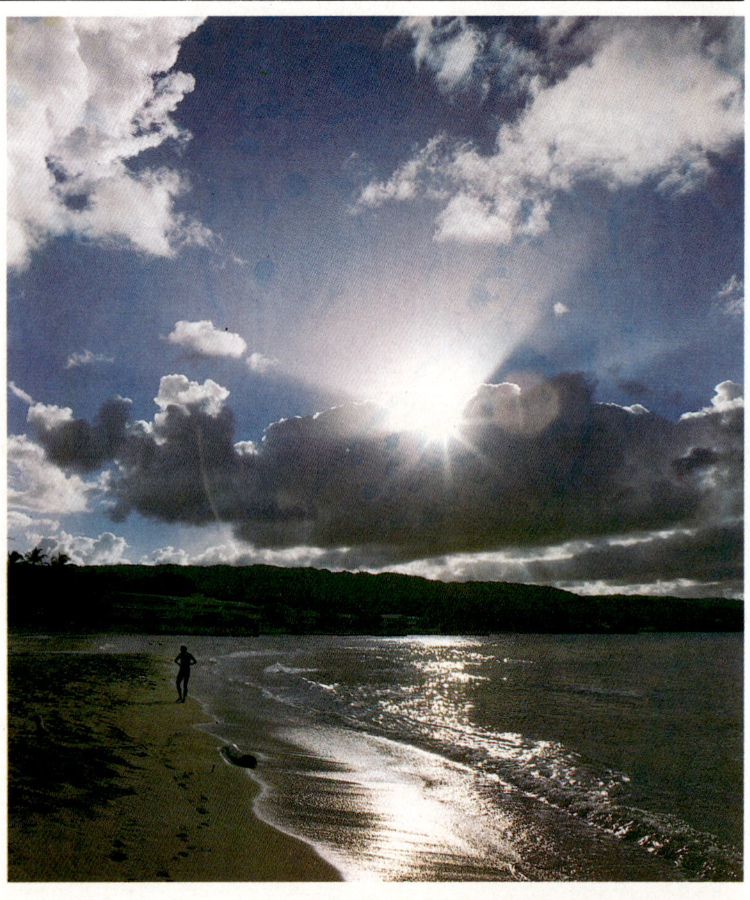

Crosstars are essentially plain, *preferably optical glass, filters with lines etched into the surface. The simplest have lines at right angles to each other – which provide a four-pointed 'star' when a light source or reflection is included in the picture area. Further lines etched between these angles produce even more points to the star effect, usually up to a maximum of 32, though two filters can be combined to give an even greater number.*

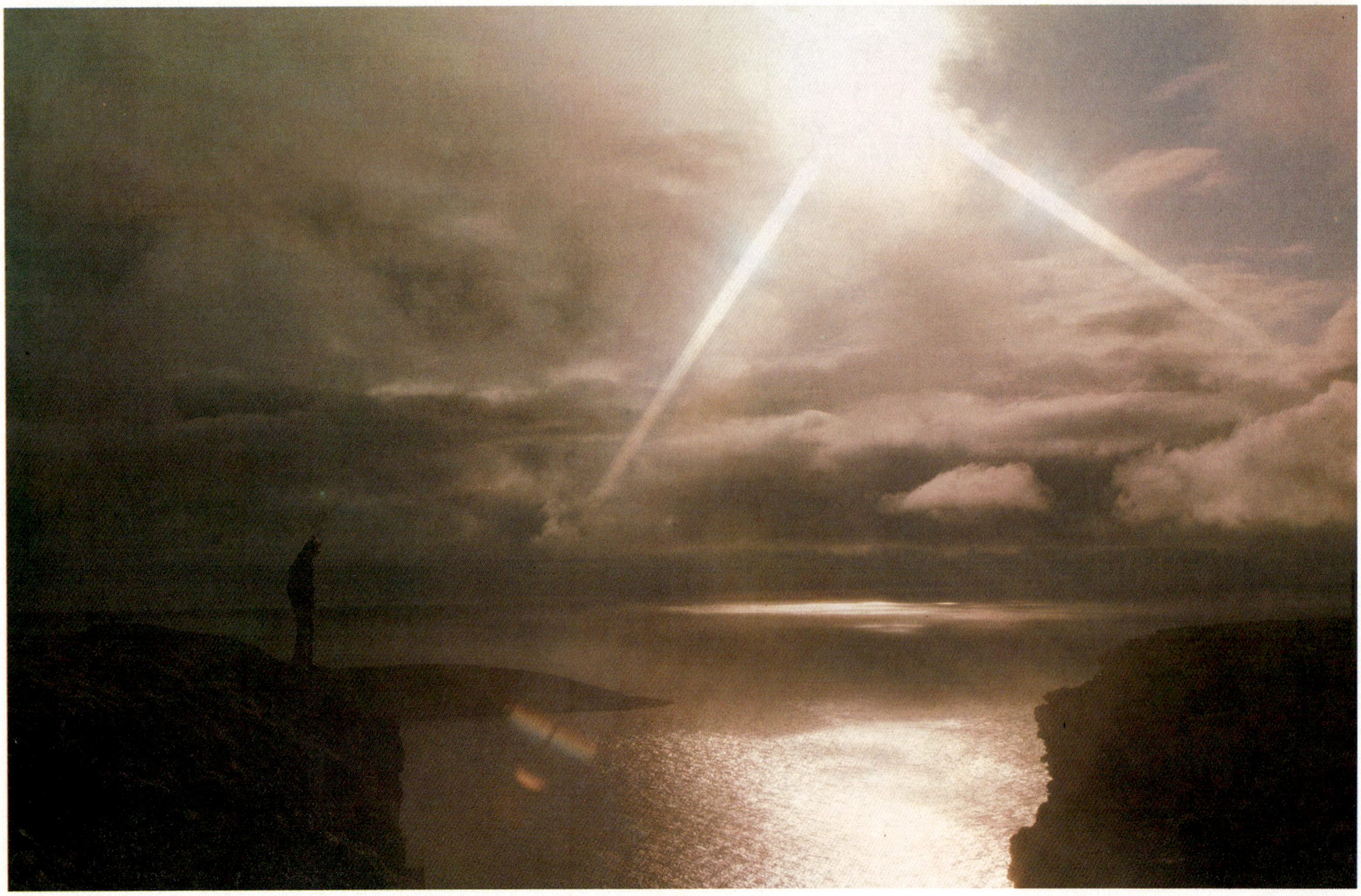

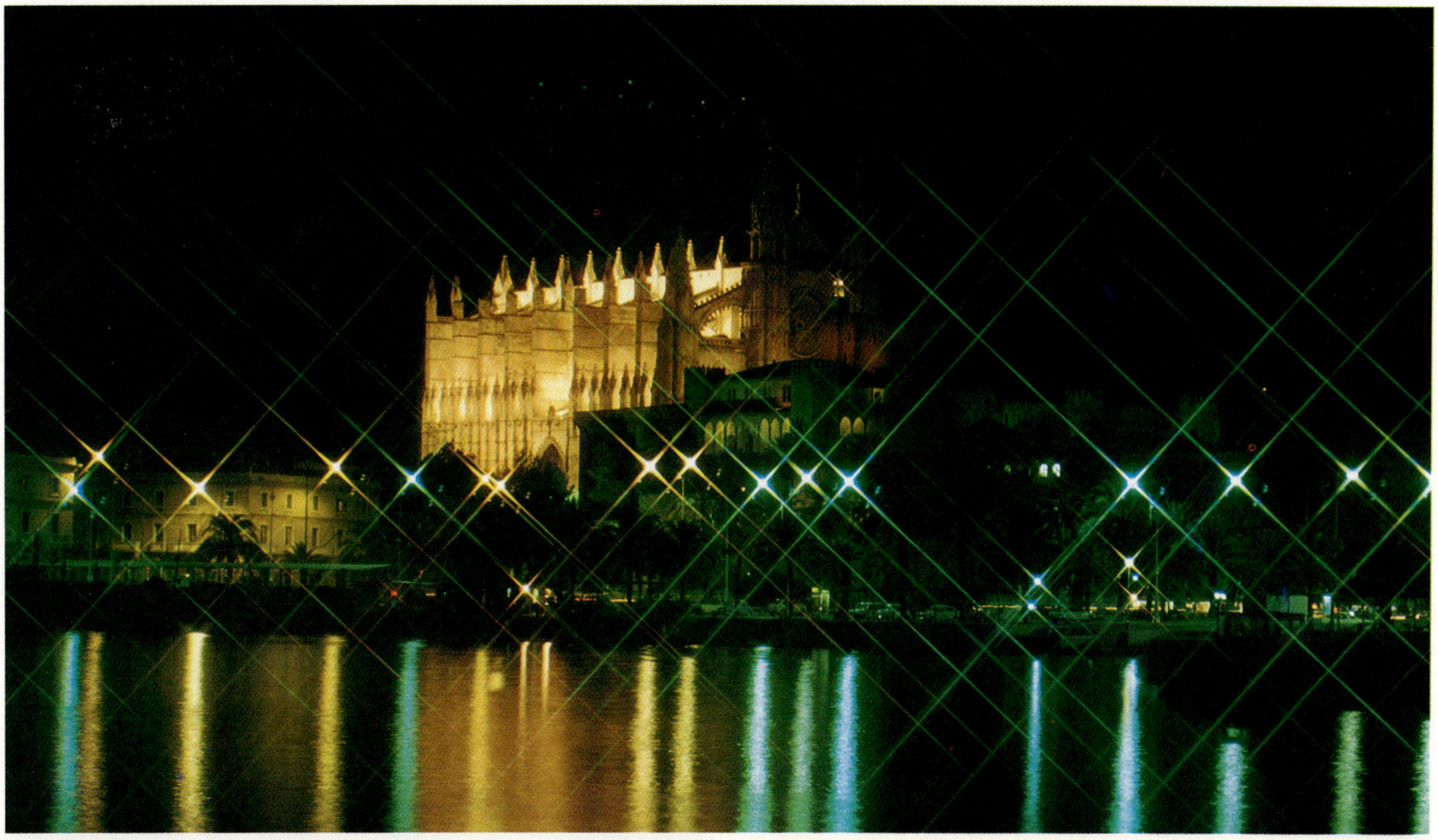

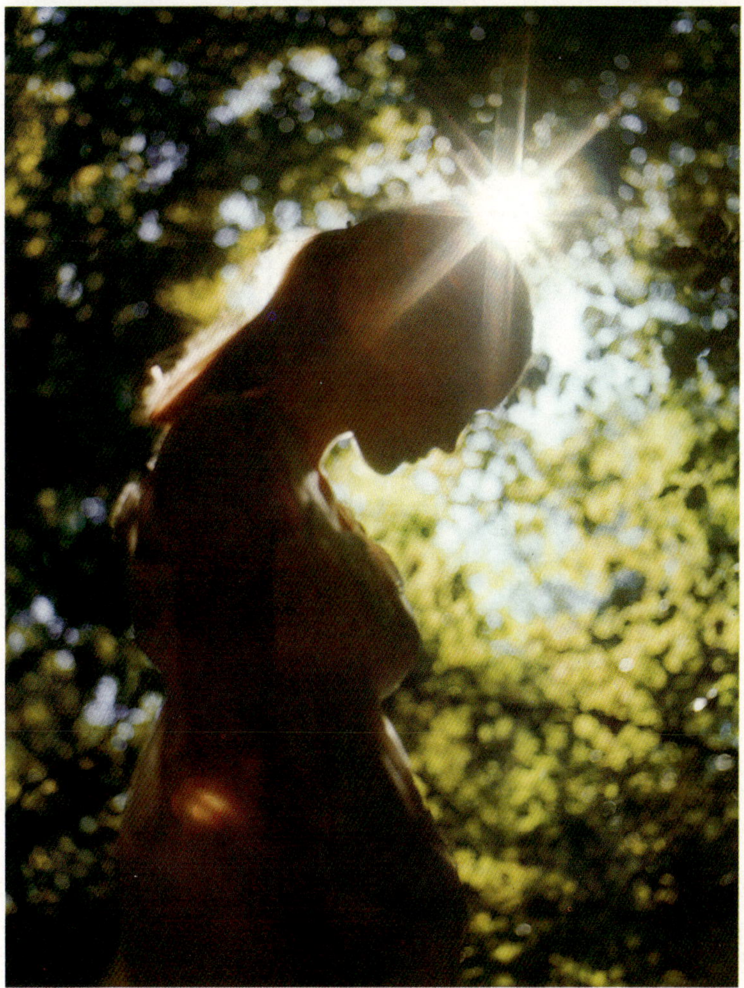

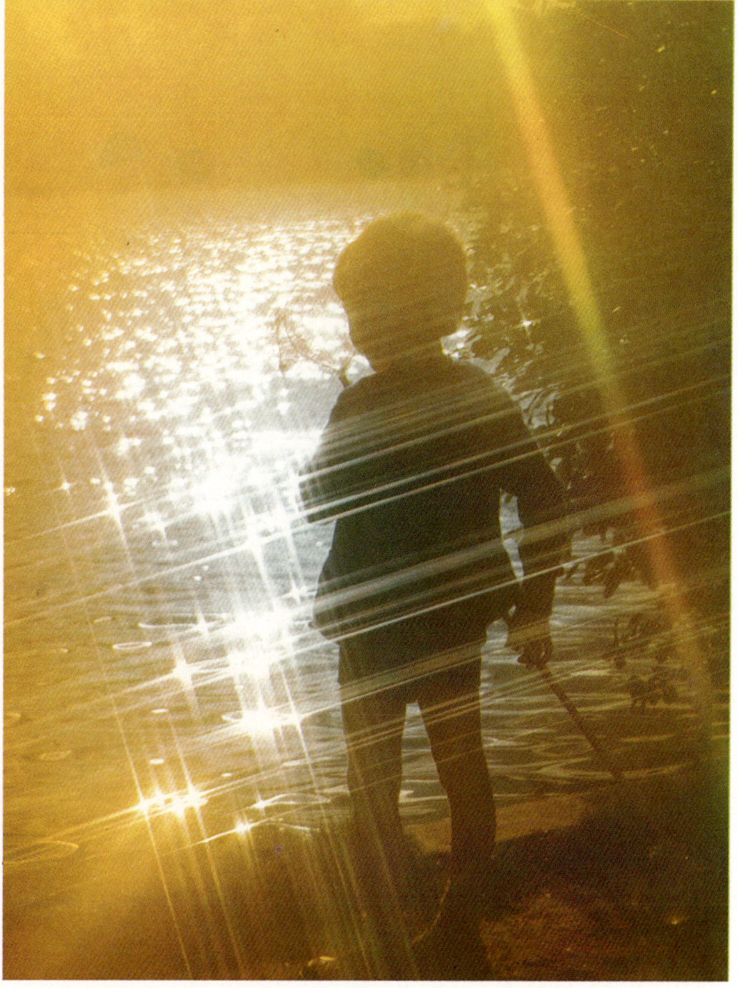

CROSSTARS

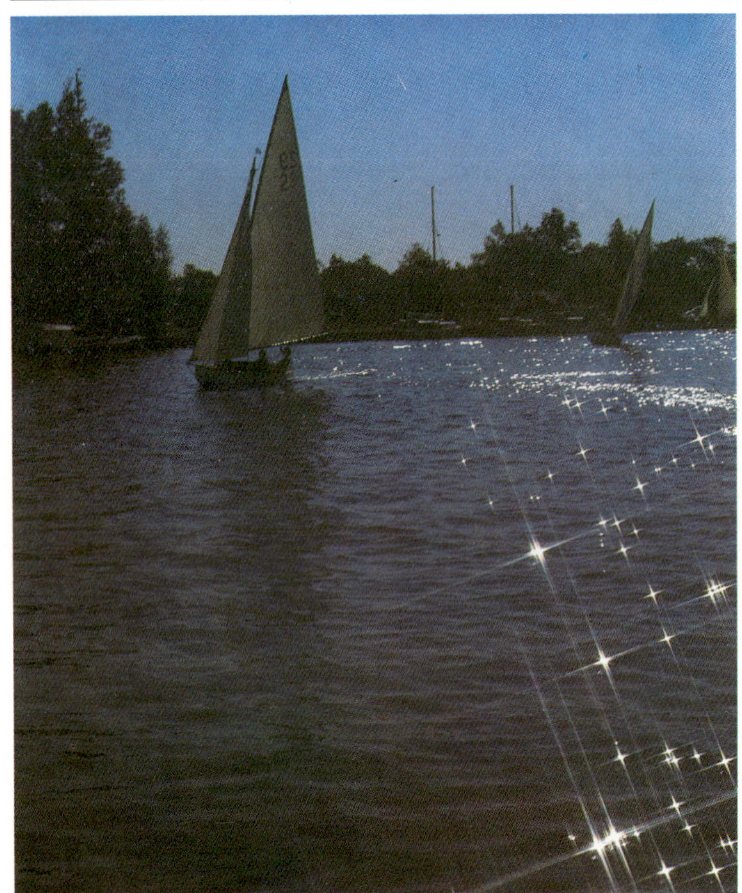

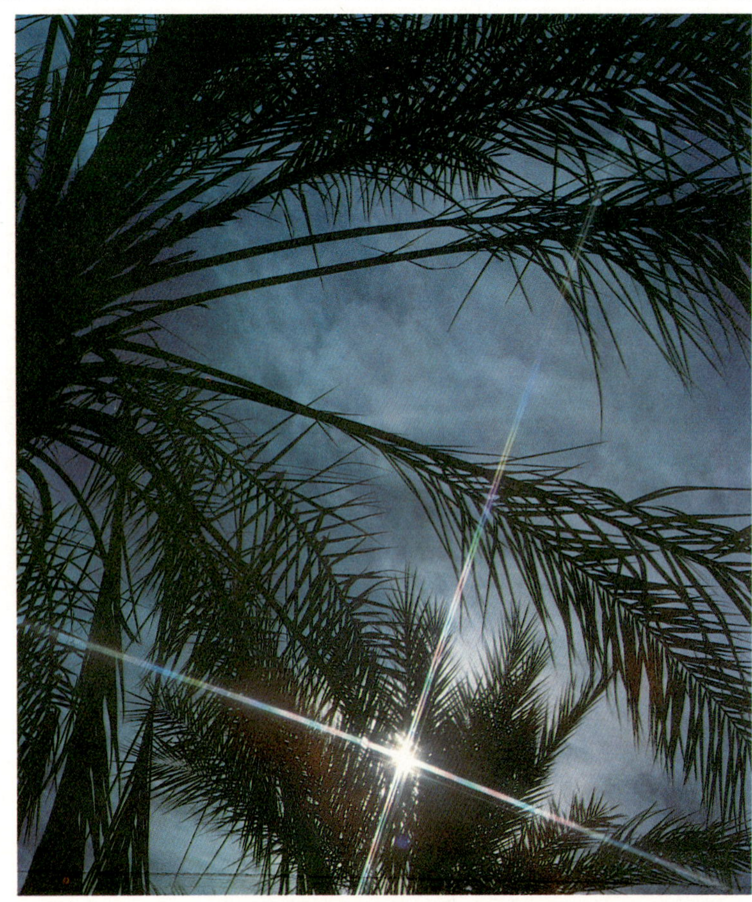

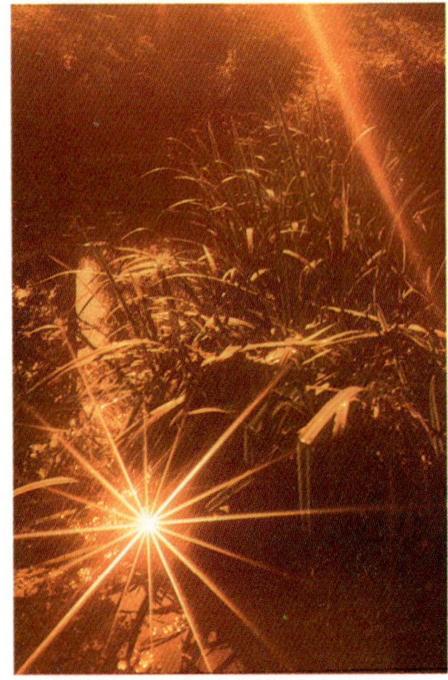

Night scenes with street lamps *and other light sources are an obvious subject for crosstars, as is the sun. Be careful, however, when including the sun in any shot; looking directly at the sun with the naked eye, or through a camera, can cause permanent eye damage. Even when the sun is partially obscured by branches or fronds* ***top right,*** *the light is still far stronger than is realised.*

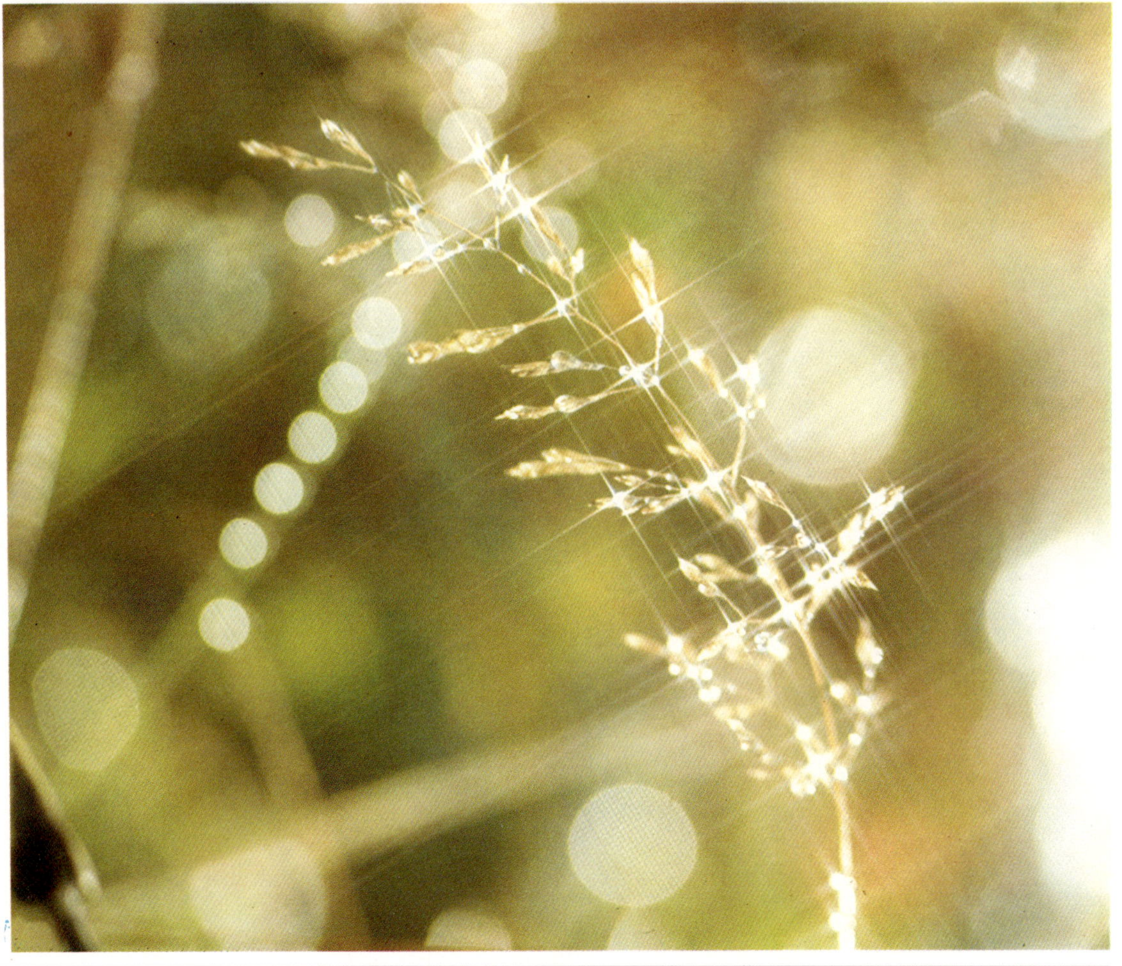

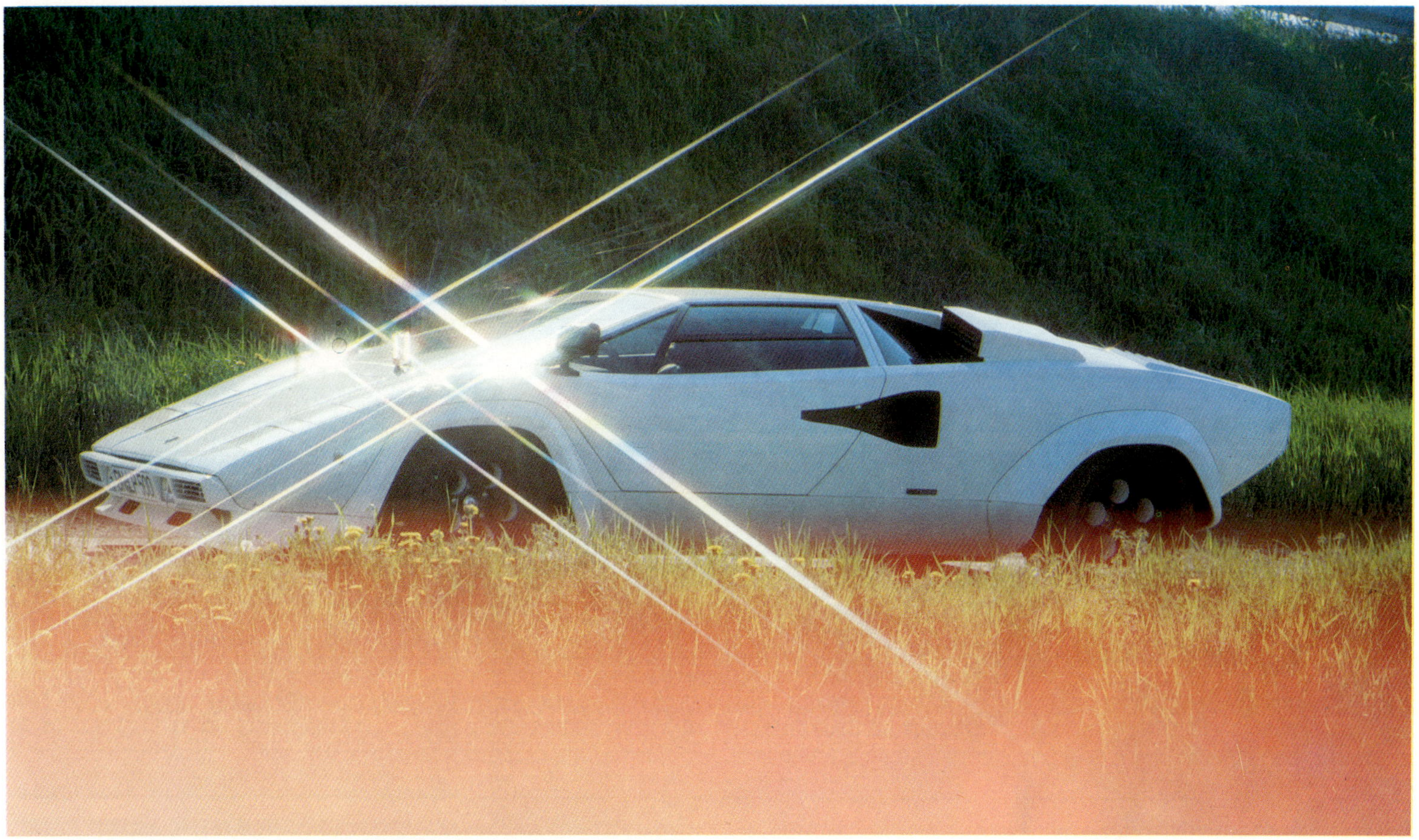

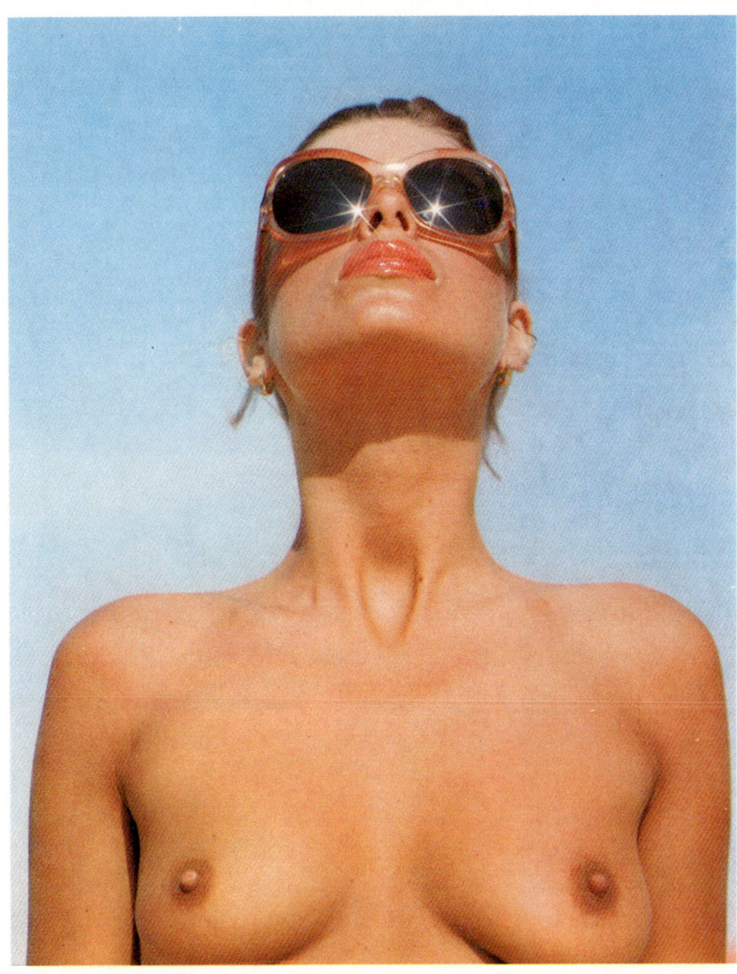

Reflections in water, whether it *be an expanse of water or droplets on flowers or grasses, can be given added sparkle by the use of a crosstar. Underexposure adds to the 'starlike' feeling, and the stronger the reflection the more pronounced will be the star. It is interesting to note that, in the shot of droplets of water on grass* ***facing page,*** *the grossly out-of-focus highlights in the background, rather than producing stars, show the actual pattern of the filter. Because of their curved surfaces, both the lenses of the sunglasses the model is wearing* ***left*** *show the same reflection of the one light source. With some crosstars it is possible to vary the angle between the rays* ***above.*** *Such attachments are usually referred to as 'varicross' filters.*

Mount and filter quality can be important. The cheapest crosstars are uncoated and fitted in a non-revolving mount, which means that they have to be unscrewed from the lens mount to change the angle of the beams. Since a light source must be included in shot, I would recommend the best filter you can afford – and use a good lenshood for the same reason. Rectangular lenshoods should be used with care, as any rotation could cause vignetting.

The lens aperture employed will affect the size and shape of the 'star,' as well as the definition and contrast of the overall image. The lens' widest aperture will produce the longest, widest star, as well as the lowest contrast. There will also be a degree of image softening. The wider the maximum aperture of the lens, the more pronounced the effect. As a general rule, it is better to shoot at about two or three stops below maximum aperture, unless you are prepared to shoot a lot of frames to know what the effect will be at each and every aperture. Under exposure is a *sine qua non,* unless the background is dark or the subject is a night scene. Crosstars need no increase in exposure.

DIFFRACTION GRATINGS AND PRISMS

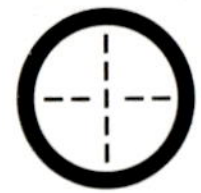
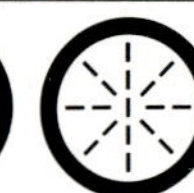
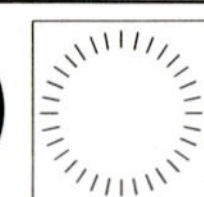
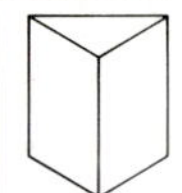

Diffraction gratings (also known as rainbow filters) work in a similar fashion to Crosstars, except that the beams emanating from a point source are rainbow coloured. This effect is achieved in several ways. By microscopically ruled parallel lines either on glass, or printed in gelatin then sandwiched between glasses, or by moulding very tiny prisms onto glass. Diffraction gratings are available which give beams in numbers from the usual 2x, 4x, 8x and 16x to 18x, 36x, 48x and even 72x. With the 'high powered' filters, a point source against a dark background is rendered as surrounded by a concentric rainbow, sometimes with dark radial interspaces. Due to the nature of the diffraction grating, it is also

Diffractors go by many *different names: Cosmos, Galaxia, Univers, Andromeda, Nebula etc. etc. They all have specially etched grid patterns which split the light in the manner of prisms but without distorting the image. They require a light source in the frame and benefit from under, rather than over, exposure. It is interesting to include the main light source and its reflection* ***above and above left.*** *The reflection, being darker, gives a different effect. The size and shape of the light source also causes differences as may be seen in the pictures* ***facing page, right.*** *A test film will provide good indications of the effects.*

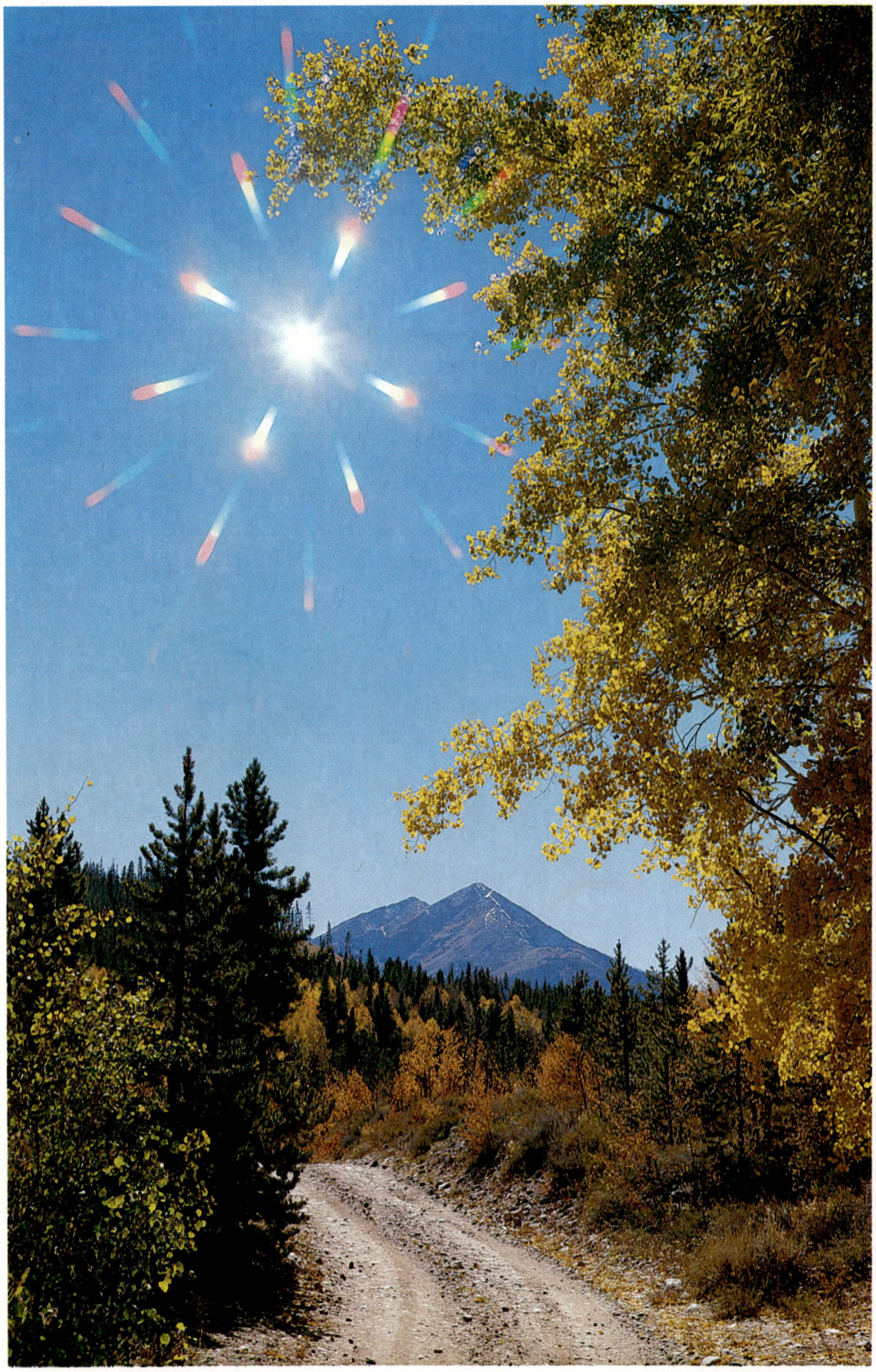

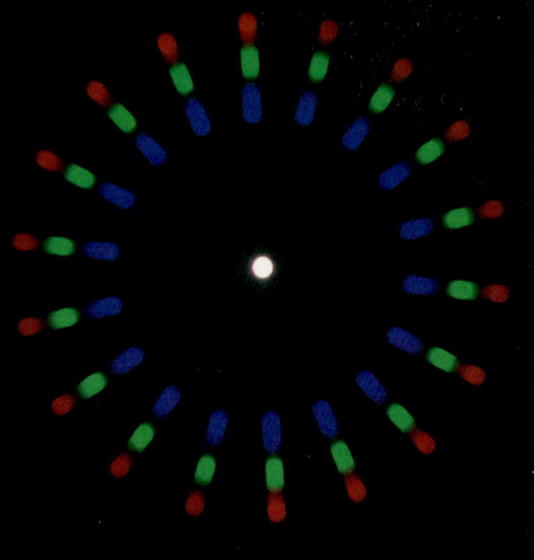

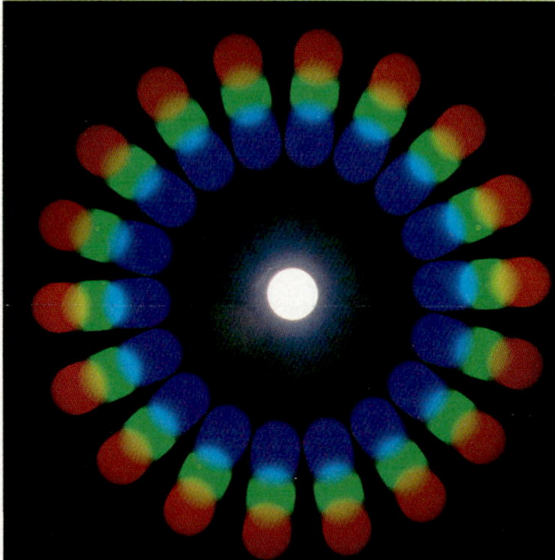

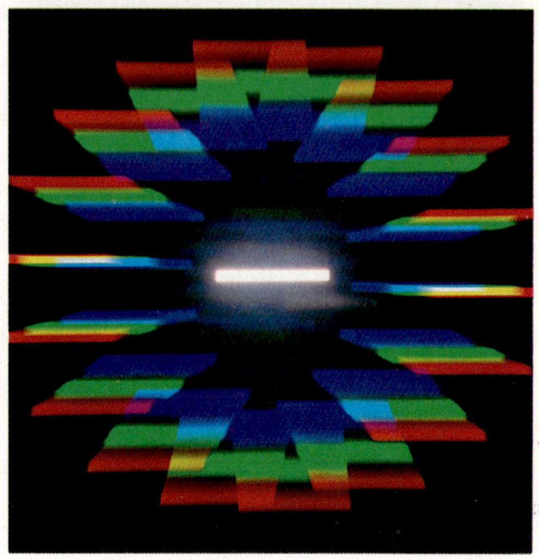

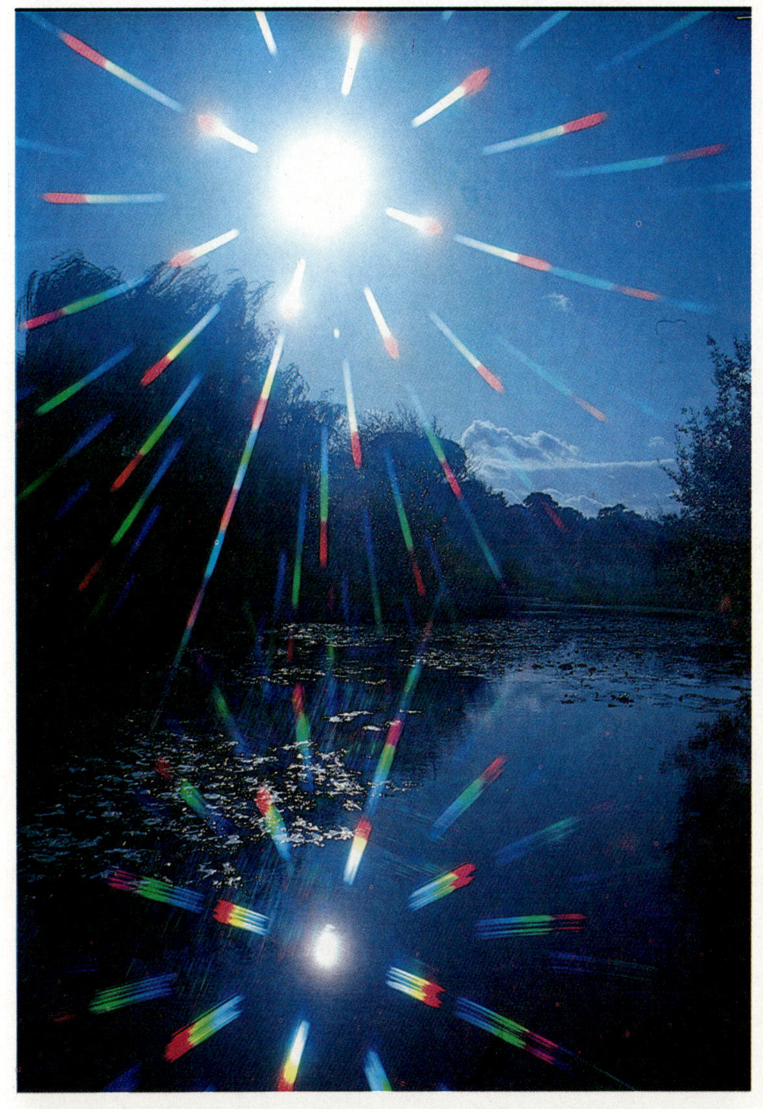

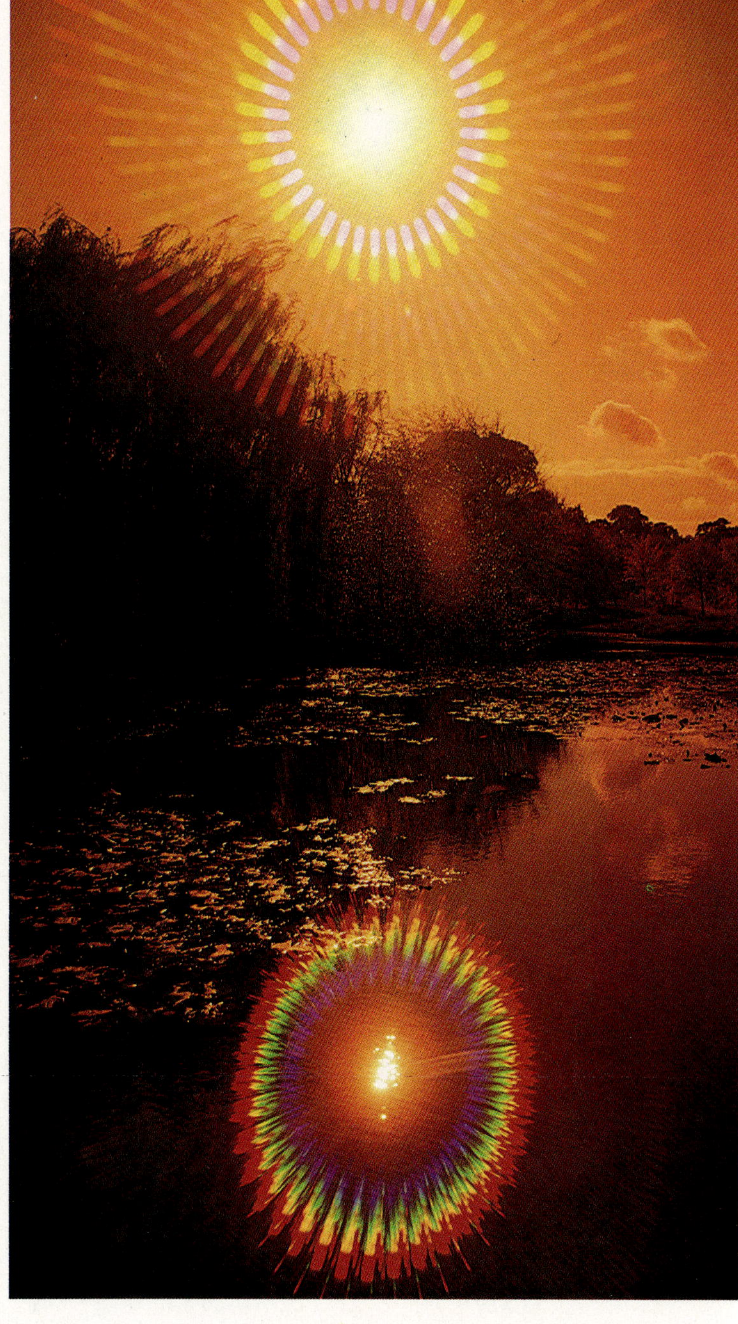

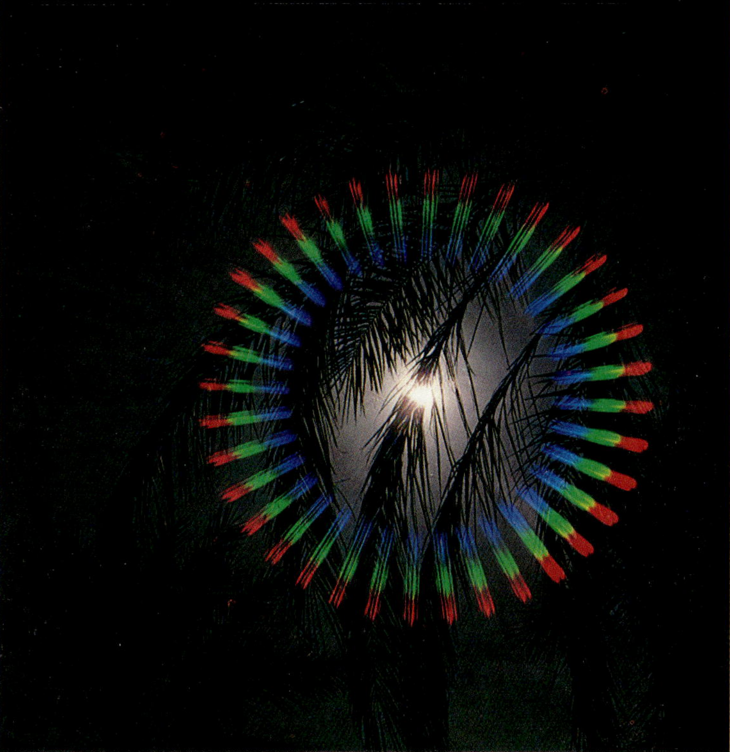

possible to produce diamond and parentheses shapes as well as variations on the wheel. All diffraction gratings have a greater effect upon image contrast and definition than do crosstars. The amount of flare produced can be drastic, though underexposure can 'cure' this. On the other hand, induced flare may add something to the final result. The choice is yours.

A prism used in front of the lens, to achieve image distortion and colour fringing, is an old idea now available in commercial form. The results are invariably somewhat abstract and without definition. They work better on longer, rather than normal, focal lengths if separation of the colours is the prime *raison d'être*. Since the image is refracted through the prism, some degree of photographer contortion will be necessary. As Jean Coquin puts it – "To photograph a subject placed in front of you, you might have to aim at the sky, the ground, or to the left or right." Prisms induce flare. Ergo, a light source in shot can be disastrous.

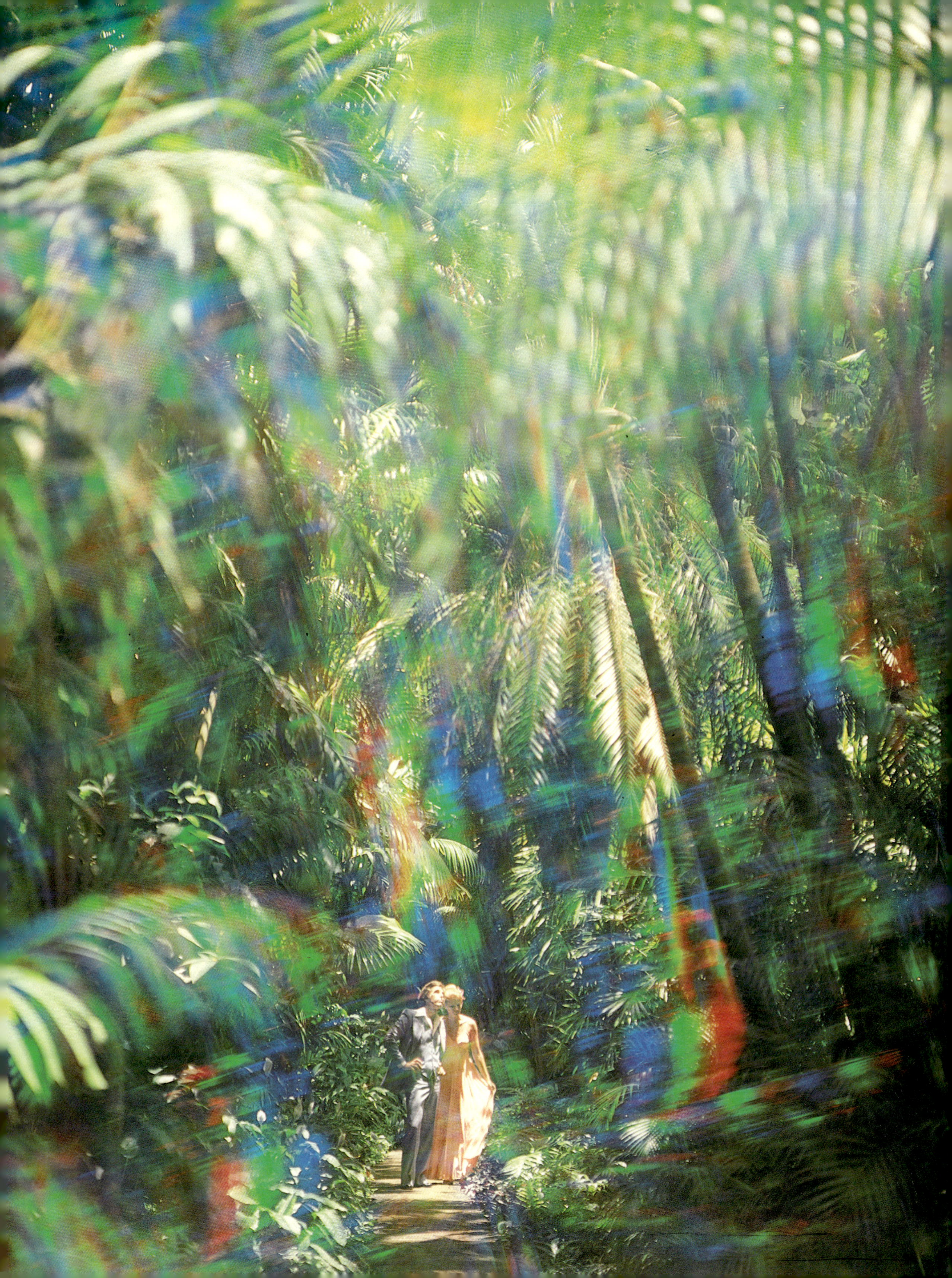

DIFFRACTION GRATINGS AND PRISMS

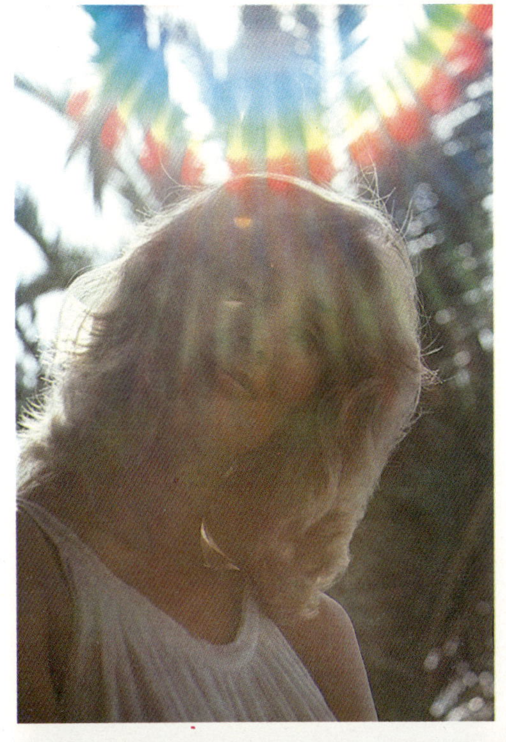

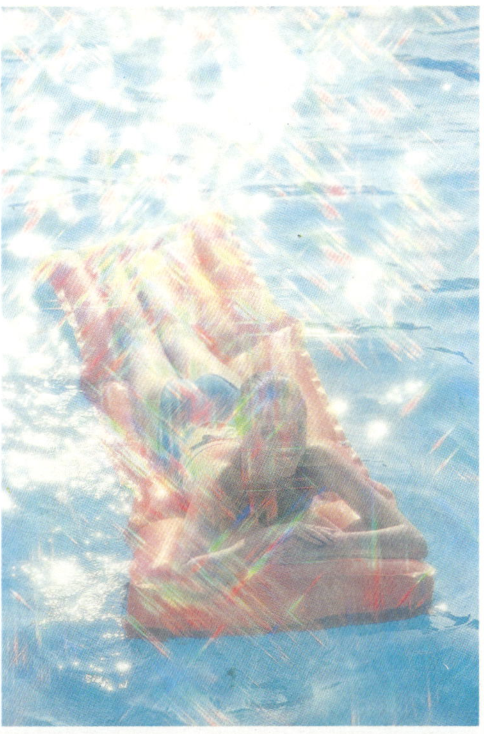

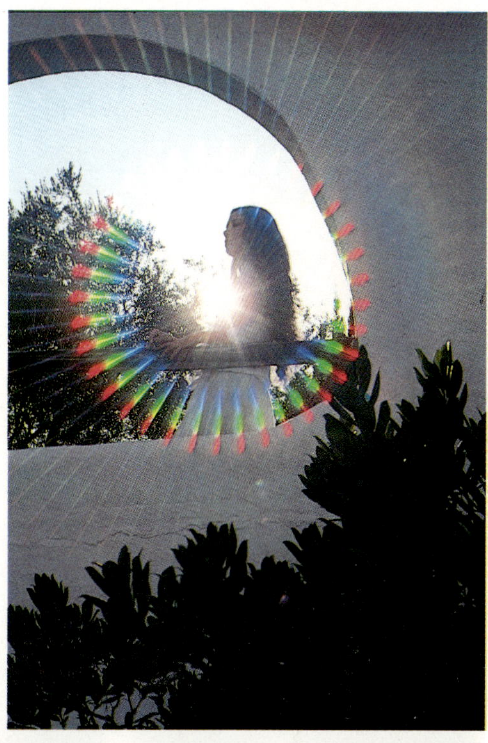

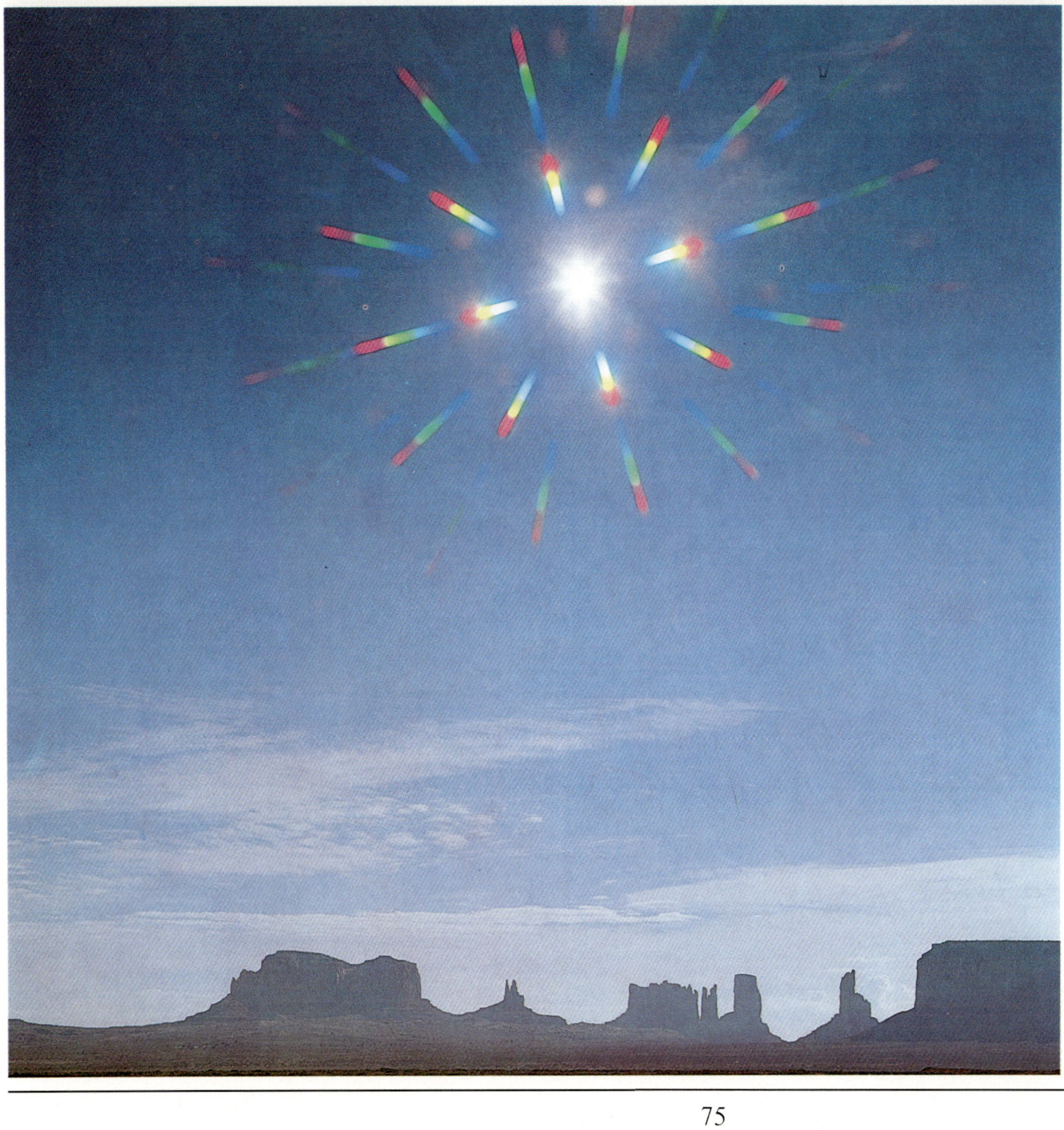

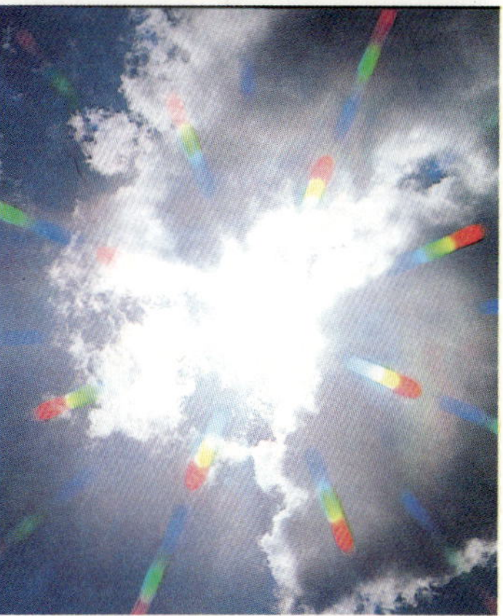

There is no doubt that the use *of diffraction gratings, by whatever name they are known, can be overdone. It would be a grave mistake to take every shot using such an attachment. But then, this is true for all special effects; it is invariably best to take one with and one without and see which pleases you best. There is no doubt that a poor shot can seldom be improved by adding an effect. The picture* ***top left*** *is ordinary, and adding colour has not altered this; it remains ordinary. Whether the picture* ***facing page*** *works well with the colours is for the viewer to decide: certainly the impression of 'walking through a rainbow' is eye catching and interesting.*

VIGNETTERS MASKS AND FRAMES

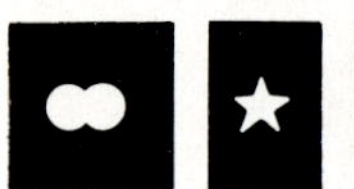
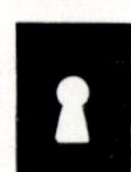

If there is one family of lens attachments which I loathe, then it is the rash of vignetters, masks or frames currently available. These are invariably sold in sets containing hearts, clubs, diamonds, spades and keyholes, etc. I cannot really see any point in photographing a nude through the latter, but then it's not my particular hang-up! The binocular cliché – formerly used in bad 'B' movies and now the province of TV – is totally incorrect, as anyone who has ever looked through them will attest. Should this not be evident, then a consultation with an optician is a matter of some urgency. Yet for all my hymn of hate, there is a use for some of these devices.

I cannot improve on the Hoyarex catalogue description of their technical mask set, so make no apologies for quoting it here. Their illustrations show how masks can be employed tastefully and to good effect.

"The Technical Mask Set consists of 15 black vinyl masks each measuring 72 x 72 x 0.3mm. There are 10 different pre-shaped masks and 5 plain masks for you to cut out your own designs. Place the masks in the Hoyarex Gelatin Holder (sold separately) and then slot into the Filter Holder in the same way as any other square Hoyarex Filter.

Strong light sources cause spectral highlights to assume the same blurred shape of the mask's perforations giving creative 'montage' effects.

The Technical Masks are particularly effective when used with telephoto lenses between 100-300mm set at the widest aperture. Using small apertures with standard and wide angle lenses has the opposite effect – to the point where the mask's effect will completely disappear. Therefore, for good results always use a wide open aperture by either adjusting the shutter speed or by using a Hoya Neutral Density filter to obtain correct exposure. As the exposure reading will vary according to the mask and lens used, it may be necessary to mount the camera on a tripod. Test shots are the safest way to evaluate the various effects and therefore assure the desired picture.

Additional sets of 15 Black Plain Masks are also available."

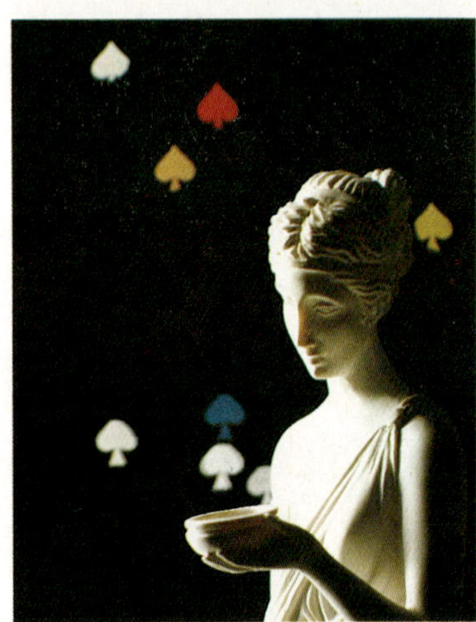

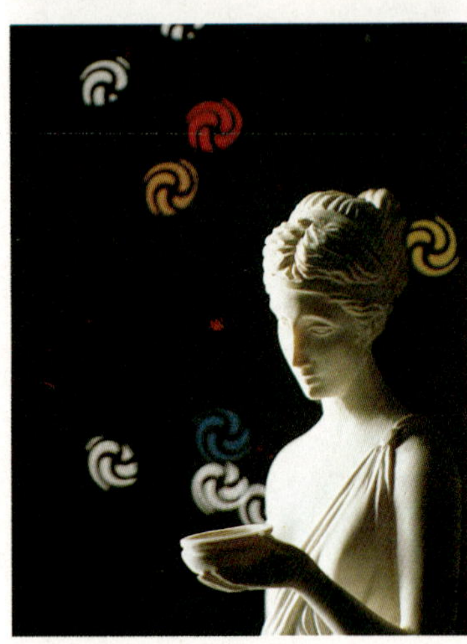

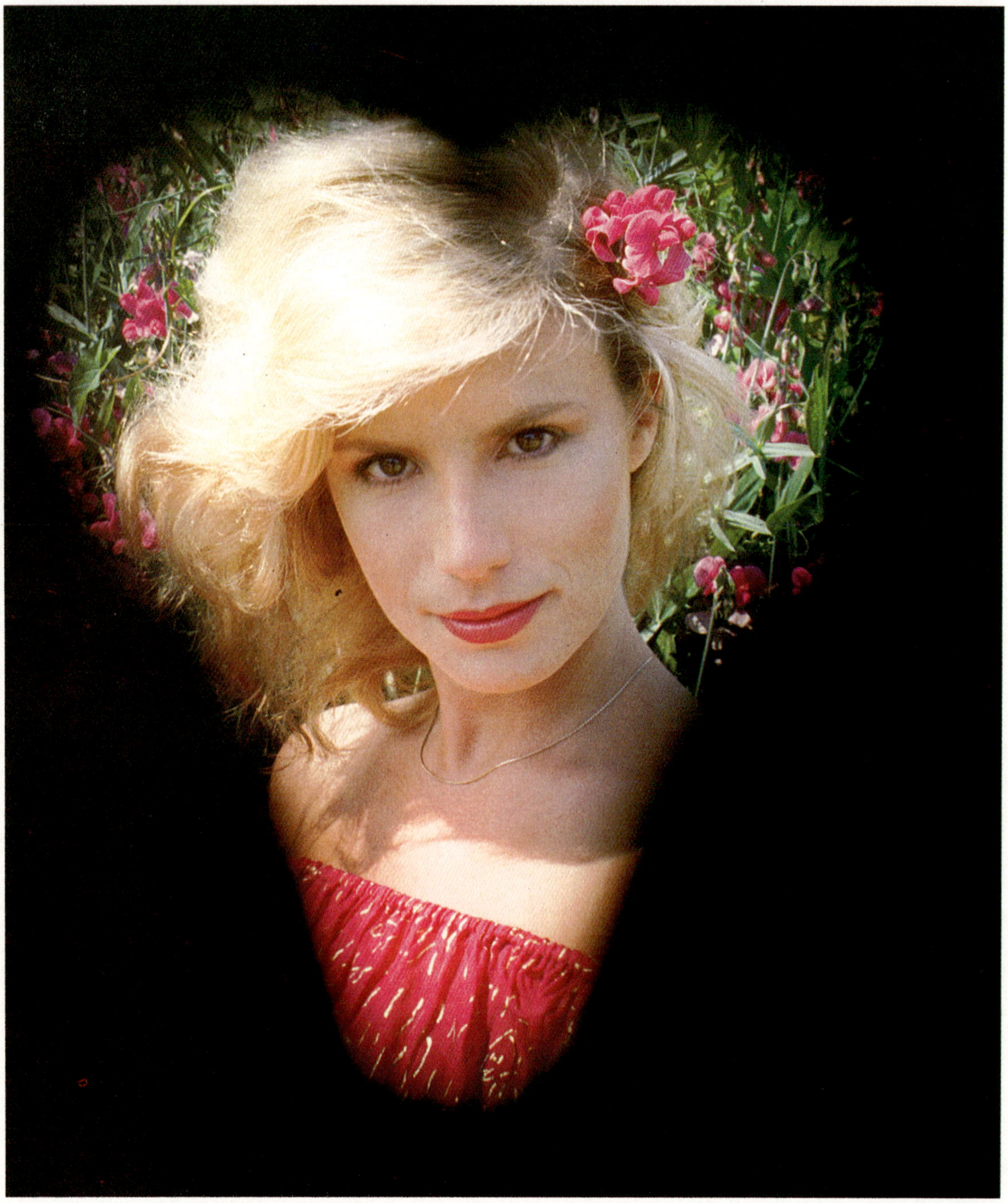

The small, cut-out shapes *provided by various special effects system manufacturers can be used to produce highlights of their own shape* ***above.*** *The more usual 'peephole' effects are also illustrated and have uses limited only by the photographer's imagination. The keyhole, however, would normally be used to look 'in' rather than 'out.'*

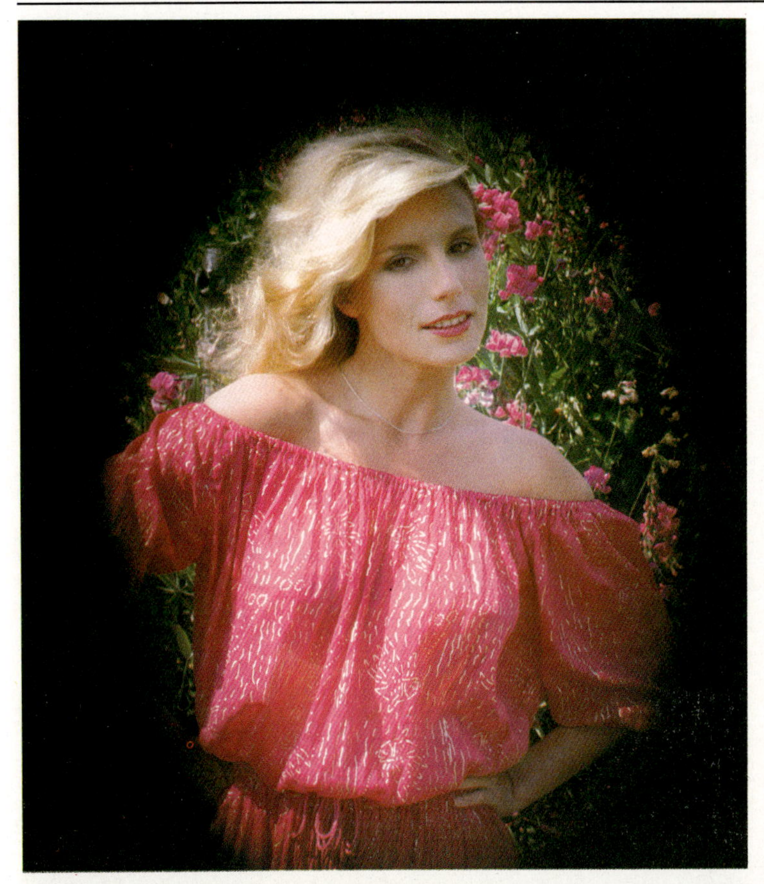

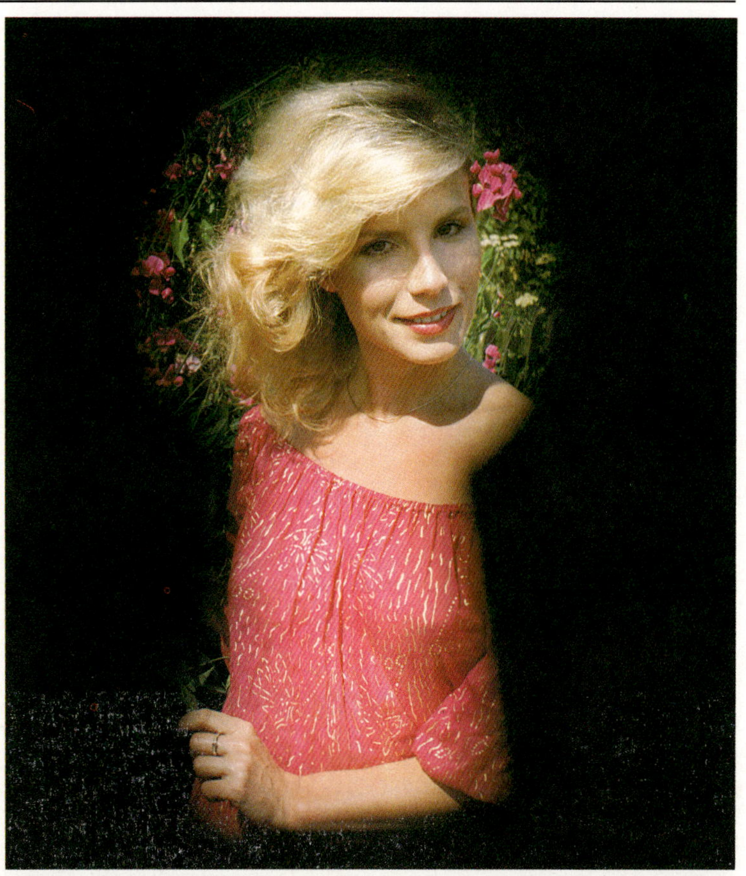

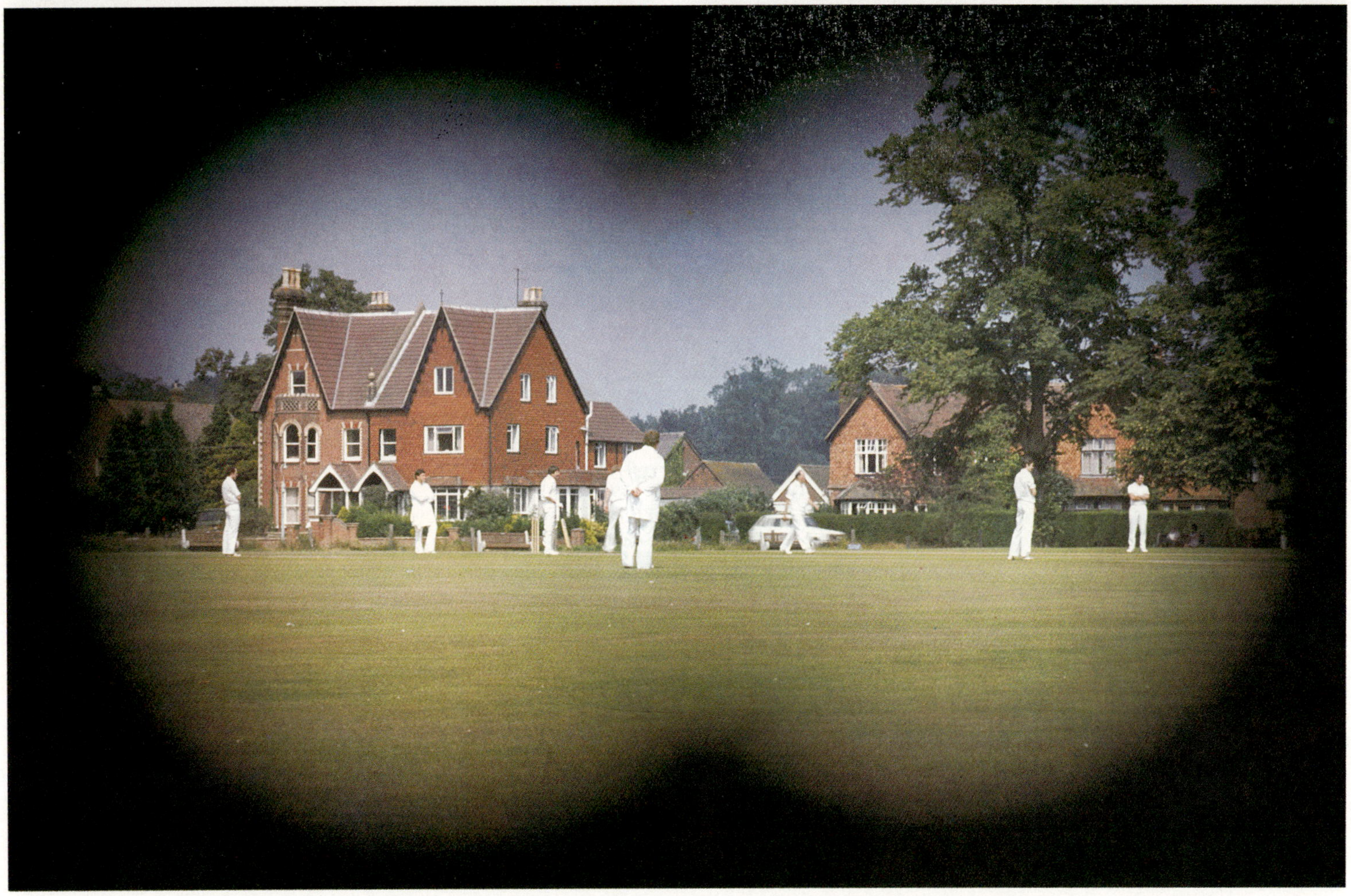

MULTIPLE IMAGE PRISMS

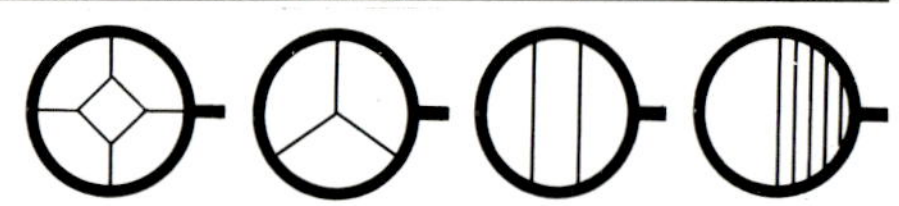

There are now at least a dozen variants of the multiple image prism on the market. For once, these were not invented by Jean Coquin, but, I am assured, originated from Spiratone in New York – out of Japan, in the early nineteen sixties. Any device which has been in vogue and used to the extent of becoming boring, will still attract a new generation of photographers sooner rather than later. The multi-image prism, perhaps more than any other attachment, fits into this category, although my feeling is that graduated filters will run a close second before long. In case it sounds as if I am anti-prism, let me assure you that I am not. Indeed the three I own have several times got me out of trouble by enabling an uninspiring subject to be rendered in a different way. As devices for editorial photography I would not be without them, even though it could well be a couple of years or more before I use one again.

Any prism attachment will produce multiple images of the original subject on film, the number of images being directly related to the number of prism facets. These can range from two to seven, with the juxtaposition of the images again relating to the arrangement of the prism faces. This gives the advantage that any prism can be immediately typed just by looking at it – ideal for secondhand bargain hunters!

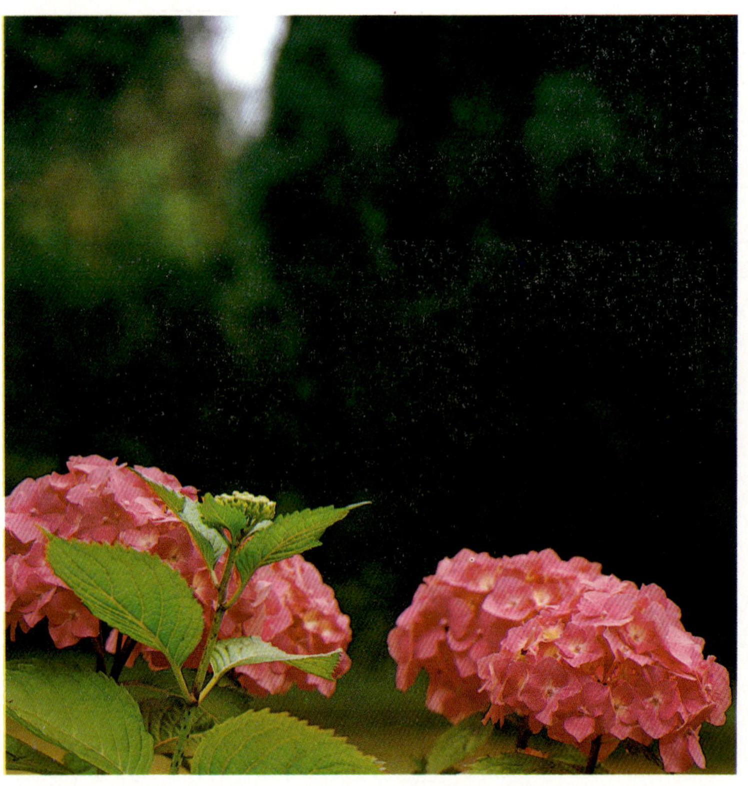

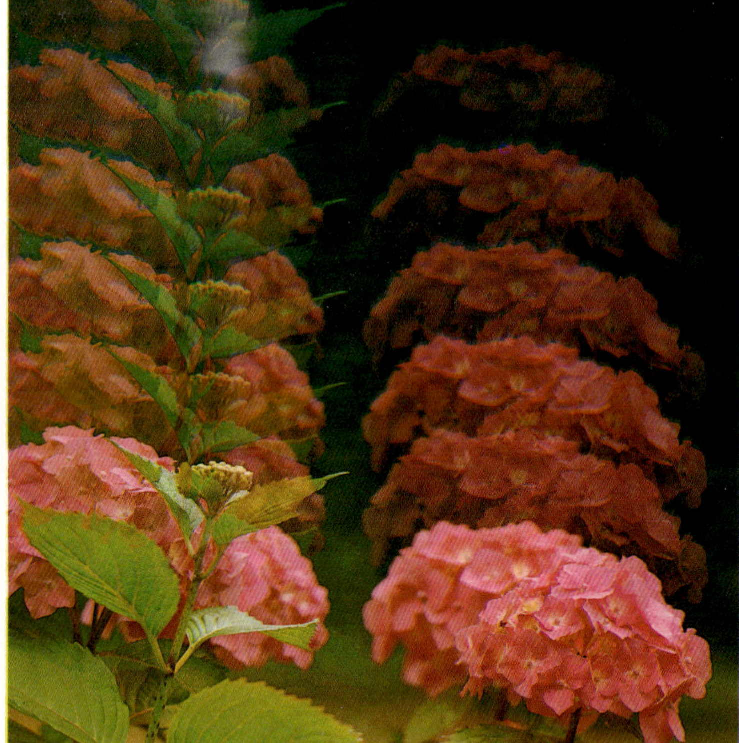

There are four basic types of prism attachments, the commonest being the kind with a plane central area. This can be circular, with anything from three to six angled surfaces radiating from it, each of which will provide an additional image to the central one. This central area can also be triangular, square, pentagonal, or hexagonal – again with the appropriate number of surrounding sectors. All of these produce a single central image, with a regular pattern of secondary images around it.

The second type of prism has no clear central area. Made only with three or four prismatic faces, a regular pattern of three or four images is produced. A rotating mount allows the triangular or square pattern of images to be moved at will around a central axis in the frame.

The third type of prism has parallel faces which provide two or three side by side images. Again a revolving mount, turned through 180 degrees, allows the images to be one above the other. Turning the mount less than this figure provides stepped images. An unusual variant of the two face parallel type is the B + W made close-up prism. This is of ca 7.5 dioptres strength – which is powerful for a close-up lens, and should only be used at small lens apertures in order to ensure adequate definition.

A fourth type of prism is the offset parallel type, more often known as a repeater prism attachment. Here the faces start from halfway across, and can be between two and five in number. This gives the effect of a stroboscopic photograph, with a 'leading' subject and between two and five extra over-lapping 'following' images. Using the rotating mount alters the image dispersion as with other parallel prisms.

The ingenious and quality B + W company have now managed to produce colour prisms. These consist of a spectrum with a choice of six faced prism (without clear central area), and a three faced parallel type. Introducing colour allows a much greater degree of subject tone variation than with a clear equivalent. Used on a white, grey or pastel subject it can produce some very startling effects.

Prism attachments can be used on any normal or longer focal length lens. With wide angle lenses there is always a chance of vignetting due to the depth of a prism mount. This will happen particularly at the smaller lens apertures. It is sometimes possible to use an oversized prism plus a step ring to get over this problem, but only with a wide angle lens of moderate angle of view, and a not too deeply recessed front element.

The choice of subject for prismatic techniques must rest with the photographer, however, as a guide, a light toned subject against a medium to dark background is likely to 'read' better than the reverse situation. For the same reason, a simple subject is likely to be the clearest, whilst anything complex could easily go towards the abstract. Opinions vary as to how far the prime lens should be stopped down. There is no doubt that a smaller aperture produces sharper images of both subject <u>and</u> prism facet

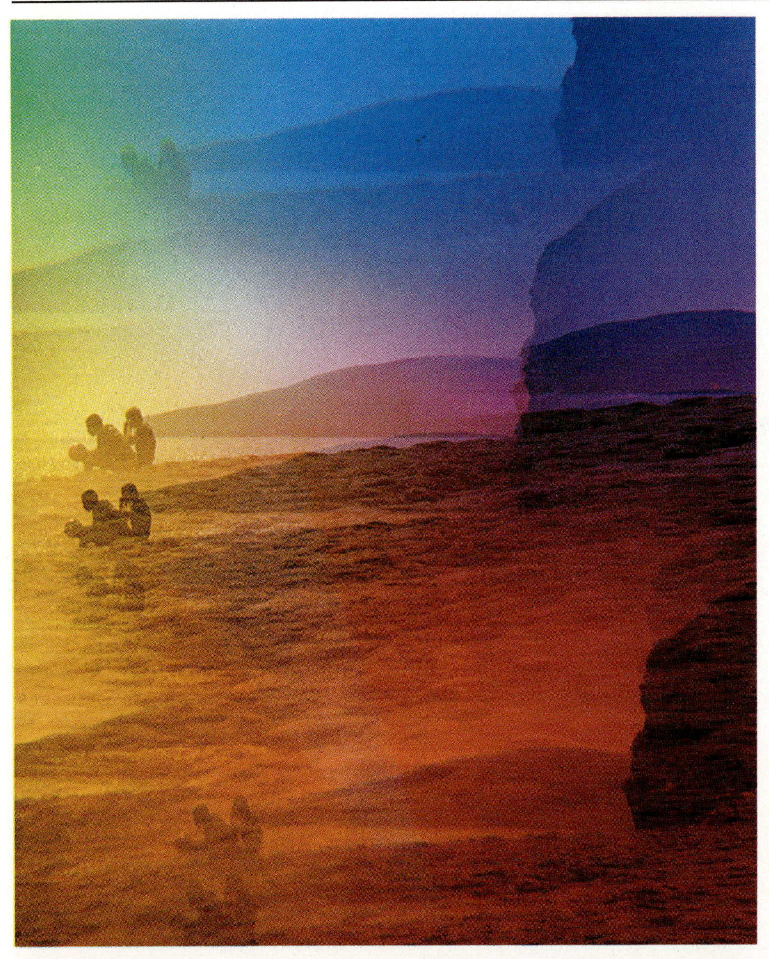

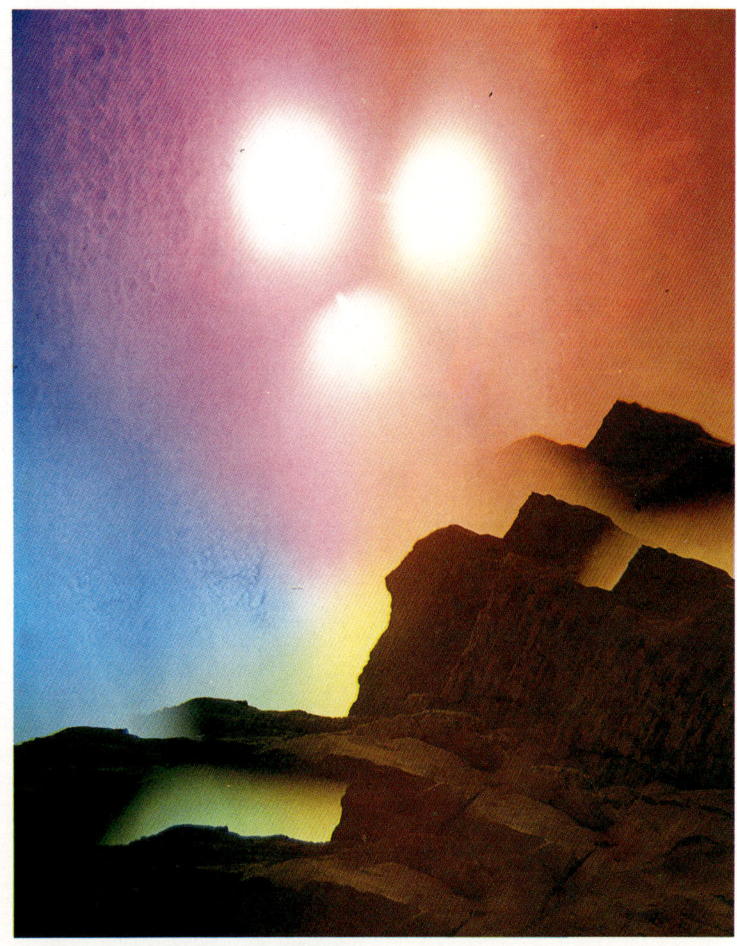

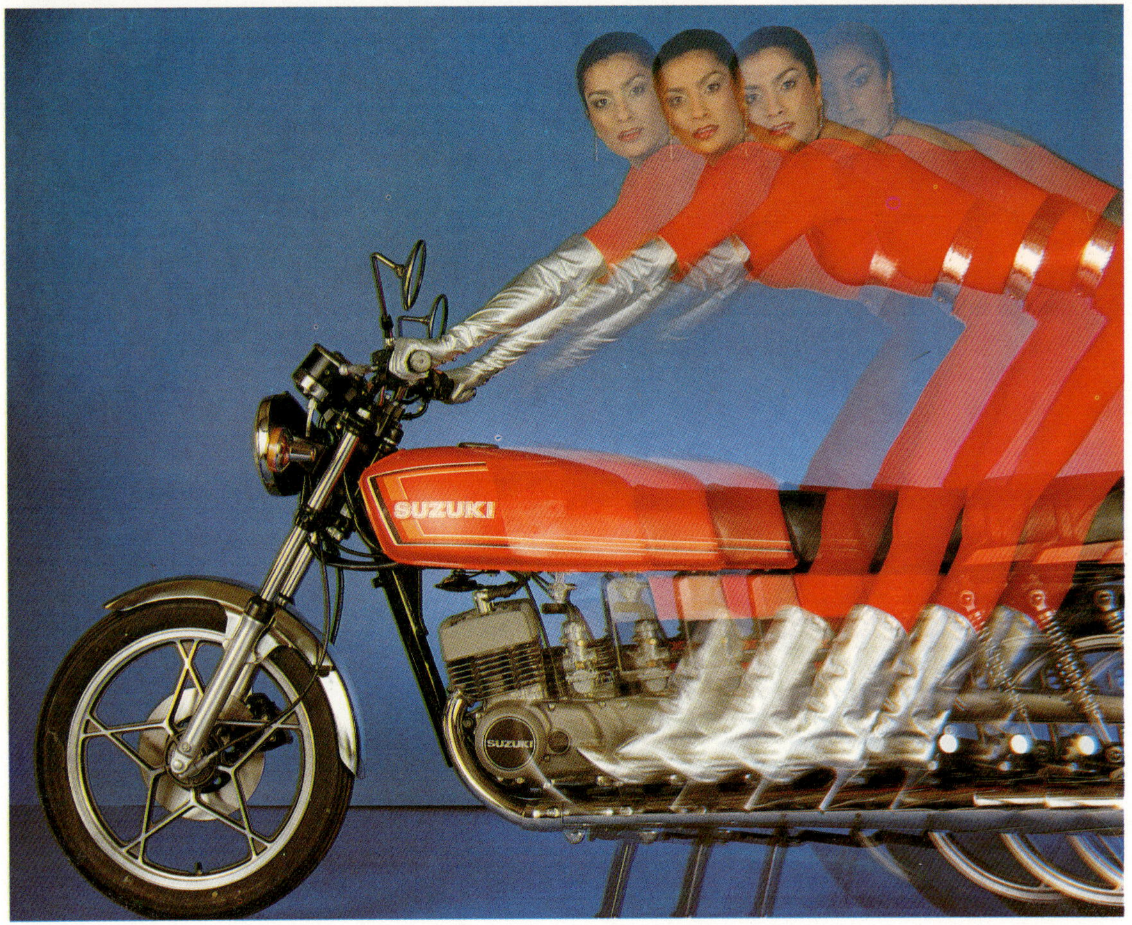

A multiple image attachment *in which the planes, or faces, are parallel is sometimes described as a 'repeater' or, maybe, a 'speed filter.' The flowers in the right picture* ***facing page*** *do, indeed, look as though they are falling because our eyes tell us that the strongest image – at the bottom – should be the latest image; therefore the flowers must be newly arrived in that position. This shot could have been taken with the strongest image at the top of the picture to give a 'magic beanstalk' effect. The studio shot* ***left*** *also conveys this impression of movement, this time across the frame. Whilst it is very obvious that neither the motor cycle nor the model are really moving, the impression is still quite strong. A multiple image prism with no clear centre, and with each segment dyed a different colour, was used to produce the two near-abstracts* ***above.*** *Where the faces meet there is an even greater multiplication of the image of the group of figures.*

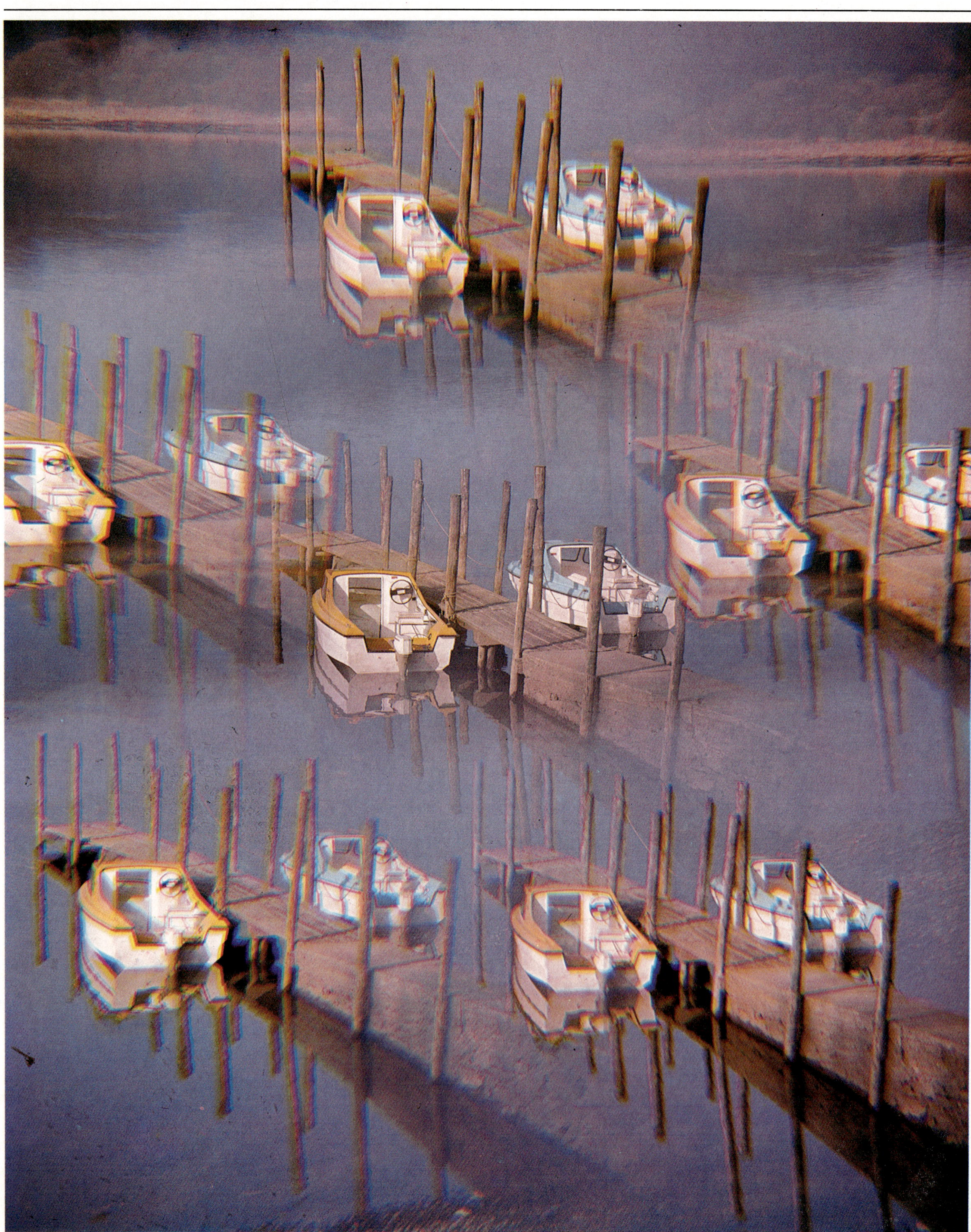

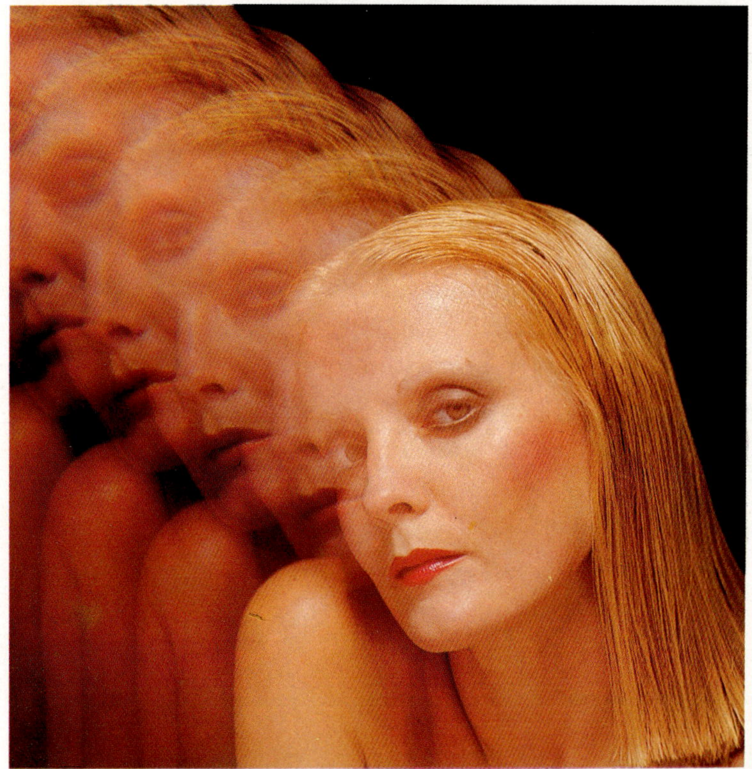

shape, as well as perhaps pulling a background into sharp focus. As with some other lens attachments, I can only suggest a three aperture trial run.

An SLR camera fitted with a depth of field preview facility saves two exposures! For the same reason, and since all prisms are fitted into revolving mounts, an SLR camera will take the guesswork out of image placement. This revolving mount can also be used to double expose in even more images. Alternatively, with the camera on a tripod and a half or one second exposure, it is possible to blur the extra images around the central image, by rotating the prism during the exposure. A prism with a central plane surface should be used, and the subject must be static. I have often been asked if it is possible to use two prisms together in order to produce even more images. The answer is a very qualified 'yes'. You may like or dislike partial images - which can occur.

Mixing dissimilar prisms can be quite interesting. The biggest snags I have found are that the resulting thickness of glass produced a poor quality image, there was vignetting with a standard focal length lens, and the prisms needed to be taped together. The advantage is that you can try the effect on an SLR - without having to use any film!

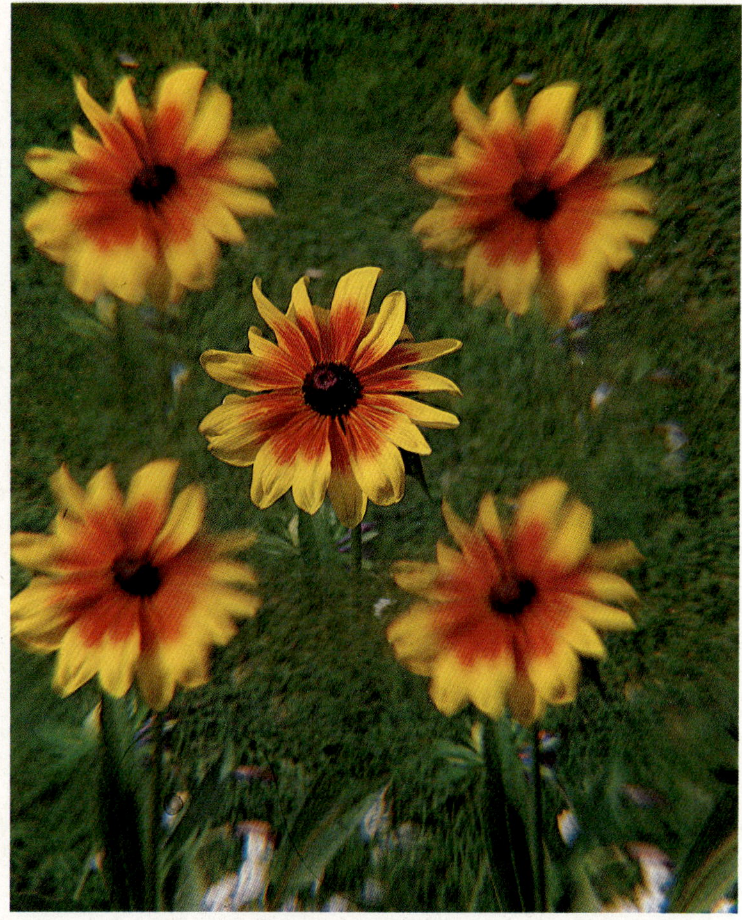

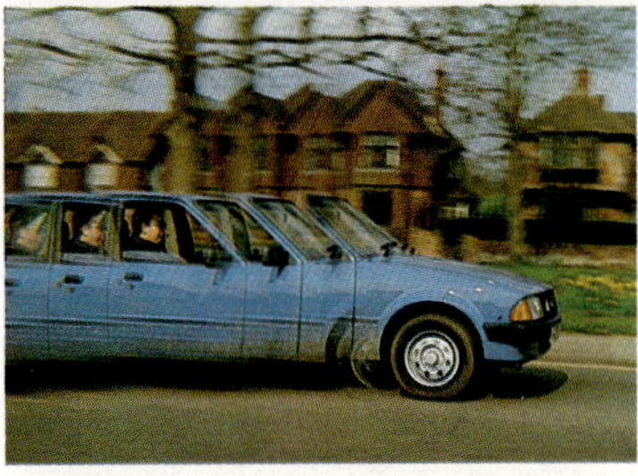

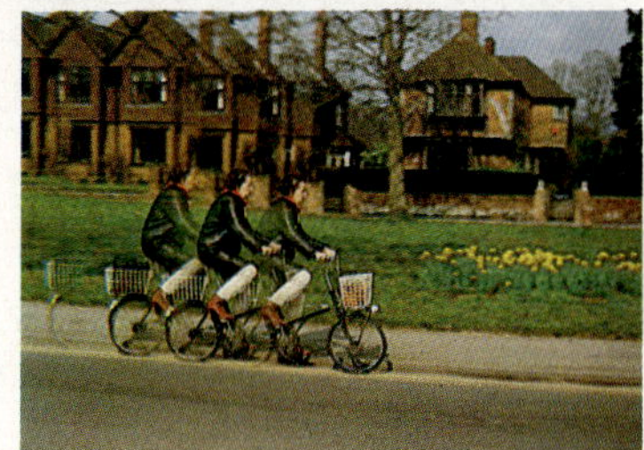

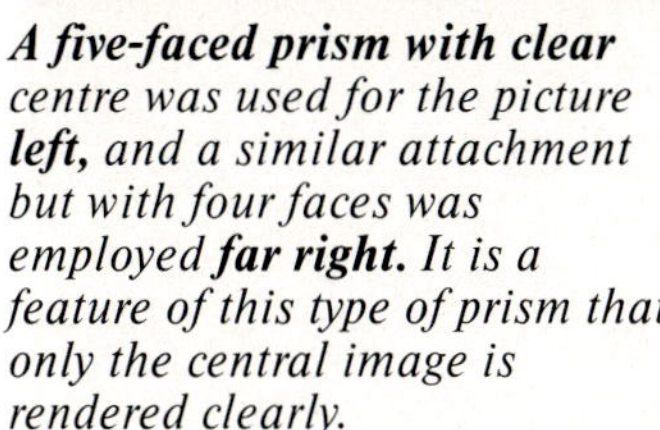

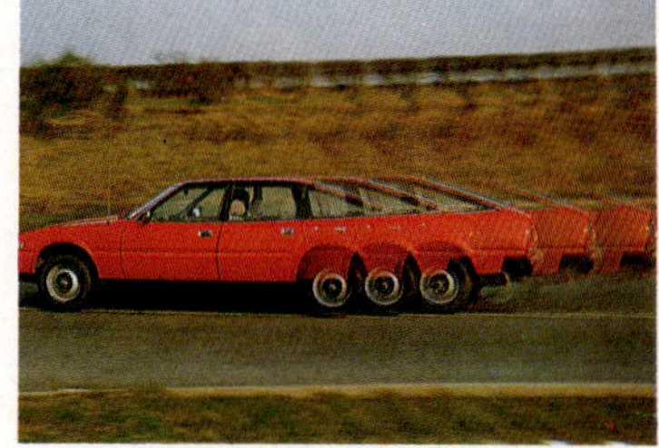

A five-faced prism with clear *centre was used for the picture* ***left,*** *and a similar attachment but with four faces was employed* ***far right.*** *It is a feature of this type of prism that only the central image is rendered clearly.*

The pictures on this page, with *the exception of the flower shot, show further examples of the uses to which the parallel-plane prism can be put. As with most of these attachments, it can usually be rotated in its mount (if not it must be unscrewed slightly in the filter thread) to position the secondary images wherever they are wanted. With parallel prisms, the closer the faces the more faces there are, and more images will, therefore, be repeated, thus giving a greater impression of speed or movement.*

DOUBLE EXPOSURE DEVICES

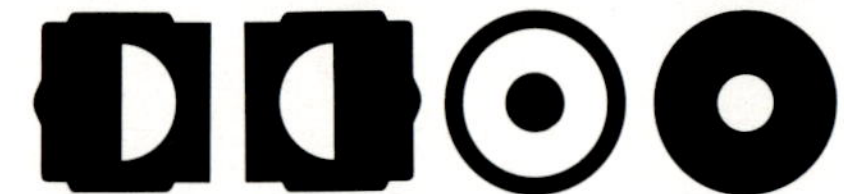

Variously known as double mask, dual image or double exposure mask, these devices exist in two forms: those which mask out half the frame and those which mask out a smaller section or shape. To use these attachments it is virtually essential for the camera to have a double exposure facility, a rewind button, or interchangeable magazines. Anything else involves marking the film leader or backing paper accurately, rewinding and re-exposing, which in the case of model shots gets silly. Yet having said this, I know of a landscape photographer who pre-exposes the full moon in pre-determined positions on numerous rolls of film. These are then taken around the world and suitable subjects double exposed in. It may be astronomically incorrect for a Hemel Hempstead moon to appear over Nevada, but who will know – or even care? Most double exposures necessitate the use of a tripod, particularly if the subject is to appear with itself. The film business, having invented the technique, still perseveres whenever a character has a double or a twin.

With a double exposure facility, or interchangeable magazine camera, the use of a double exposure mask presents no problem. Failing this, the rewind button can be depressed, the shutter wound and the second exposure made. The disadvantage of this method is that the film can move between exposures. Even by taking up the slack in the film cassette and taping over the rewind knob before the second exposure is made, there is still the chance of up to 2mm error. In the cases of either a straight double exposure mask or a shape mask, this becomes a hit or miss operation. The cliché of a girl's head appearing in a bed of

Cokin double exposure masks *were used for both these subjects; the picture* ***right*** *with the double mask, which blanks out the central portion of the frame, which can then be re-exposed using the second part of the attachment. For the shot* ***below*** *the sliding double exposure device was used. Note that the slightest movement of the tripod-mounted camera results in a double image in the centre of the picture.*

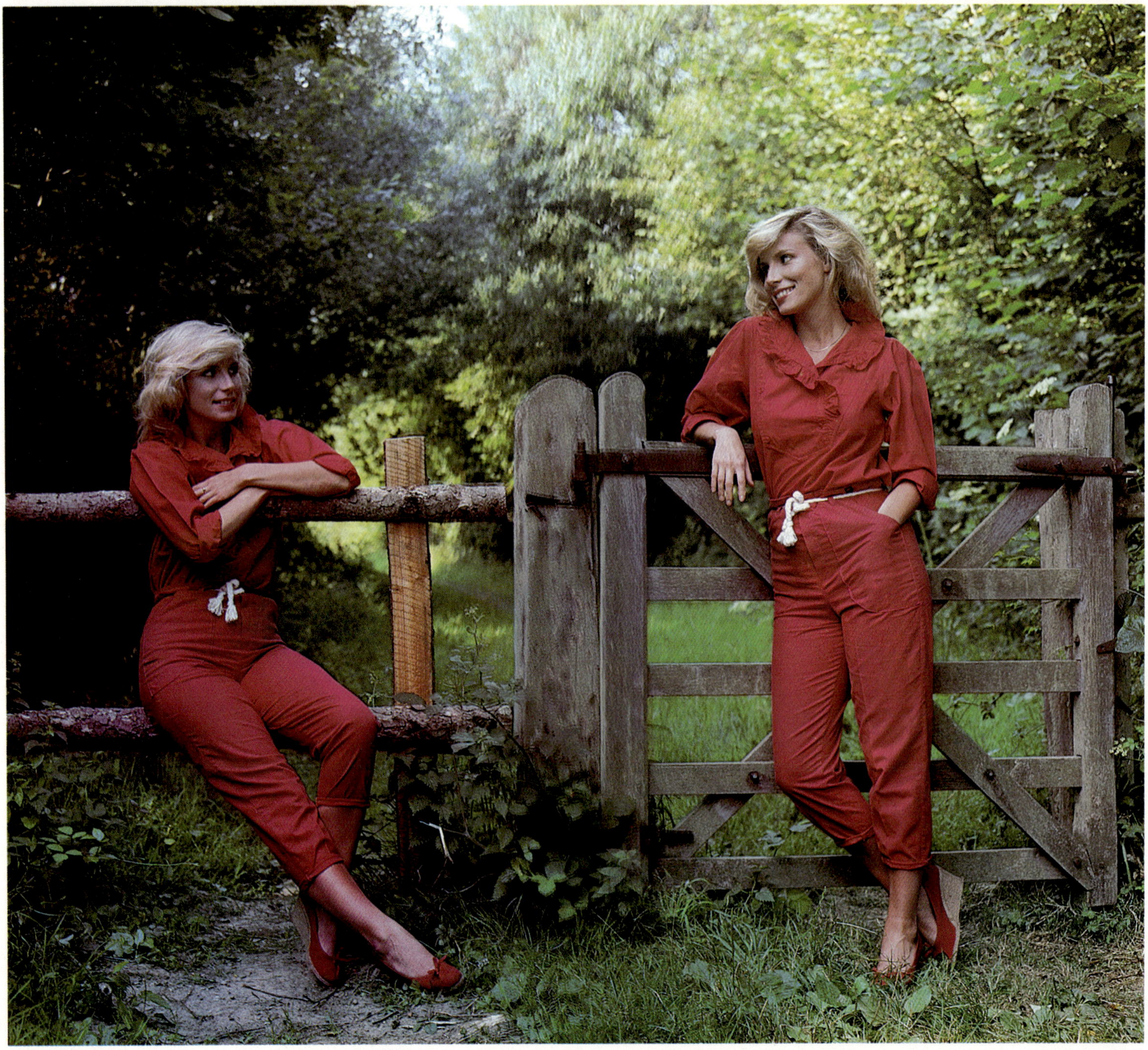

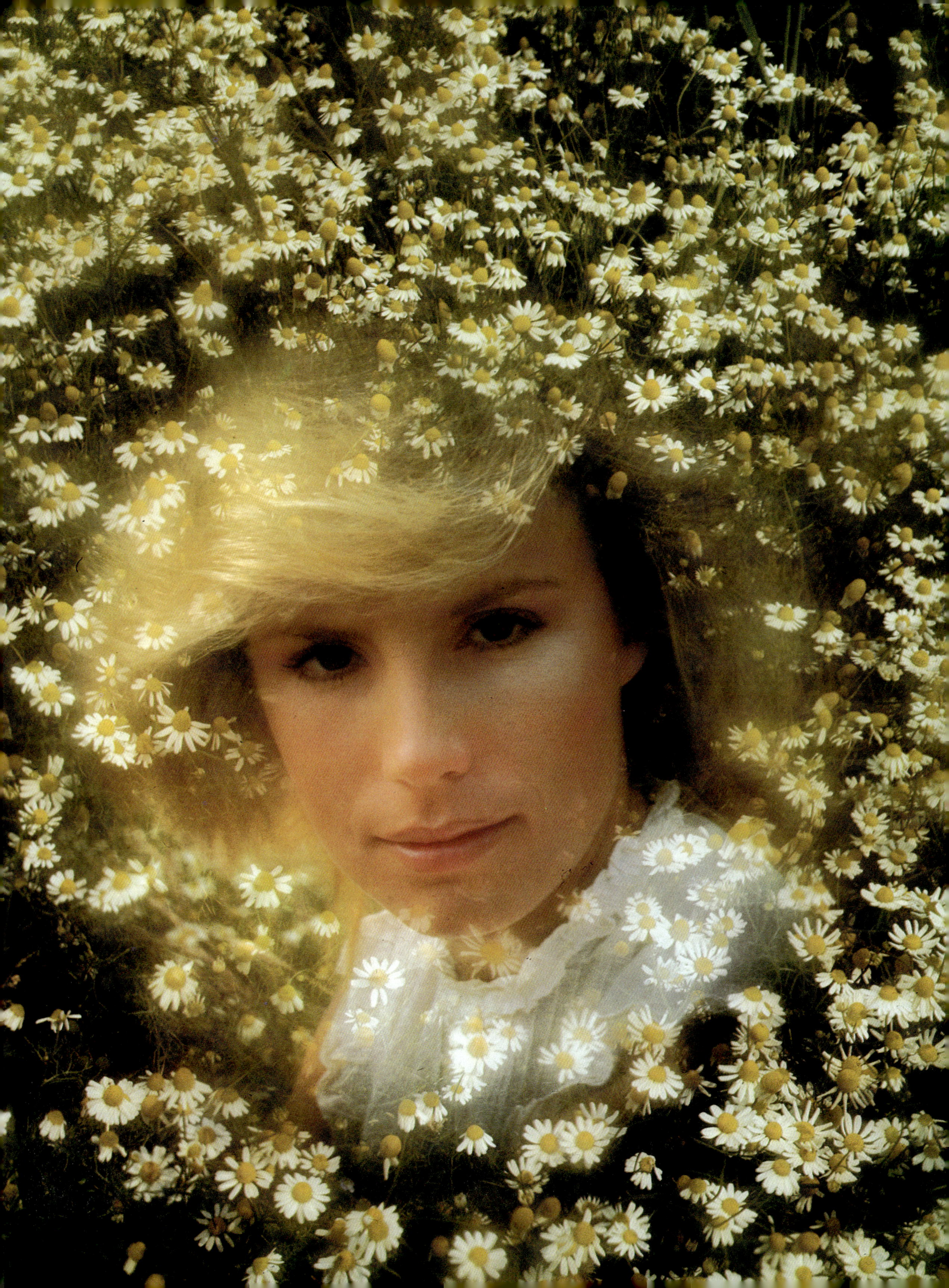

DOUBLE EXPOSURE DEVICES

flowers will not be affected by a millimetre error, though a degree of planning is necessary in order to have both girl and flowers in close proximity.

All double exposure masks work on a replacement basis. The first exposure is made with either half of the frame blanked off, or a shaped mask is used to perform the same function. The blanked off half of the frame is then re-exposed by sliding the attachment across the frame. In the case of a shaped frame, its negative shape is replaced by its positive or vice versa. In either situation the masks must register with each other.

The aperture and focal length of the lens employed has a distinct bearing upon the image overlap, or lack of it. As a guide, a wide angle should be used at between f4 and f5.6; a normal lens at between f8 and f11, and a telephoto (or long focus) between f11 and f16. As with so many other lens attachments, a wide angle will produce a sharper cut off, whilst a tele will be more diffuse in this respect. A depth of field preview facility and a grid focusing screen help to gauge alignment and final result. Medium and large format users can always check out with a Polaroid.

Exposure readings must be checked and held before the attachment is fitted, as otherwise over exposure from a false reading will result. Finally, a dark or complex background will tend to disguise any masking error. A black background allows the use of deliberate image overlap.

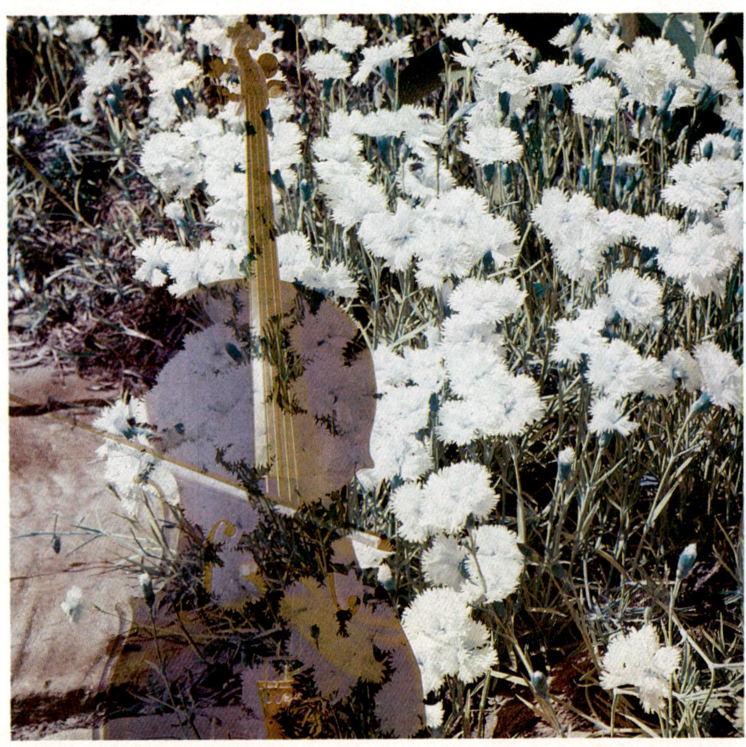

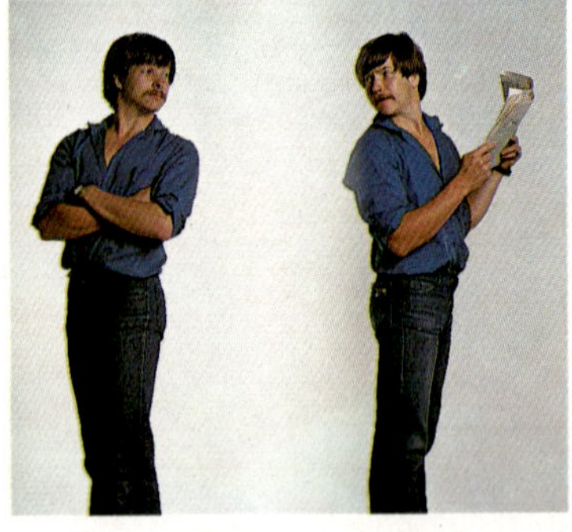

Above is another example using *the double exposure attachment. This can also be used to take images one above the other, as well as side by side. A child up a tree, for example, can look down on itself sitting on the grass. The other two pictures on this page are the result of straightforward double exposure in camera. This requires the provision of some means of disconnecting the film drive between exposures, usually by means of a double exposure button or lever on the camera. Failing this, the rewind button must be held in, the rewind knob held securely, and the lever wind operated. The pictures* ***facing page*** *are the result of exposing a film on shots of the moon, rewinding, repositioning the film exactly in the camera, and making the subsequent exposures.*

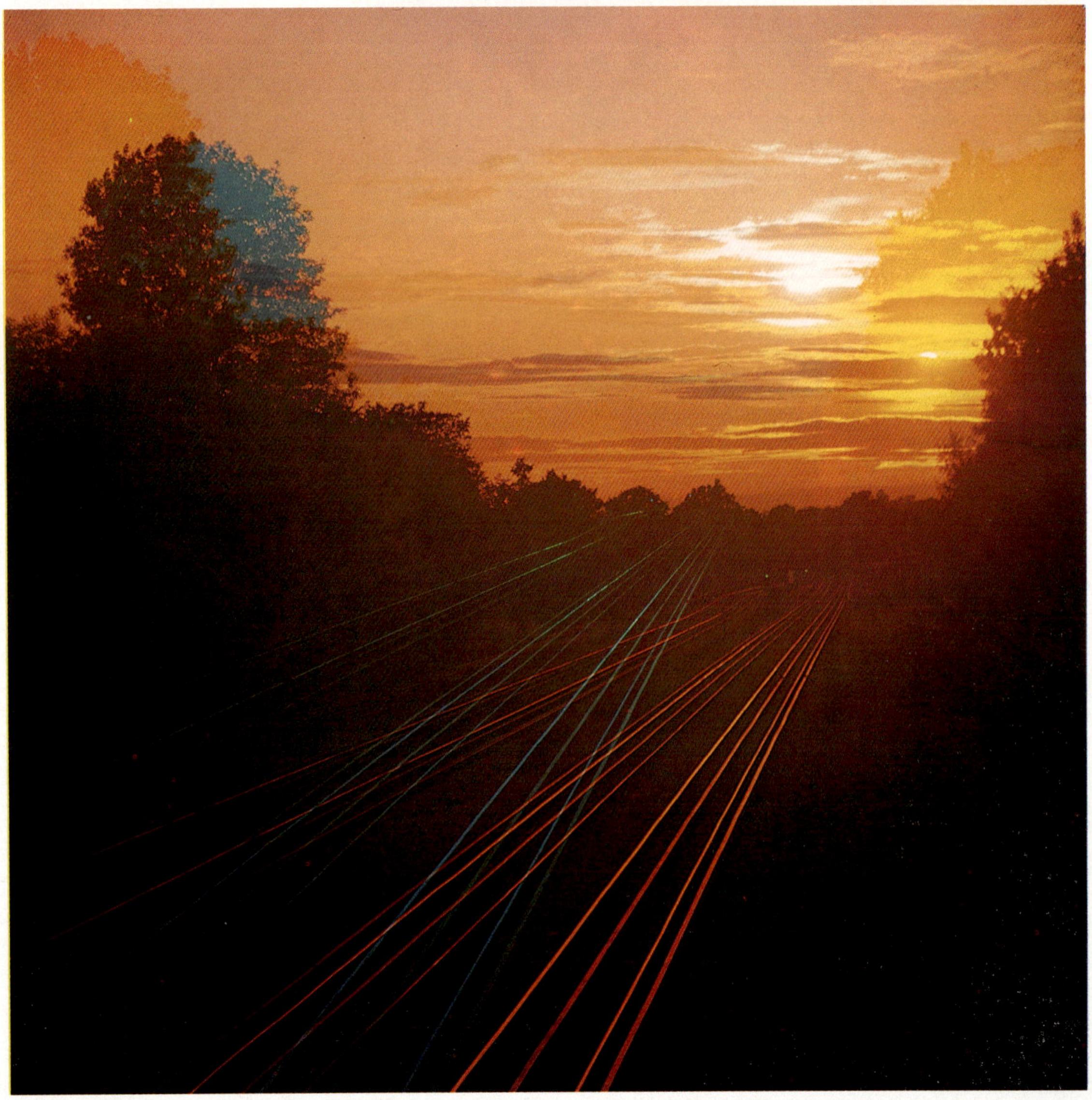

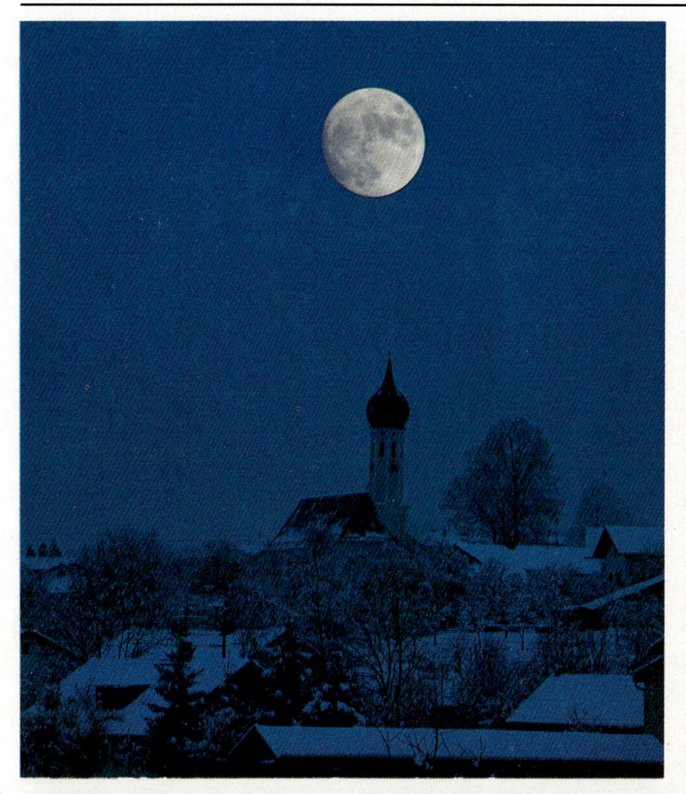

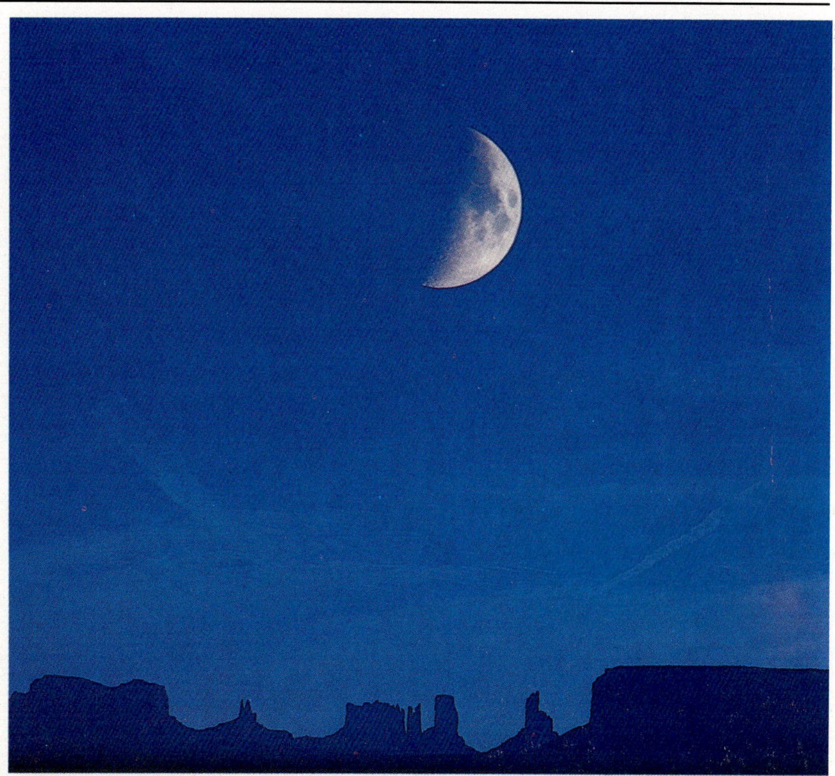

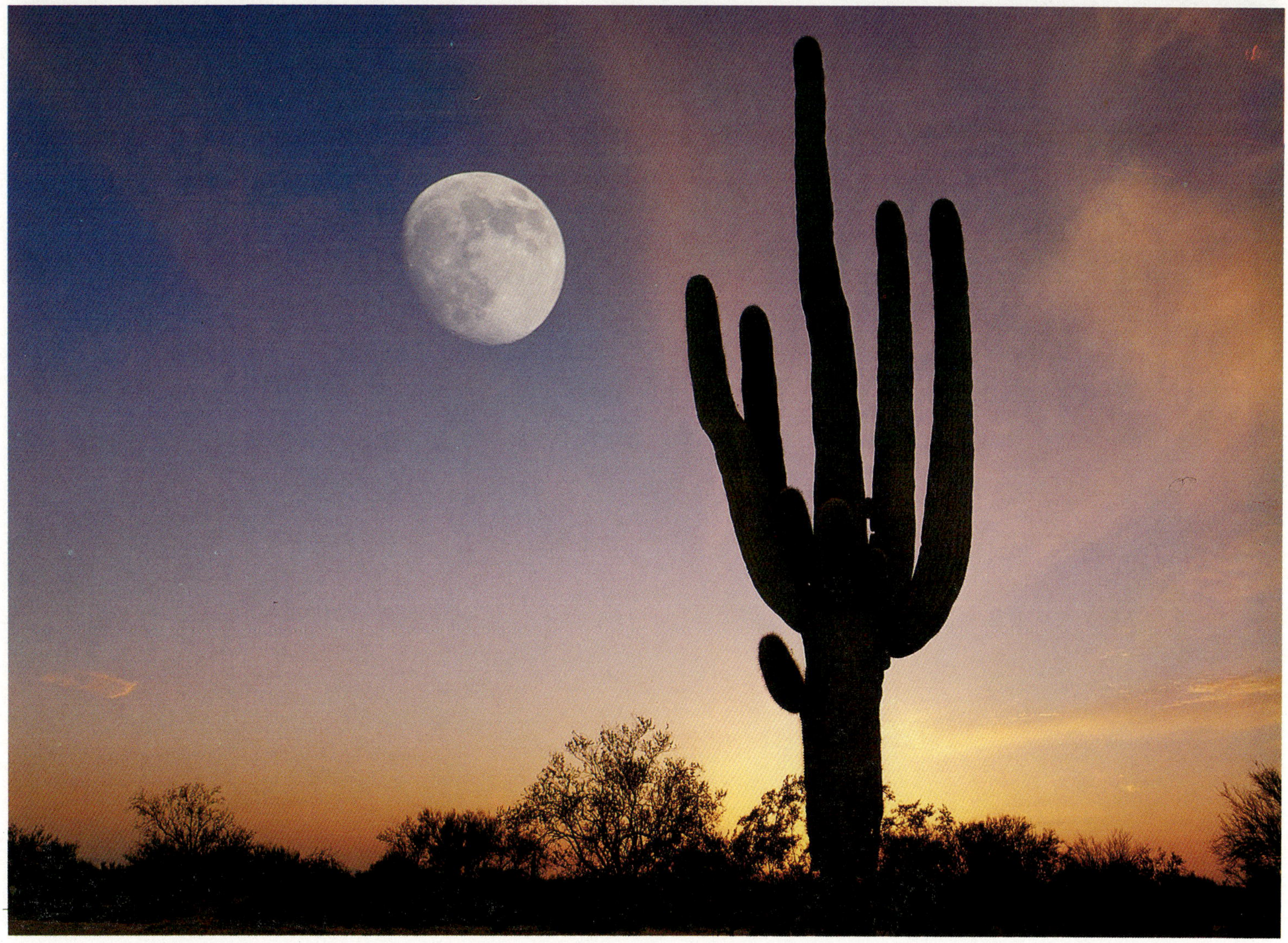

DOUBLE EXPOSURE DEVICES

To take the multi-coloured *waterfall* ***facing page,*** *the photographer divided the total exposure by the number of different colours he wanted in the finished shot. This required a neutral density filter to increase the exposure to manageable proportions. It was then a matter of mounting the camera on a tripod and making a series of exposures on the*

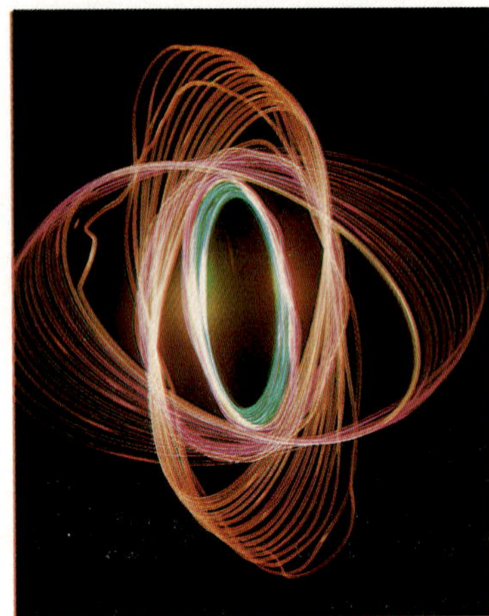

same frame, each through a different coloured filter. Thus, if the exposure was, say, four seconds at f16, each exposure was made at one second. Waving the camera about with the shutter open, in front of a point light source, was the method used to create the abstract ***facing page top left.*** *Several exposures were made on one frame, each through a different coloured filter. A similar method was used for the shots* ***above and right,*** *but this time the camera was securely mounted facing upwards, a torch was attached to the ceiling with string and swung in a circular pattern, and the shutter opened. Again, several exposures were made through coloured filters. A light, or lights, covered with coloured gels and moved around to create a pattern, with the camera shutter open and the studio blacked out, was followed by a flash exposure on the model to produce the shots* ***facing page bottom.***

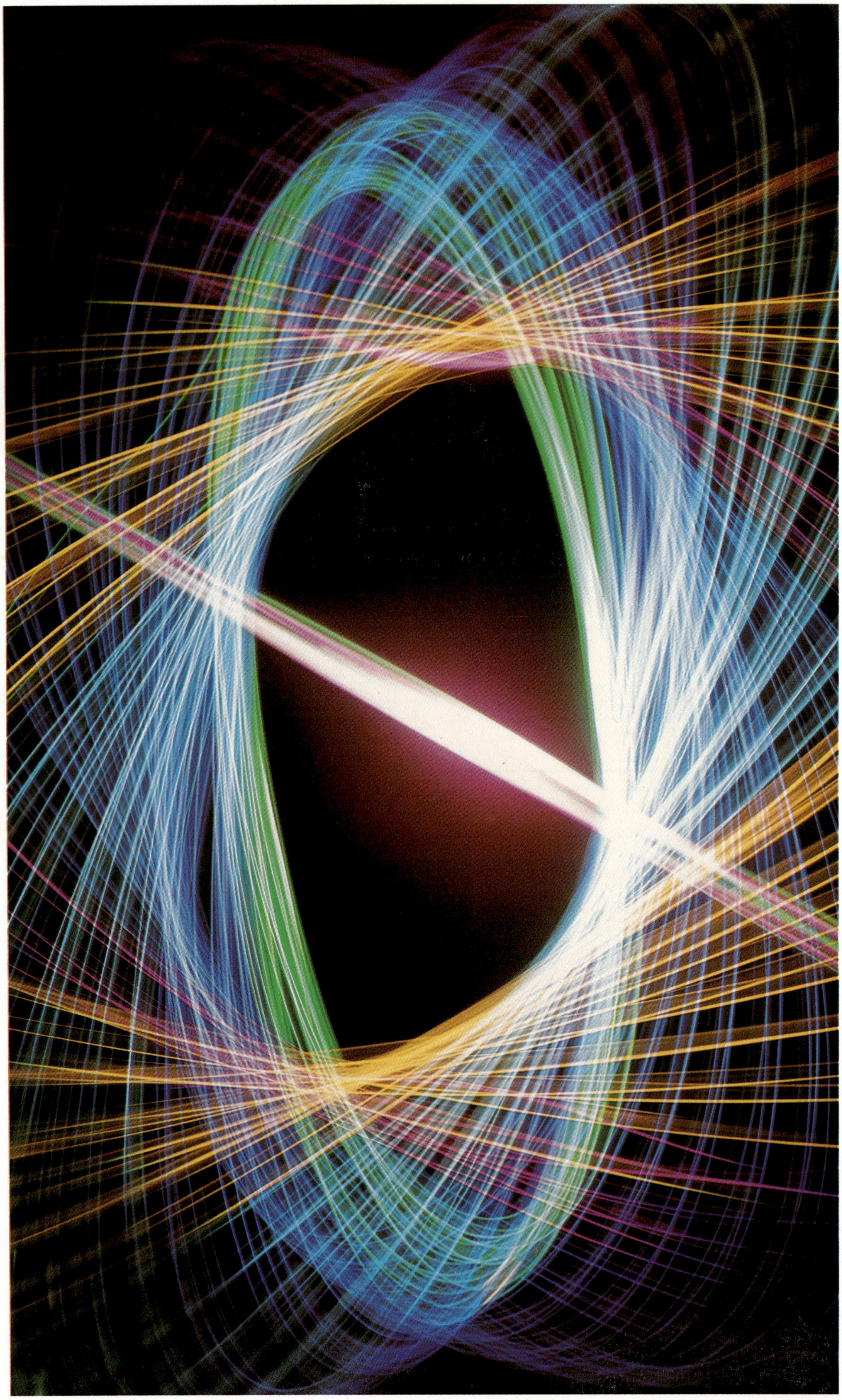

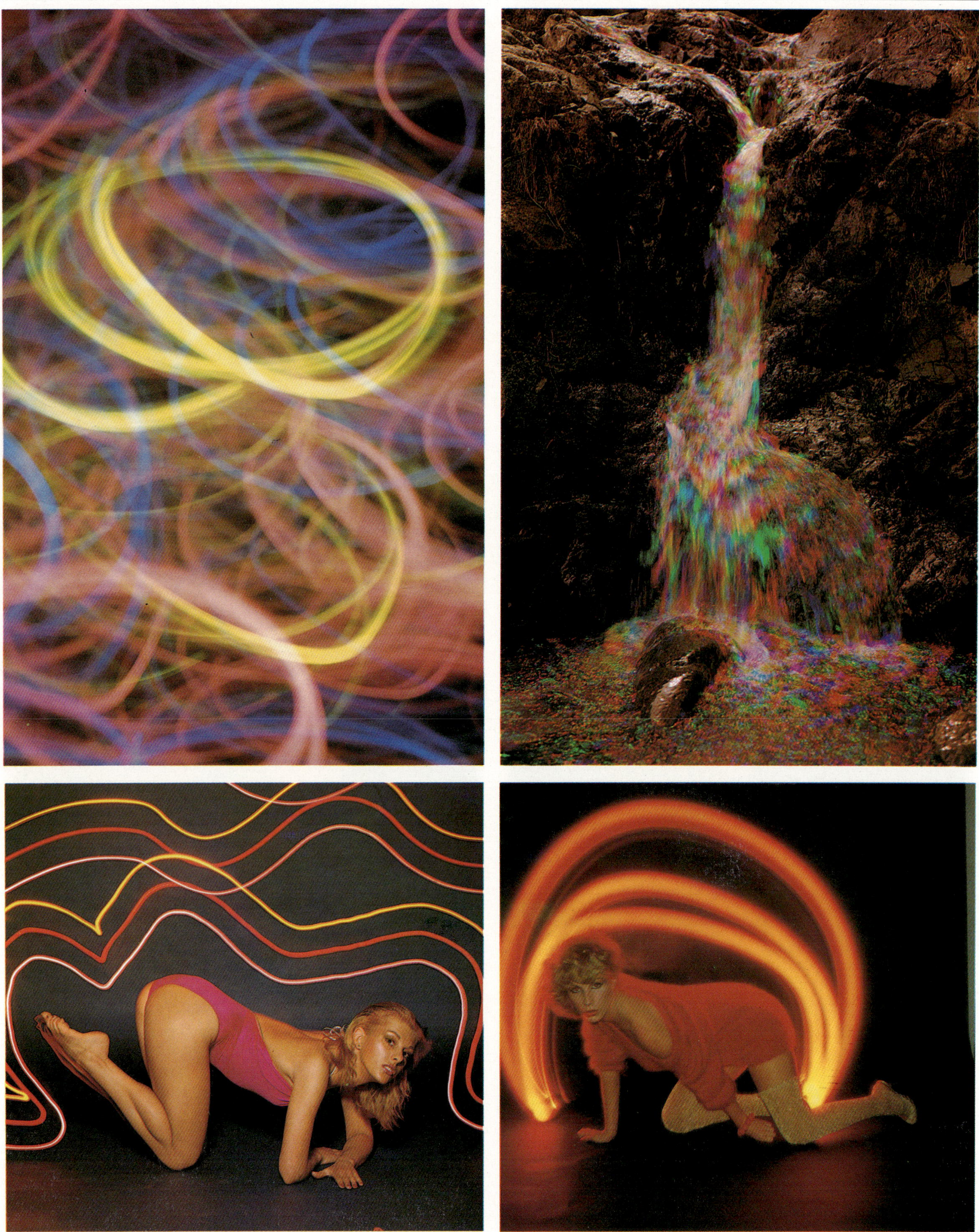

DO IT YOURSELF

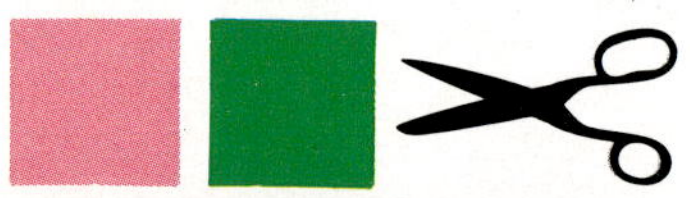

No matter how ingenious attachment makers become, there is always some photographer producing a do-it-yourself gadget. Realising this market, there is even a Cokin creative filter set, which can be hacked about at will. Perhaps the following story does not really come into the lens attachment category, yet it illustrates a point. Some years ago I knew a travel photographer who had a triangular pegboard device which fitted his camera from a tripod bush (apex) to forward of the lenshood (base). The holes in the pegboard could be filled with grass, flowers and/ or fitted with a square frame. This miniature garden was used to hide the foreground of unfinished hotels. With a beach attachment likewise, and the frame (suitably decorated), provided a nice surround for head shots of pretty girls. As all of

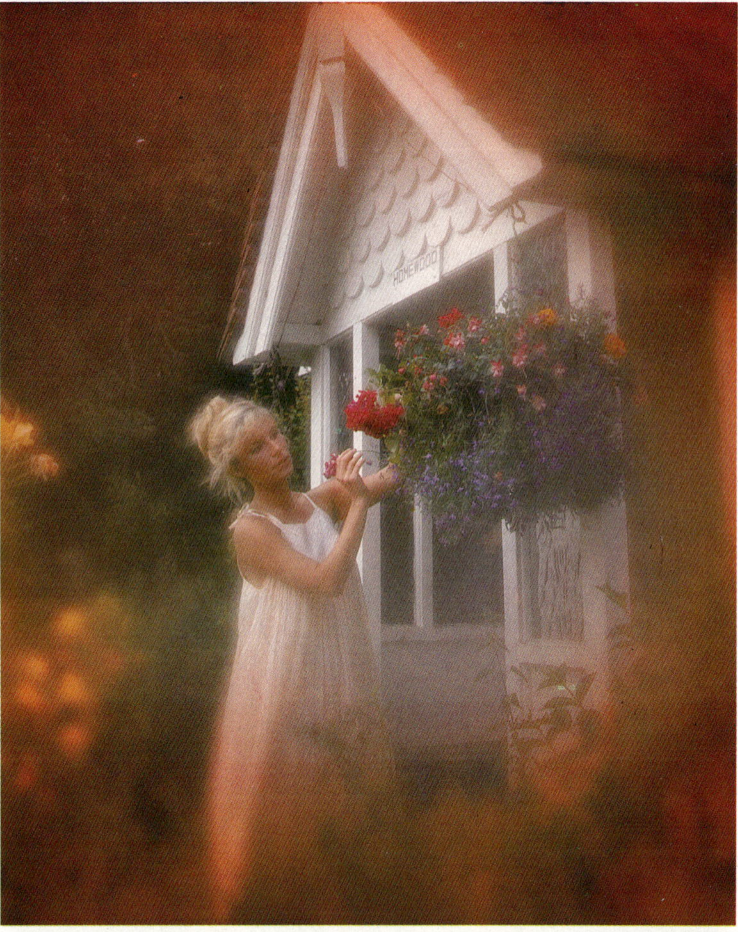

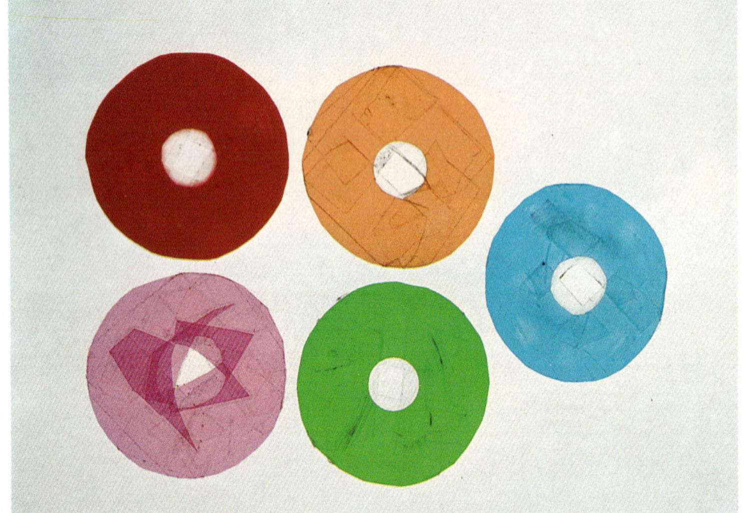

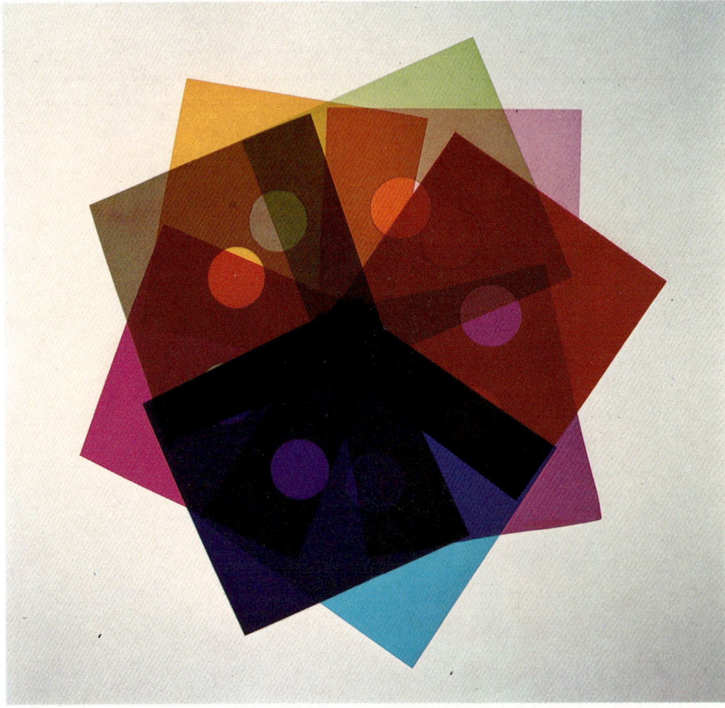

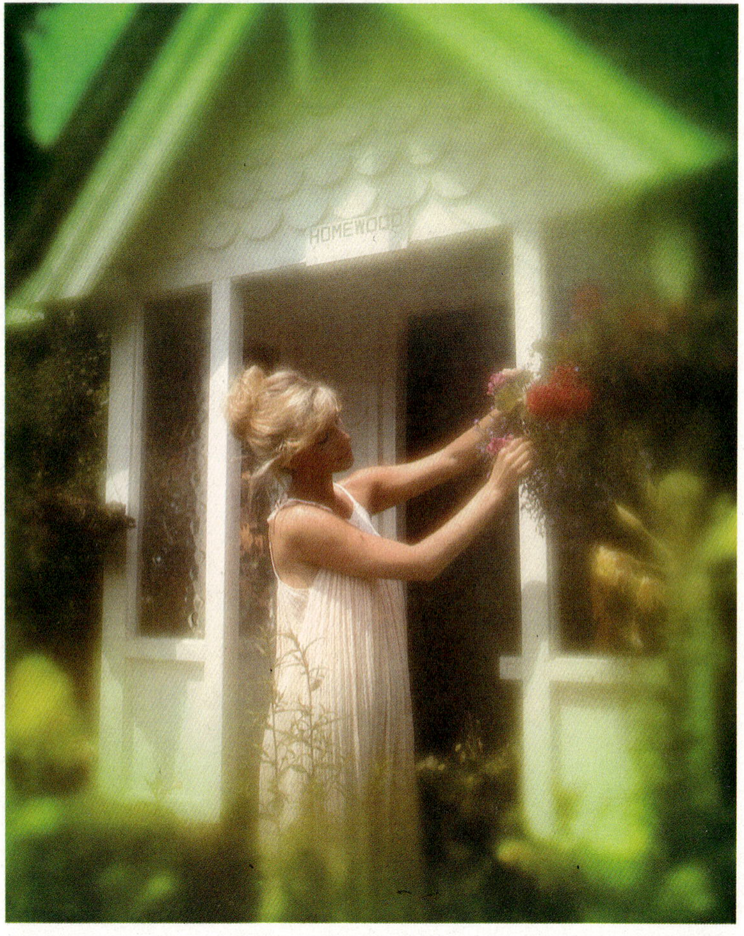

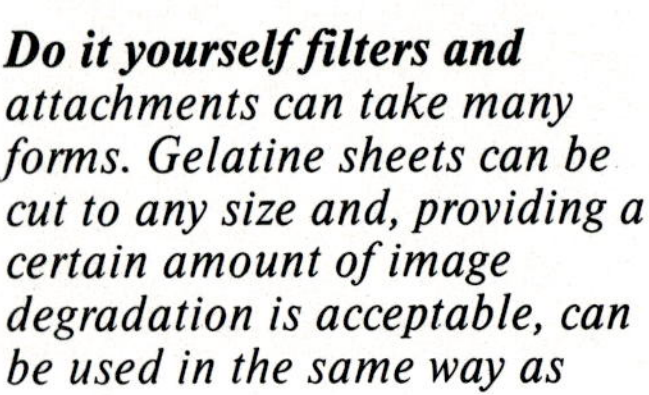

Do it yourself filters and *attachments can take many forms. Gelatine sheets can be cut to any size and, providing a certain amount of image degradation is acceptable, can be used in the same way as ordinary filters to colour the subject. Transparent tape can be added to increase the softening effect and holes can be cut quite easily, as above, with the aid of an engineers compass scriber.*

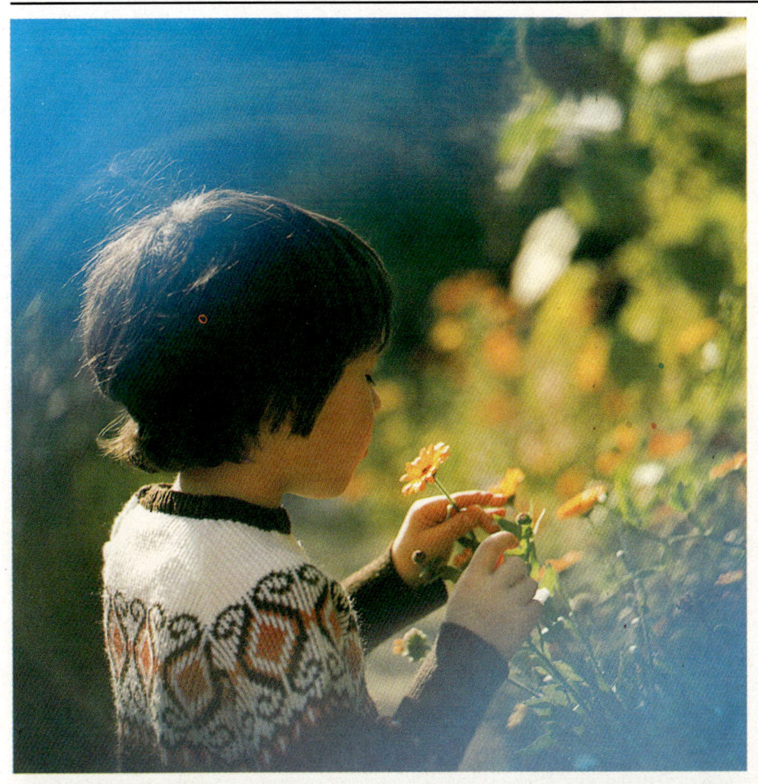

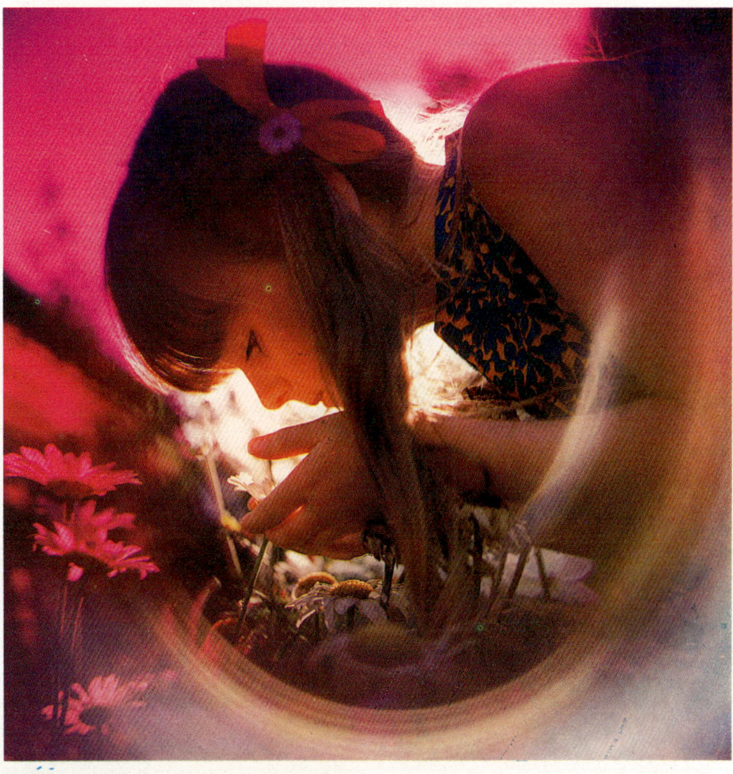

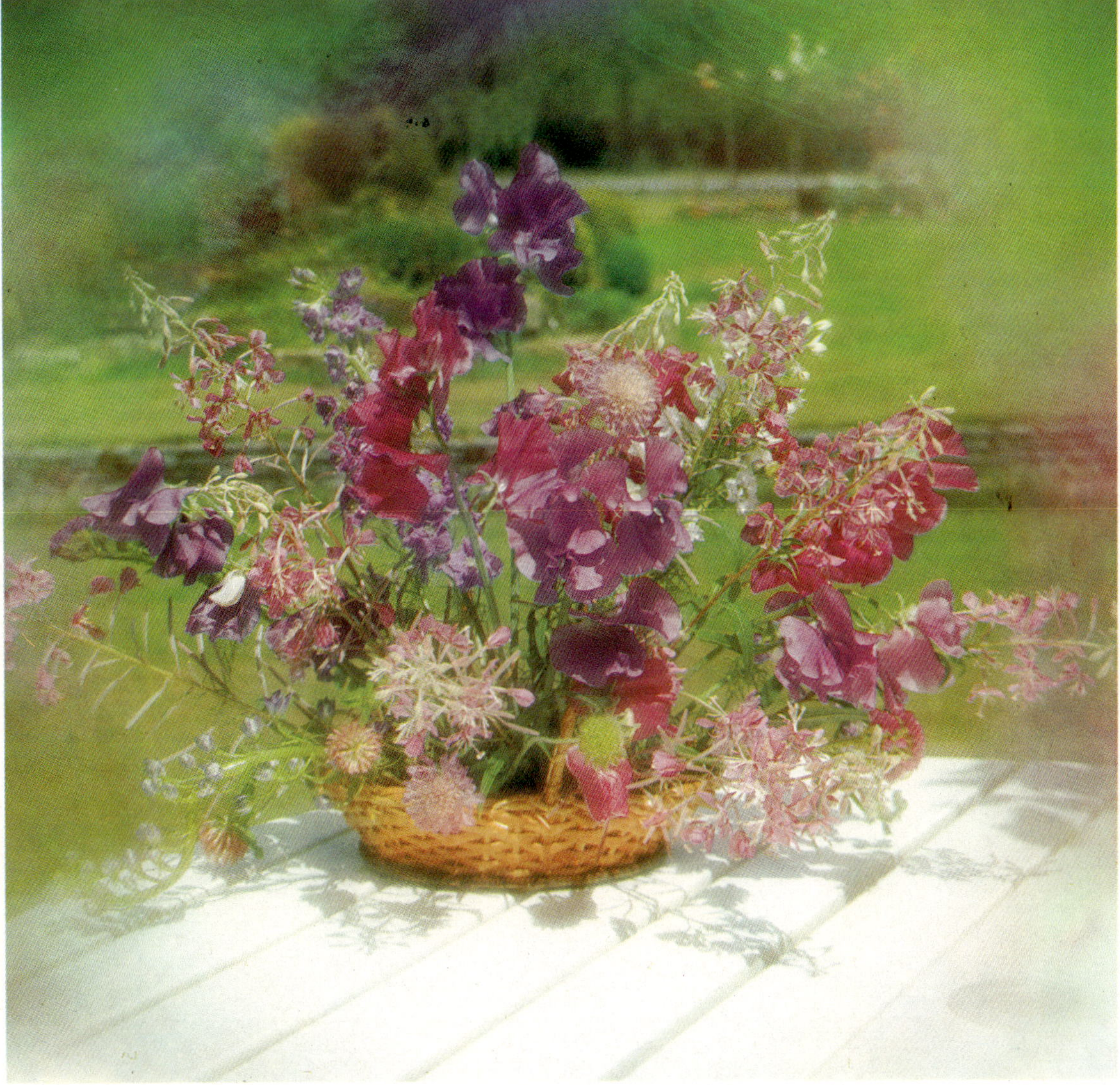

The effects that can be achieved *using the types of filters shown can be very similar to those obtained using proprietary items. They can be cut circular, to fit standard filter holders, but it may be found that changing from one colour to another is a fiddly, time-consuming business. A simpler method is to hold the squares of gel in front of the camera lens – though this requires that the camera is a single lens reflex. Several such squares, with or without an aperture cut in the centre, can be fixed at one corner by the use of a paper fastener, as in the illustration. By this means several filters are always to hand and hardly any space is taken up in the gadget bag. The more scratched the filters become, the more useful they are to soften and degrade the image and to scatter light. As an alternative, if no single lens reflex is available, a 'tube' can be fashioned from the gel, which fits over the lens mount. A little experimentation is required to determine the correct length, but both the pictures* ***above*** *were taken using this method.*

this could be used hand held, he preferred it to his previous portable foreground technique of carrying a table, cold drinks and sunglasses etc, in his car.

One of my favourite gadgets is the 75mm diameter base of a cut glass tumbler. Salvaged from a washing-up accident, it fitted neatly into an old lens hood. Attached to a standard or wide angle lens it turns mundane subjects into colourful abstracts. There is no point in focusing but the effect does change with the lens aperture used. 'Cut glass' transparencies have been sold for record, book and brochure covers, as well as for backgrounds to an audio-visual presentation. You can try this effect by inverting a complete tumbler over the lens.

Not yet manufactured is the 'gizmo'. Inspired perhaps by an American who used a tube in order to 'think' images on to a Polaroid film? The gizmo consists of a cardboard (or metal) tube about twice the length and diameter of a standard lenshood. Lined with mirror plastic – or aluminium cooking foil – it enables head shots of pretty girls to be surrounded by interesting abstract shapes and colours. It is better if the model is framed by colours and shapes to start with, though even a street background will do. It is essential to use a wide shooting aperture and it helps if the gizmo is adjustable for length.

Speckle filters consist of various coloured – or all the same colour – gelatin spots, casually arranged around a clear centre

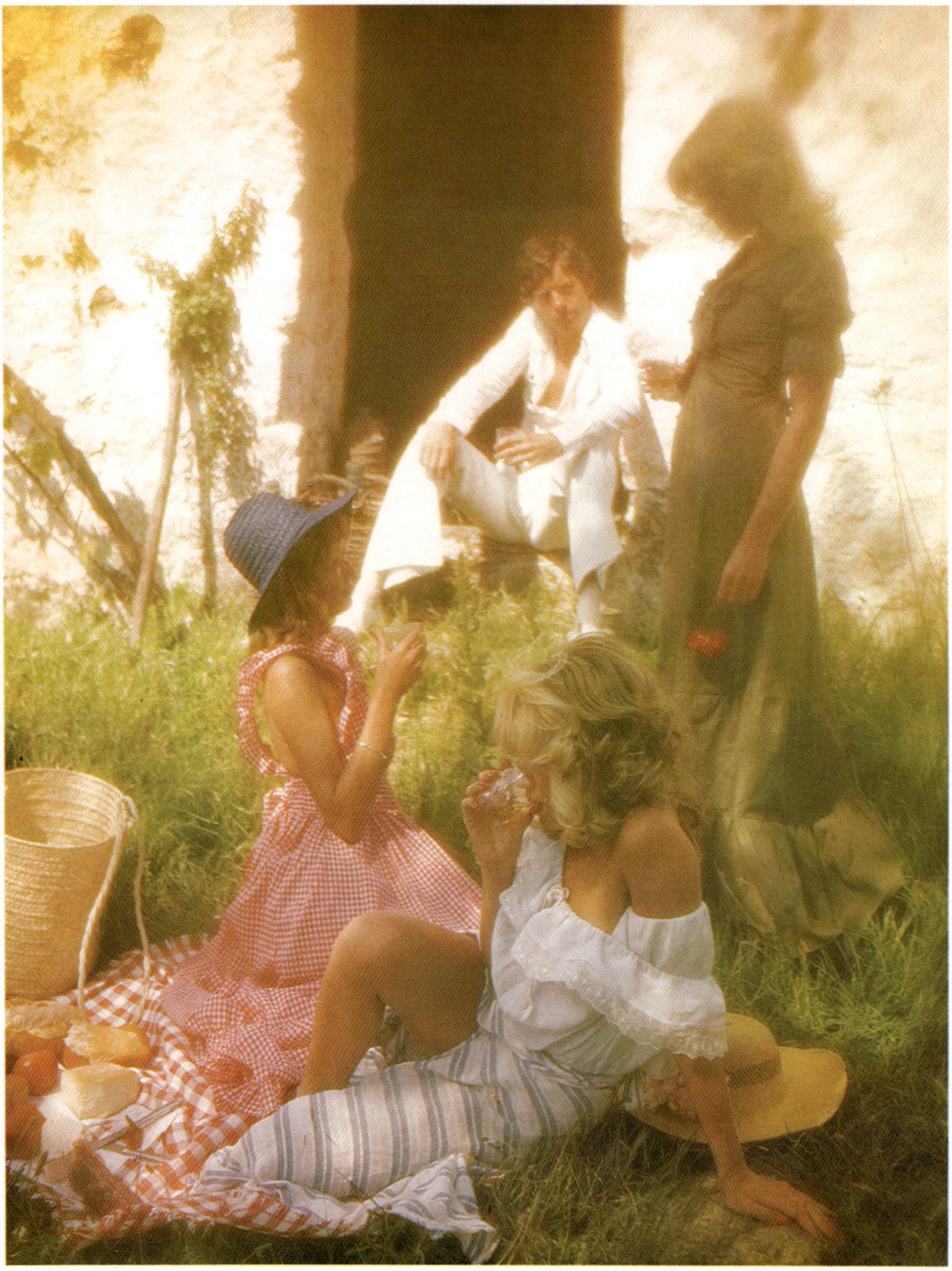

The 'Romantic' image is one *that lends itself to soft focus, degradation of image, and so on. It may seem ridiculous that we go to the expense of buying lenses that offer superb, biting sharpness, and then go to considerable lengths to destroy that sharpness – but such is*

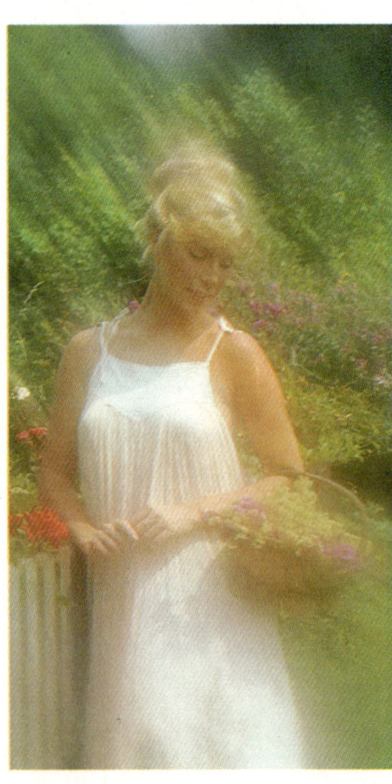

fashion, in photography as in anything else – and you have the advantage of sharpness for subjects that require it. Be careful in your choice of colours. Try not to introduce jarring colours, either in filtration, clothing, props or setting when attempting such pictures. The overall feeling should be one of calm and tranquillity. Smart clothes do not blend well with the idea, and this is why rather old fashioned, soft clothing features so much in settings like these. The minimum depth of field should be used; sharpness in the background is normally to be avoided.

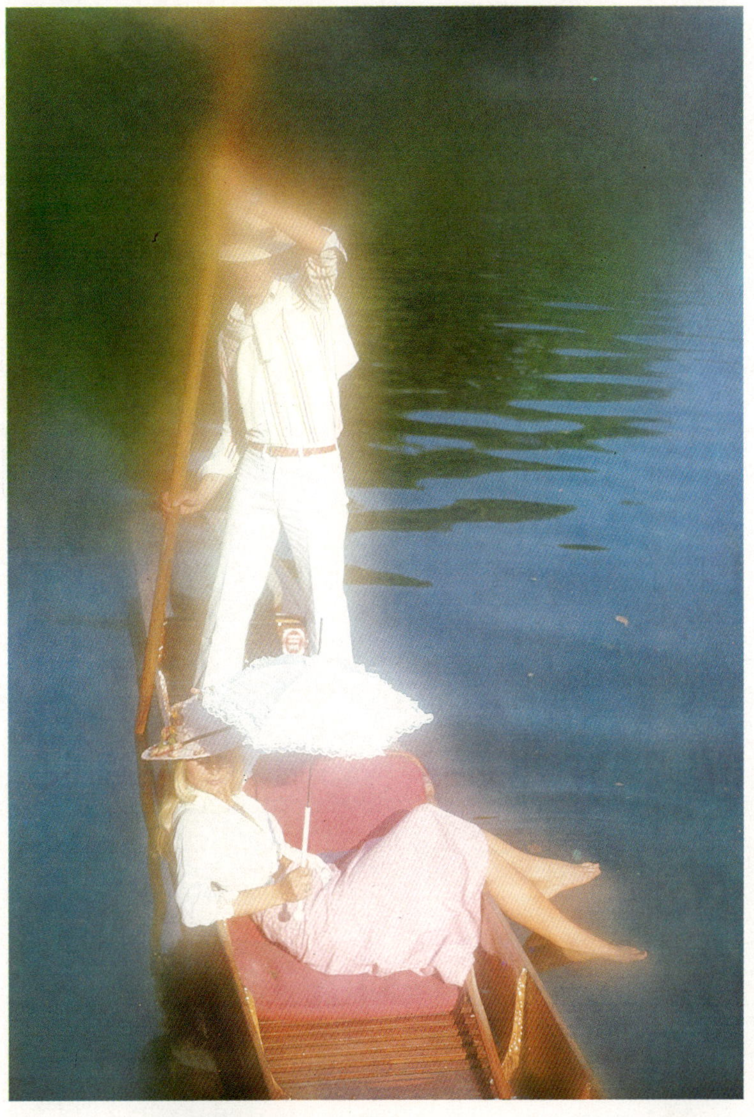

area. These spots can be cut out with scissors (larger) and/or produced with a ring binder paper punch (smaller), and then bound between lantern slide cover glasses, or in a 6 x 6cm slide mount. I have also seen this type of filter produced by using self adhesive clear plastic on a cover glass, a scalpel then being used to cut a clear centre area.

A Kaleidoscope filter is produced by the same means but the gelatin, or acetate, is cut into triangular or oblong shapes. Toy kaleidoscopes can be modified for photographic use although the image quality of the main subject will be poor.

Both speckle and kaleidoscope filters can be taped to the front of a lenshood in the absence of a suitable holder. They should be used at a wide lens aperture, as smaller openings will bring the filter into sharper focus.

In a similar vein is the use of an unwanted colour transparency – again with a hole cut in it. This should be at least 6 x 6cm, or part of a 5 x 4" as otherwise it will not be big enough to cover a lenshood aperture.

Speckles, kaleidoscopes and old transparencies all work well in conjunction with a gizmo, particularly if the main subject is photographed against a white background. I could also mention home-made distortion filters, and how to produce your own graduated filters, to say nothing of stripeys – but then one has to leave something to the imagination of others, doesn't one?

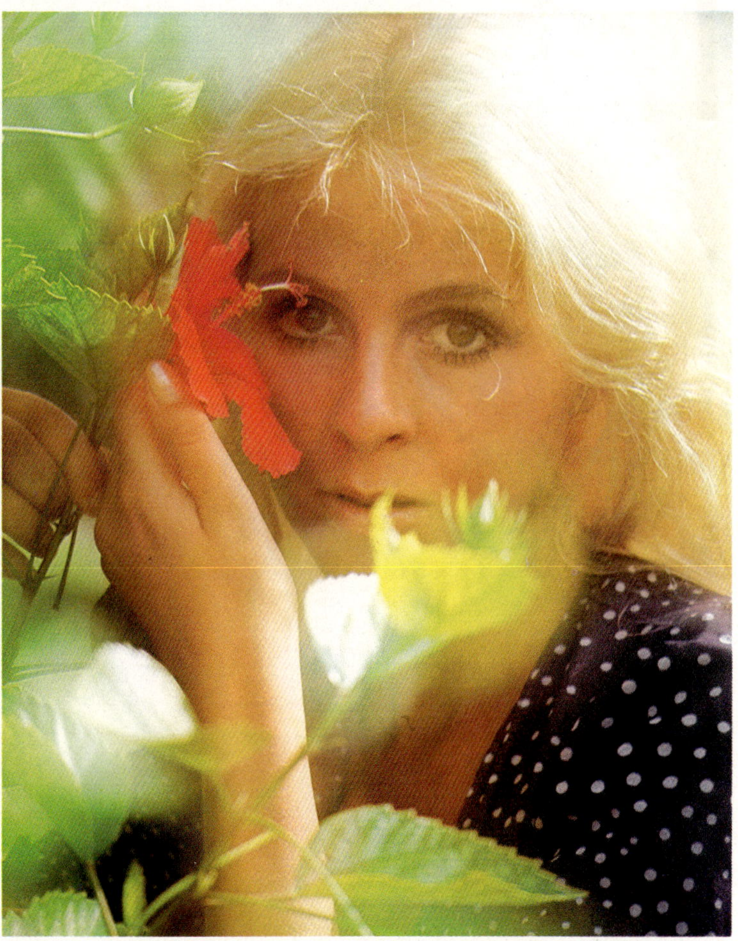

Filters you make yourself may *not be as predictable as the manufactured variety; they may not always produce the result you expect, but they will invariably produce 'different' pictures. If that is what you want, then sweet wrappings, crumpled cellophane, nylons and net curtaining can all be used – the limit is your imagination and ingenuity.*

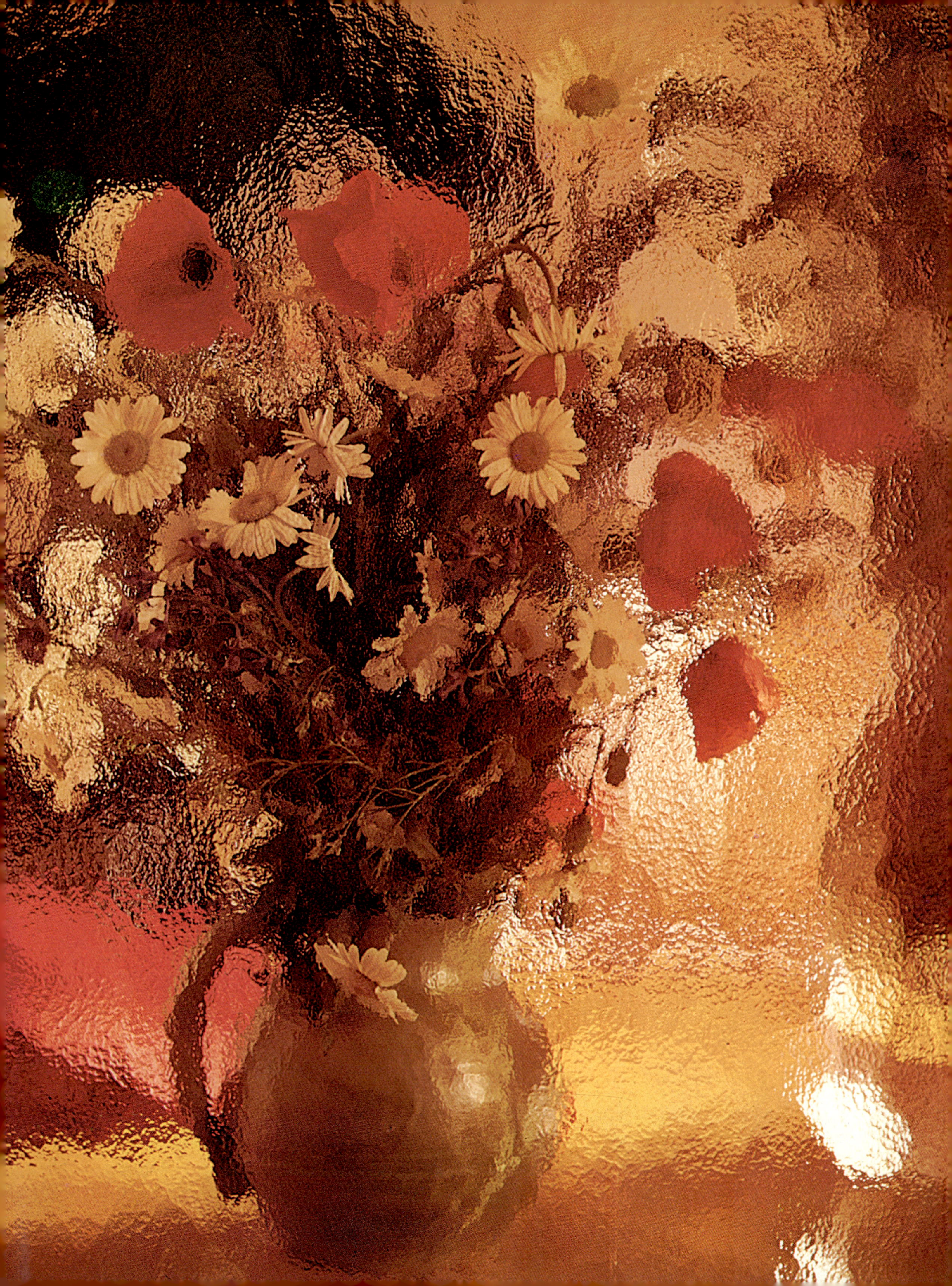

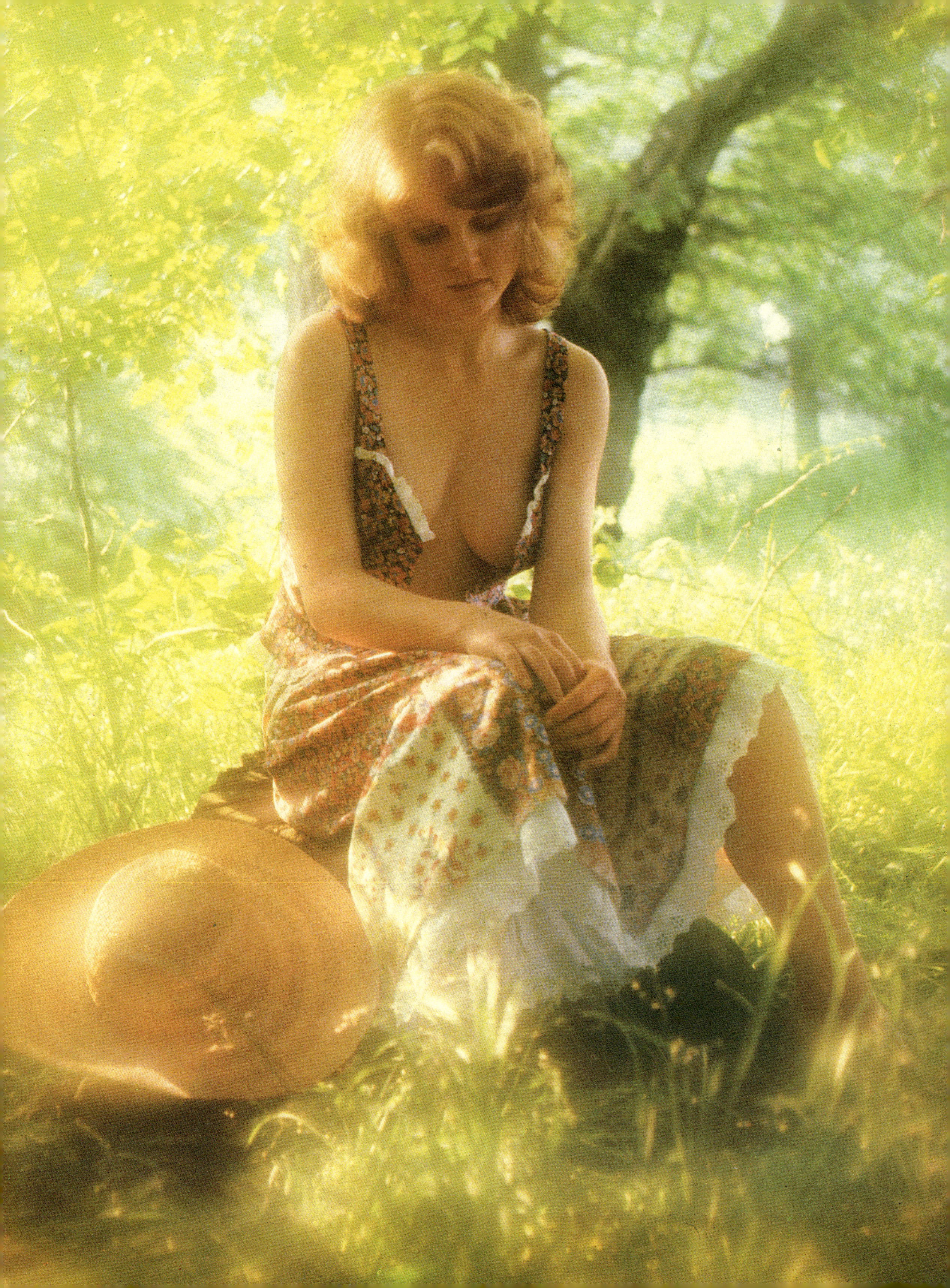

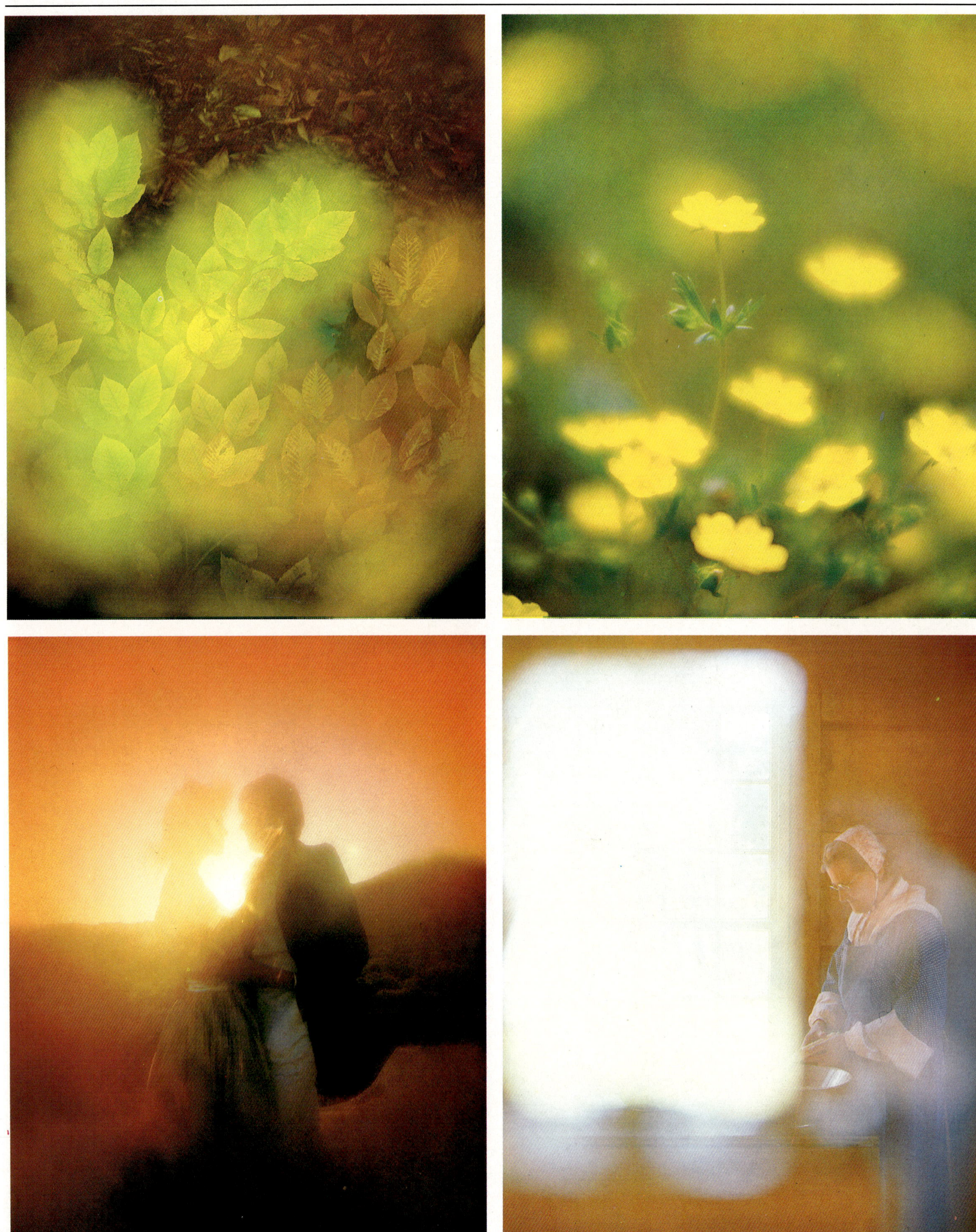

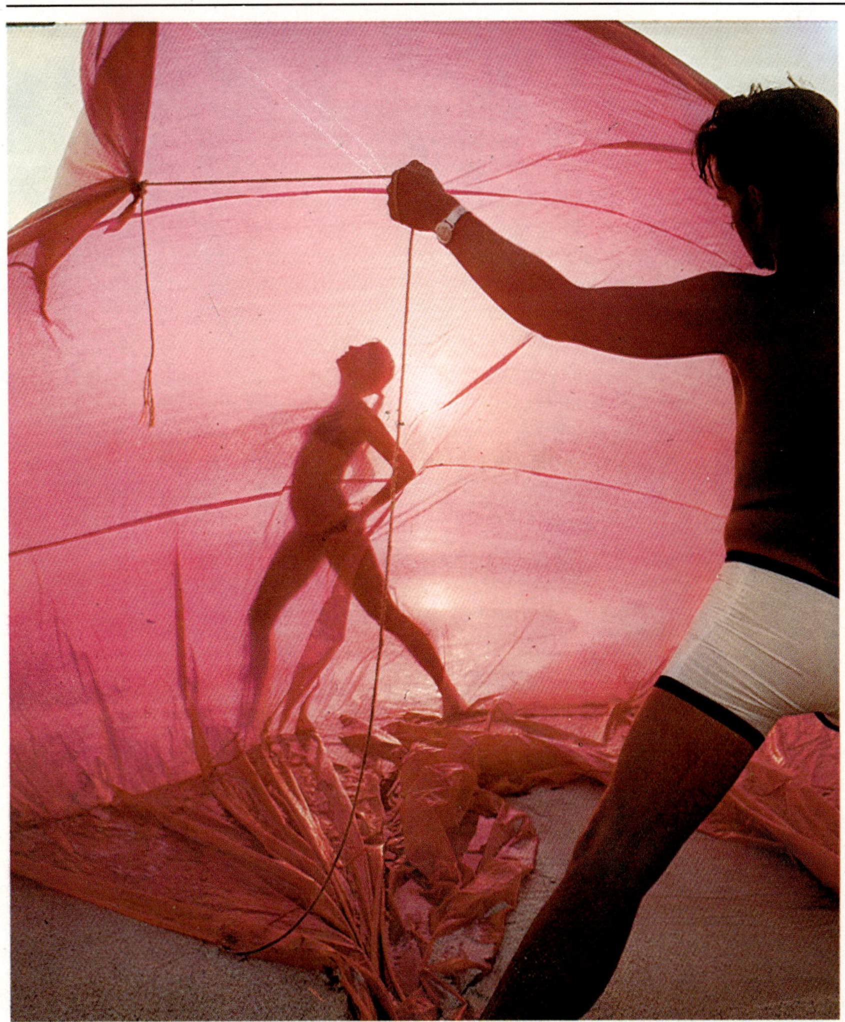

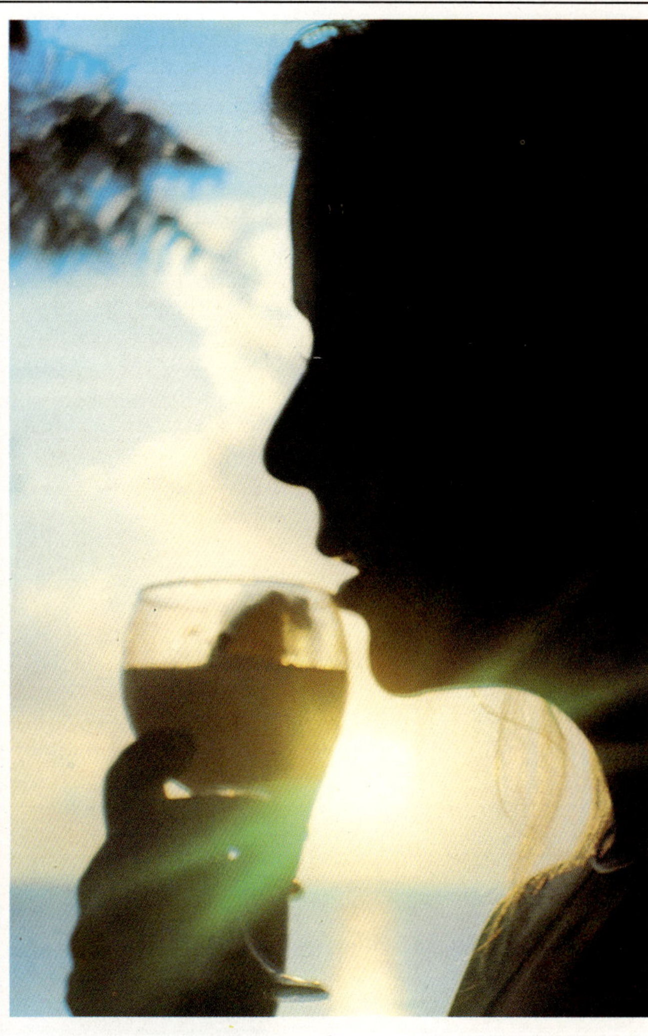

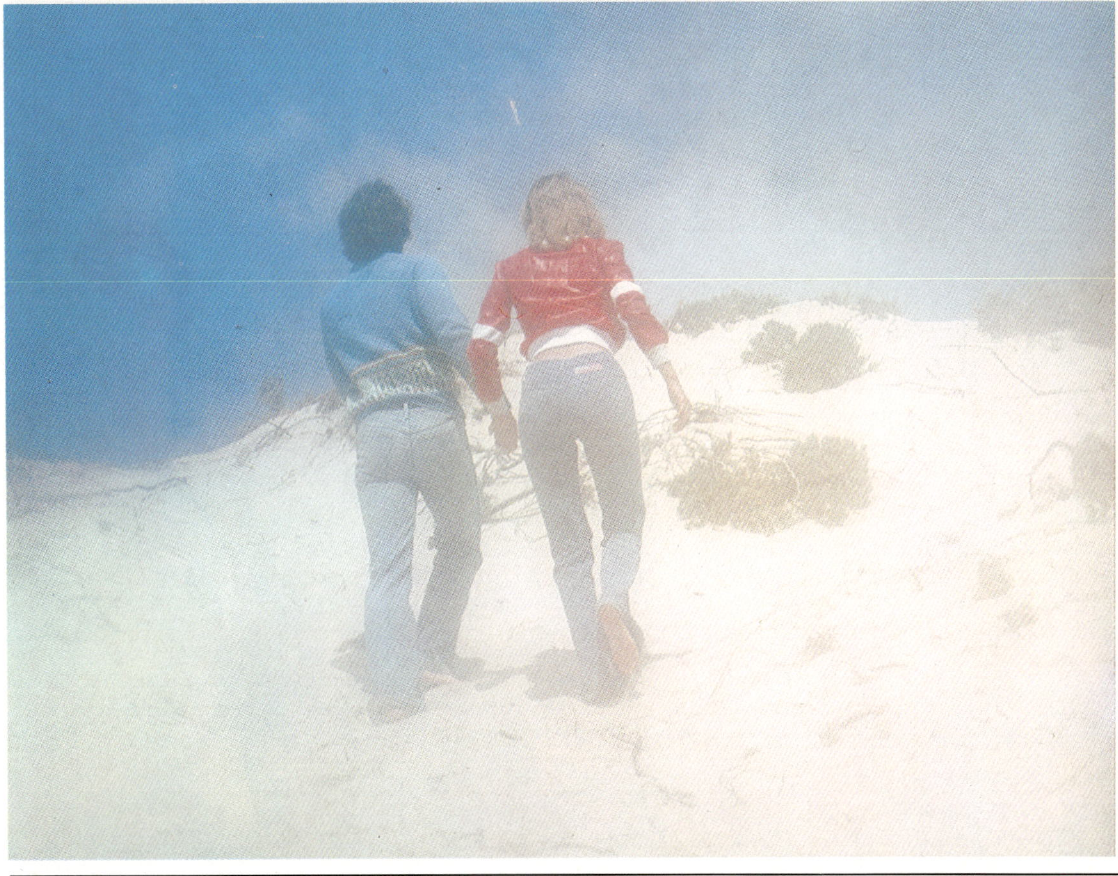

The picture on the facing page *has something of the look of an impressionist painting. It was produced by standing a sheet of hammered, frosted glass, such as is used for bathroom windows, in front of the subject. Note that the flowers closest to the glass appear relatively undistorted compared with those further away, which become merely coloured shapes. The picture* ***above left*** *shows, better than words, how imagination and ingenuity can produce a striking image. A blue gel with cut out centre, held well in front of the lens* ***left*** *transformed a rather ordinary shot. The same technique was used for the picture* ***above,*** *exposure being calculated for the background so as to preserve the silhouette. Notice how the yellow of the sun has combined with the blue of the gel to create the green flare under the glass. Moving the camera, or the gel, even a few inches would have changed the feeling completely.*

CLOSE-UP LENSES

There are two ways to achieve close-ups. The first is to extend the distance between lens and film plane by means of extension tubes or bellows, and the second is to use a close-up lens. The former needs adjusted exposure when a TTL metering system is absent, whilst the latter does not, under any circumstances. Extension tubes or bellows can achieve subject/image ratios of 1:1 with ease. Close-up lenses are not really satisfactory at ratios of more than 1:4.

For many years close-up lenses were known by the generic name of Proxars – a trade name of the Carl Zeiss company who did so much to popularise the idea. The range was then nos. 1, 2 and 3. These figures correspond to a dioptre, which is a focal length of one metre. Strangely perhaps, a two dioptre lens has a focal length of half a metre, a three dioptre of a third of a metre and so on. Unfortunately, what was a nice standard of measurement has not been adhered to by many manufacturers, so that one maker's number four lens could be number four in his range and not necessarily of four dioptres. I can only suggest that you check maker's figures before purchase.

The optical result of adding a close-up lens to a prime lens is effectively to shorten the focal length of that lens, which means that the combination can focus closer within the range of the existing focusing mount movement. Most close-up lenses come with a table which at least shows camera to subject distances of an approximate nature, when a standard focal length lens is set to infinity or its closest focusing distance. Leitz, in their traditionally precise manner, also give reproduction ratios, field sizes and depth of field for whichever lenses in their range are suitable. Dioptre strengths range photographically from 0.25 (weakest) to 10 (strongest). There have been 20 dioptre lenses made, in an attempt to reach 1:1 subject/image ratio. These were so strong that the results were awful, the same unfortunately being true of many of the 10 dioptre lenses around.

The quality of close-up lenses varies as much as with any other lens. The best will be made to the same standard as the makers camera lenses, be multicoated and fitted in a precision mount. After all, you are in effect adding an extra element to your prime lens, with all that this entails, and this is what you pay for. The very best close-up lenses are achromats, which are of two element cemented construction. Using two glasses of different refractive indices allows for greater corrections to be made. This is not of great concern if your subject is a flower or a kitten's head, but if the original is linear and you need edge definition, then an achromat is essential.

Close-up lenses are not suitable for every type of prime lens. Few (if any) 50mm f1.4 and no f1.2 lenses are suitable candidates. After all, this is not what they were designed for. Exactly the same is true for wide angle lenses where there is a good chance that fall-off in illumination and vignetting will occur. The exceptions to this are the non-retrofocus wide angle lenses used on rangefinder focusing cameras, which can be used with close-up lenses. However, there are then framing problems.

Three component sets of close-up lenses can be used in combination which allows even closer camera/subject distances. As long as one realises that this is adding perhaps three extra elements and six air/glass surfaces to the prime lens, and that there will be a decrease in contrast and resolution, then this is fine. A flower subject, for instance, could still be attractively rendered.

Zoom lenses, with a shortest focal length of 70mm and up, can be used with close-up lenses, though most now seem to have a built-in macro facility anyway. Like longer telephotos and long

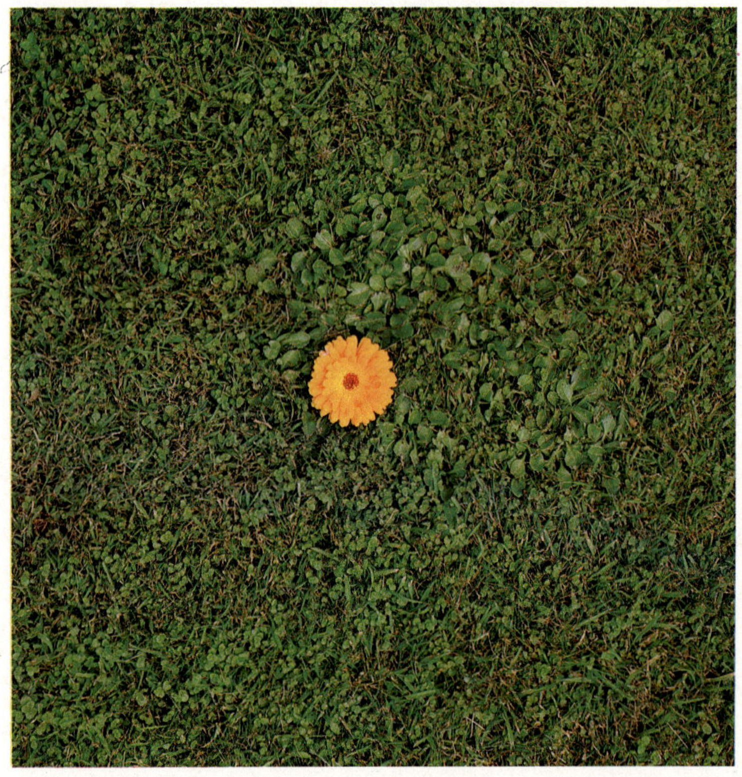

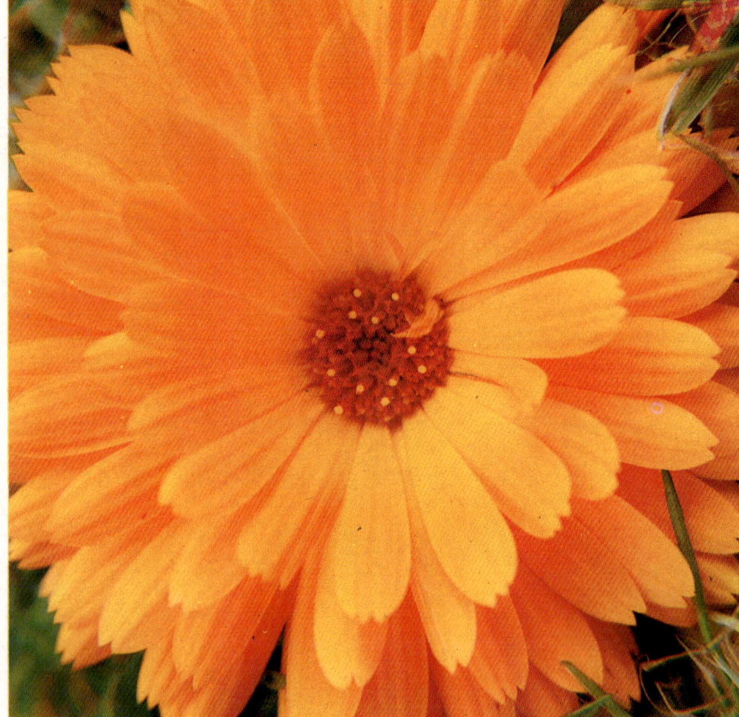

For ultimate quality, extension *tubes, bellows and/or a well-corrected micro lens are unbeatable for close up work. Bellows and tubes, however, do have the disadvantage that, because of the increased extension between lens and film, valuable film speed is sacrificed. Shallow depth of field, or long exposure times, have to be accepted. Light, easily carried and used close up lenses, therefore, are very useful items indeed and can provide acceptable quality. Closest focusing distance with a Hasselblad and 80mm lens is shown* ***above left,*** *and* ***above and right*** *the dramatic difference that can be achieved with close up lenses.*

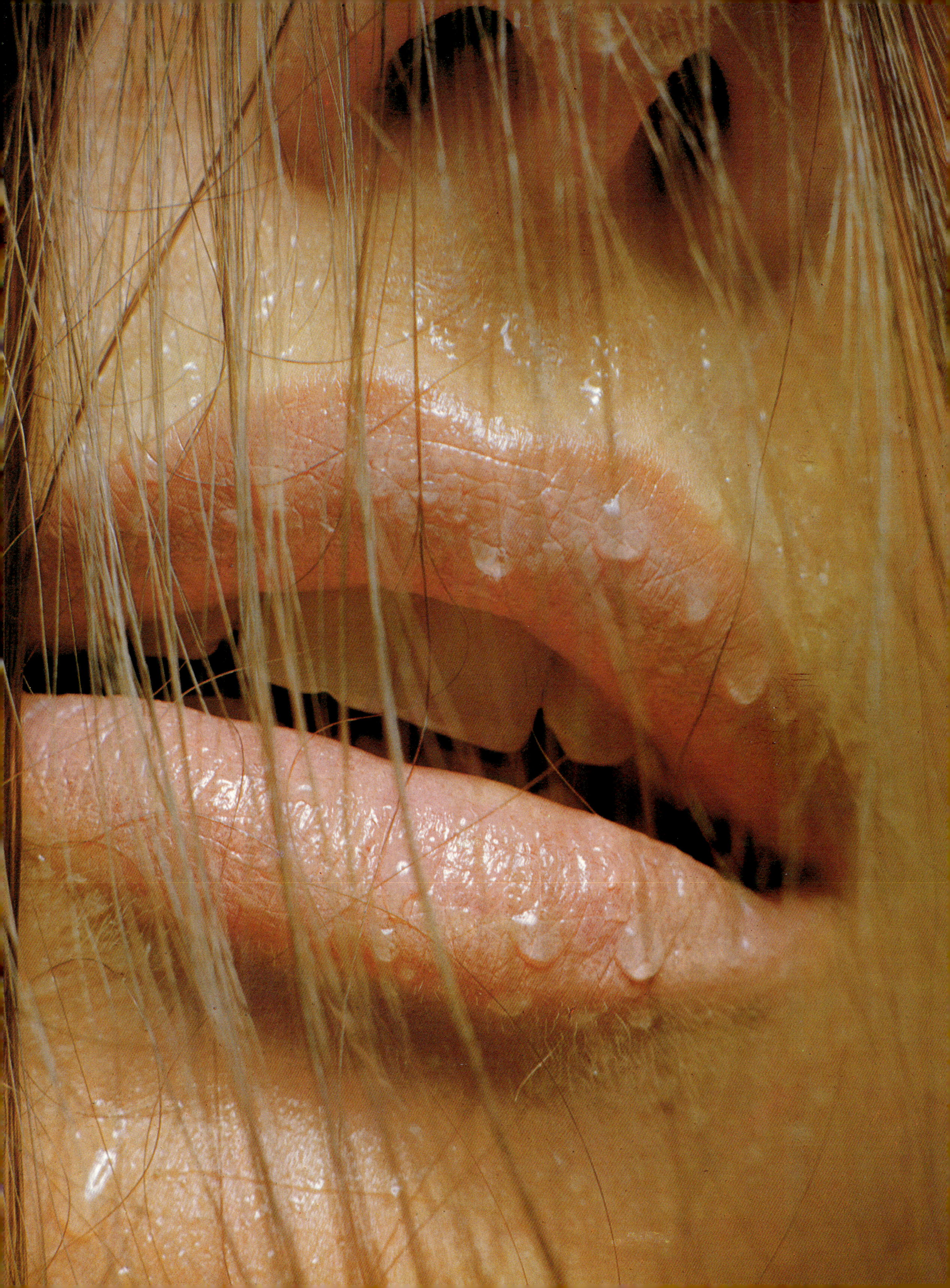

CLOSE-UP LENSES

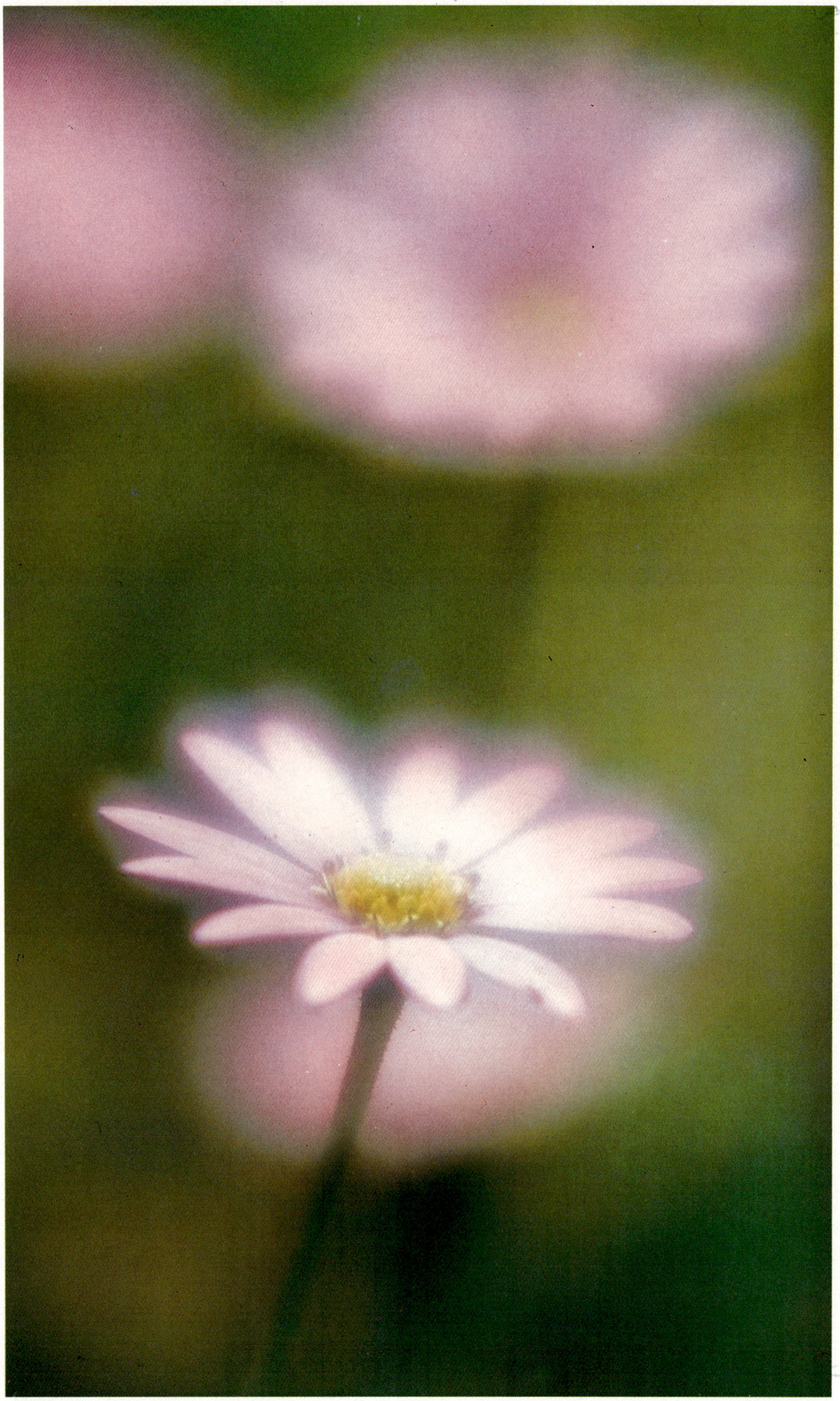

***Patience, timing and** anticipation are important requirements in taking close ups such as those **below, right and bottom.** Creatures that appear to move relatively slowly*

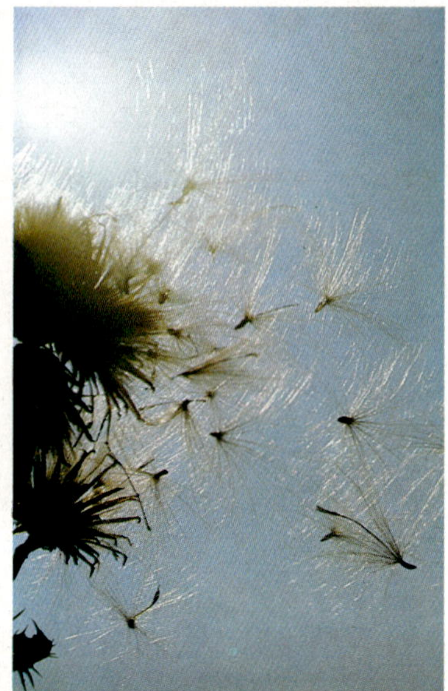

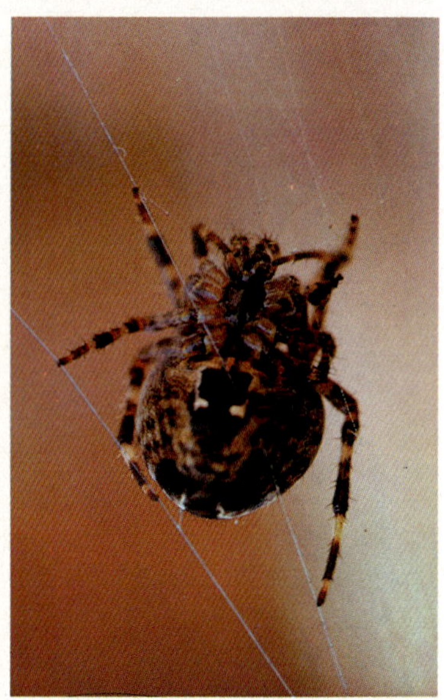

*actually move much faster than is realised, and the lack of depth of field can make them appear as meaningless blurs. Flowers are favoured subjects for close ups. They allow ample time for composition to be considered and are very beautiful in their own right. Soft focus lenses, or diffusers, can be combined with close up lenses **left** to create soft, ethereal subjects of considerable appeal. The shot of marbles in a glass jar **right** was taken using a Bronica SQ and +3 close up lens. All pictures on these pages were taken hand-held.*

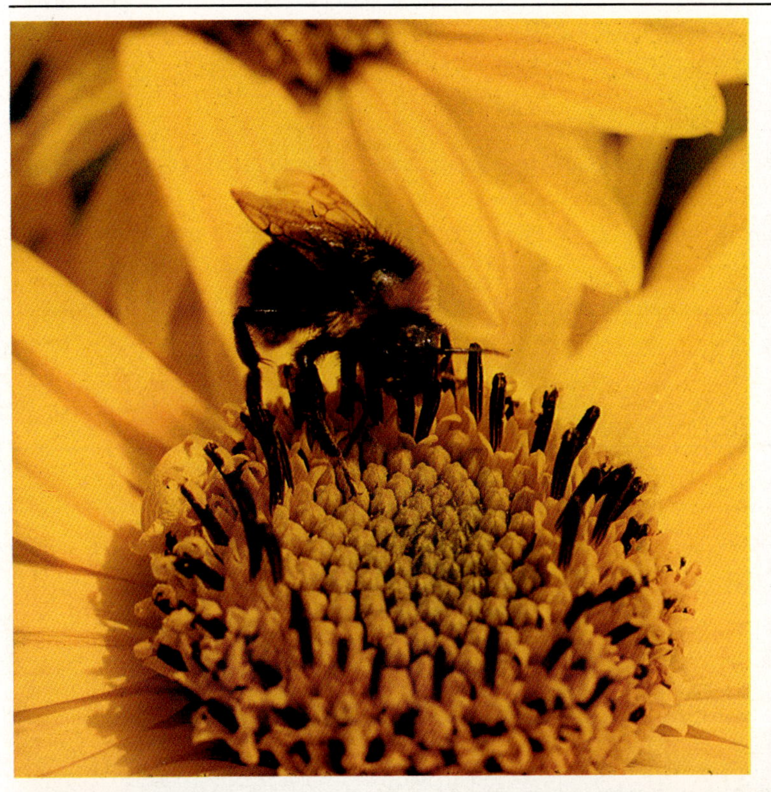
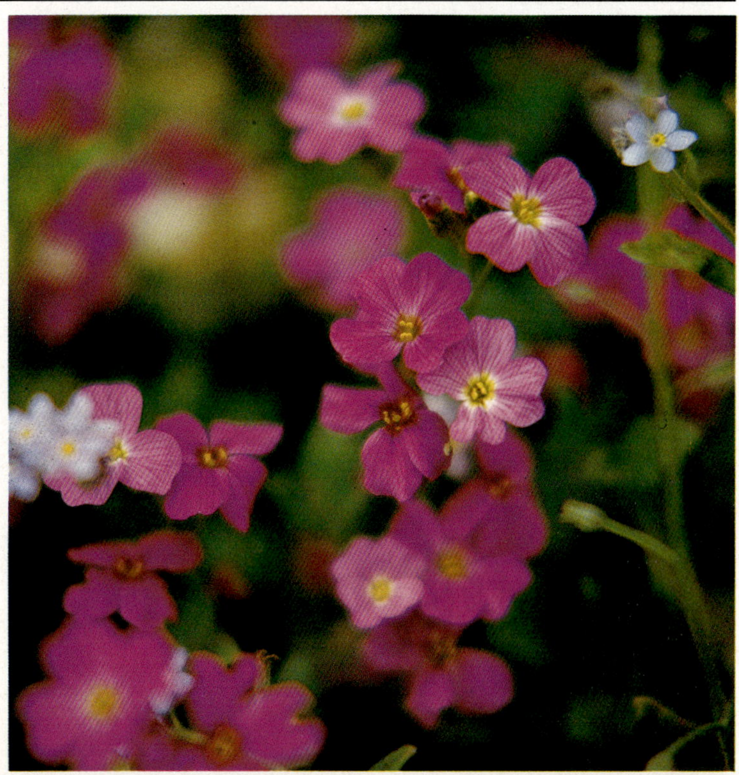

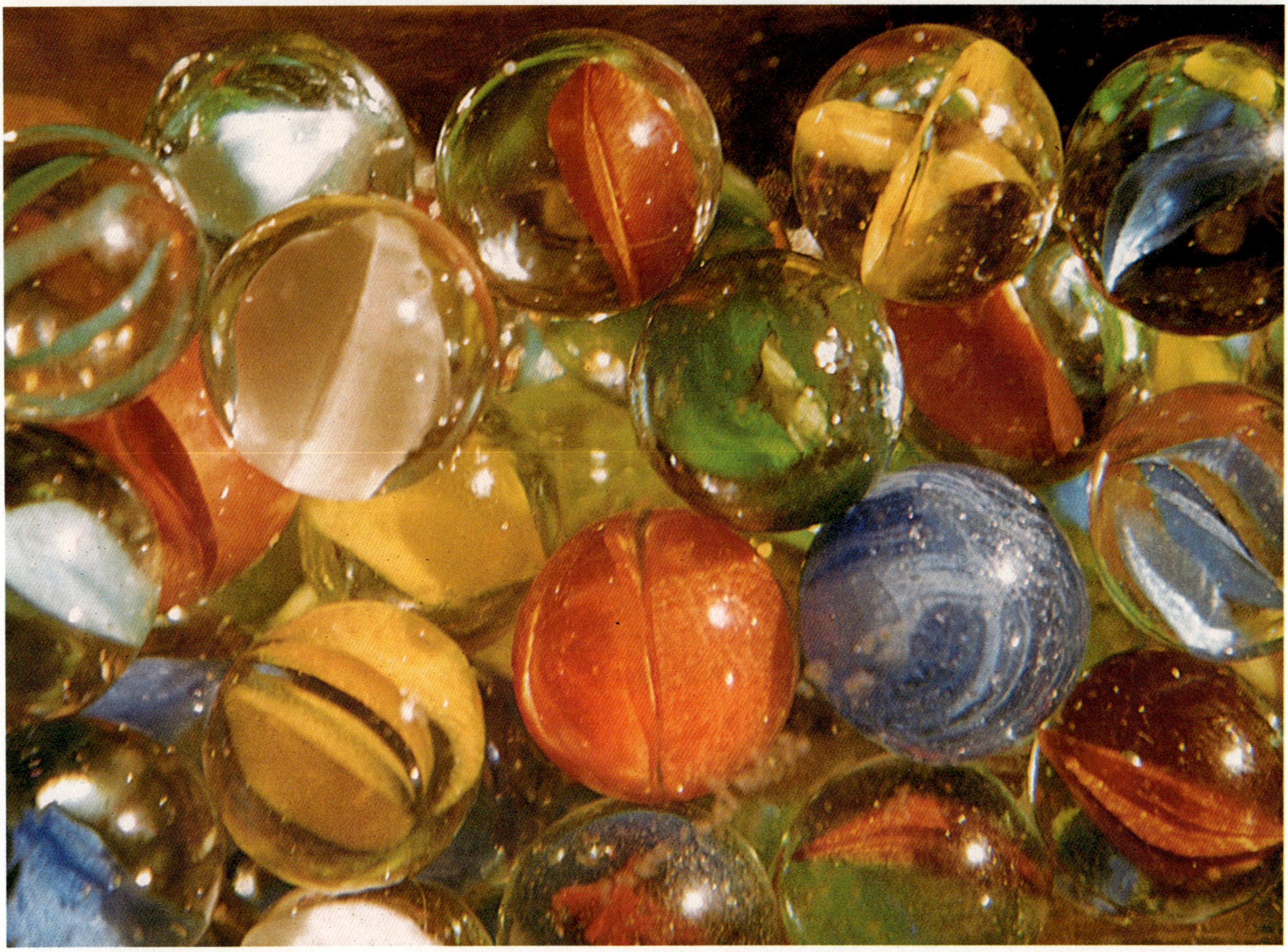

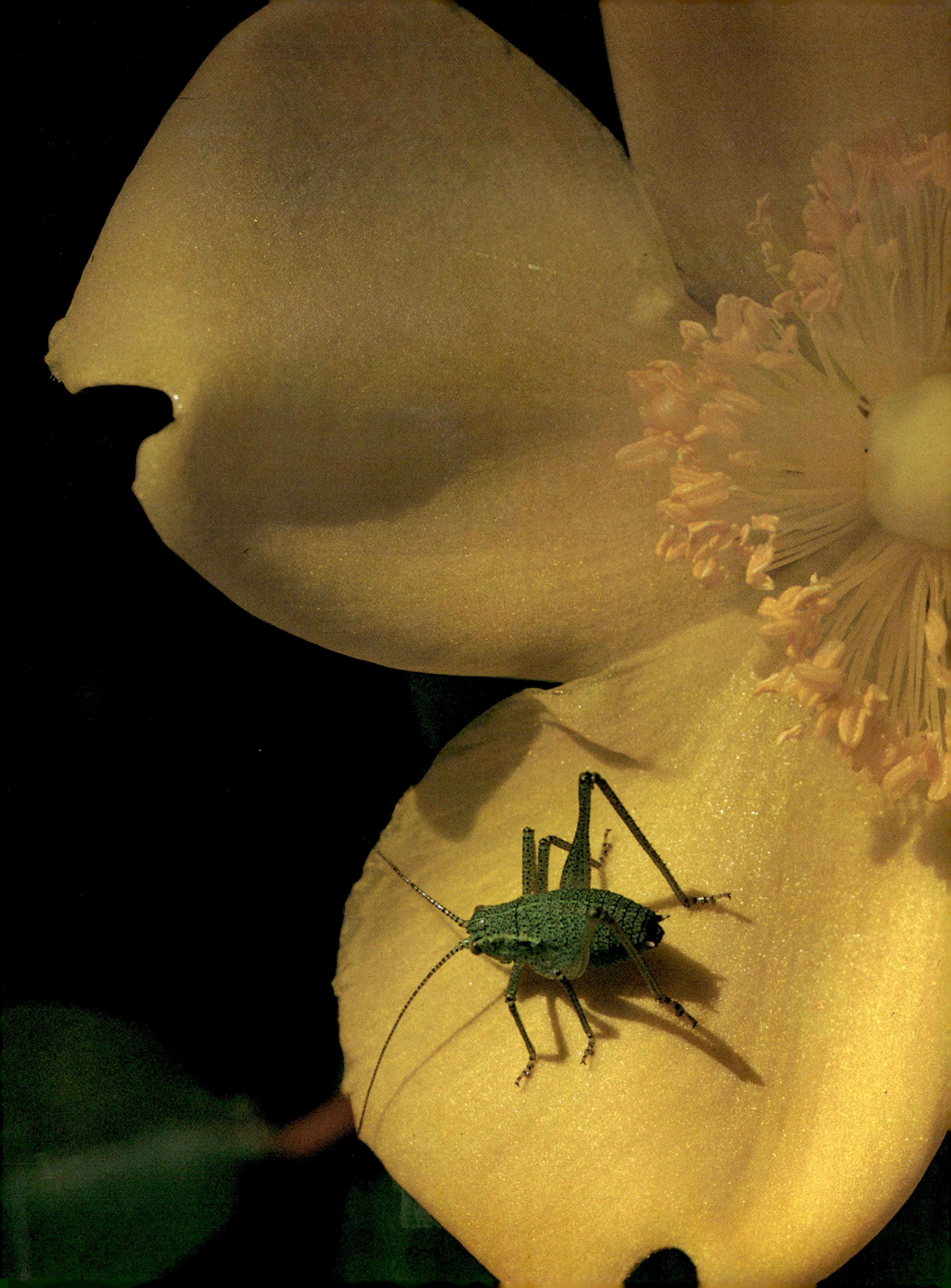

CLOSE-UP LENSES

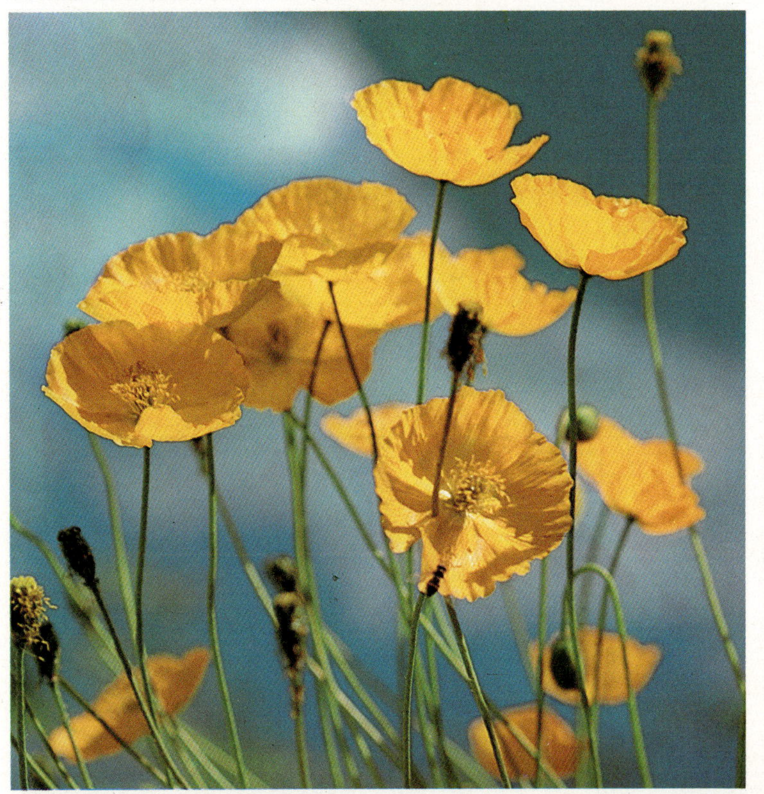

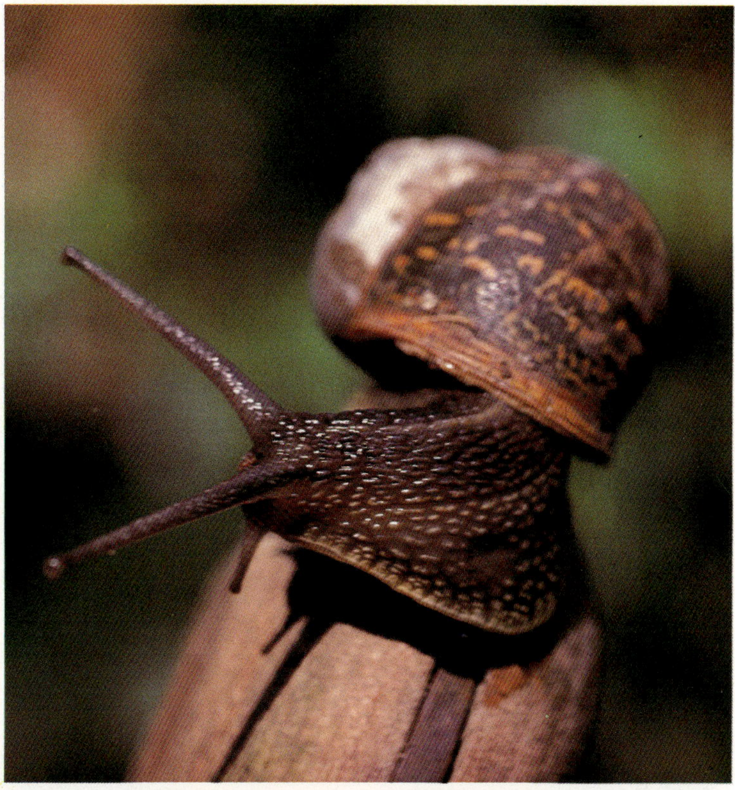

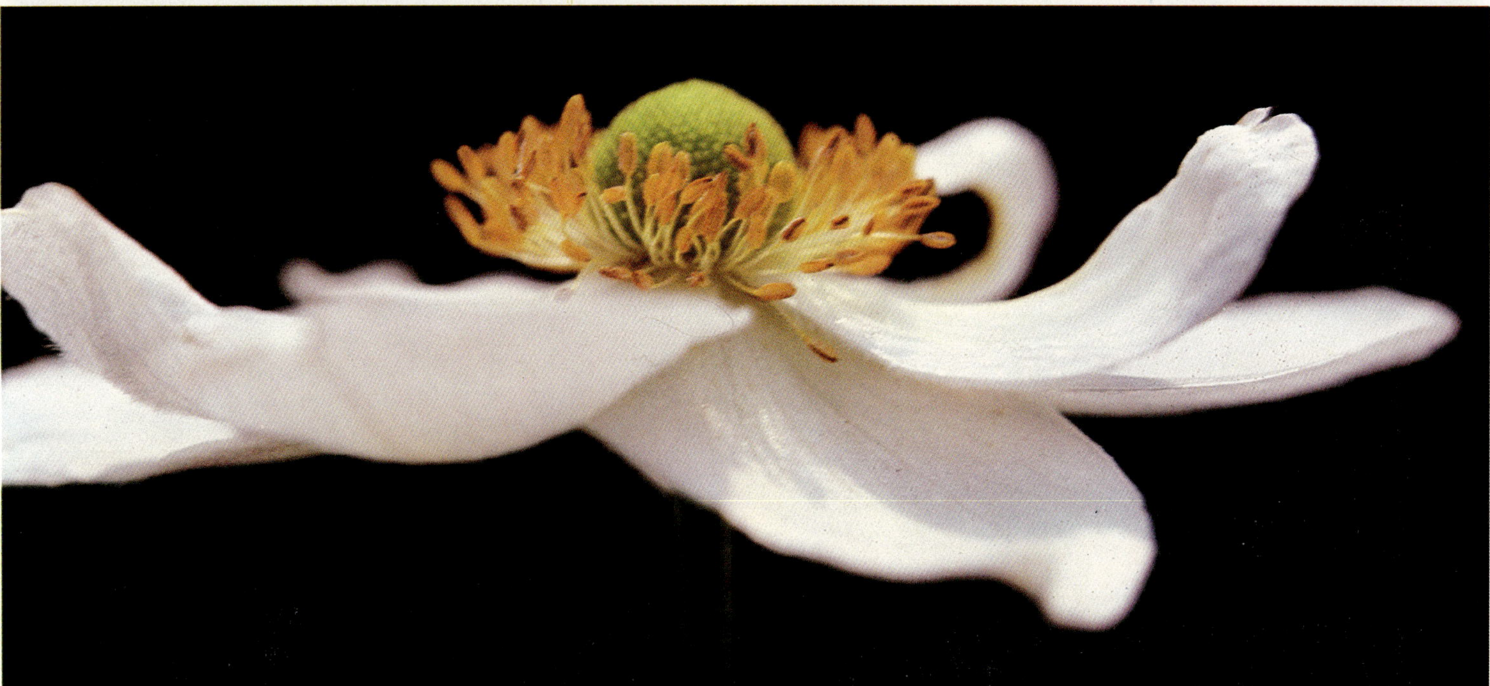

focus lenses, zooms use the fractional dioptre accessory lenses. If there is any disadvantage at all, it is that good, large diameter close-up lenses need good, large diameter bank balances to finance them – but then so do big filters.

Anyone who has taken close-ups will know that the biggest problems are lack of depth of field and working in your own shadow. For these reasons I tend to use close-up lenses mainly with modest apertured lenses in the 90 to 150mm focal length range. Not only do they stop down to f32, but are also a nice compromise in the subject stand-off distance. I also have a preference for long focus rather than telephoto construction for reasons of definition.

__With subjects parallel to the__ film plane __left,__ the shallow depth of field inherent in close up work can be used to maximum advantage. Otherwise you should focus on the part of the subject __above and top right__ that contains the most detail, interest or importance.

Macro-zoom attachments have been around since the sixties, and perform much the same function as a 50/55mm prime macro lens. Like early zoom lenses they do not hold focus between settings, though with any close-up work, it is easier to move the camera backwards and forwards for focusing. Fitting a macro-zoom attachment to a macro lens can be a startling experience. At the closest setting the subject will be literally inside the macro-zoom lens mount. There is, as always, a price to be paid for convenience. The macro-zoom accessory is bulky and more expensive than a set of reasonable quality close-up lenses, against which it does not compare too favourably in either definition or contrast, unless used with a prime lens of simple construction, in order to cut down the total number of lens elements between subject and film.

Split field lenses are an ingenious combination of half of a one, two or three dioptre close-up lens and a half empty filter mount. What these can achieve is a close-up of a foreground subject with a view to infinity in the top half of the picture and render both sharp at the same time. To do this, set the camera lens to infinity and then move the camera backwards and forwards until the foreground subject is sharp. Small apertures produce the most satisfactory results. The effect is similar to that which can be produced with an ultra wide angle lens, but without the extreme perspective. Split field lenses can be used turned through ninety degrees so that a foreground object can be to one side of the shot, or turned through a further ninety degrees to allow, say, overhanging flowers to be rendered as sharp as the background.

It is also possible to focus a subject through either 'half' in order to blur the other half of the picture. In this case use a larger, rather than a smaller, lens aperture. Since half of this attachment is 'open', a good lenshood will help to avoid a 'join' showing. A variation of the split field lens is the eccentric spot attachment made by B + W of Germany. This consists of an eccentrically located clear circle within a close-up lens. A rotating mount enables a distant subject to be blended into a close-up shot – within the confines of radial movement and format shape.

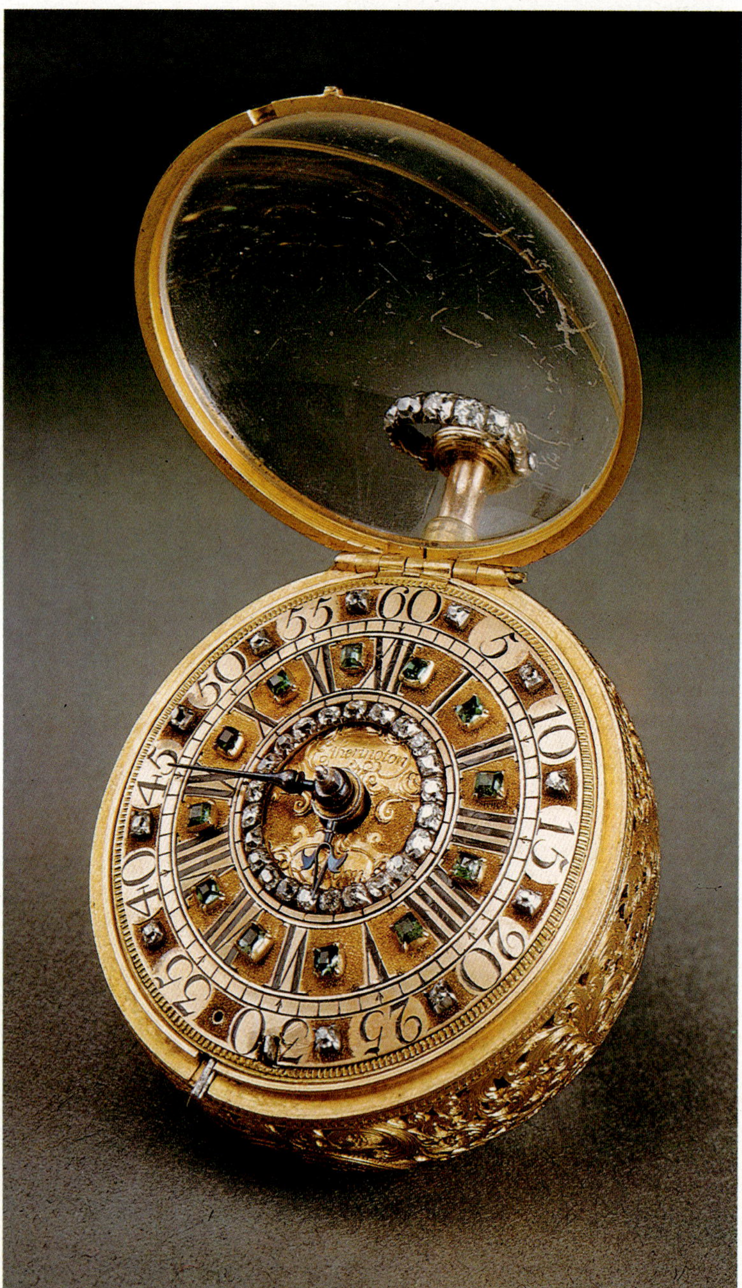

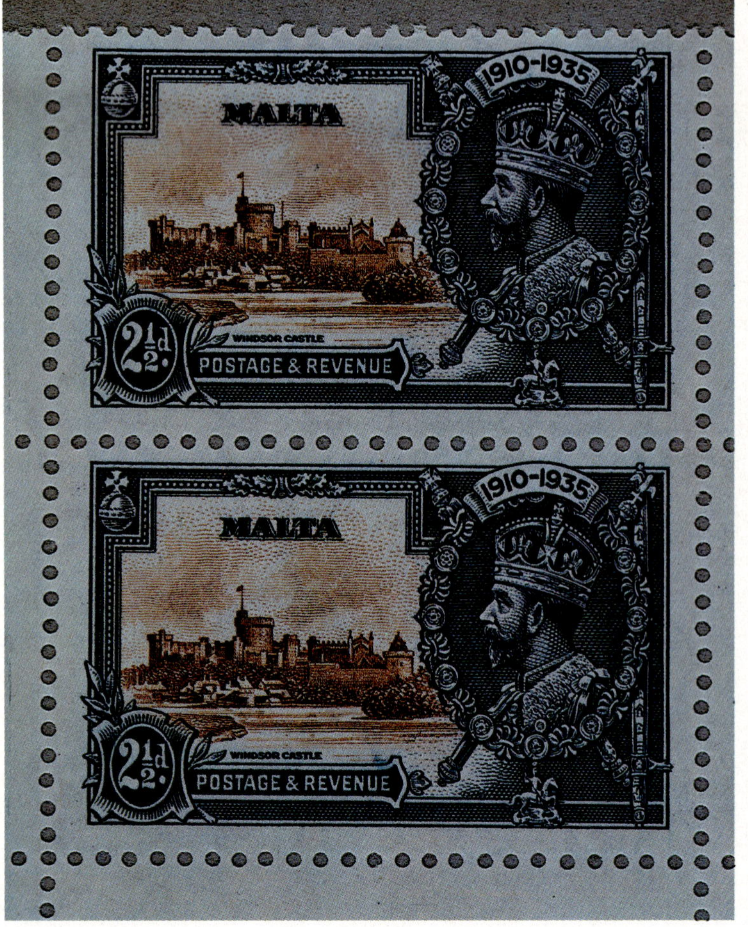

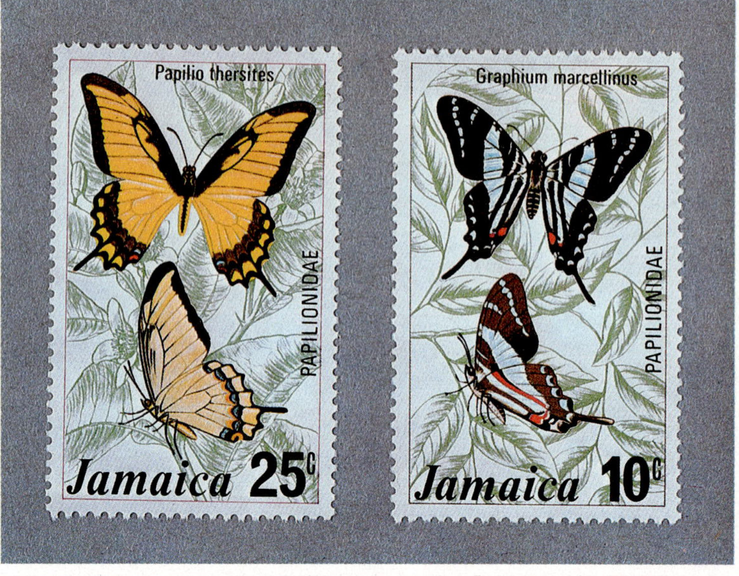

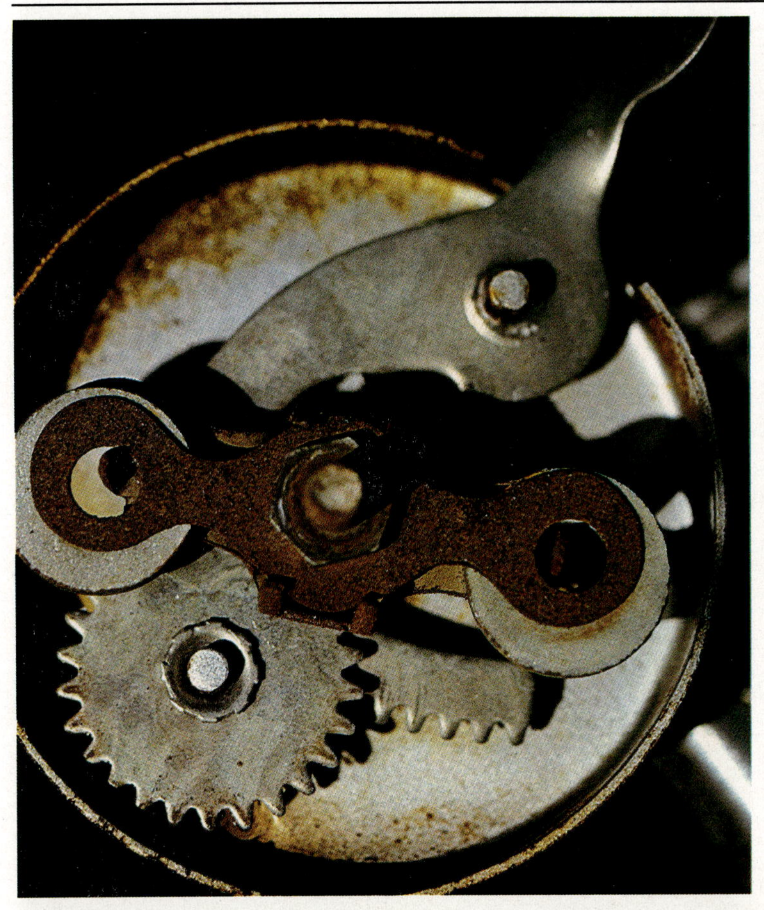

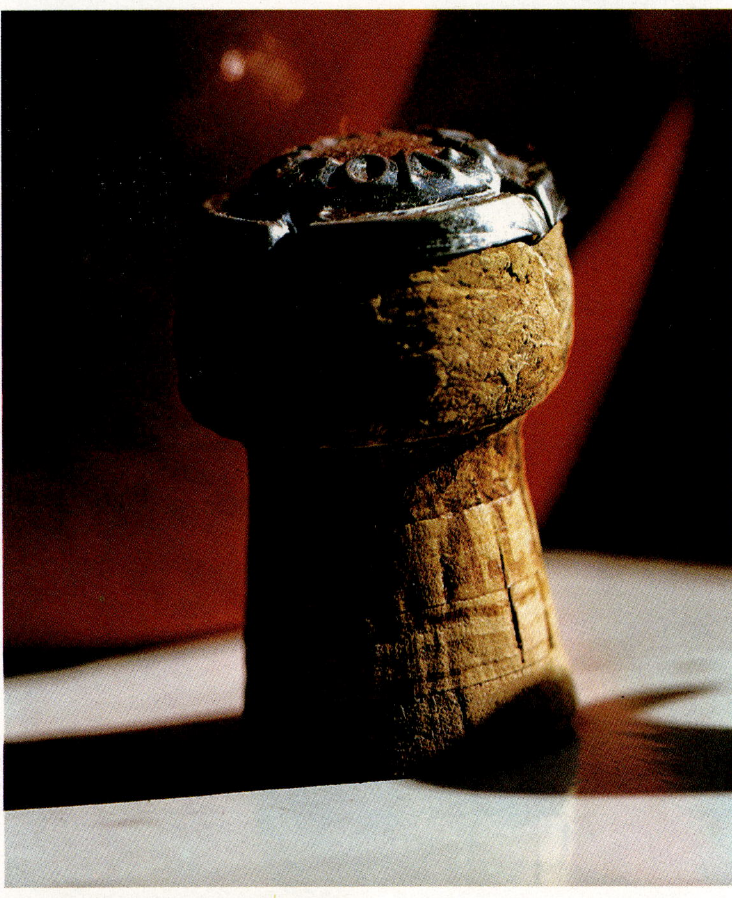

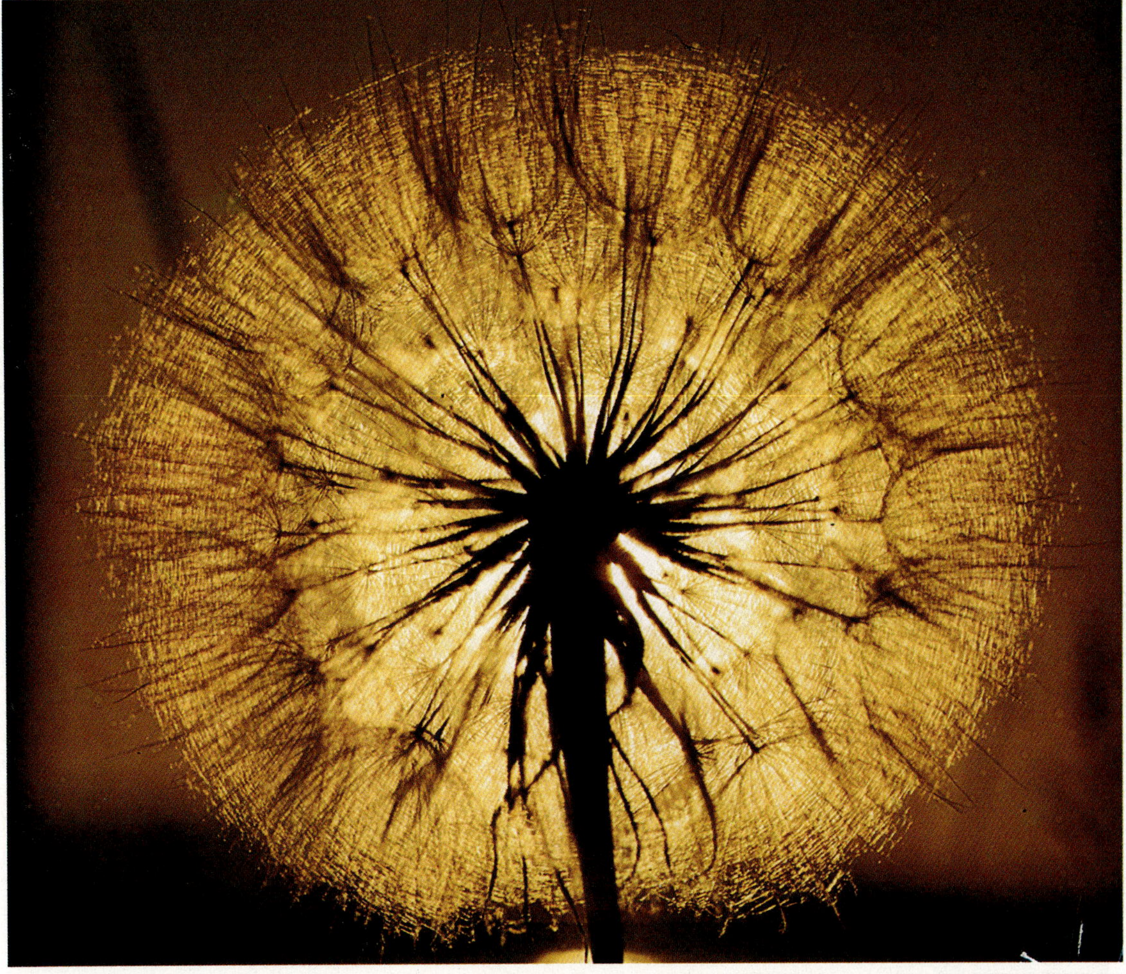

Of all the attachments we can *buy to fit on the front of our lenses, the close up attachments provide us with by far the most dramatic change in the way we view our surroundings. Suddenly, our photography takes on another dimension; the ordinary, everyday things we always took for granted can be viewed, and recorded, in an entirely new way. The commonest items take on a new significance; the rusty old bicycle bell becomes an engineering abstract, and the champagne cork reveals its texture when sidelit. A dandelion seed head is transformed into an object of even rarer beauty when positioned directly in front of a light source such as the setting sun or a street lamp. Close up photography is also an exceptionally accurate way of recording a collection of small items such as jewellery, stamps, coins, matchboxes or whatever. Such a photographic record, besides being useful as a reference, is also very valuable in the case of insurance claims made on items lost or stolen.*

CLOSE-UP LENSES

Given plenty of light, *permitting the use of a small aperture and fast shutter speed, close ups are quite easy. It is when the light is low and we cannot stop the lens down far enough to render sharply the depth of even a shallow subject, such as a moth* ***below right,*** *that we need the small, front-mounted flash units* ***right*** *specially designed for close up work.*

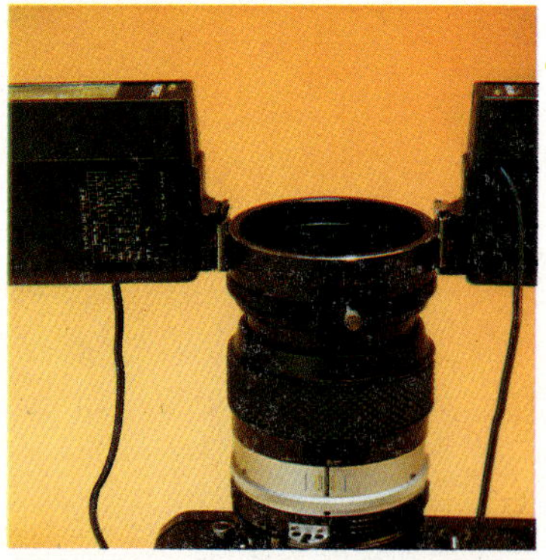

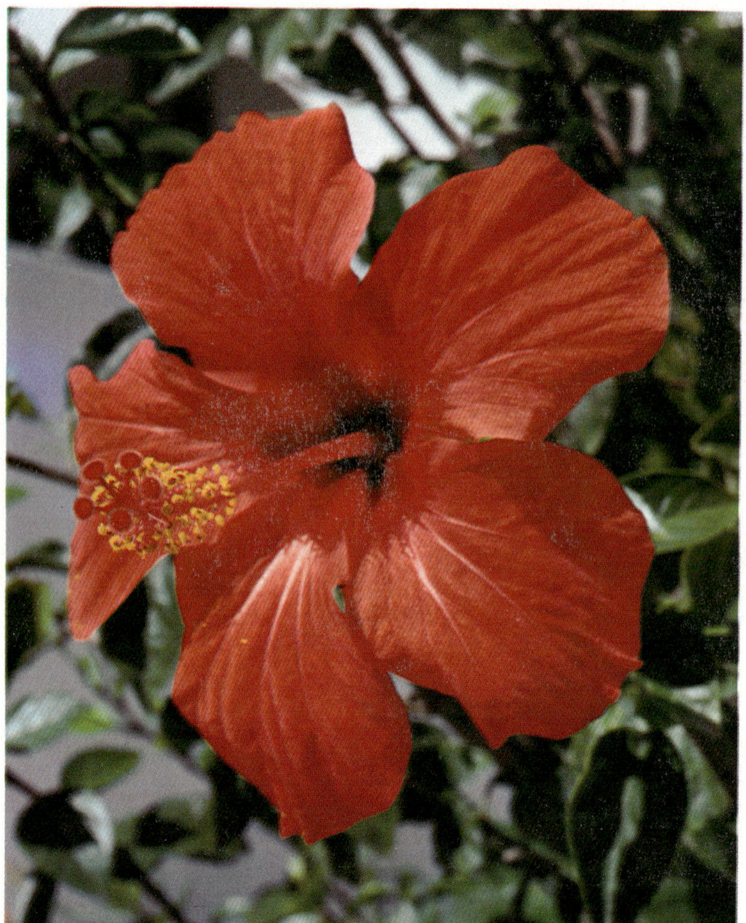

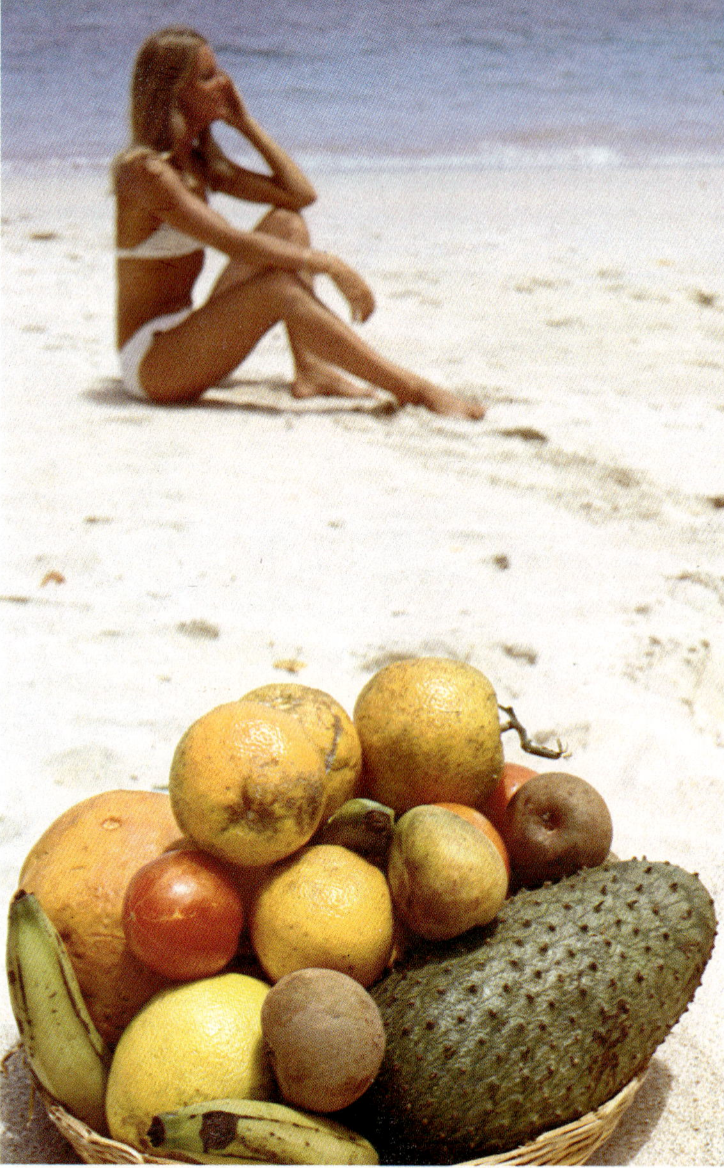

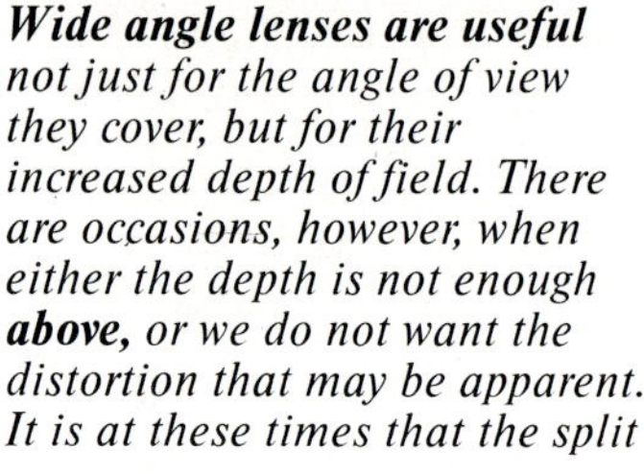

Wide angle lenses are useful *not just for the angle of view they cover, but for their increased depth of field. There are occasions, however, when either the depth is not enough* ***above,*** *or we do not want the distortion that may be apparent. It is at these times that the split field close up lens comes into its own* ***facing page.*** *This item is essentially half a close up lens – in varying strengths – and, used carefully, it can be most effective. Bear in mind that there will invariably be an out of focus band between near and far subjects.*

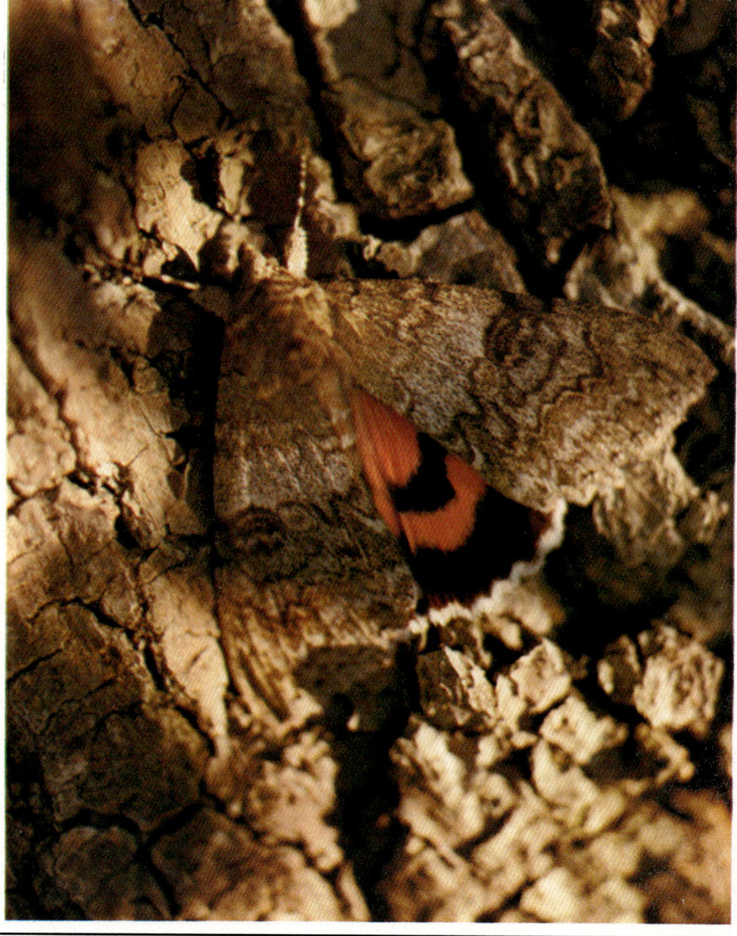

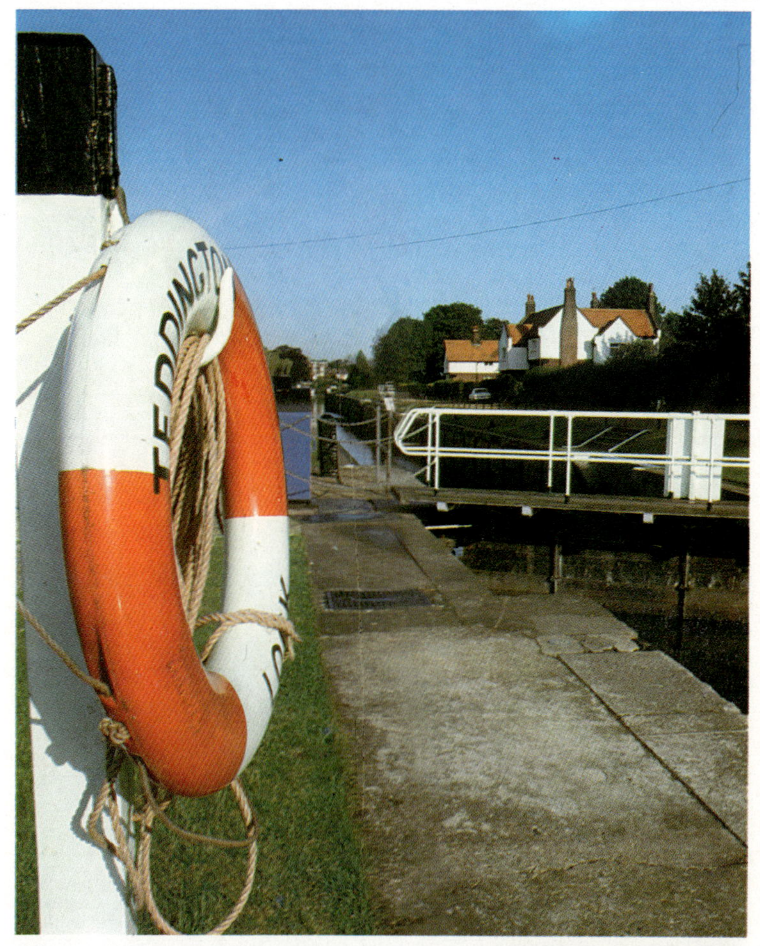

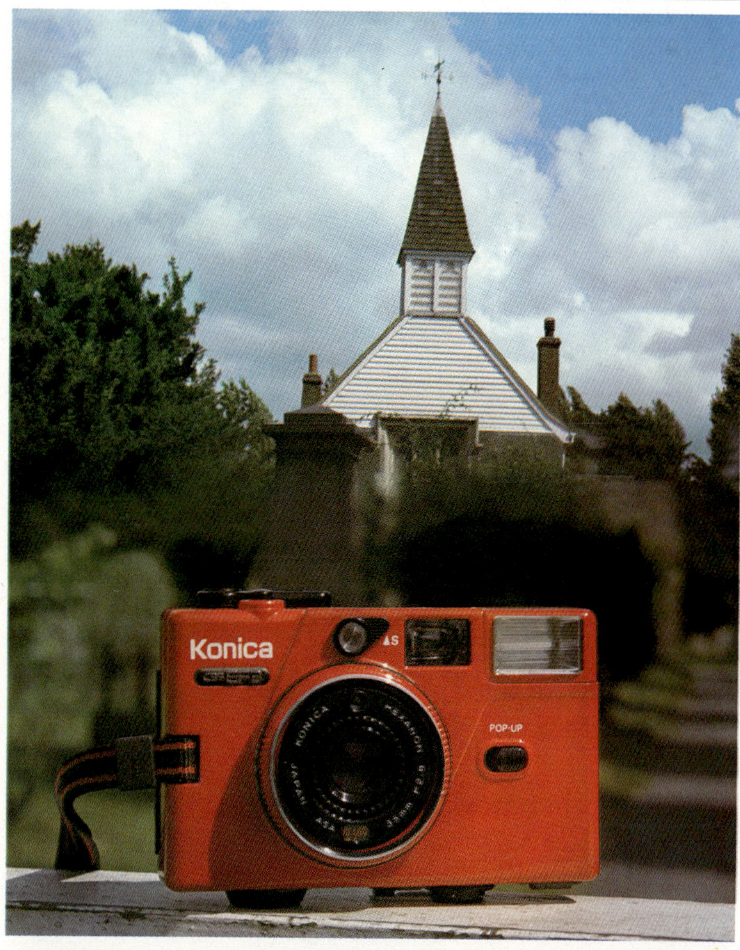
Konica
POP-UP

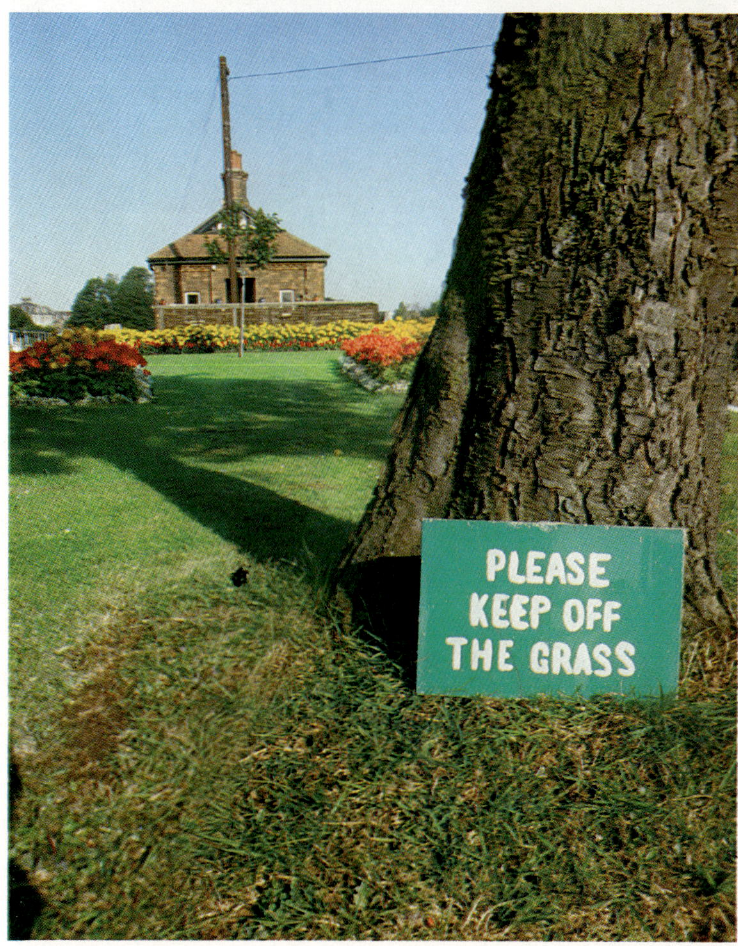
PLEASE
KEEP OFF
THE GRASS

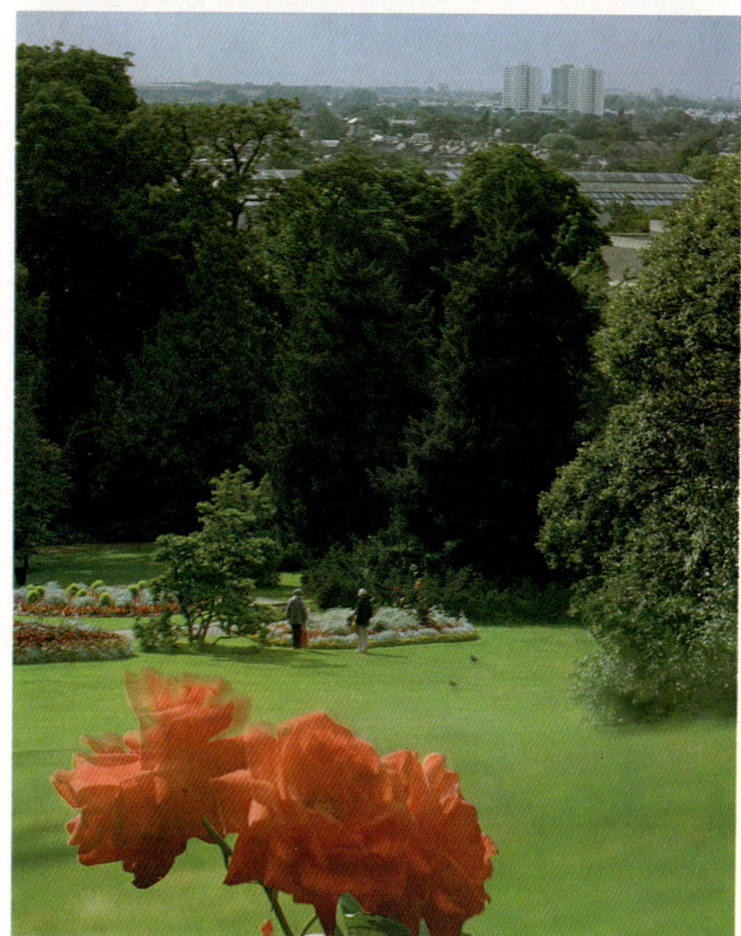

WIDE ANGLE AND TELEPHOTO ATTACHMENTS

Wide angle and telephoto attachments were produced in the first instance to enable owners of fixed lens cameras to keep abreast of those with more expensive equipment, at least in creative terms. Mainly a post-war phenomenon, these devices have been marketed for Instamatics, Polaroids, various rangefinder cameras and even single and twin lens reflex cameras. They are still around today.

Wide angle converters increase the angle of view of a standard lens by between 25% and 35%, or in approximate terms, turn a 50mm standard lens into a 35 to 30mm. Telephoto attachments have been made which increase the standard lens' focal length by 50%, 100% and 400% respectively. These lenses were often sold as a pair. In the case of a non-reflex camera, a double format viewfinder was supplied, or sometimes an adaptor which clipped over the camera's existing viewfinder. TLR's were provided with an extra viewfinding lens. The performance of these attachments can only be described as adequate – the telephotos being much better than the wide angles, where edge definition of a sort only becomes possible at small apertures, and curved distortion of straight lines is always present. For those who are happy with enprints and a simple camera, these attachments will provide an extra dimension at low cost. The experimentally minded will also have some fun.

Monocular attachments are in effect half of a pair of binoculars with a filter ring fitting. They are usually 6 x 35 rating which amounts to about 300mm focal length and f16 maximum aperture. Those made for the Zeiss Contaflex SLR camera were surprisingly good within the optical limitations imposed. All monoculars are clumsy to operate on a camera, but function normally when used with the eye.

Anamorphic, or wide screen attachments, emanate from the world of cinematography. These compress the image in one dimension, and stretch it in the other. A normal ciné frame ratio of about 1⅓:1, can be stretched to 2½:1, or more, depending upon the make of lens used. An anamorphic projection lens is used to 'restore' the image upon the screen. Some of these attachments can be fitted to a 35mm SLR. The resulting distortion of the image is not dissimilar to that produced by a prism, but without colour fringing and with rather better definition. They work best on subjects like the interior of a forest, or anything else long and thin, but they are not too good for photographing people! Anamorphic attachments are still available new at a reasonable price.

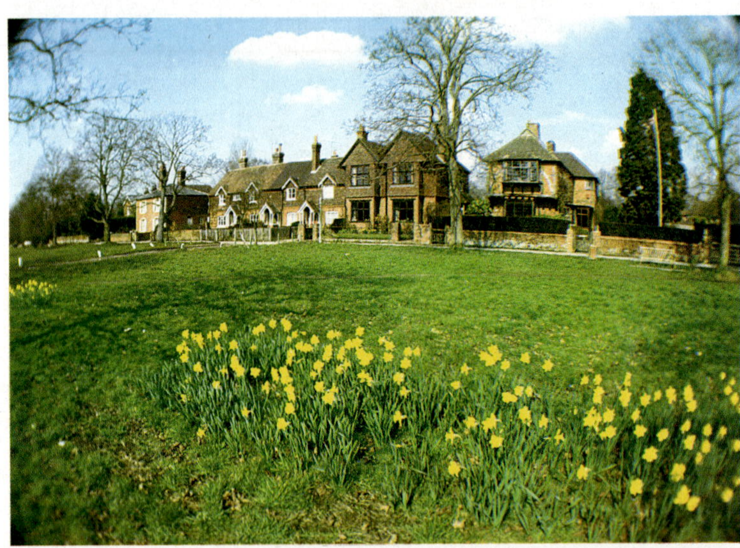

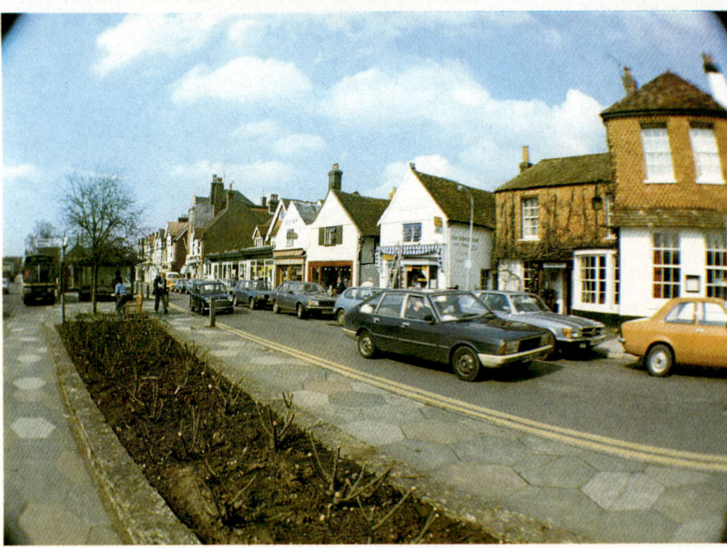

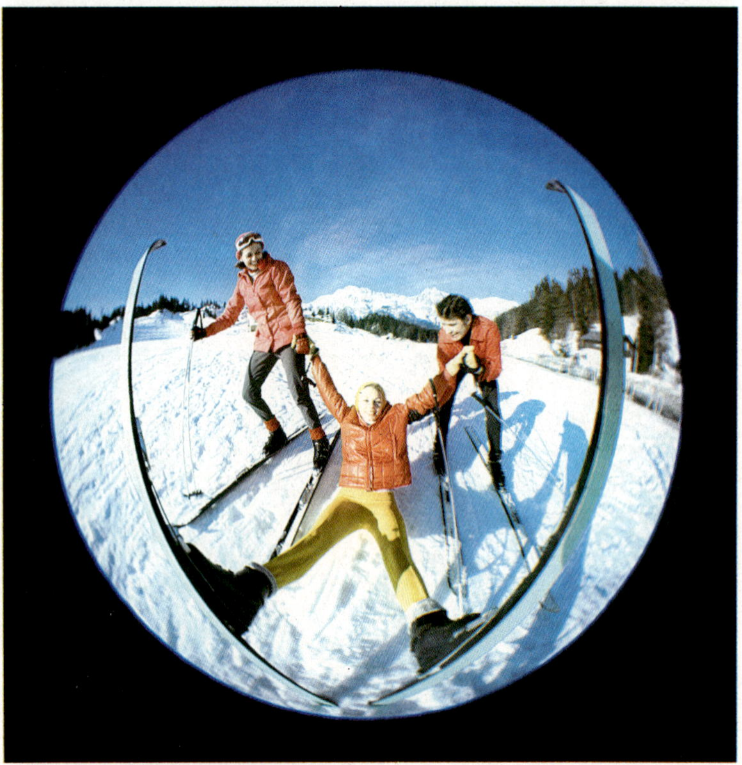

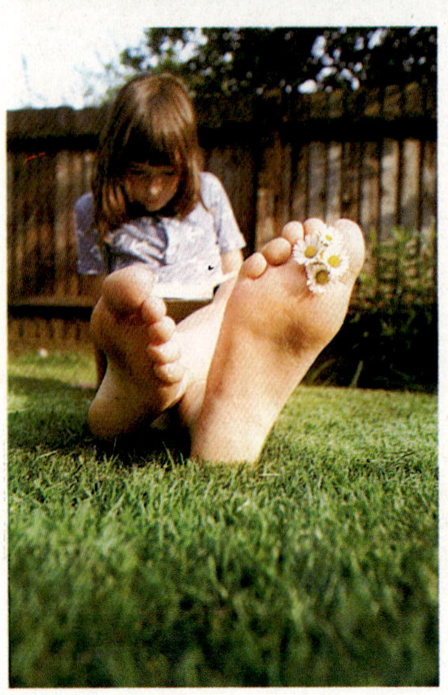

Telephoto and wide angle *attachments can be used as cheap alternatives to prime lenses on SLR cameras, or as the only means of altering the view of a fixed lens camera. The pictures* ***left and far left*** *show the effect obtained with a wide angle attachment on a standard focal length lens. Different perspective can be achieved with such attachments fitted to wider or longer objectives. Vignetting and fall-off in image quality is a characteristic that should be allowed for, and this can be cropped out at a later stage.* ***Above:*** *Fisheye attachments produce exaggerated views and distort nearby objects.*

FISHEYE AND SUPERWIDE ATTACHMENTS

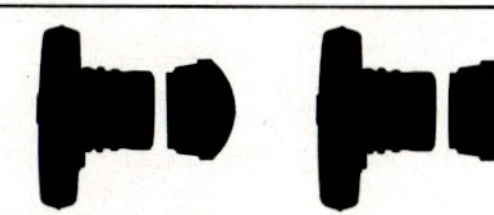

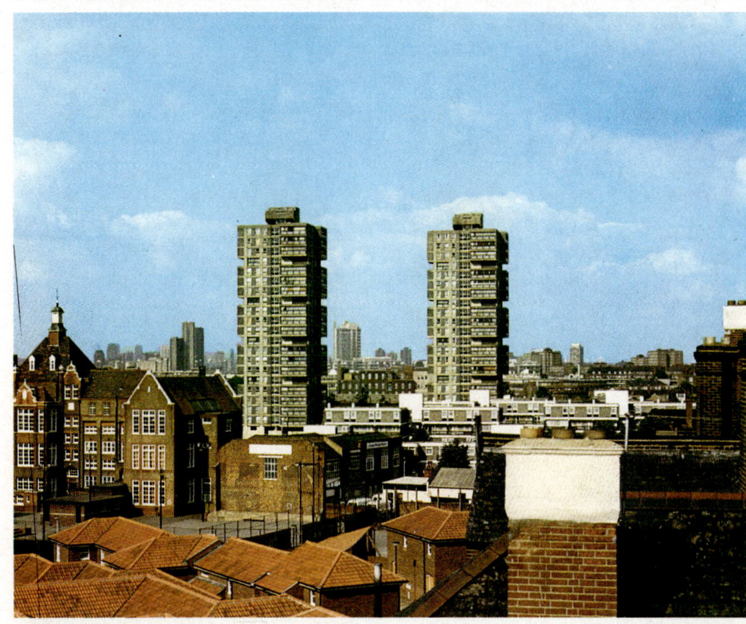

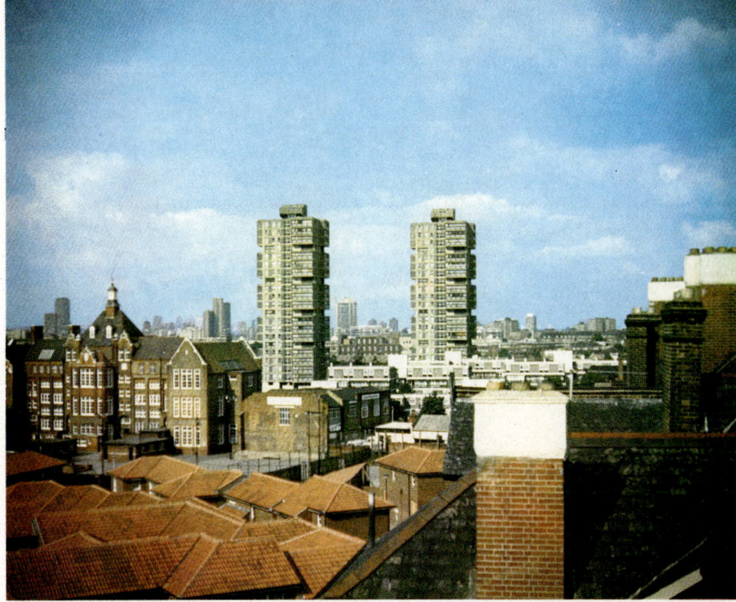

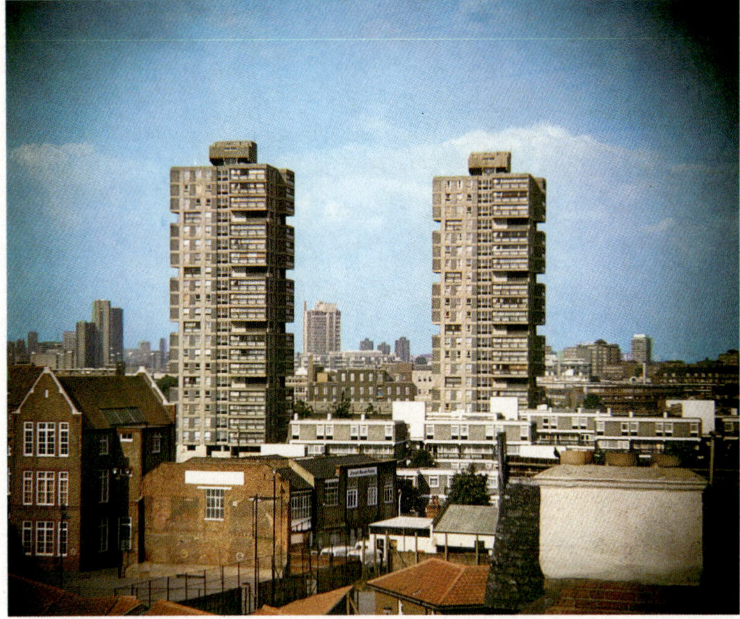

Fisheye and superwide lens attachments share a common function in that their effect upon a prime lens is to increase the angle of view of that lens, and also to render straight lines as curves. This statement must be qualified in that a horizontal or vertical line, falling exactly in the centre of the picture, will be rendered as a straight line. However, each few degrees of camera tilt will promptly render that line progressively more curved. The maximum angle of view of these attachments varies between 110° and 180.° This is increased towards the maxima stated by the use of a short prime focal length lens, or decreased by using a longer than normal focal length.

In the former instance, the classic, circular fisheye image will be produced with the use of say 20 – 28mm focal length lenses on 35mm format. The only variation will be the size of the circular image on the negative or transparency, not the included angle of view. A 180° attachment needs a larger prime focal length in order to fill the frame, and provided that the maximum filter mount diameter of the prime lens used is not above about 58mm, then these attachments can be used on 6 x 6cm, 5″ x 4″ or even 10″ x 8″ formats!

There are two distinct types of fisheye/superwide converters. Those which affect exposure and those which reputedly do not. All the 180° converters which I have examined reduce the effective aperture of the prime lens in proportion to the focal length of that lens. As an example:– the Kenko/Cosmos attachment for 180° pictures requires any prime lens to be used at its maximum aperture. A conversion scale on the lens, shows that a 35mm focal length + attachment will have an effective maximum aperture of f5.6, a 100mm lens becomes f11 and a 200mm lens becomes f22, etc. etc.

As all attachments need to be stopped well down in order to achieve any degree of definition at the edges of the field encompassed, it follows that a large format user could well be working at an aperture of f256.

The newer 110° fisheye/superwide attachments are primarily designed for TTL 35mm cameras, where any induced exposure increase is automatically catered for. When used on larger format cameras, they still work admirably but exposure compensation is necessary, certainly when working from a hand-held meter or with electronic flash. Since most professionals also check out exposures with Polaroid film, they are less likely to make mistakes in this area.

Both types of attachment can be a useful creative tool, witness the fact that the top lens manufacturers produce both as prime objectives. Whether you like the results or not is a subjective matter, yet as a professional, I would hate to be without some sort of fisheye facility. But then I only have to use it once a year in order to justify its continued existence.

When it comes to choice of subject matter, high curvature lenses with their inherent distortion are better employed with inanimate, rather than animate, subjects. At best, the family dog, portrayed as having a huge rubber 'hooter' and miniscule body, will accept the resulting mirth as being a sign of affection. The human family member portrayed likewise, could well not share the same emotion. It takes a lot of self confidence to accept a parodied image.

Although wide angle and *telephoto attachments generally impair the resolution of the camera's lens, they can nevertheless be used on many occasions when fine detail and straightness of line is not an essential. With such devices fitted to a viewfinder camera, it is of course necessary to compose the picture via a matched accessory viewfinder. The pictures, from top, show the effect of using a standard lens, wide angle and tele attachment.*

VARIZOOM

From HAMA in Germany, although made in Japan, the impressive Varizoom attachment shortens or lengthens the focal length of the prime lens by 25%. Designed for use with 35mm format lenses of 100mm focal length and above, it would appear that the prime use of this attachment would be for zoom effect shots. Yet when taking photographs from a fixed position, the focal length variation could well be of paramount importance. I have used the Varizoom on a Hasselblad, for which it was not designed, with the following effect. There is vignetting with the 150mm Sonnar lens at apertures below f5.6, unless either of the 16 on backs are used to give a 6 x 4.5cm or 4 x 4cm superslide format. With the 250mm Sonnar there was no problem.

This table (of rounded off figures) gives you some idea of focal length changes when using a Varizoom:

Focal length of prime lens	Zoom range with attachment
100mm	75 - 125mm
135mm	100 - 170mm
150mm	120 - 180mm
200mm	150 - 250mm
250mm	200 - 300mm
300mm	225 - 325mm
400mm	300 - 500mm
500mm	375 - 625mm

The Varizoom is not suitable for use with the compact mirror (catadioptric) lenses now on the market or with focal lengths of less than 100mm, as vignetting will occur.

The multi-coated Varizoom specification is sophisticated enough to utilise moving elements, therefore the barrel does not extend with focal length changes. However, the attachment is a varifocal rather than a true zoom, in that the focus does not hold between minimum and maximum settings. In practice this is of no great disadvantage, least of all in terms of cost/effectiveness!

One extra bonus is that when used at its 'wider' setting, a closer focusing distance between camera and subject is possible: not a macro facility but still useful. Series 7 filters may be used between the attachment and the prime lens by means of a special ring. Alternatively, there is a standard 58mm front thread. I would recommend a larger than 58mm lenshood, by means of a step-up ring for the shorter prime lens focal lengths.

The makers state that no exposure adjustment is necessary with this attachment.

Subjects like these can be *produced with the aid of a zoom attachment, which must be operated through its range during exposure. This sounds easy, but timing is important. The camera must be tripod mounted and, if there is action in the frame it works best if it is towards the camera position* ***below*** *and the centre of the shot is positioned to one side. With static subjects, such as the vase of flowers* ***right,*** *the situation is easier. Again, the camera must be tripod mounted and the zooming action very smooth, with half the exposure completed before 'zooming.' Changing focus has a similar effect as, of course, does a zoom lens.*

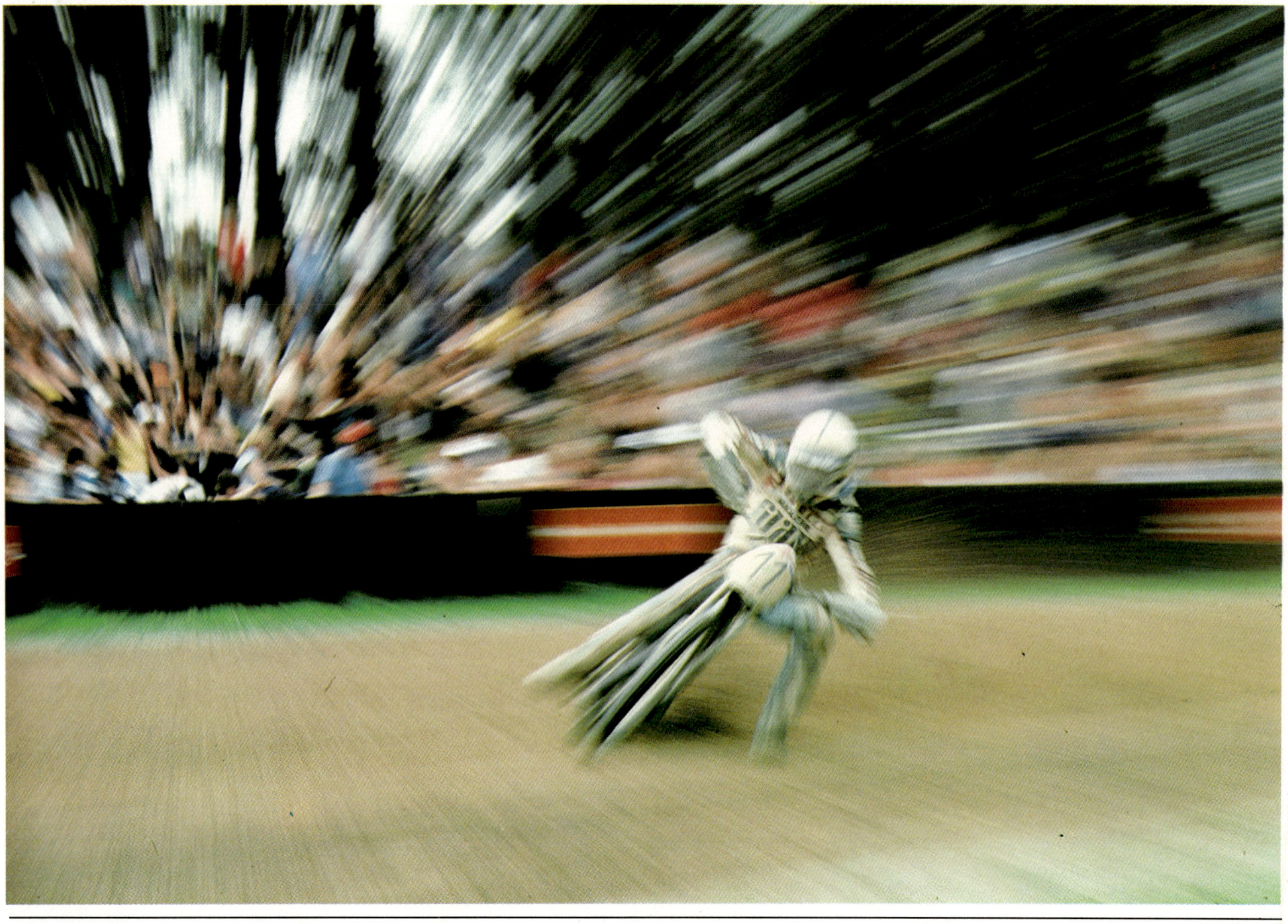

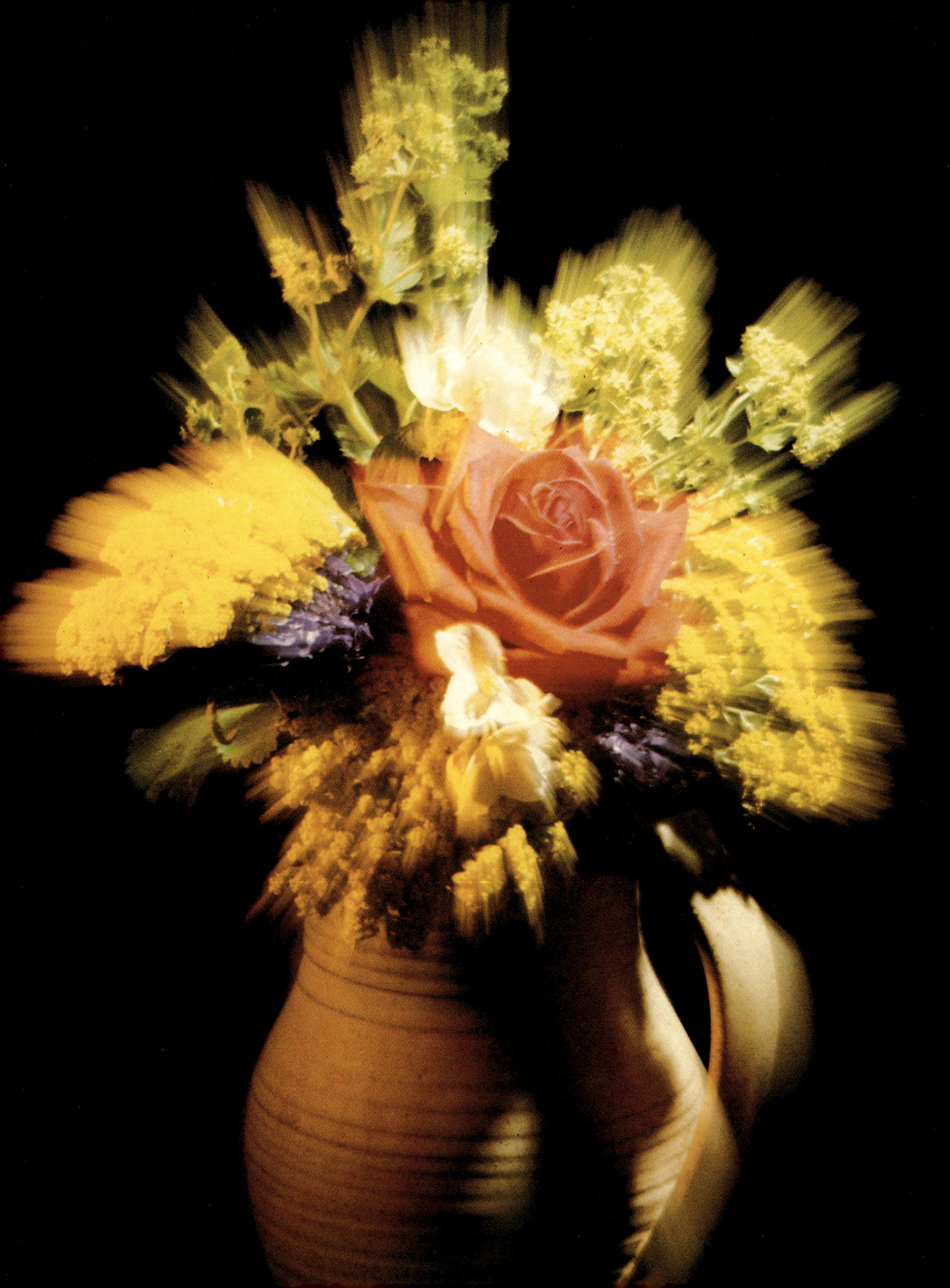

SOFT FOCUS ATTACHMENTS

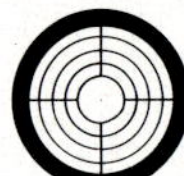
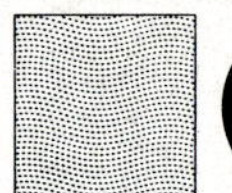
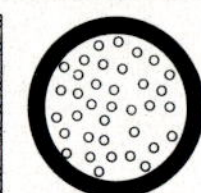

For almost as long as lens designers have been computing sharper and sharper lenses, photographers have tried to destroy that resolution for various reasons. Indeed, the lens manufacturers, realising this need, gave in gracefully and designed special soft focus lenses – a situation which still exists. Those of us who have a penchant for soft focus, or would like to try it, do not normally go straight out and buy a special lens. It is for this reason that soft focus attachments have been made, thus allowing for experimentation or the occasional need.

Why should any photographer wish to produce soft focus effects when surely those days are left behind? Perhaps, like stereoscopy or romanticism this is a cyclical occurrence. It could be tied in to the world of fashion, nostalgia or the rediscovery of an era in the cinema. Yet in spite of this there has always been an element of practicality. Portraiture, for reasons of human vanity, has always been the most prolifically practised subject in all forms of graphic art – including photography. Whereas the painter could ignore the passage of time when portraying ladies of an 'un'certain age, the camera could not. I have long conjectured that this was the reason for the discovery of soft-focus lenses, later for negative retouching, and nowadays make-up for T.V. appearances.

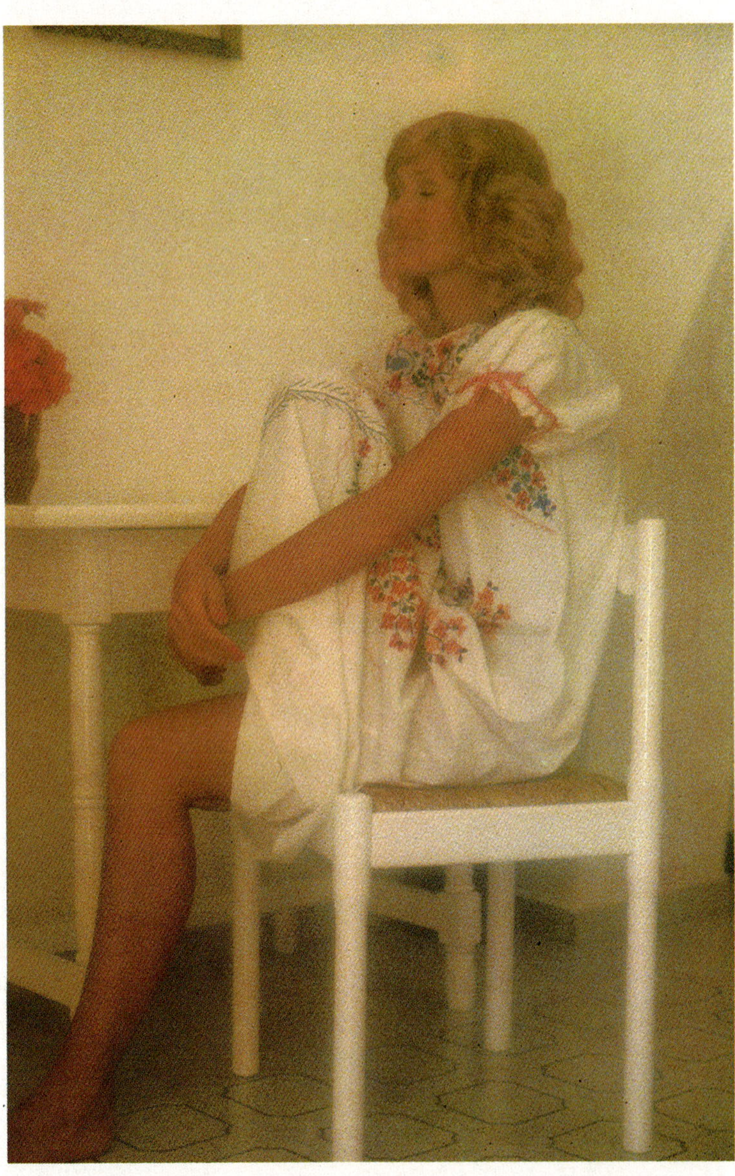

I once assisted a very famous portrait photographer, who had been commissioned to photograph the chairman of an internationally respected company. It was my juvenile misfortune to deliver the finished results. Lord M. just happened to be in his office and told me to wait. "Rubbish," he exploded. "The man's made me look like a bloody baby. Take them back – and don't you dare send me a bill!" Needless to say, Lady M. was delighted with her pictures from a previous sitting. The moral of this story is, by all means use soft focus for landscapes, children, the ladies or whatever else suggests, but never for masculine portraits.

Soft focus lenses and accessories are both fascinating and infuriating to use; no two are exactly alike in effect. There are three co-related factors in soft focus work which must always be taken into consideration if the best results are to be obtained. The first is the degree of enlargement of the final result, the second is the taking aperture of the lens, and the third is the strength of the diffusing medium.

In the days when a portraitist always produced the same sized final print, it was easy to control the degree of diffusion. Likewise, Hollywood in the twenties and thirties was working to a standard screen magnification. This is also true today for the transparency enthusiast filling his forty or fifty inch screen at every showing. The photographer who prefers prints will find that a soft focus picture which is 'correct' at enprint size will be over the top when he makes a 10 x 8″ enlargement. Conversely a negative which produces a 'correct' 10 x 8″ print will be too

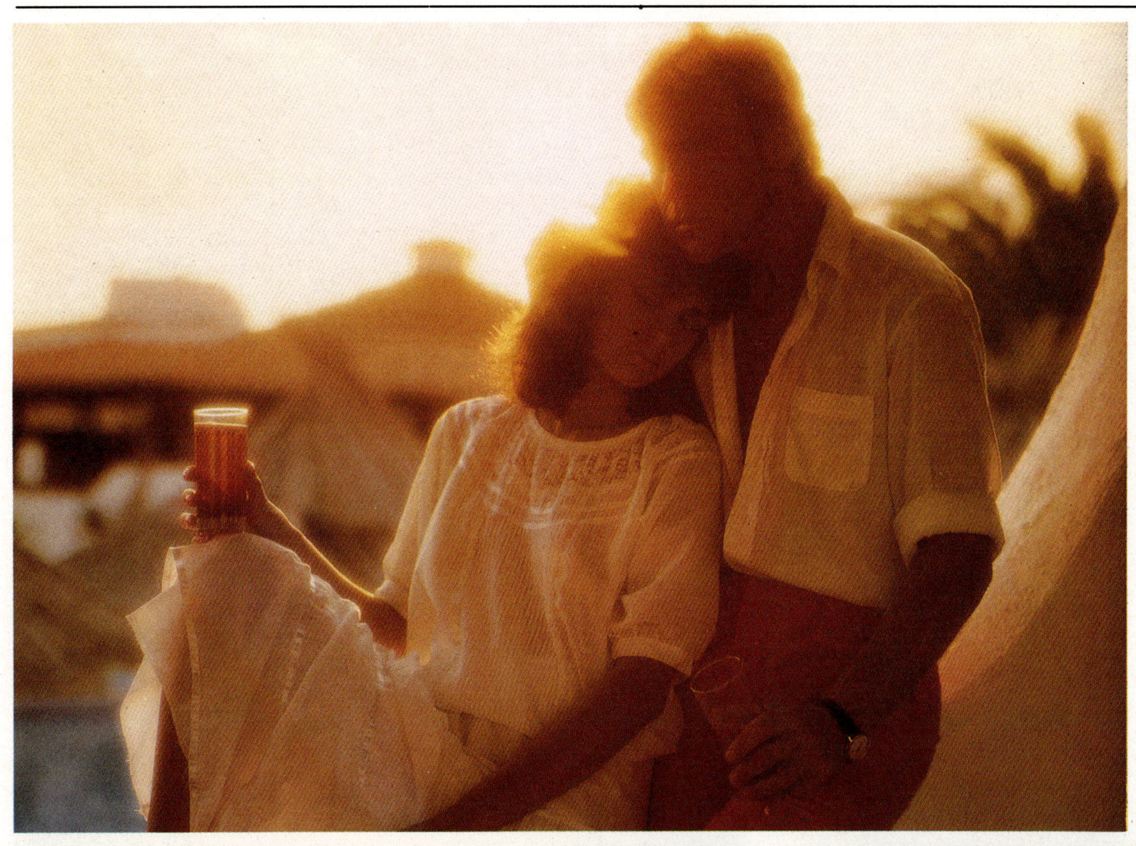

***Backlighting, particularly with** the light source within the frame, degrades the photographic image to some extent. This is one reason for the development of multi-coating, but not even the very best multi-coating methods can entirely prevent some degree of flare. For the purposes of soft focus rendition this is all to the good; we can use this image degradation, add a pale pastel filter, plus a soft focus attachment if desired, to produce very soft images. With the subject in indirect light **facing page right** it is surprising how little effect a weak soft focus filter has. In these circumstances it is sometimes necessary to use every means we have to achieve the softness we want. For the shot **facing page left** a medium strength soft focus plus a fog filter and a crosstar were used. Without highlights, the crosstar served as a second soft focus filter!*

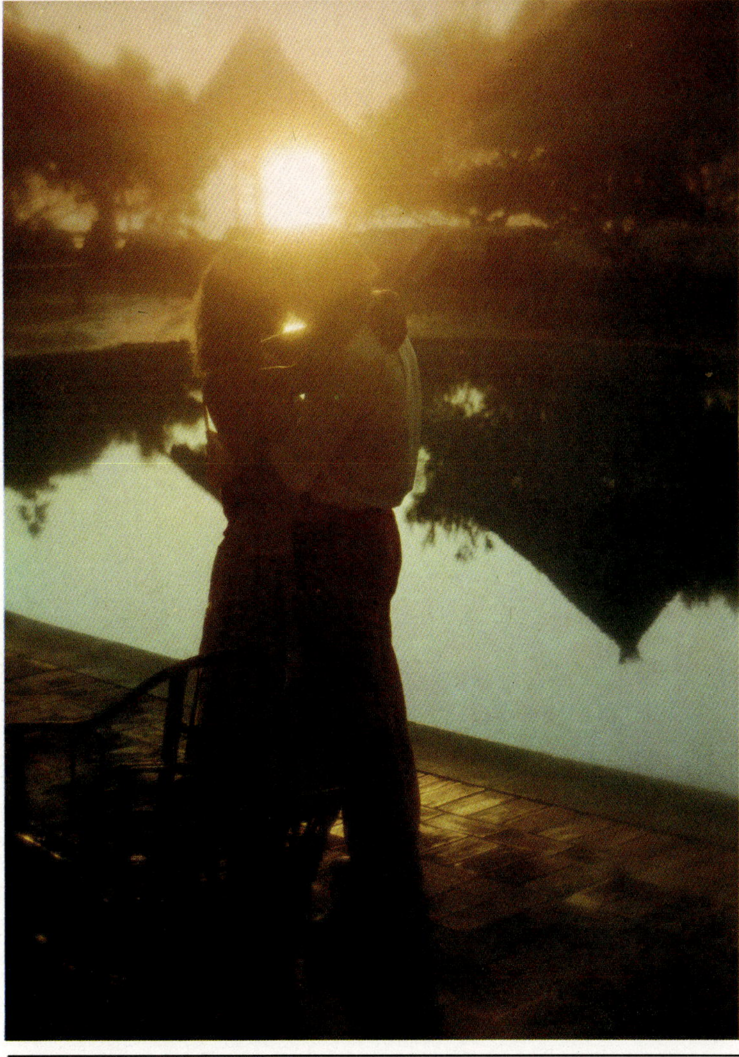

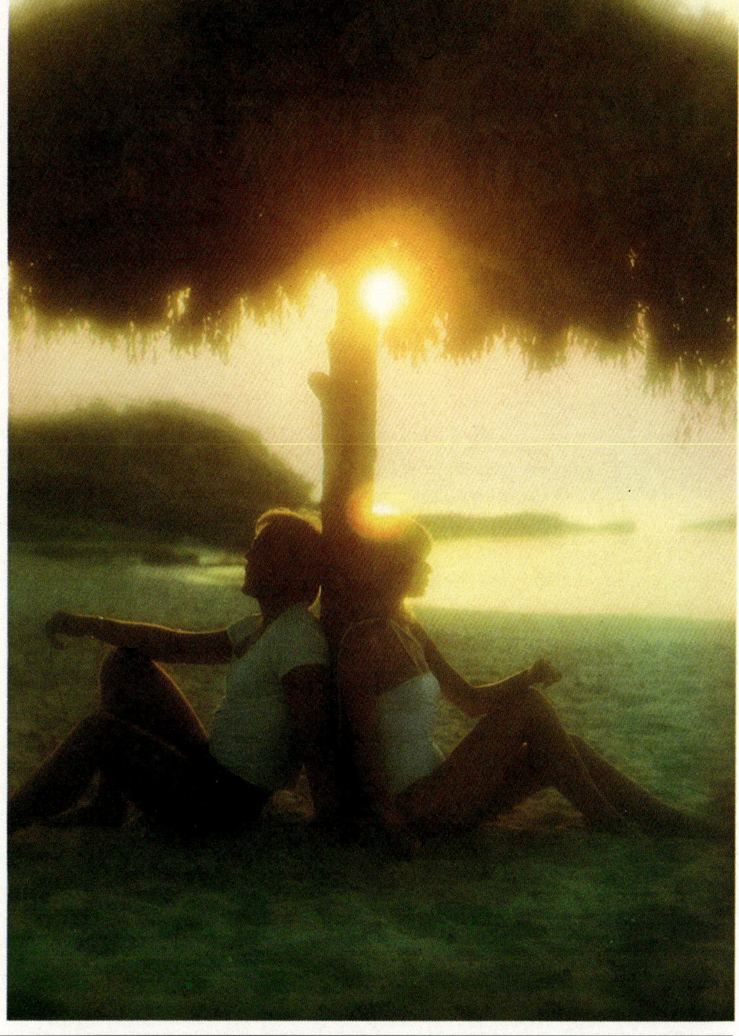

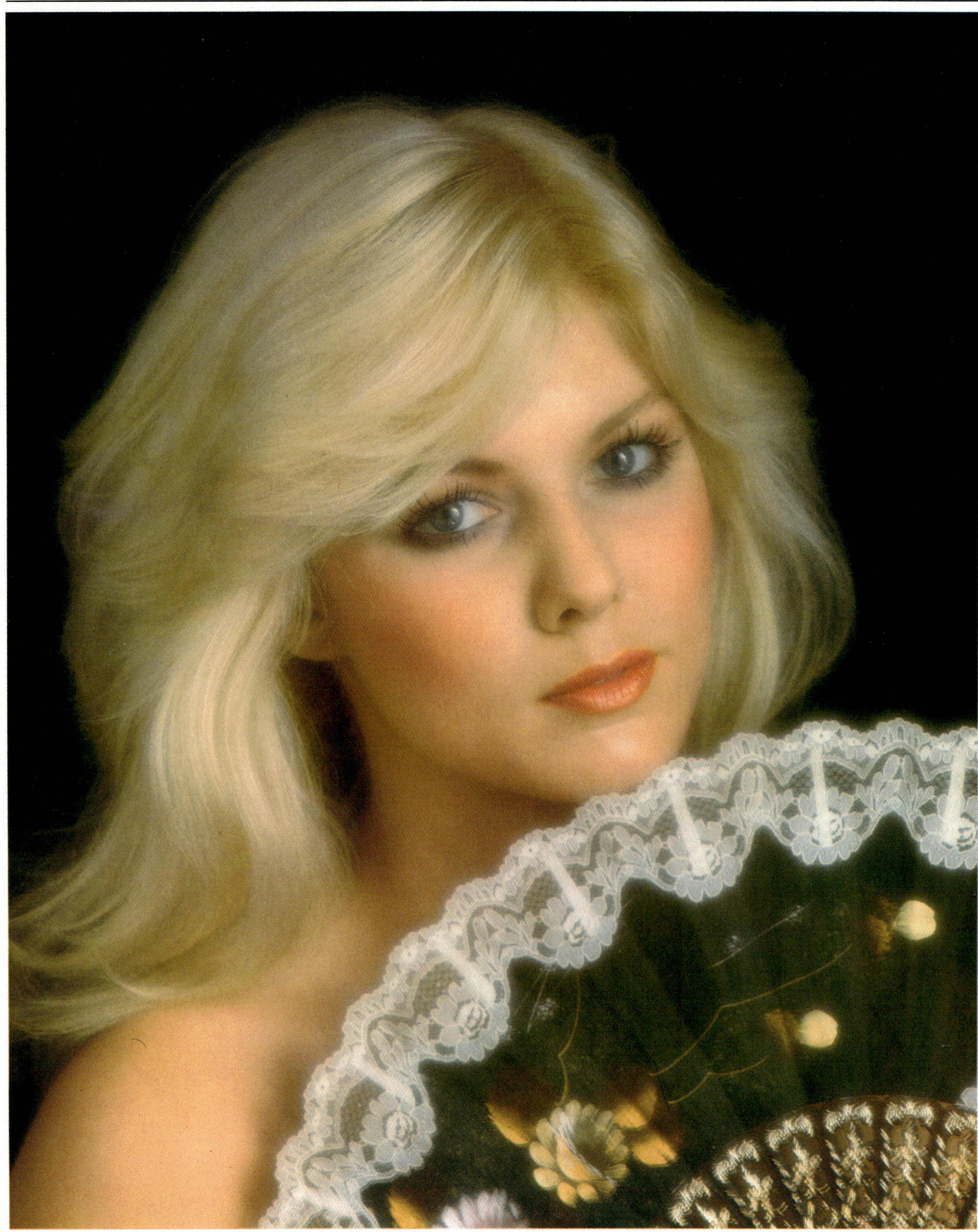

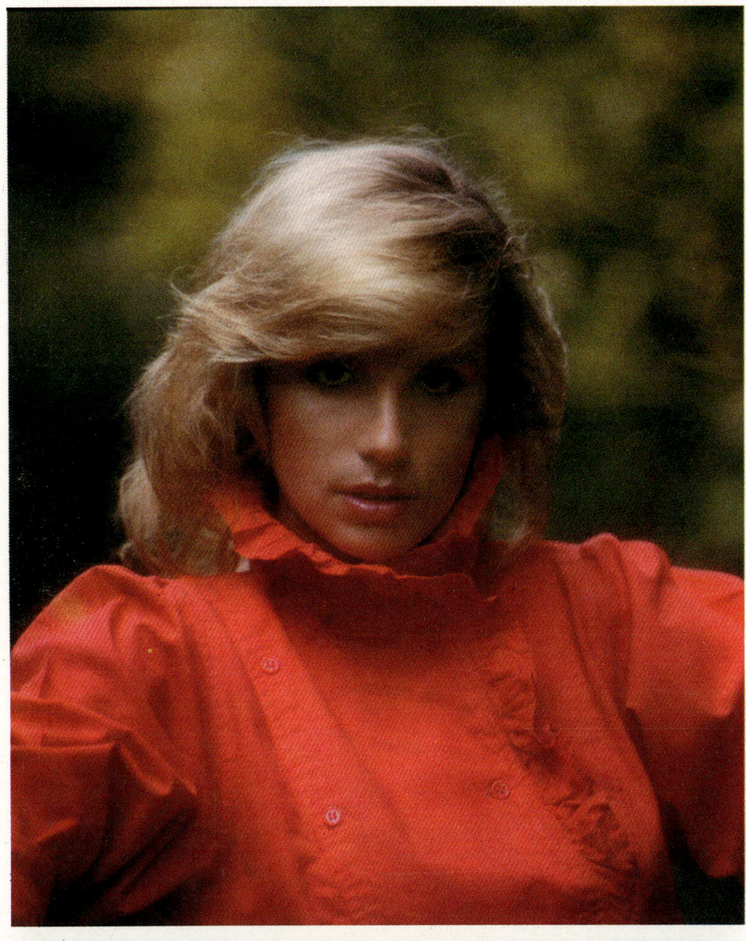

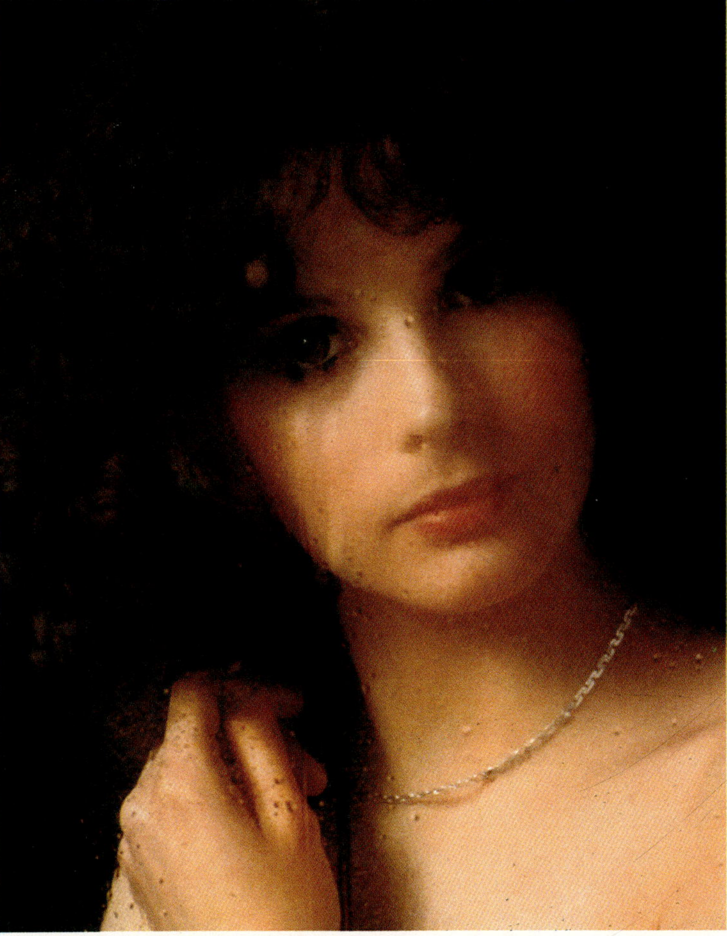

sharp at enprint size. This situation can, however, be easily overcome. Most soft focus attachments work in the same manner in that the degree of image diffusion and flare is greatest at maximum lens aperture, becoming relatively less as the aperture is reduced. A print worker can therefore make two, or more, negatives at different apertures thus allowing for all eventual degrees of enlargement. The alternative is to make three negatives with different strengths of diffuser, all at the same taking aperture. The better makers market three grades of soft focus devices for just this reason.

As soft focus attachments induce some degree of flare at wider apertures, this sometimes needs to be taken into account. In the studio it is possible deliberately to use more contrasty lighting than usual. Expressed as a ratio, when using colour materials, this would be in the order of 1:3 instead of a more usual 1:4 maximum contrast between highlight and shadow areas. On the other hand, you may wish to produce a soft, high key effect. In this case use your normal lighting set-up. A hard backlight, bare bulb (or electronic flash), out of sight and facing camera, behind the model's head, will add to the effect. By the same token, outdoor portraits taken against the light – with preferably a dark background, can be effective for blondes and brunettes alike.

Before moving on to comparisons between the different soft focus attachments, just a word about diffusion in the darkroom. It would be nice to think that it is always possible to 'add' soft focus to any shot at this stage. Unfortunately, the effect is to spread the shadows into the highlights instead of the other way round. This may at first seem a nonsensical statement, but a practical test will show the very obvious difference. The compromise – and it is just that – is to diffuse for part of a print exposure. Usually a quarter or third is sufficient, though it all depends upon the type of diffuser employed, and the end result desired.

One of the earliest accessories for soft focus effects was the Modulo. This has the appearance of a UV filter engraved with a series of concentric rings. The strength depends upon the number of circles engraved. A modern variant also has radial lines engraved from the outside of the smallest circle to the edge of the glass.

Concentric soft focus 'filters' are very sensitive to lens aperture. To go beyond two stops from maximum in a number one, or three stops in a number three, will produce hardly any effect – unless the degree of enlargement is big, although this can vary slightly from manufacturer to manufacturer. This type does, however, have the advantage that contrast loss is low and definition good.

Other attachments of this type are crosstars and diffraction gratings. Whilst not intended to be soft focus devices, they will perform this function when used at wide lens apertures. The degree of diffusion depends upon the number of rulings – or put another way, the number of 'points' they are intended to produce. Image contrast is lower than the Modulo type and decreases as the rulings increase.

Portraits of women have for *many years proved ideal subjects for the use of soft focus. The highlights spread into the dark areas to a greater or lesser extent depending on the strength of the soft focus attachment used. Because of this spreading of light areas, light subjects* ***facing page*** *are preferable to darker ones* ***above left.*** *It is not always necessary to use a soft focus attachment to create a soft focus effect. The shot* ***left*** *was taken using a sheet of plain glass, which was lightly sprayed with water, between the subject and the camera.*

SOFT FOCUS ATTACHMENTS

The commonest soft focus attachments around now are of the dimples and pimples types. Since the introduction of so many organic glass (i.e. plastic) filter systems, it has become easier to introduce the kinds of imperfections which will give a soft focus effect upon film. In its mildest form, the dimpled type resembles the glass from an anti-Newton ring slide mount glass. In fact one of these can be used over the camera lens for a mild soft focus effect. Dimpled glass – or plastic, is available in several grades, the finer types only being suitable for 35mm work, whilst the heaviest tend towards the image flattening quality of a fog filter. The pimple type has a raised moulded pattern upon one surface. The shapes of the pimples can be round, elliptical or diamond. The effect is both to soften definition and to induce light scatter to lower contrast. To my mind these are the most satisfactory soft focus attachments, as the better glass types – like the superb Hasselblad Softars – can be used stopped down to small apertures without losing much effect. The optical clarity allows for an image quality approaching that of a true soft focus prime lens, although of a necessarily different nature.

The last category of commercially available diffusing attachments is the differential soft focus type. These consist of a close-up lens with a centre area ground flat, or sometimes cut out. The effect of this is to induce a soft image with very out of focus edges to the negative or transparency. They are very sensitive to lens aperture, and if stopped down more than a couple of stops will start to produce an odd double image. This can be used creatively but is no longer soft focus in the accepted

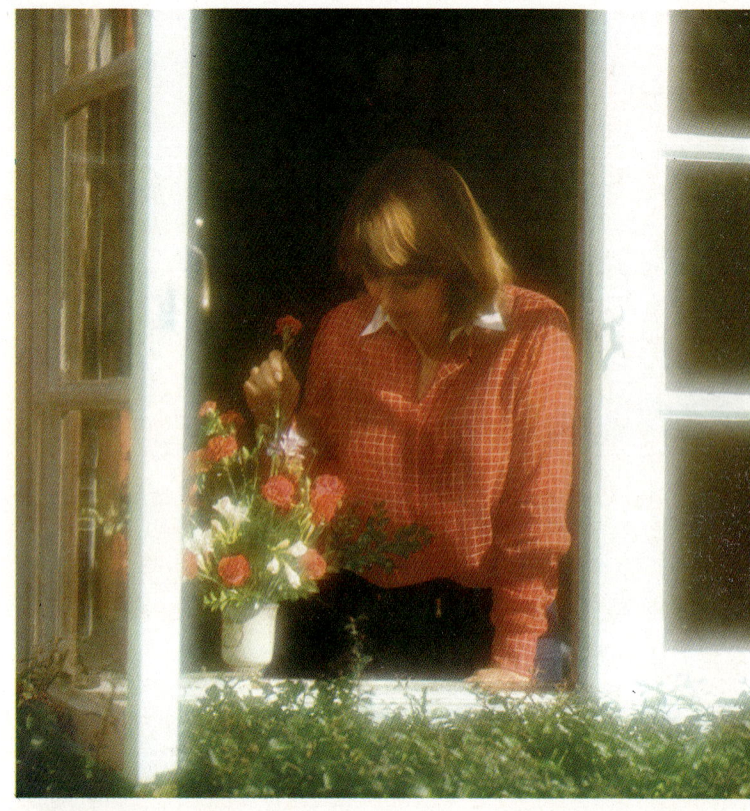

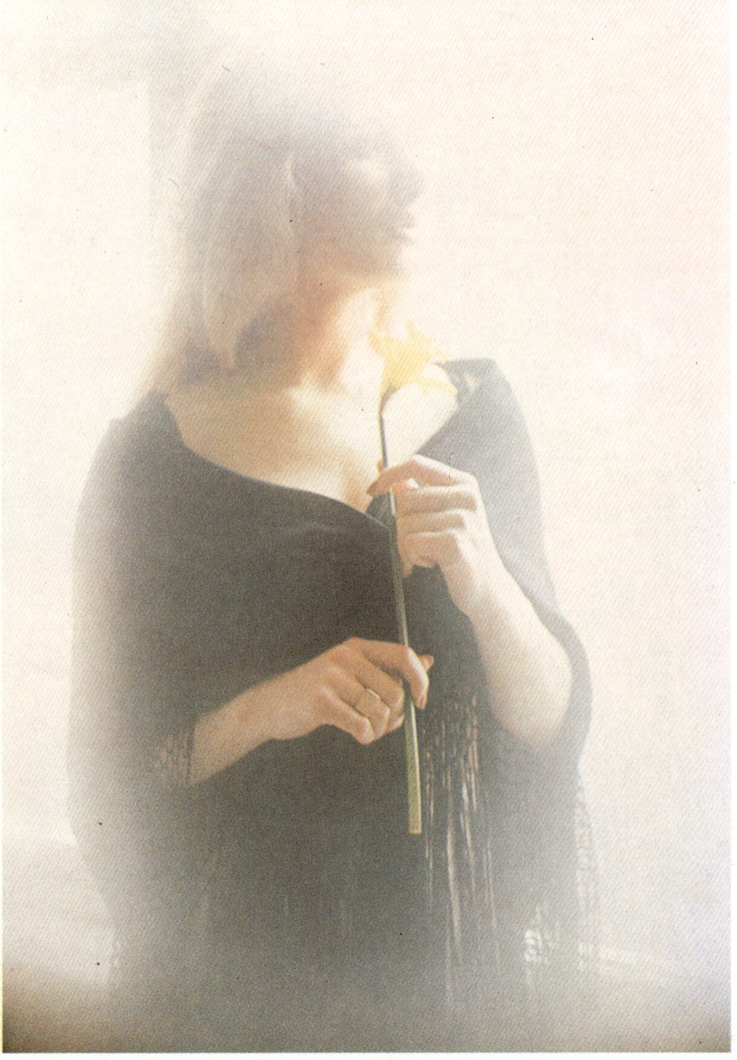

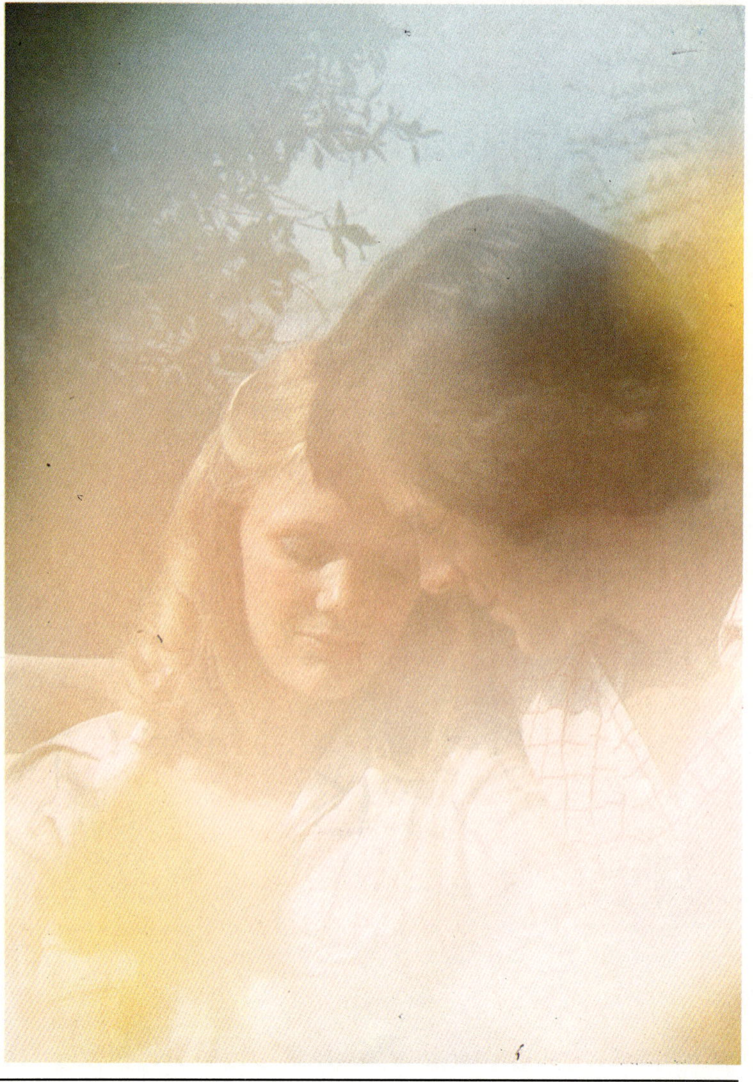

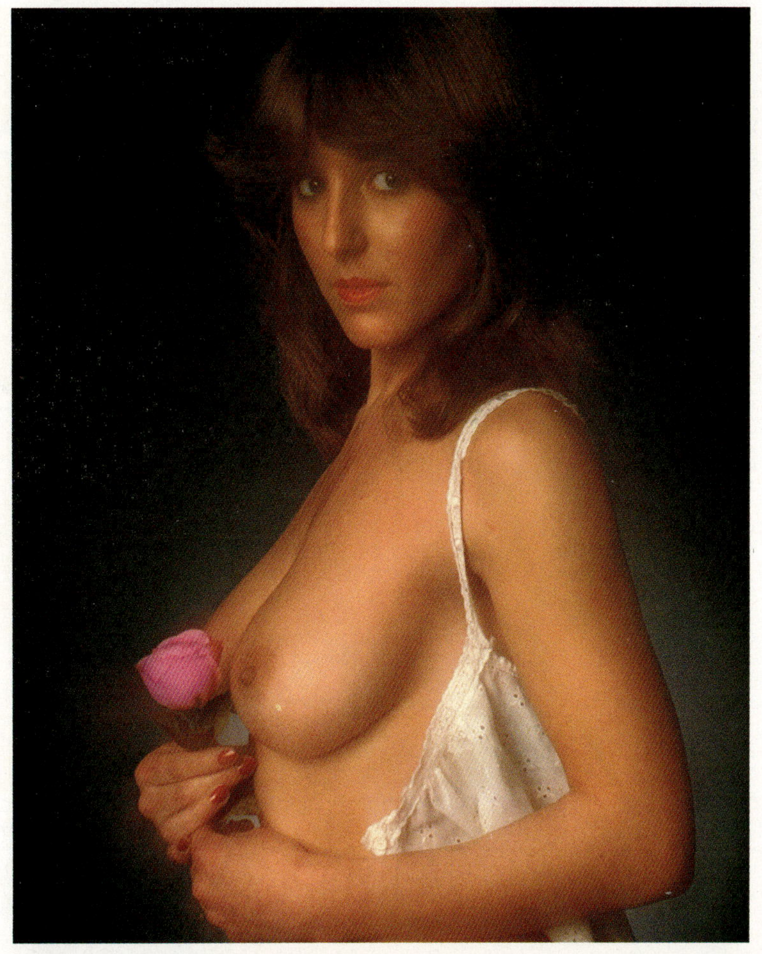

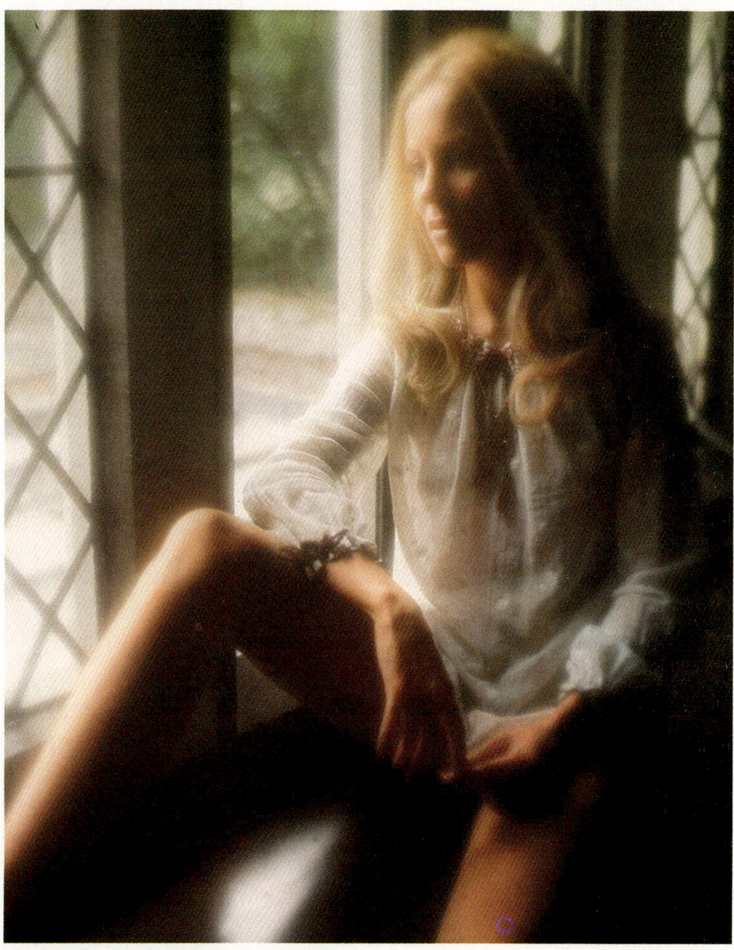

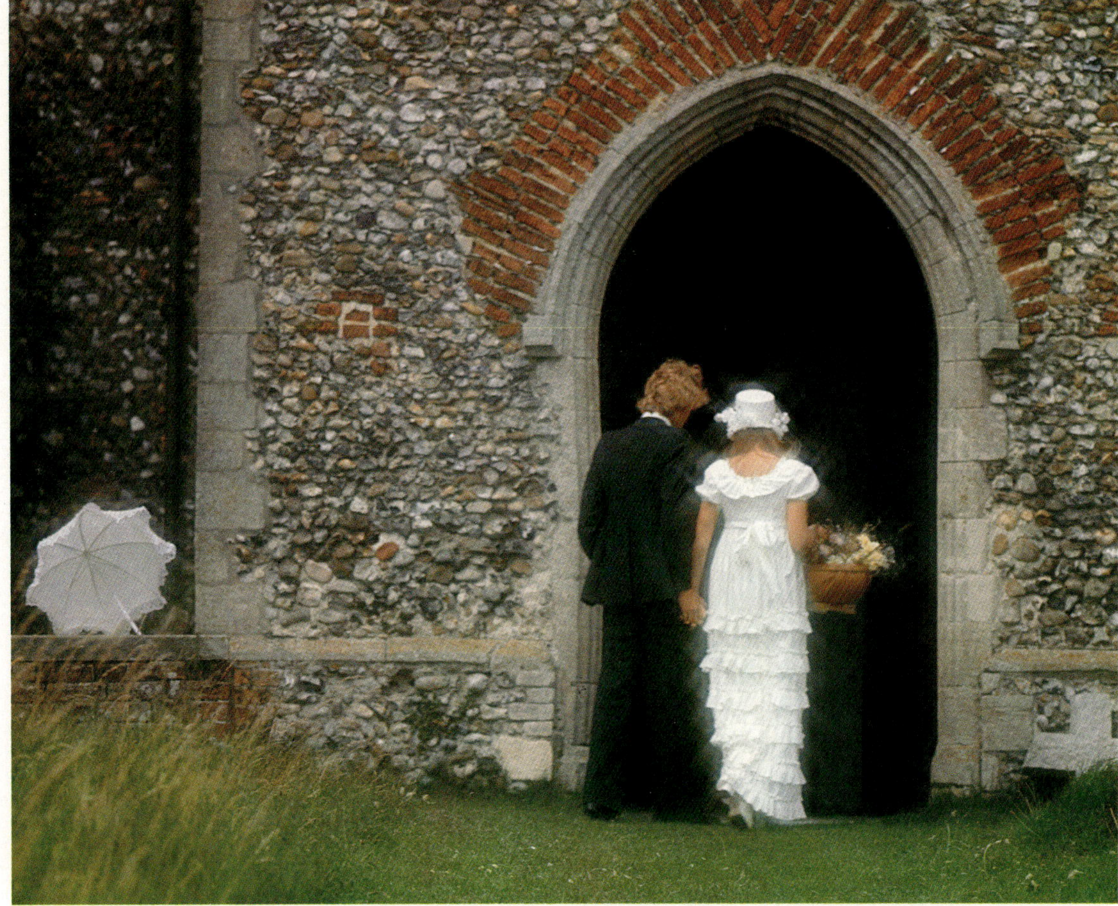

The degree of soft focus used *obviously affects the mood of a picture considerably. It can vary from an almost imperceptible softening to a dreamy, hazy feeling as shown on the* ***facing page, lower pictures.*** *Soft focus is something we happily accept when it is used to portray girls, or couples, in a romantic and rural-looking setting but it works much less happily in a bustling town or city environment. Weddings, however, whether in town or country, usually make ideal subjects for soft focus treatment. Backlighting adds to the effect, enhancing the spread of light. Soft focus can, of course, be combined with other effects filters to, for instance, accentuate pastel colours. Except with such subjects as romantic couples, never use soft focus in shots of men, particularly portraits; it looks quite out of keeping with the subject and is invariably unacceptable to him. This applies equally to older men, whereas older women will usually find the effect flattering and pleasing.*

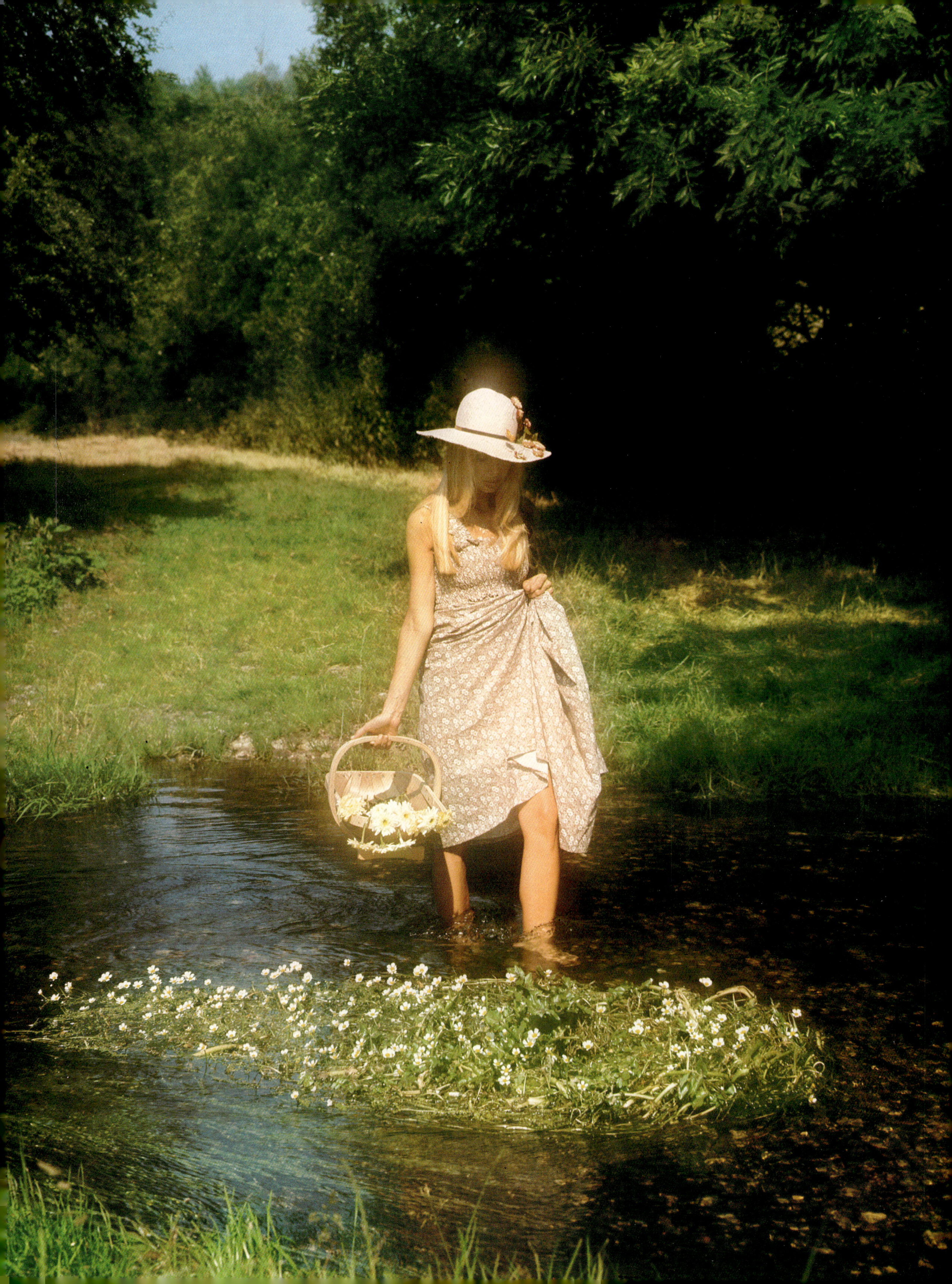

SOFT FOCUS ATTACHMENTS

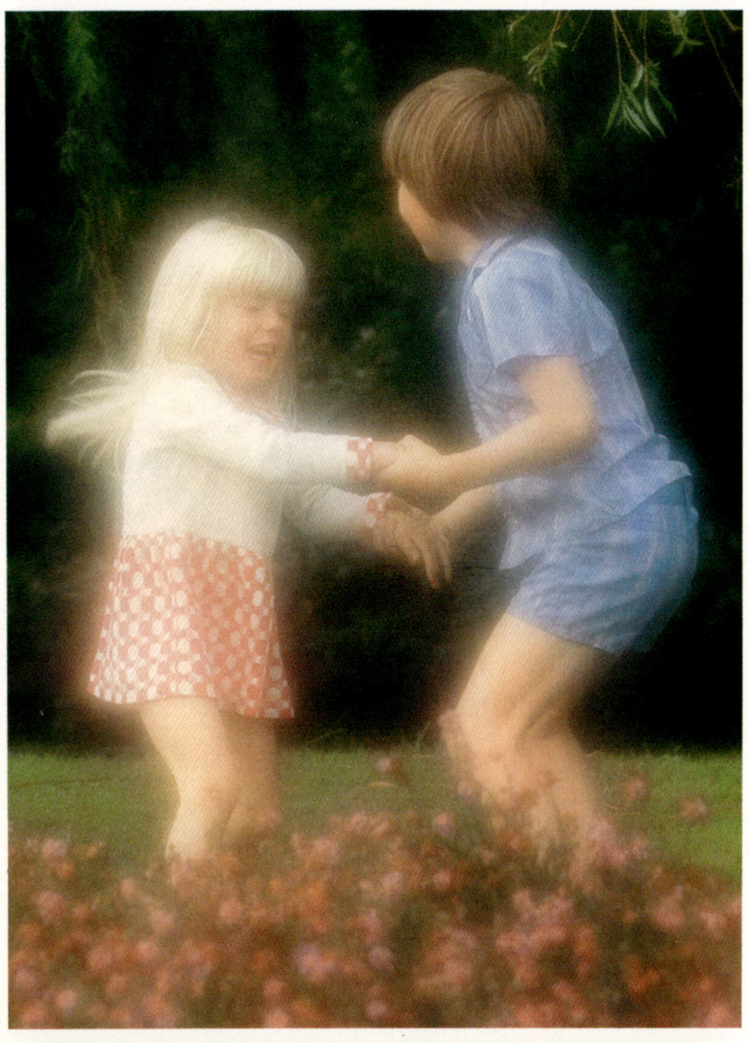

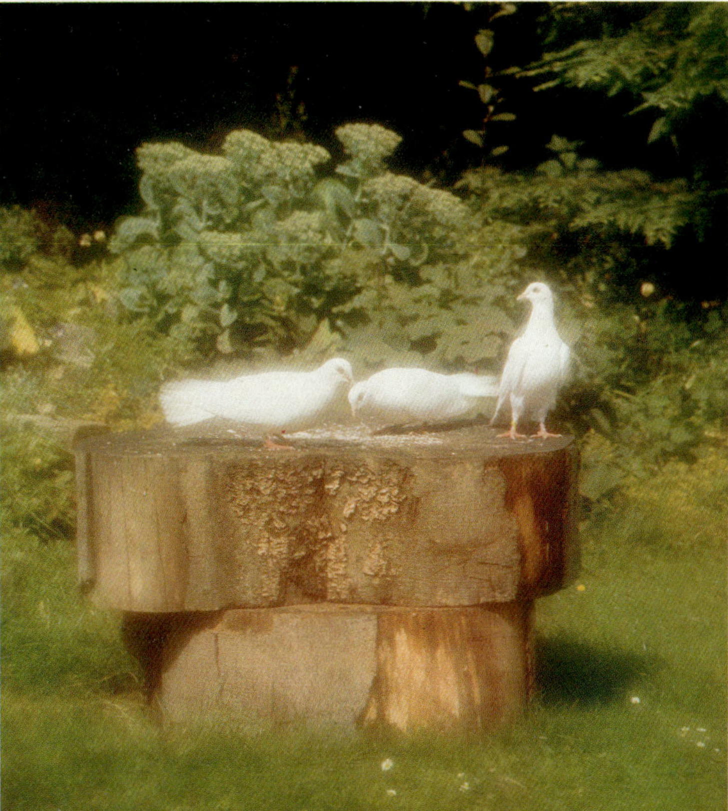

sense. Where these devices are most useful is when attempting a portrait against a confusing background. The effect here can be to render this as very out of focus and thereby more acceptable. The result is not dissimilar to focusing a wide aperture lens on a SLR, but with a degree of soft focus added. In bright light it will probably be necessary to add a neutral density filter in order to retain a sufficiently wide lens aperture.

Do-it-yourself soft focus has been around for a very long time. Prewar articles in the photographic press would describe how crumpled cellophane from a cigarette packet was taped over a lenshood, and then, in order to retain some definition, a lighted cigarette was used to burn a small hole through the centre of the cellophane. This technique is still used in studios today, particularly since the size and shape of the centre hole can be varied so easily. A smoker always has a soft focus facility available.

Of more recent type is the lady's stocking over the lenshood, again with the cigarette burn centre aperture. Unlike crumpled cellophane, the denier and colour of stockings will effect the degree of soft focus and can induce colour cast. Warm tone nylons can give the effect of an 81 series filter in combination with soft focus! I know of several professionals who have gone to the expense of having their favourite nylon 'combination filter' cemented between glass and put into a filter mount. This is one attachment that nobody has yet marketed.

Vaseline smeared over an old UV, or skylight, filter became a vogue in the sixties which still continues today, even to the extent that coloured Vaseline is now sold in photographic shops.

The use of Vaseline as a diffusing medium gives an effect quite unlike anything else. As a starting point, leave a quarter of an inch clear aperture in the centre of an old filter and apply the Vaseline in a circular pattern. Radial smears will add to the effect.

An alternative is to apply greasy finger prints in regular or irregular pattern but again leave a clear centre aperture – unless you are after drastic effect. Do not use Vaseline on any filter glass which you intend to use again in its normal role, as its mount will have to be dismantled for thorough cleaning. Regular exponents of this messy technique invariably have an attachment made up which will hold a $2\frac{1}{4}$ x $2\frac{1}{4}$ or $3\frac{1}{4}$ x $3\frac{1}{4}$ inch lantern slide cover glass in front of the camera's lens. Vaseline can be removed with lighter fuel, followed by washing-up liquid and warm water.

Another D.I.Y. technique is to use clear nail varnish for spots, circles, radial lines or in combination. I would recommend experimentation on cover glasses before attacking even an old UV filter, as nail varnish dries fast and requires a lot of acetone to remove it completely.

Sellotape over a large lenshood was immediately popularised when Lord Lichfield appeared in a T.V. programme. He used an old photoflood reflector, painted matt black inside, and with two inch clear Sellotape criss-crossed over its front. Again a central aperture should be allowed, in this case of a square or diamond shape. There is nothing to stop you using thinner Sellotape over a standard lenshood, though the results will be different. A wider lens aperture and a longer than standard focal length lens must be used with a large hood, otherwise there is a very real danger of the Sellotape being rendered sharp.

It would be hard to imagine *better ingredients for a romantic subject than those in the picture* ***facing page.*** *A woodland setting, a stream, flowers and a beautiful girl have been given just the right degree of soft focus to enhance the mood. We associate doves with peace, hence this is another subject* ***left*** *that works well when softened, as do children – particularly when engaged in relatively peaceful pastimes!*

LENSHOODS

It was not long after the birth of photography – well, about forty years to be precise – that photographers discovered the advantages of using lenshoods. Admittedly, most lenses in the earliest days only consisted of between one and four elements, and since coating was still a hundred years or so away, perhaps they should be forgiven for their ignorance.

In spite of deeply recessed lens mounts on some of the cheapest cameras around, camera manufacturers no longer follow the dictum of their forbears: 'Keep the sun behind you', but instead offer automatic focus/exposure/flash, or build in a motor wind as a means of taking better pictures. Expensive and in many ways less effective!

I am always amazed that tourists toting expensive gear – often with several extra lenses in a case – have still to discover the use of a lenshood. Whether one should blame manufacturer or dealer, or both, is a matter for conjecture, yet surely the cost of a collapsible rubber lenshood is now so low as to be almost ludicrous. That this simple item could be omitted from any purchase is beyond my comprehension, but then perhaps I am preaching to the converted. Even in the earliest photographic literature the photographer was exhorted to keep the sun behind the camera, or alternatively, to use his hat to cast a shadow over the lens. Easy enough when most cameras were mounted on a tripod, otherwise there was the need for an assistant, preferably one who wore a hat – and understood about keeping out of shot.

The coming of the 35mm miniature camera with its flare-prone, wide-aperture lenses, brought about a greater awareness generally for the necessity of a lenshood. Accessory hoods of the push-on/clip-on/knock-off type were produced in profusion for the amateur market. Professionals, after the first flush of enthusiasm, went back to not bothering. The aggravation of losing so many knock-off hoods was simply not worth the effort.

Built-in lenshoods have been a feature of larger focal length lenses for some time, and are now appearing on standard lenses. These are the ultimate in terms of convenience, yet because of the design parameters imposed by the dimensions of the lens mount, are often not as efficient as a previous accessory lenshood fitted to the same focal length lens. A further disadvantage is that when a filter, or close-up lens, is fitted, the built-in lenshood becomes proportionately shorter and consequently less efficient. Reversible lenshoods are yet another Leitz innovation from the early 1930s. A hood of this type is invariably deep, wide and, in consequence, very effective.

In ultimate terms of efficiency, a lenshood should be the same shape as the camera format. It is, of course, easier to produce a circular lenshood shape which is why we are stuck with them. There have been compromises between shape and format in the past. The earliest Leitz lenshood, from the nineteen twenties, was a circular shape with a rectangular cut-out in front. This was ultra efficient but meant that the hood had to be a) removed to adjust the iris diaphragm setting, and b) aligned when replaced.

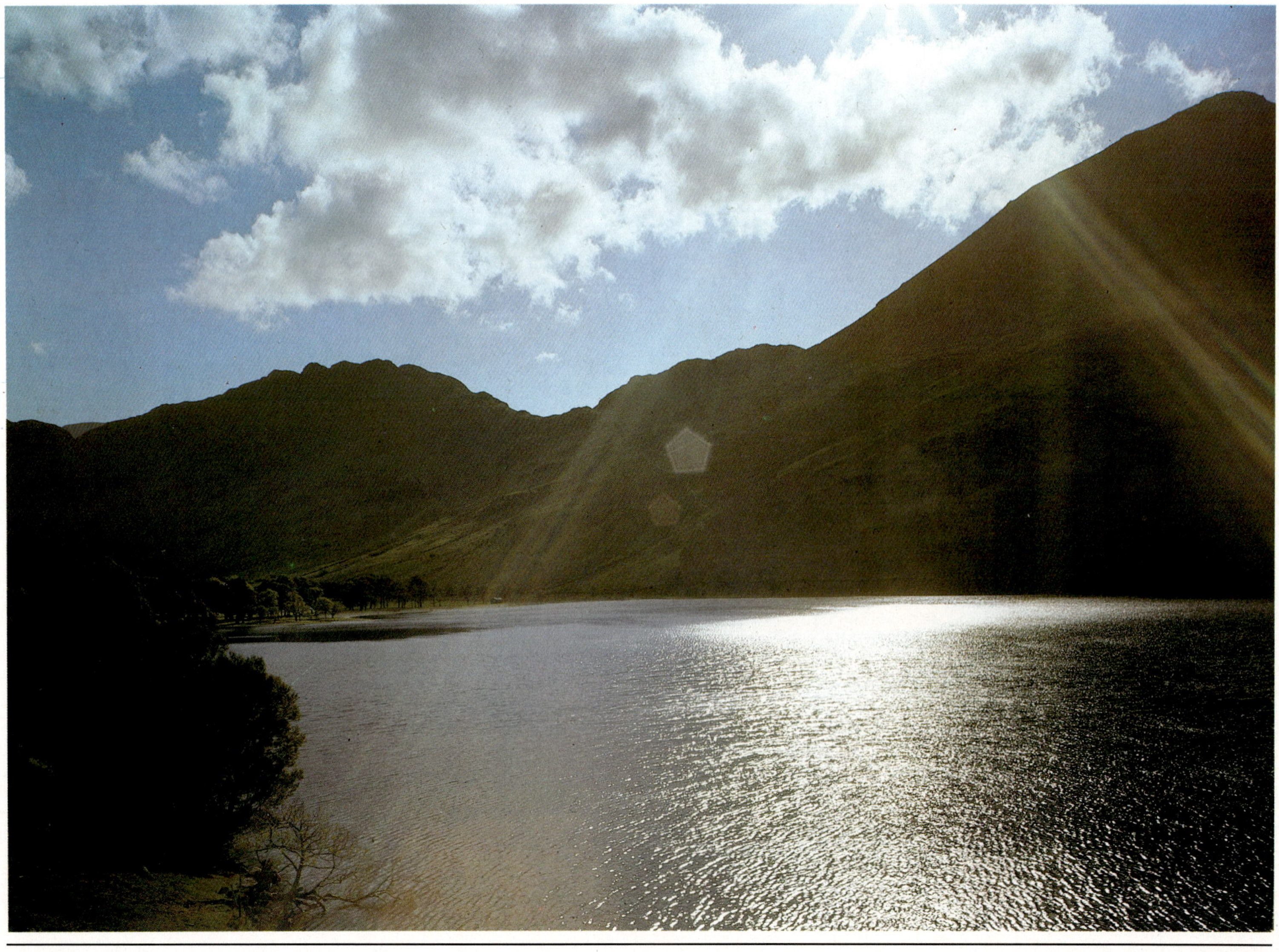

***Flare, caused by a light source** - often the sun - being in, or just out of frame, spoils many photographs. Even if flare patterns are not evident **facing page,** image quality invariably suffers. Sometimes we may deliberately wish to include such flare but, if not, a good lens hood of the correct length for the lens in use, is essential.*

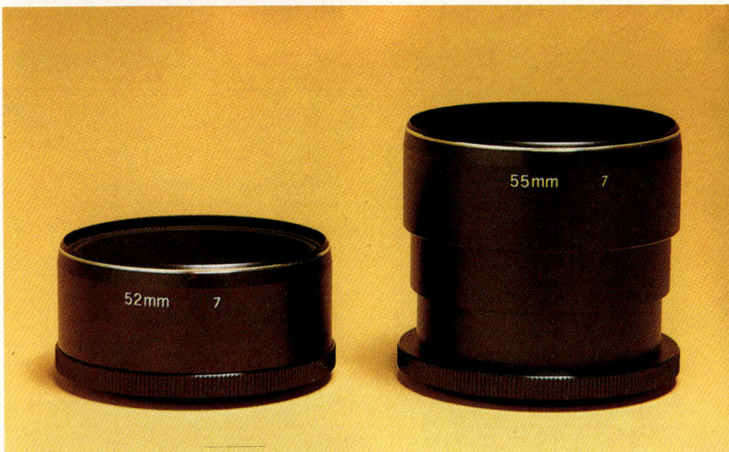

*Lens hoods come in a variety of sizes and types. A wide angle lens requires a short, wide hood **top** to avoid vignetting, and there are extending models available **above.** The best, albeit most expensive lens hood is probably the bellows hood **left** which is adjustable for practically all lenses.*

It was superseded by a conventional round hood. Some years later Leitz produced larger, round lenshoods with a cut-out back. This reduced the amount of cut-off in the rangefinder/viewfinder windows. Similar hoods have been made by Zeiss, Nikon, Canon and Hoya. Although designed for lenses of up to 100mm focal length, all these hoods were so shallow that they were more appropriate to wide angle lenses. This still applies to the current hoods of this type.

Square and oblong hoods are rather rarer, and usually only available for medium format rollfilm cameras. Invariably with a bayonet mount to avoid skew problems, this type can be compact and efficient - providing that filters etc. are not used on the inner bayonet. The most unusual of these hoods which I have encountered, was an oblong hood with a rotating mount, designed for the 6 x 6cm Praktisix SLR camera. The logic defeats me but it worked well in practice!

Wide angle lenshoods are often neglected by photographers, and certainly when you look at their skimpy dimensions, and sometimes price, this is understandable. Yet the manufacturers do not make these for fun. Under certain circumstances every little helps. Retrofocus wide angle lenses having large areas of glass in front and lots of elements behind, are prone to flare. Even a necessarily shallow lenshood can prevent a side or top light source from getting into the lens elements. There is also the consideration of affording physical protection to the somewhat vulnerable glass surface. An oversized, and therefore deeper lenshood, can often be fitted to a wide angle lens by means of a step-ring. This may not be as convenient to carry but will be more efficient.

Telephoto and long focus lenses, particularly those with a built-in hood, are the biggest offenders when it comes to inefficiency. As an example: A current proprietary 300mm lens that I own has a lenshood of 30mm length - or 10% of its focal length. A 1950s 312mm telephoto lens was fitted with a 100mm long lenshood as standard, this being over 30% of the focal length. What is more, it needs it! Test pictures taken with the late multi-coated lens, showed a marked increase in contrast when it was fitted with the 100mm hood of the earlier lens.

The first reference I can find to an extendable bellows lenshood is in the James A. Sinclair catalogue of 1910. (It was still available thirty three years later!) Movie cameramen started using this type of hood very early on and still do, but then, look at even a sub-standard format ciné lens, and note the depth of the lenshood. This concern with avoiding lens flare spread into professional photography during the nineteen fifties. Larger format camera makers like Sinar, Arca and Hasselblad began to produce the square compendium, or professional lens shade, as an optional accessory. In recent years this trend has even spread into the 35mm market, through the aegis - literally, of Ambico, who, as far as I know, were the first to produce an oblong bellows hood for still photography. Most hoods of this type have filter provision, either for cemented in glass, gelatins in holders, or nowadays, various plastic devices. Invariably there is also provision for a front mask, à la Leitz, for the longer focal lengths or for specialised cut-out shapes. In practice, a bellows lenshood can be adjusted for maximum efficiency, with any focal length between super wide and ultra long, and at any camera/subject distance between infinity and macro.

A depth of field preview control on the camera is essential to avoid cut-off at smaller lens apertures. Large format hoods are also adjustable in line with camera movements. If the bellows lenshood has any disadvantage it is simply one of bulk, though some units are now made which can be folded for greater portability. All controls are lockable.

The last type of lenshood is basically a filter holder with a (usually) optional lenshood. This is the basis of Cokin, Chromatek, Hoyarex and other filter systems. Filter holders of this type date back a long way, though to the ingenious Jean Coquin must go the credit for their current popularity. Nikon, Hama and Hoya all produce high precision gelatin filter holders with the option of add-on circular lenshoods. These can be suitable for super wide to telephoto lenses. Gelatin filters of 75 x 75mm or 100 x 100mm can be used depending upon the maker. Even Kodak, with its ultimate gelatin filter range, have produced the crude Portré filter holder/lenshood device for many years.

One last word pertinent to lenshoods, and this concerns the blackness of the interior. At one time the better lenshoods were lined with black felt, which, although this could pick up fluff, when kept clean was very black indeed. Modern hoods, with machined interiors sprayed matt black, are not as efficient. They can, however, be lined with black felt. Bellows hoods, though again not as black as felt, by their shape alone will absorb any unwanted light.

COPYING AND DUPING

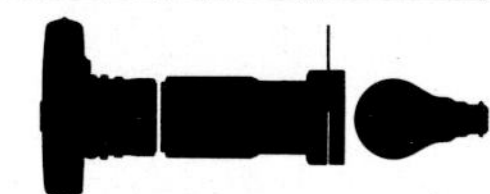

Just because the sun goes in or it's a lousy day, is no reason to hang up the camera or your filter collection.

All of us have seen what can be done with transparency duping, where there is always a chance that the shot which didn't quite come off could be saved or at least changed into something more acceptable. With the advent of cheap transparency copiers, some of which use the camera's standard lens, there is now no real excuse for the photographer not to try his hand at this technique. In the last resort, there is always the possibility of changing a colour image into black and white – or even vice versa, with the aid of a bit of darkroom magic!

Some of the simpler slide copiers can only use filters behind

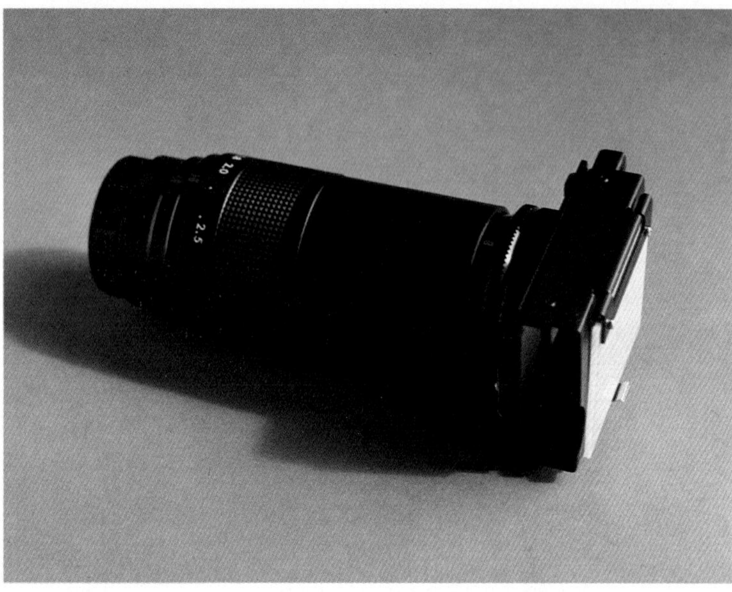

the transparency to be copied. This is fine for colour correction and other filters, 'grads,' vignettes, centre and colour spots, and any other attachment which is larger overall than the transparency. Because copiers of this type have a translucent diffuser behind the transparency, the effect of a centre spot or shaped mask will not be as marked as in a camera original.

Alternatively, filters and attachments can sometimes be used between the camera's prime lens and an add-on slide duplicator. This invariably affects the focus setting and it may be that the combination will now only focus closer than 1:1. There is also a possibility of vignetting. Gelatin filters can be cut to fit inside the adaptor if required, in which case there will be no focus shift.

Professional slide duplicators like the Illumitran, Elinchrom and Repronar are as versatile as their hefty price tag suggests. The fact that a filter or attachment can be placed between the lens and the subject transparency is a bonus also shared by a conventional bellows unit. In consequence, soft focus, fog, centre and colour spots, varipol and half colour filters may now be used as in a normal picture taking role.

With any of the simpler transparency duplicating devices, the choice of light source is left to the photographer. Whilst daylight or artificial light are the naturals – since a TTL metering system can be used – there is a lot to be said for a constant source, i.e. a small electronic flash unit at a fixed distance from the transparency to be copied. Although this means a certain amount of experimentation with a 'standard' transparency, in the long term it is a better method.

Professional transparency duplicators often use the substitution system. Exposure measurement of the subject transparency is made with a tungsten lamp, the reading from which is then 'translated' into the correct exposure for the electronic flash used in the final exposure. There is nothing to stop the ingenious from adopting the same method, once the exposure parameters have been ascertained.

Whichever type of slide duplicator is used, there are certain filters and attachments which simply cannot work. These include normal polarisers, infrared and ultraviolet filters, whilst diffraction gratings and crosstars can only be employed by double exposing a separate light source into a dupe or black and white negative. Multiple image prisms and some centre focus attachments will invariably record areas outside of the subject

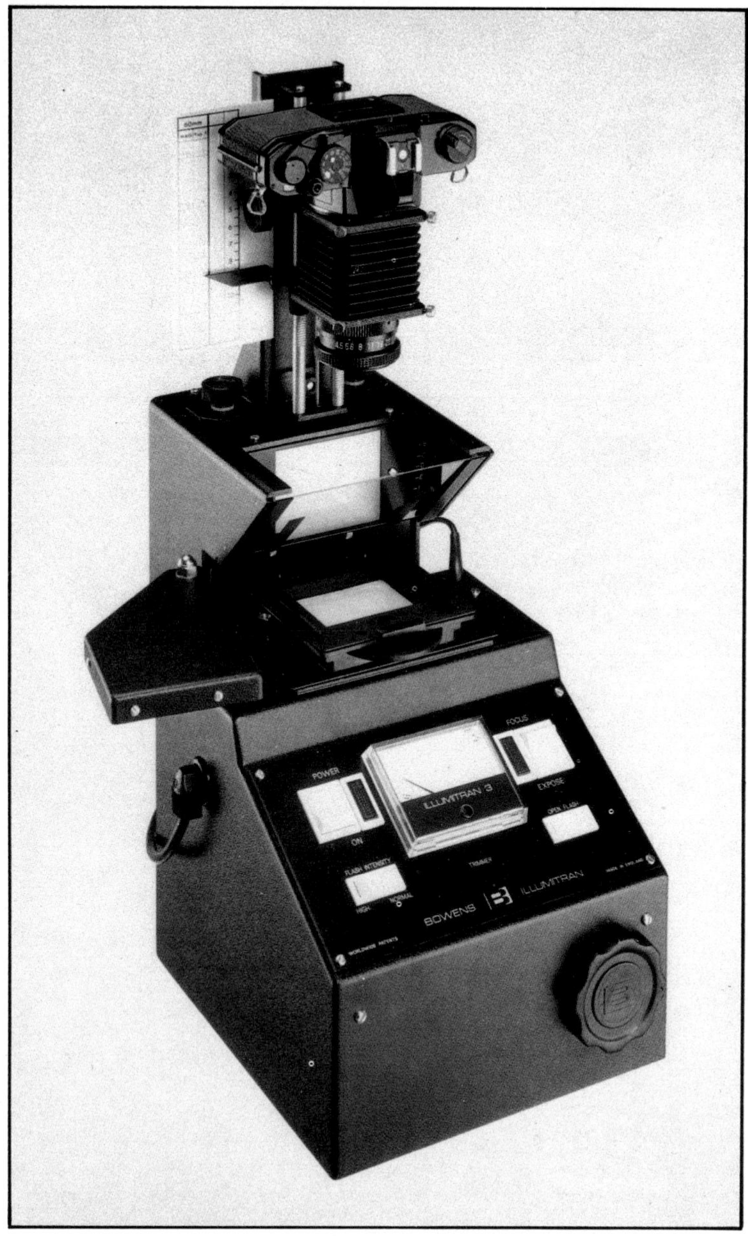

Above left is an Ohnar *transparency copying device that may be fitted with adaptors and thus to the camera body. This particular example contains its own lens system and has zoom facility to allow for enlargement of portions of a transparency. The Bowens Illumitran* ***above*** *is a much more sophisticated and costly version of a similar item which includes its own electronic light source plus focusing lamp. With the simpler unit a light source for exposure must be provided, usually a small electronic flash.*

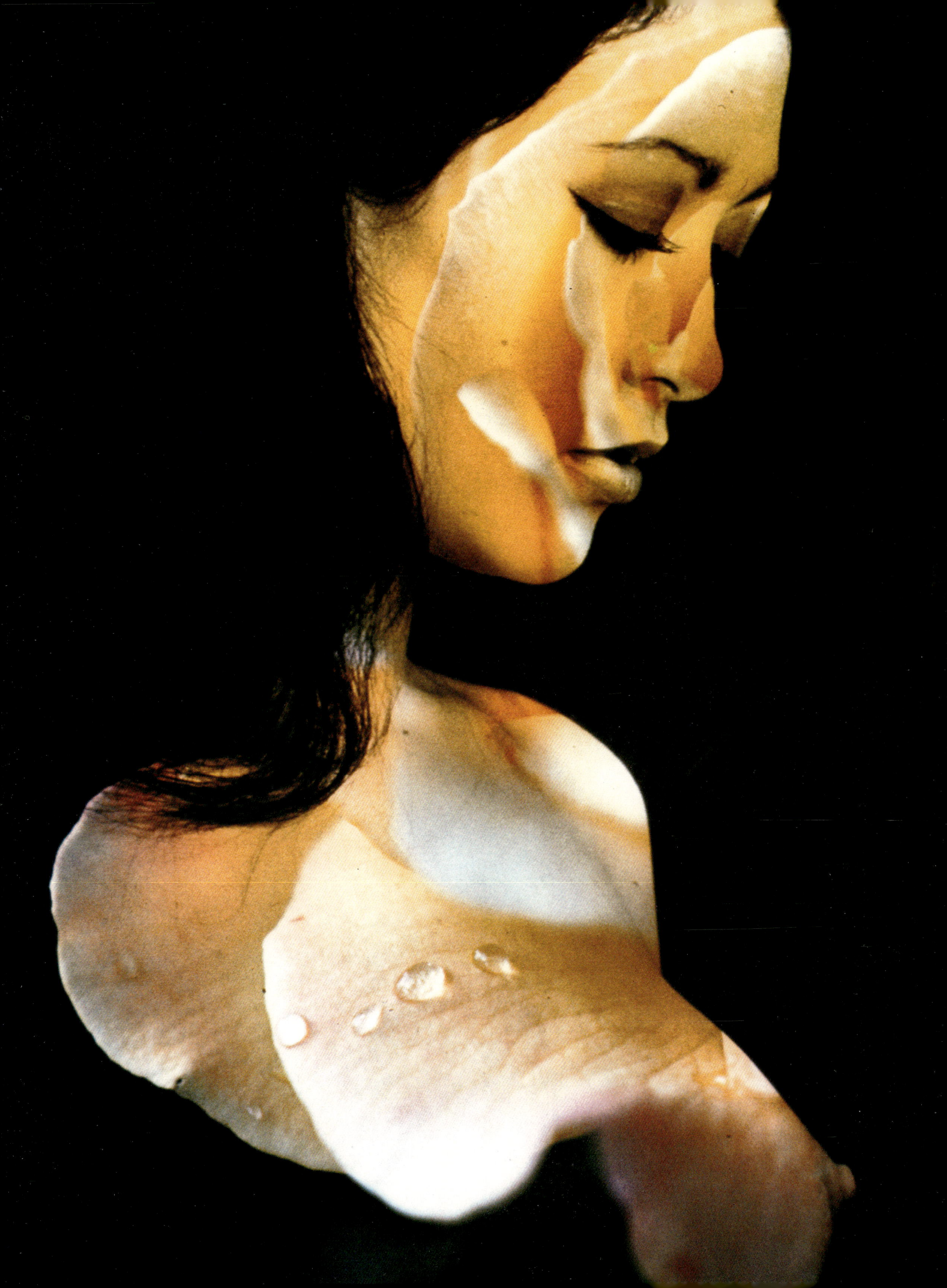

COPYING AND DUPING

***Transparencies can be copied in** several ways. There is the sophisticated copier, and the simpler version, featured on the previous page and, of course, copies can be made by making a negative and producing positives from this. It is also possible to copy a projected image. This requires that the camera and lens be set up as close to the optical axis of the projector as possible. With any of the direct copying methods a colour filter, mask or another slide can be combined with the first to create one single transparency in which both images are combined. Many photographers who are interested in duping take photographs specially to use later in combination with another shot. A sheet of kitchen foil, shot through various coloured filters, or with a zoom lens, may not make an exciting subject alone but, in combination with an existing, or yet to be taken, transparency it can provide a very different result. Experimentation is the only way to gain experience.*

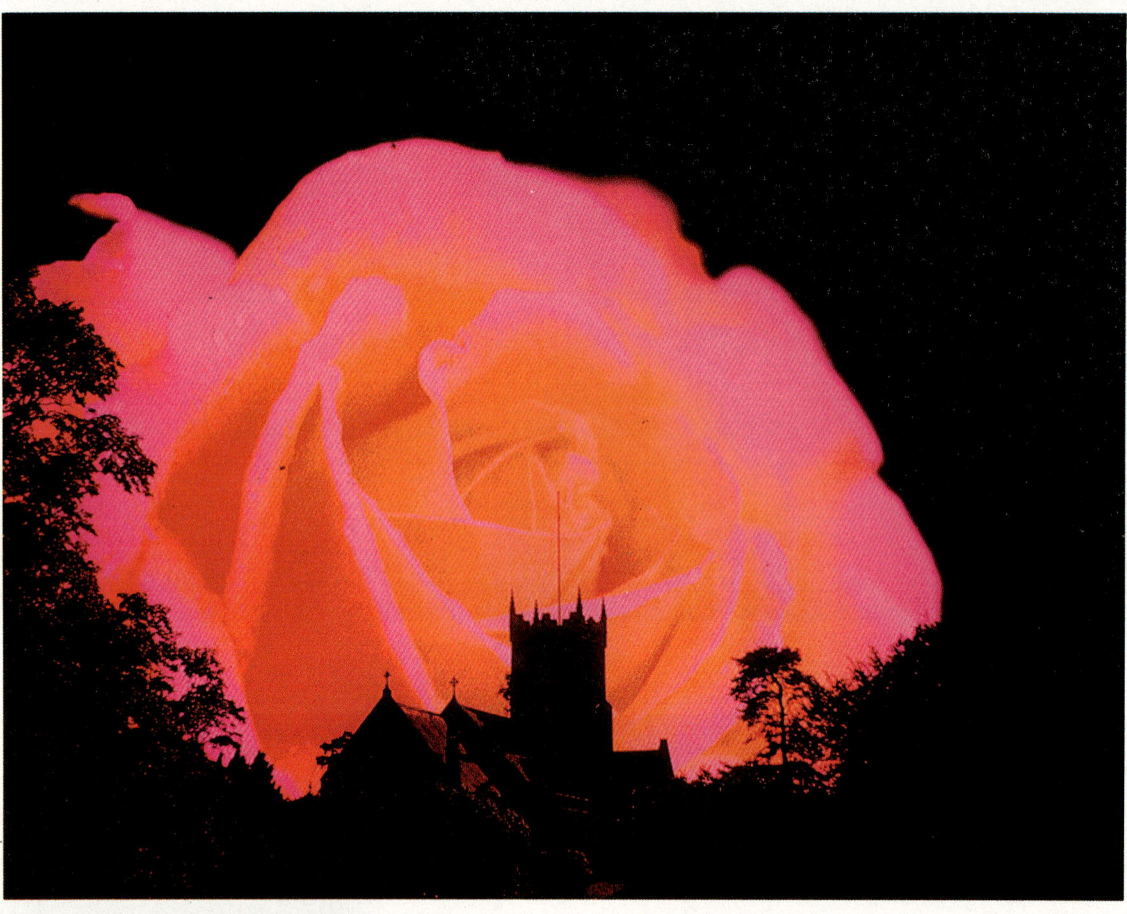

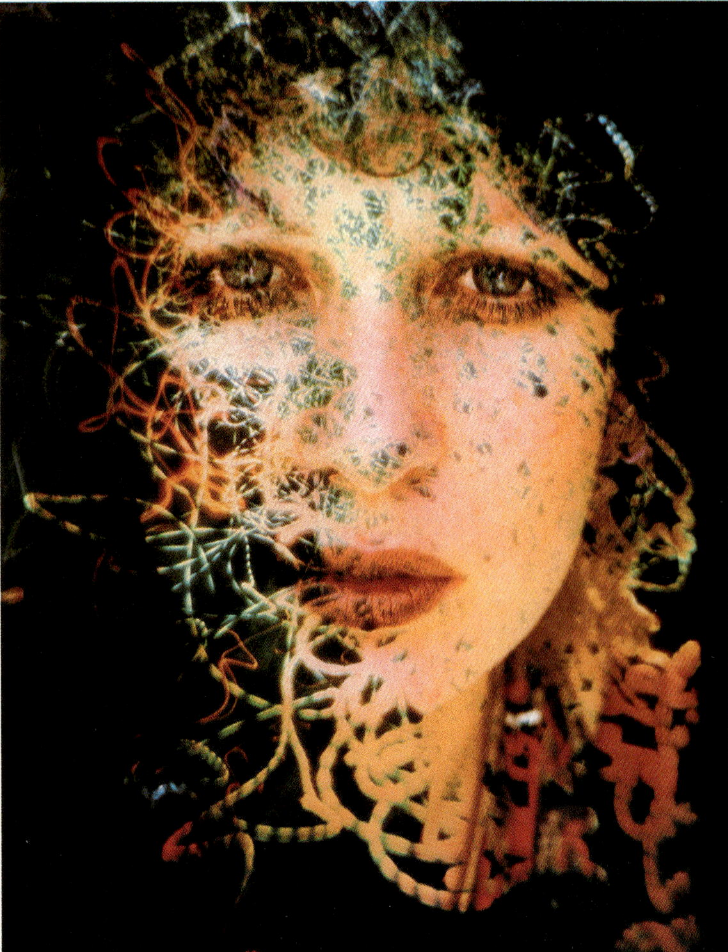

transparency, as do fisheye and superwide attachments.

The most useful items from the camera bag are Wratten CC colour correction filters, which can be used to alter a colour cast. Light balancing filters such as the 80 or 85 series will only act as a colour filter. A transparency exposed by a totally wrong light source cannot be corrected to normal. This is simply a matter of not being able to put back what is not already there! The same is true for an over-exposed transparency but not for one which is under-exposed. In this case a one, to one-and-a-half, stop error in exposure can often be corrected to a surprisingly high degree. There may be a need to use a colour correction filter if the degree of under-exposure has produced a colour shift in the subject rendering.

The lighter 81 'warming' filters may be used just as in their normal camera role, whilst the blue 82 filters are also useful for the apposite function.

Unfortunately, with any copying process there is an inevitable increase in contrast, which may or may not be acceptable. Several manufacturers make special transparency duplicating films of lower than average contrast. These are only available in bulk lengths, which means loading your own cassettes! A compromise is to use either Kodachrome 25 or, conversely, Ektachrome 160 or 200, these being of slightly lower contrast than other films in the range. All E6 films can be cut in processing by a half stop (maximum), which also reduces contrast. There will be a colour shift towards blue (about CC 10 blue), which must be allowed for.

Provided that your camera has double exposure facility, there is another contrast lowering duping technique which avoids special film or processing. This is known as flashing. The method is to make one exposure of the copier light source with a very heavy neutral density filter, followed by the correct exposure for the transparency to be copied. I must emphasise that this

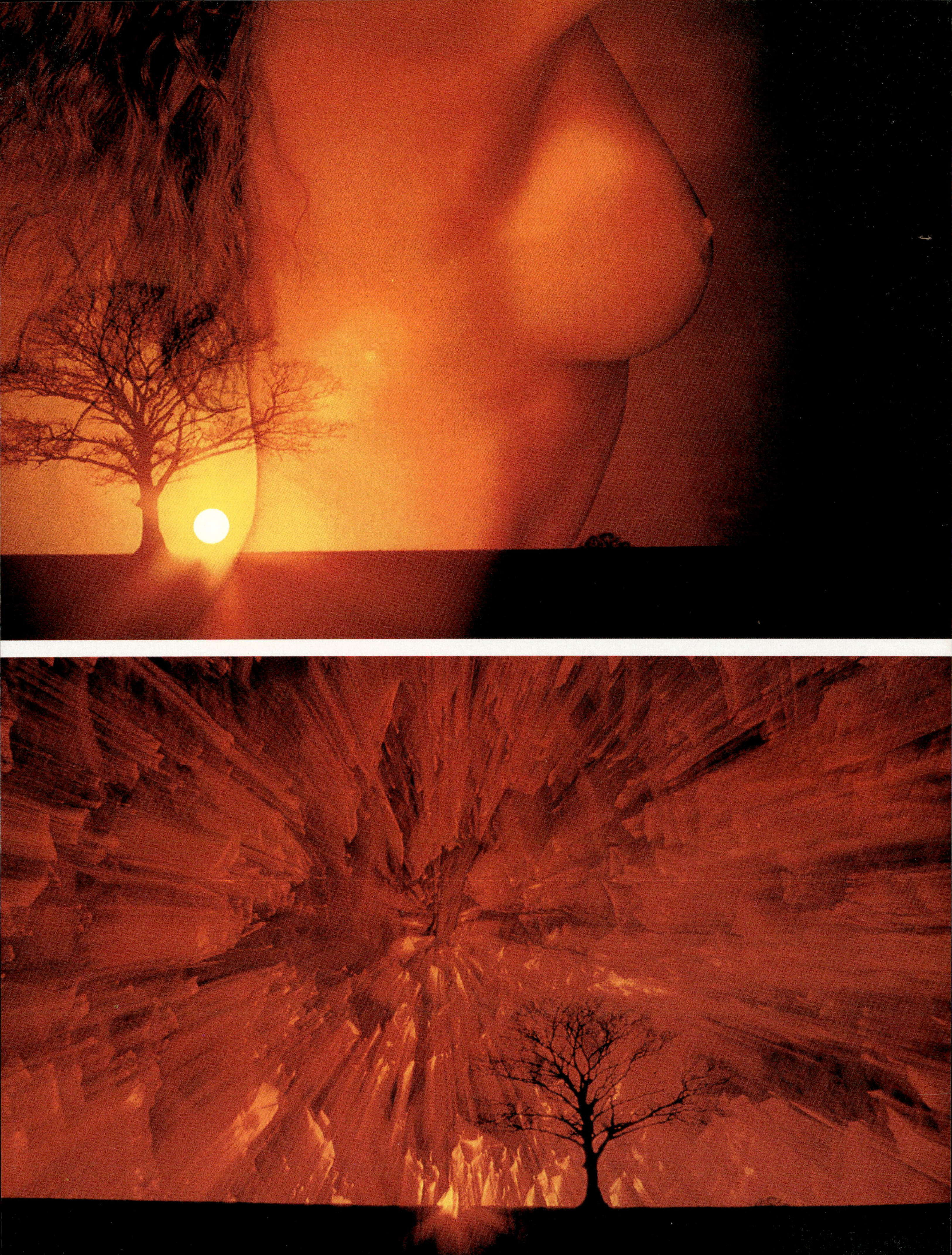

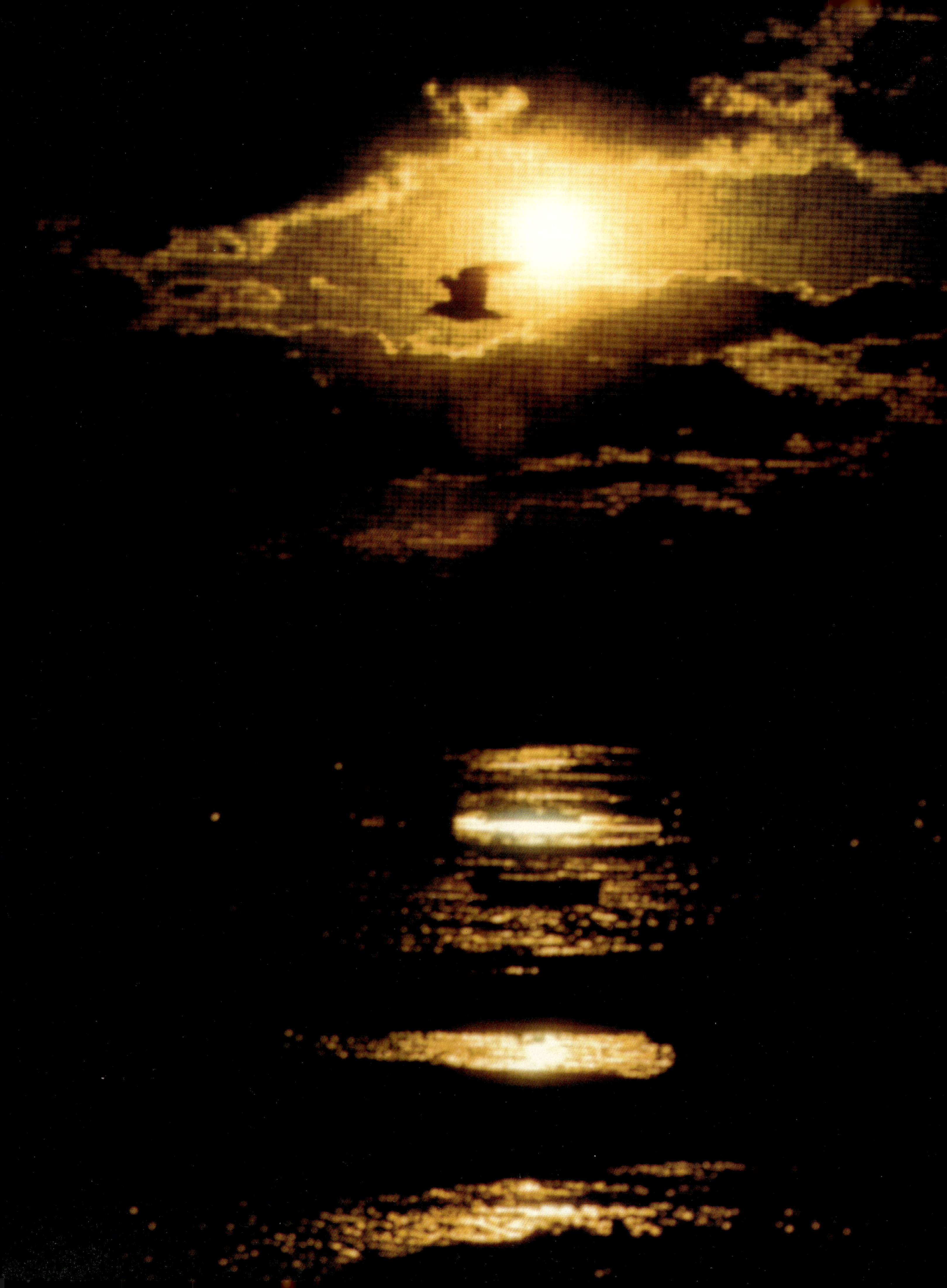

COPYING AND DUPING

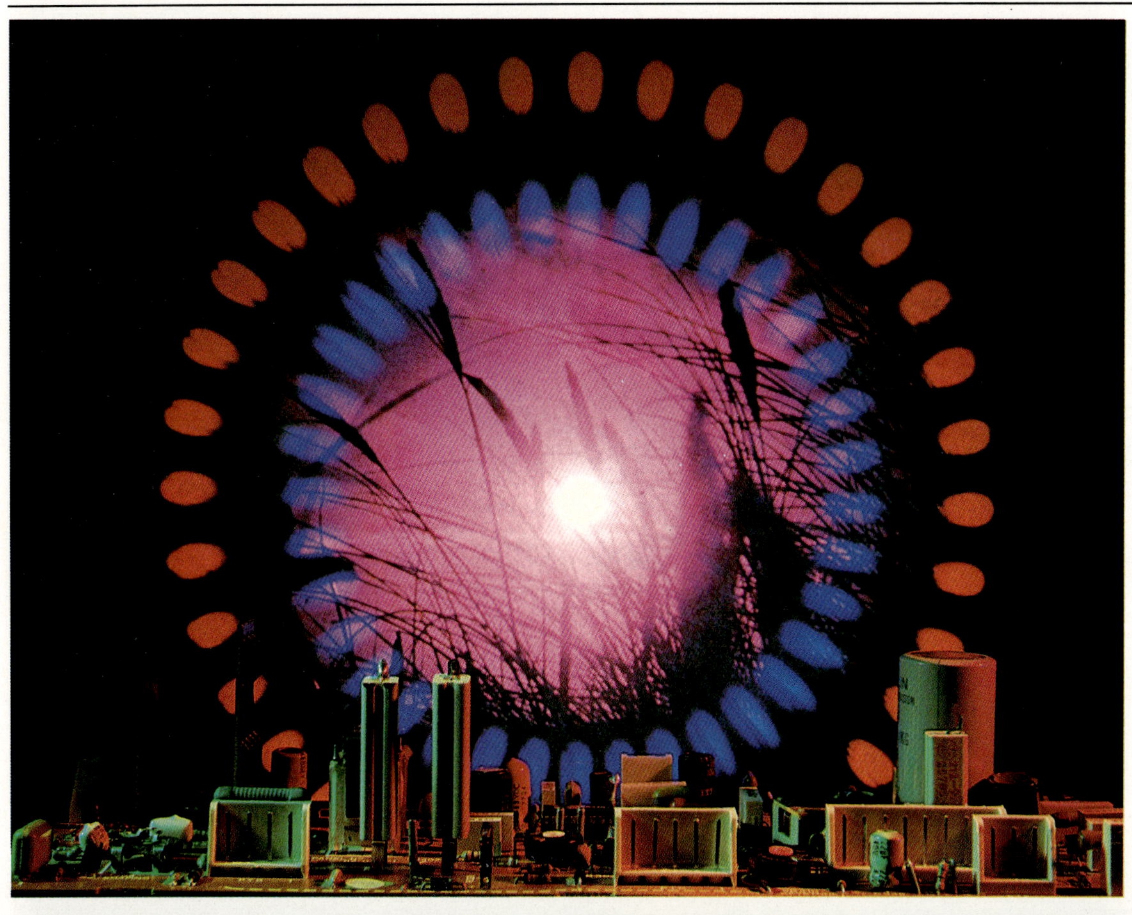

Facing page is an example of a *transparency duped together with a texture screen. These screens are available in a wide variety of patterns to suit all types of subject. A quick glance at the pictures on* ***this page*** *suggests that they show a city skyline. This, of course, is what they are intended to suggest. They are, in fact, electrical components mounted on a circuit board, combined with transparencies of special effects filters and* ***left,*** *also with an outdoor shot which was also filtered! The possibilities presented by a duping set-up, of whatever type or simplicity, are almost endless. As the owner of one of these pieces of equipment, you will find yourself looking at all kinds of subjects with a view to duping. You may even build up a library of such shots, to while away the long, dark evenings, but not, hopefully, at the expense of your photography!*

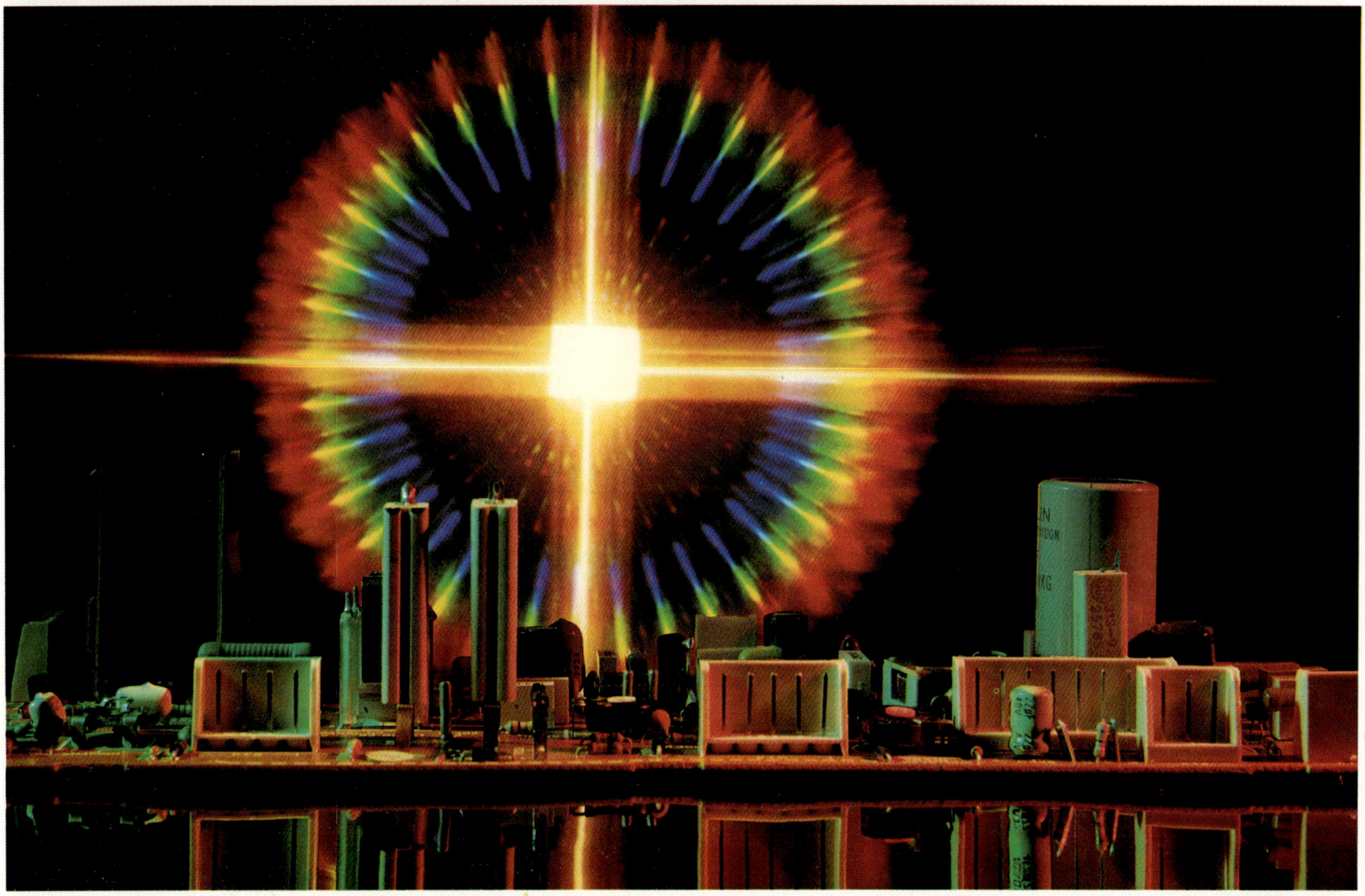

combination does require a certain amount of experimentation, as the ND filter density directly relates to the ASA speed of the copy film. As a guide, start with 64 ASA film, a Wratten ND 3.0 filter (1000 x factor) and make the flashing exposure at one stop less than for the second exposure. As with any duping technique, it pays to keep copious notes for future reference.

When copying colour transparencies on to black and white film, the same techniques may be used. Once more, high speed film is of lower contrast than slower film. Exposure and development may be altered for contrast reduction: the usual method is to over-expose by one stop and reduce development by 20%.

When copying a colour transparency on to colour negative film for the eventual production of prints, it is better to use internegative film (only available in bulk rolls), if colour fidelity is important. Flashing again gives a slight improvement but alterations in exposure and development will cause colour shifts which often cannot be corrected. Now that a soft grade of colour paper is available, home printers have fewer problems with excess contrast than in days gone by.

There are ways of using filters to change a black and white image into colour. Excluding the specialised techniques of tone separation, most photographers are happy enough to use the methods used by audio-visual producers and colour supplement art directors. This entails monochromatising a black and white image so that it blends tonally with a colour presentation or picture spread. It is as simple as copying a black and white print on to colour film, using a single filter to add colour. It can be as easy as using an 85B to produce sepia tones, or a Wratten 30 for magenta, or an 80B to give blue, and so on, according to the effect required, or to taste, or sometimes lack of it! Strongly coloured and pop filters also tend to obliterate tone and sometimes apparent definition.

Many camera filters can be used on the enlarger, whether to modify an enlarged 'duplicate' transparency, Cibachrome, Ektaflex or other colour, or black amd white print. In each case the nature of the process must be taken into account. For instance, a graduated orange filter will work on the enlarger for an enlarged transparency, Cibachrome or Ektaflex (positive) print, but will induce a lighter complementary coloured area in pos/neg colour print, and in black and white will have the effect of totally holding back the added graduated area.

Monochromatic colour effects can be produced with camera filters on the enlarger, particularly when colour heads simply do not have this range or depth of hue, to say nothing of the 'mixes' available elsewhere.

Spot and fog filters, soft focus devices, vignettes and masks can also be used. The latter is better placed over the subject negative or transparency when mechanisms allow. Even anamorphic and superwide attachments may be used over the enlarger lens (with a suitable mounting ring), to induce distortion in the image. Such are the joys of projection images.

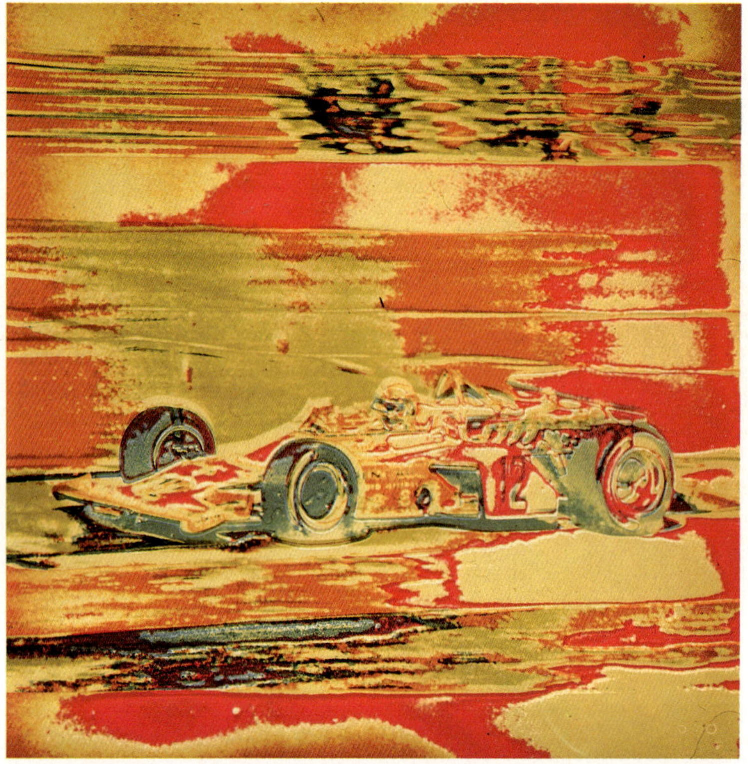

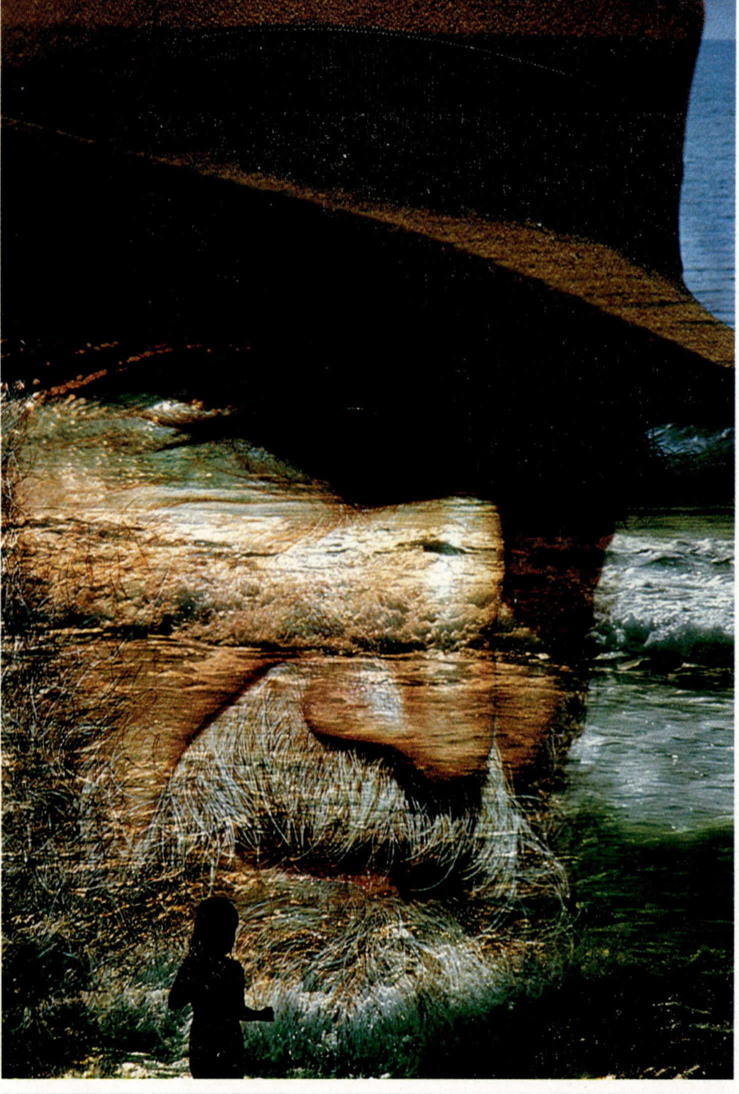

***Photography, without any** tricks, is capable of producing evocative images. Combination duping **right,** in which one subject is superimposed on another, can reinforce the idea. The best of these pictures leave something for us to think about. Is the old man remembering the child he was? Or a child he once knew? Or does the picture tell us what the child will become? What has the sea to do with it? Is the memory pleasant or tragic? Solarisation and posterisation are other avenues open to the darkroom worker. There are many different methods of achieving these results, all of which can then be duped, singly or in combination.*

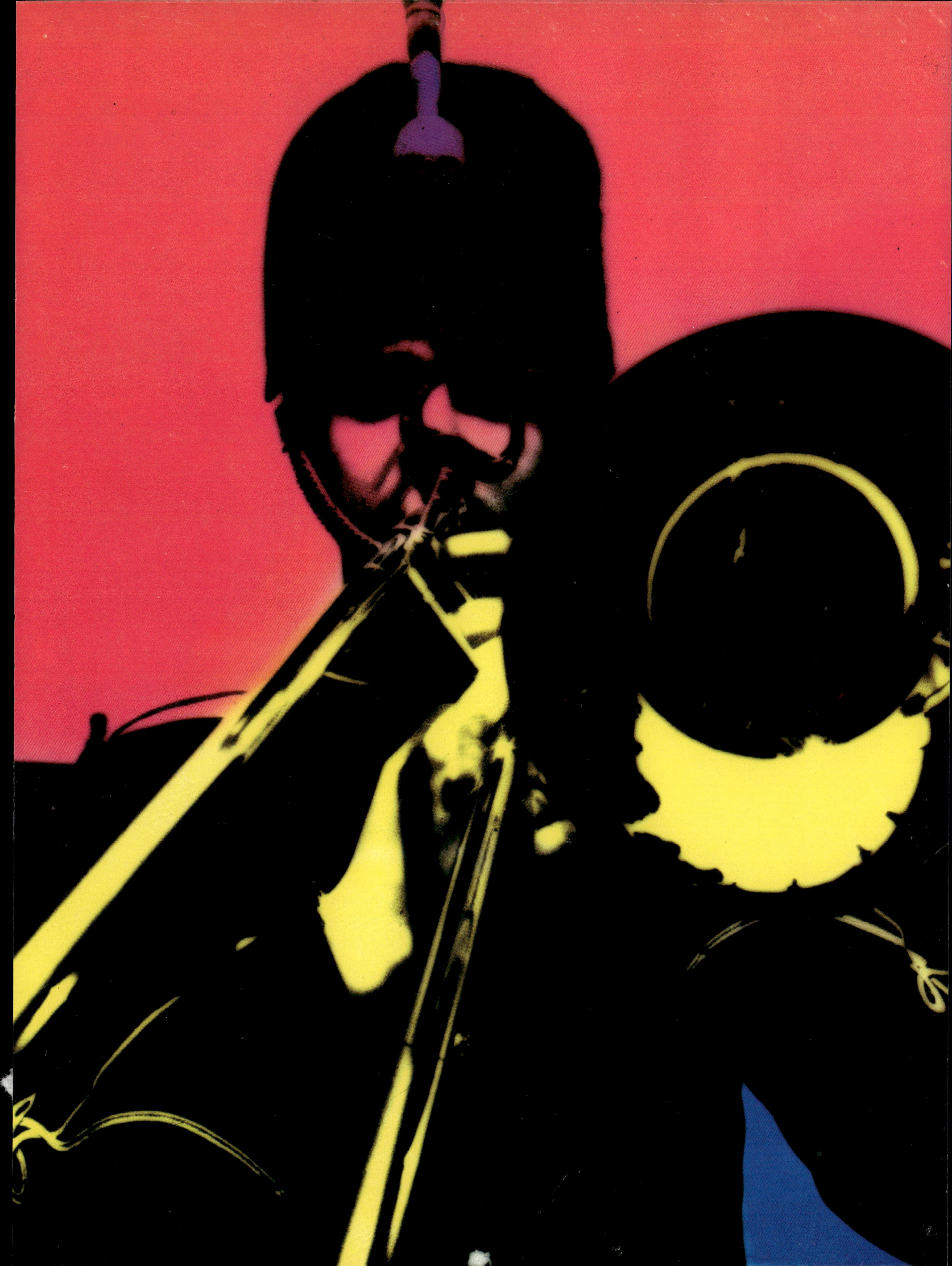

ACKNOWLEDGEMENTS

The publishers would like to express their grateful thanks for technical information and for the loan of equipment to:

Eumig (UK) Ltd
Introphoto Ltd
Kodak Ltd
Leeds Camera Centre Ltd
Photax (London) Ltd
Polysales Photographic Ltd
Russell's Cameras, Wimbledon

Our special thanks to Mayfair Photographic Suppliers (London) Ltd for technical information and the loan of the **cokin**® filter system.

First published in Great Britain 1982 by Colour Library International Ltd.

Colour separations by FERCROM, Barcelona, Spain.
Display and text filmsetting by Acesetters Ltd., Richmond, Surrey, England.
Printed by Cayfosa and bound by Eurobinder - Barcelona (Spain)

ISBN 0 86283 016 8
COLOUR LIBRARY INTERNATIONAL